# THE ANARCHIST WAY TO SOCIALISM

# THE ANARCHIST WAY TO SOCIALISM

Elisée Reclus and Nineteenth-Century European Anarchism

Marie Fleming

CROOM HELM   LONDON

ROWMAN AND LITTLEFIELD
Totowa, New Jersey

© 1979 Marie Fleming
Croom Helm Ltd., 2–10 St John's Road, London SW11

British Library Cataloguing in Publication Data

Fleming, Marie
    The anarchist way to socialism
    1. Reclus, Elisée
    2. Anarchism and anarchists —
        France — History
    I. Title
    335'.83, 0924      HX894

  ISBN  0-85664-867-1

First published in the United States 1979
by ROWMAN AND LITTLEFIELD, 81 Adams Drive, Totowa, N.J.

ISBN  0-8476-6158-X

Printed and bound in Great Britain

# CONTENTS

# ABBREVIATIONS

| | |
|---|---|
| AEN | Archives de l'Etat, Neuchâtel |
| AFJ | Archives de la Fédération Jurassienne |
| AHG | Archives Historiques du Ministère de la Guerre, Vincennes |
| AN | Archives Nationales, Paris |
| Archief ER | Archief Elisée Reclus |
| BFJ | Bulletin de la Fédération Jurassienne |
| BN | Bibliothèque Nationale |
| BPU | Bibliothèque Publique et Universitaire, Geneva |
| CIRA | Centre International de Recherches sur l'Anarchisme |
| Dossier ER | Dossier Elisée Reclus |
| Fonds ER | Fonds Elisée Reclus |
| IFHS | Institut Français d'Histoire Sociale |
| IISG | International Instituut voor Sociale Geschiedenis |
| IWMA | International Working Men's Association |
| MEW | Marx Engels Werke |
| NA | Nettlau Archives |
| NAF | Nouvelles Acquisitions Françaises, Bibliothèque Nationale, Paris |
| Papiers ER | Papiers Elisée Reclus |
| P.Po. | Archives de la Préfecture de Police, Paris |
| PV du CFJ | Proces-verbaux des séances du Comité fédéral jurassien |

TO THOSE I LOVE

# PREFACE

Elisée Reclus was an important figure in European anarchist circles from the 1870s, the time when the anarchists began to be distinguished from the wider socialist movement. In the late nineteenth century he contributed to the radical direction which the anarchist movement assumed and consistently supported the adoption of increasingly extreme measures. Unwavering in his hostility to the bourgeois state and party-political action, he relentlessly upheld the principle of propaganda by the deed, even when it was used to justify the terrorism which plunged Europe into a virtual state of panic in the early 1890s. The anarchist historian Max Nettlau wrote a biography of Reclus in 1928, but admitted that it represented only a first stage in coming to terms with the subject.[1] Since the publication of Nettlau's work, much new material has come to light, in particular police files and unpublished correspondence. Reclus' contribution to the development of late nineteenth-century European anarchism has, however, still received little attention from scholars.

Not only was Reclus known as a committed anarchist. He achieved worldwide acclaim as an early proponent of the scientific study of human geography. As author of the monumental nineteen-volume *La Nouvelle Géographie Universelle* (The New Universal Geography), he was the somewhat reluctant recipient of gold medals from both the Paris Geographical Society (1892) and the Royal Geographical Society of London (1894). His interest in geography can be traced to 1851, the very year in which he first put forth his social and political views in written form. As time went on his social and political thought and his theories of geography became ever more closely inter-related, until they achieved a final synthesis in his posthumously published *L'Homme et la Terre* (Man and the Earth), the six-volume conclusion to *La Nouvelle Géographie Universelle*. He considered that, while the general nature of the data in his geographical and his social-political studies might vary, its generic quality remained the same. Nor was there any significant distinction between the methods of analysis employed in each. The links between the two areas of enquiry deserve close attention. It is worth noting his remark to the Dutch socialist, Ferdinand Domela Nieuwenhuis: 'Yes, I am a geographer, but above all I am an anarchist.'[2]

Reclus was particularly close to developments within the European anarchist movement which lasted from the late 1870s to 1894. His moral and financial support was of critical importance for *Le Révolté*, the anarchist paper founded by Peter Kropotkin (1879 to 1887), and he exercised a considerable influence over its contents and administration; the same was true for *La Révolte* (1885 to 1894). The value of such activity is not to be under-estimated. Because European anarchists came to reject all formal organisational ties, newspapers assumed many of the functions normally performed by an organisational structure; in particular, they provided the forum for discussions on theory and practice, giving continuity to an otherwise disparate movement. *Le Révolté* and *La Révolte* enjoyed a central place among anarchist papers. In the beginning, from 1879, the former carried sober, well-written pieces which helped to sustain the nascent movement. Even when anarchism later gained in momentum and more flamboyant (though generally short-lived) papers came into existence, *La Révolte* was able to carry on the tradition of its predecessor and continued to be most highly regarded. It expired only with the collapse of the movement in 1894.

As writer of a variety of pamphlets and numerous articles, Reclus' influence extended to many parts of the world; his works appeared in a number of languages, French, English, Russian, Dutch, Hungarian, Italian and Spanish. He achieved particular success with the well-conceived and persuasively written pamphlets *Evolution et Révolution* and *A mon Frère, le Paysan* (To my Brother, the peasant). As a respected figure in the world of journalism outside anarchist circles, he wrote prolifically on all kinds of contemporary developments. While he was recognised as an able scholar and a keen social critic, many of his 'non-anarchist' colleagues, however, tended to see his politics as evidence of a curious personality trait which did not generally find expression in his scholarly work. They were mistaken, of course, but such an assessment meant that he was able to reach many people who were largely unaware of the ways in which his anarchist views informed his scholarship. Late in life, as a teacher of geography at the New University in Brussels, he drew the attention of a wide number of eager, young people. He ennobled their cause, many anarchists said, with his powerful mind and clear thinking.[3]

The outstanding characteristic of Reclus as seen by his comrades was his success in living up to the principles of the anarchism which he espoused. Kropotkin was not alone when he stated that the man was an anarchist 'to the deepest recesses of his mind, to the smallest fibre of his being'.[4] 'For me', wrote Max Nettlau, 'he represented a true realisation of anarchy.'[5] 'Elisée Reclus', said Johann Most, 'I count as one of the greatest inspirers since I became an anarchist.'[6] Reclus was a person who came to justify violence and terrorism, while at the same time managing to impress all who met him with the generosity, the kindness and the sense of toleration of a saint. His humility was legion; one after another of his friends have testified their astonishment that the renowned geographer and anarchist theorist should be able to conduct himself with such a lack of pride and affectation. Elisée Reclus had 'the strength of character, the power of endurance and the vision of a Prophet of old', wrote one admirer.[7] He 'remained to the last as direct and straightforward as a child, saying exactly what he thought, and living up to it', was another observation.[8] Throughout his long life and increasingly so towards the end of it, Reclus, by his very existence, made it more 'reasonable' to believe that anarchism could become a reality. For many anarchists, he had become incorruptible, living proof of human perfectibility. Not even Kropotkin came anywhere near achieving such a position.

This book introduces the views of an important anarchist theorist whose contribution to late nineteenth-century European anarchism has been almost completely neglected by scholars. The central position which Reclus held in the movement would alone be sufficient justification for a study of his thought. However, such a study also provides a basis for a general re-assessment of European anarchist thought, because it contributes to an understanding of important dimensions of anarchist theory and practice which have not been well understood. The anarchist conception of the state, the nature of oppression and revolution, the role of violence and terrorism — these and other questions will be subjected to careful scrutiny. One of the underlying themes of the book is that the social and political theory of Elisée Reclus was the product of an interaction of utopianism and science, two strands of thought frequently taken to be mutually exclusive. I am using the term utopian in its traditional sense to refer to a vision of a new society wherein social and political forms would have reached an ideal perfection. In this sense Reclus was the heir of community-makers such as More, Campanella, Morelly and Mably. On the other hand, he was also an enthusiastic advocate of a scientific method which revealed the existence of social laws working through the people, although independently of them. The interesting thing is that, for Reclus, the use of the scientific method, however rigorously applied, did not weaken his utopian dreams, but on the contrary, served to strengthen them. In fact, Utopia was removed from the realm of dreams and placed squarely on the centre stage of the real world, for science, as the independent arbiter of truth, held out the promise that utopia would become ever more realisable. Within this context of utopianism and science, I shall show that Reclus' legendary generosity and kindness towards others and his justification of violence are logically consistent, both being derived from his all-embracing social and political theory.

The approach which I have taken breaks with many traditional interpretations of anarchism by resisting an emphasis upon the continuities in the thought of the anarchists. In particular, I have not opted for a 'conservative' interpretation which would have represented Reclus as an anarchist from youth, and his theorising as a number of shifts correlated with the prospects of revolution. Instead, I suggest the importance of objective historical conditions in the shaping of the anarchist position. Such an examination is essential, I believe, because his social and political thought was crystallised in response to specific historical events, especially in the period from 1870 to 1871. The dialectical interplay of event and theoretical response is, therefore, crucial to an understanding of the nature of the theory. My point is that I am using historical context not merely to enhance the analysis, but as an essential part of it. That is not to say that I deny the importance of the continuities in the thought of the anarchists; indeed, as I show, they should be adequately represented.

My contention is that up to 1871 Reclus was approaching a position in which he was prepared for at least temporary accommodation to the bourgeois order, even that he was coming to a more permanent support of parliamentary institutions. I shall argue that he was beginning to see that the 'battle for democracy' might be won through outwitting the liberals in their own arena, and that these options were abruptly closed with his emotional and intellectual revulsion following the savage repression of the Paris Commune. In short, his bitter hostility towards the bourgeois state and his rejection of all party-political activity developed from 1871. Herein lies the tragedy, as I see it. Reclus, who had an uncanny sense of the power of the people in the movement of history, also developed a political theory which denied them access to a set of institutions through which they might achieve real political gains. By way of implication this book raises the question of the significance of the Commune for the development of the anarchist movement itself, partly because Reclus was to become an influential theoretician and the archetypical anarchist, but also because the men who were to launch the movement were part of a generation who shared similar elements in their responses to the events of 1870 to 1871. Needless to say, not everyone will agree with the notion that ideas and their evolution have social-psychological causes, reflect social-political events, and have to be seen within the context of a social, economic and political world. To those people I can only say that I hope this book will spark discussion from which all may benefit.

There are many friends, advisers, archivists and librarians throughout Western Europe who very generously helped me at the various stages of my work and to whom I owe a debt of gratitude. I should like to mention Chimen Abramsky, Jean Maitron and Albert Sadik. James Joll has been a constant source of inspiration. I am very grateful to Jacques Reclus, grand-nephew of Elisée Reclus, who very kindly provided much useful advice. Vincent Wright contributed intellectual stimulation, patient guidance and friendly encouragement during those years in which he supervised an earlier version of this study as a PhD thesis at the London School of Economics and Political Science. Since my return to North America, I have accumulated further debts. Both Dominick LaCapra and Richard Vernon read the earlier version of my work and offered helpful suggestions; S.J.R. Noel helped me clarify a number of points. My sincerest thanks are extended to the secretarial staff of the Department of Political Science at the University of Western Ontario, as well as to Teresa Cerny who typed the final manuscript. A special word of gratitude is due to Robert Gellately, whose intellect and generosity I have shamelessly exploited at every stage. None of the above shares responsibility for the errors which remain.

The study was made possible through the financial assistance of the IODE, the Canada Council and the Central Research Fund of the University of London.

Marie Fleming
University of Western Ontario
London, Ontario

## Notes

1. Max Nettlau, *Elisée Reclus: Anarchist und Gelehrter* (Berlin, 1928), pp. 171–2n.
2. Quoted in H. Roorda van Eysinga, 'Avant tout Anarchiste' in *Elisée Reclus (1830–1905), Savant et Anarchiste* (Paris–Brussels, 1956).
3. See especially Joseph Ishill, *Elisée and Elie Reclus: In Memoriam* (Berkeley Heights, 1927), *passim.*
4. Peter Kropotkin, 'Elisée Reclus' in *Les Temps Nouveaux,* July 1905.
5. Nettlau to Jacques Gross, 17 July 1905, *Fonds Jacques Gross, IISG.*

6. Quoted in Pierre Ramus, 'In commemoration of Elisée Reclus' in Ishill, *Elisée and Elie Reclus*, p. 125.

7. Anne Cobden-Sanderson, 'Elie and Elisée Reclus' in Ishill, ibid., p. 43.

8. William, C. Owen, 'Elisée Reclus' in Ishill, ibid.,  p. 127.

# INTRODUCTION

Anarchism is a term that elicits a wide range of responses, and its utility
is steadily being diminished, as new and different meanings continue to
be attached to it. In conventional usage it conjures up visions of chaos,
confusion and disorder, and is frequently equated with the actions of
urban guerrillas, plane hijackers, even common criminals. In this book I
am concerned with its historic use as a term to denote the theory and
practice of a social and political movement which developed in late
nineteenth-century Europe. For a number of years this movement was
perceived as a threat to the continued existence of the established order,
a threat all the more frightening because anarchists often adopted the
most radical means — violence and assassination — in an effort to
achieve their ends. Academic interest was soon aroused by this most
perplexing contemporary problem, although once the anarchist
movement appeared to have been successfully repressed, scholars turned
their attention to the analysis of the more enduring social democratic
movements. Within the last few years, however, there has been a revival
of interest in anarchism, in part reflecting a general reawakening of left-
wing thought and practice.

Much of the recent scholarly work on European anarchism has been
devoted to the activities of self-professed anarchists and to the 'proto-
political' affiliations within which they worked. Great gains have been
made in clarifying the activities of individuals and groups associated in
one way or another with anarchism as it grew and, for a time, flourished
in the late nineteenth century.[1] Although it would be less than just to
under-estimate the findings of such research, there seems to me to be a
salient weakness running through it, namely an inability or an unwillingness to re-assess the essentials of anarchist thought. Certain unwarranted
assumptions and clichés continue to pervade most thinking on the
subject. Before proceeding to an analysis of Reclus' thought, I wish to
review the main lines of traditional research on anarchism, to make
explicit the principal assumptions, and to suggest why they should be
questioned.

The notion that there is an 'anarchist' way of viewing the world
first appeared in the late nineteenth century. To be sure, there had been
people calling themselves anarchists around the mid-nineteenth century
— Pierre-Joseph Proudhon and Anselme Bellegarrique are notable examples

15

– but these were isolated individuals within a still vaguely defined radical opposition rather than representatives of a widespread movement. A general awareness of an 'anarchist' position did not exist until after the emergence of its representatives in the late 1870s.[2] Even before these individuals had become fully conscious of the nature of their beliefs, observers had singled out hostility to and rejection of government as the most striking characteristic of their thought and had seized upon the term 'anarchist' as the most apt description of it. In the beginning some of these people who were thus branded adopted the name only reluctantly. James Guillaume, a prominent spokesman within socialist revolutionary circles, argued in 1876 that the terms 'anarchist' and 'anarchy' expressed only a negative idea 'without indicating any positive theory' and led to 'distressing ambiguities'.[3] Guillaume was pointing out to his comrades that the use of the term anarchist would emphasise their opposition to bourgeois government and the state – which was true – but would also deny their socialism, that is what they were *for*. Despite such misgivings, there came to be little point in a continuing resistance, since increasingly they came to be designated as 'anarchists', by both friends and foes. In 1878 Reclus, in his customary search for the advantages of a *fait accompli*, said that the term might even aid their cause, in so far as it would provide them with a certain notoriety and attract attention.[4] In any event, the name stuck, and from the late 1870s the anarchists were to develop a movement of some consequence. By the end of the 1880s and especially in the period of the attentats of the 1890s, some self-professed anarchists sought to carry out savage assaults on the political order.[5]

Anarchism initially appeared to contemporaries to be a new phenomenon. Almost immediately, however, it came to be seen not so much as a branch of the socialist movement, but rather as an embodiment of a peculiar way of looking at the world, the product of an imagination which longed for a stateless and utopian solution to all social ills. Marxist condemnations of the utopian ('unscientific') nature of anarchism are well known. But contemporary non-Marxist scholarship also played a most important role in highlighting utopian elements within anarchism. A good example of how 'informed' opinion was attempting to reckon with the still early movement is contained in the study made by J. Garin in 1885. Garin claimed that 'these [anarchist] doctrines are not new; they have existed for all time, and not only does one find the same ideas, but even the same ideas expressed in the same terms'.[6] He was comforted by the 'banality' of the theories, which in themselves, he believed, were perfectly harmless and even 'natural' intellectual diversions for philosophers.[7] The problem in his own day, as he saw it, was not that such ideas were being discussed – this had been going on since the time of the ancient Greeks – but that they had seized the imagination of people who were ignorant enough to believe that they could be put into practice and sufficiently stupid to make the attempt.

> The problem is that these utopias, excusable because they are natural, are being made concrete, that is to say into doctrines of application. What the philosophers resolve in this or that sense, a speculative problem, is of little importance ... But the worker is not capable of savouring this pleasure of thought, and when social and political convictions are involved, the conviction leads to action, and the solution demands to be applied; it dictates immediate demands, it becomes a goal to attain.[8]

What was novel about the 'new' anarchism was its apparent appeal to groups and individuals outside the usual handful of utopian dreamers (frequently restricted to intellectuals) which could be found at any time in society. To suggest this departure from tradition was also to raise the important question of the possible social consequences, even in the unlikely event that anarchists substantially increased their following. Garin's response was to demonstrate the powerlessness of their ideas by depicting what were regarded as two unsuccessful attempts to implement anarchist theories in the past: that of Mazdak in Persia in the sixth century and that of the German Anabaptists in the early sixteenth century.[9] In a word, Garin sought to convey, by way of a simple history lesson, the reassuring thought that anarchist ideas were not new at all, that they could exercise very limited appeal, and that if and when they actually won a mass following, they led inevitably to self-destruction. Such utopianism in action was bound to fail in terms of bringing about significant change. Garin was, I believe, correct in sensing elements of utopianism within anarchism, but wrong in his dismissal of the theory as a repetition of traditional utopian schemes. He failed to perceive the essential nature of this peculiarly nineteenth-century variety of utopianism. The specific nature of Reclus' utopianism is a central question and will be examined throughout the book.

The explicit focus on the utopian nature of anarchist views as expressed within Garin's analysis was somewhat relaxed in the 1890s as observers attempted to come to terms with the bombings and assassinations committed in the name of anarchism. There was a conscious effort by people such as Cesare Lombroso and Félix Dubois to probe the psychology of the anarchists of their own day rather than to speculate upon their spiritual ancestors.[10] Essentially, their approach, when it did not simply denounce anarchists as outright criminals, described them as individuals with a peculiar psychological make-up, thus tending to reinforce earlier notions that certain personality types throughout the ages had fallen prey to an anarchist view of the world. Dubois' study demonstrates an effort not only to observe the anarchists of the late nineteenth century, but also to trace the origins of such behaviour at least back to the Anabaptists. Even though the 'establishment' bias of most analyses was embarrassingly evident, the authors claimed a high degree of objectivity and 'science' for their work. A greater detachment was achieved in such accounts as those of Ernest Alfred Vizetelly and E.V. Zenker which appeared, interestingly, after the anarchist threat had subsided, in the early part of the present century.[11] By then the events of the late nineteenth century could be more comfortably related to previous experience, that is, they could be seen as a reappearance, albeit in a rather savage form, of an age-old phenomenon.

By the turn of the century the view was firmly established that anarchism — understood as a yearning to break with governmental authority and to destroy the state — had a long heritage, with precedents reaching back to ancient Greece. One writer could even imagine how the lineage of the anarchists might be traced back to Adam or to the cave dwellers of prehistoric times.[12] The historically minded have been generally content with Zeno, the ancient Greek Stoic philosopher, followed by various early Christian sects and the Gnostics of the twelfth and thirteenth centuries. Some have claimed that anarchist views featured prominently in Wat Tyler's Rebellion of 1381, the activities of the Adamites in the fifteenth century, and especially in the rising of the German Anabaptists in the early sixteenth century. Certainly, there is no shortage of anarchistic personages from the eighteenth century onward; the Curé Jean Meslier, Diderot, Rousseau, Anarcharsis Clootz, Jacques Hérbert and Babeuf have all been seen as in some way representative of anarchist views.[13] Within this context the activities of the Kropotkins and even those of the Ravachols (Ravachol was the most notorious of 'anarchist' terrorists) appeared to be susceptible to explanation.

Accounts of anarchism written after 1900 generally maintained that there were indeed continuities observable from ancient Greece to modern Europe, though a second major tendency, that of distinguishing more sharply between modern anarchism and its forerunners began to emerge as well. The outstanding contribution to this debate was made by the German judge Paul Eltzbacher.[14] His 'scientific' attempt to grasp the essentials of anarchist thought first appeared in 1900 (French 1901), and was quickly accepted as the standard work. His 'impartial' treatment even found him favour with the anarchists; writing for the readers of the *Encyclopaedia Britannica* Kropotkin recommended it as 'the best work on Anarchism'; and in 1960 it was re-issued by *Freedom*, the journal which Kropotkin helped to found. Eltzbacher's views have become such a commonplace that they have been incorporated into almost every study of the subject up to the present day – a regrettable development, as we shall see.

Eltzbacher set out in a 'scientific' way to find the common denominators which linked representatives of modern anarchism. He selected the 'representatives' not upon the basis of any objective criteria, but rather examined the thought of those whom (informed) public opinion of the time regarded as the principal exponents of anarchism. As we have already noted, however, public opinion, prior to Eltzbacher's appearance, had already determined that the essence of anarchism was its anti-statism (broadly defined) and that all views which were hostile to the state were of necessity intimately related. Thus, it was a foregone conclusion that he should isolate the 'negation of the State' as the only common element in 'anarchist' thought. He was not led to question the utility of linking bodies of thought in this way, even though he made the important discovery that this negation of the state had 'totally different meanings' in the various exponents of anarchism. Eltzbacher mistakenly believed that the subject of his study was the nature of anarchism; in fact what he was doing was investigating people's perceptions of its nature. His work had the effect of sanctioning already existing beliefs.

Eltzbacher has also been instrumental in establishing the identity of those individuals who are considered representative of 'modern' anarchism. Largely as a result of his study, it has become conventional wisdom that this phase begins with William Godwin, and that the 'Seven Sages of Anarchism'[15] are Godwin, Proudhon, Max Stirner, Michael Bakunin, Kropotkin, Benjamin Tucker and Leo Tolstoy.[16] Even a cursory examination of the views of these men raises serious questions concerning the wisdom of such a grouping. Godwin made some startling statements, but many contain little more than verbal resemblances to those of the anarchists of the late nineteenth century. He was an isolated thinker who worked from utilitarian principles and may have been more akin to J.S. Mill than the European anarchists.[17] Under Eltzbacher's typology, it is correct to regard Tucker as an anarchist, but he had no significant connection — spiritual or otherwise — with the Europeans. He may have borrowed those aspects of their views which he could synthesise into his own individualist philosophy, but this does not necessarily mean that his thought comes anywhere near that of Kropotkin.[18] Tolstoy was a curiosity; his 'Christian' anarchism rested upon premises totally unacceptable to the decisively atheistic West Europeans, and it would be difficult to reconcile his spiritual approach with their 'rational' theories. Stirner gained a short-lived notoriety in the 1840s, while Kropotkin articulated views which were shared by a sizeable number of committed anarchists in the late nineteenth century. Moreover, Stirner is the epitome of almost everything which revolutionaries of Kropotkin's tradition came to oppose.[19]

Besides reinforcing contemporary assumptions about the nature of anarchism, and establishing the genealogy of anarchist thinkers, Eltzbacher's interpretation, by its very success, has had two further consequences. One has been the implicit rejection of the importance of the socialist impulse within the thought of the European anarchists. That this has affected our perception of the nature of anarchism can be easily detected in our continuing habit of juxtaposing the terms 'anarchist' and 'socialist'; there is a tendency to speak of 'anarchists and socialists' as if the latter did not include the former. In his widely acclaimed *History of Socialism*, Harry Laidler's very choice of words not only provides an excellent example of the assumption of a dichotomy between anarchism and socialism, but moreover, he dismisses the importance of late nineteenth-century anarchism for an understanding of socialism by dealing with what are considered to be its main principles in a long footnote.[20]

There is no question that those people who participated in the late nineteenth-century European anarchist movement perceived themselves as socialists. In 1873 Kropotkin insisted: 'There is not the slightest doubt that among different socialists of the most varied shades [and he was including socialists of an 'anarchist' persuasion] there exists a rather complete agreement in their ideals.'[21] Reclus similarly commented upon the kinship of all socialists in 1882, years after the anarchists had become a distinct group within the socialist movement.[22] Many anarchists sought public recognition of their socialism by attempting to infiltrate the Second International from its founding in 1889 until the London Congress of 1896. However, even though their socialism has been recognised by outstanding scholars such as James Joll[23] and by

sympathisers such as Daniel Guérin,[24] this has not led to a questioning
of the validity of the old categories. It is important to consider the
argument of the great sociologist Emile Durkheim. In his study of
socialism, which, unfortunately, he did not complete, he constructed a
framework in which the essential ingredients in socialism were its
'economic concepts', while political concerns in turn were extensions of,
or derivations from, the economic.[25] A reconsideration of the principles
of late nineteenth-century European anarchism will, I feel certain,
establish that the emphasis upon government and the state is secondary
to the interest in the social-economic structure of society.

Another major consequence of Eltzbacher's interpretation is the distortion of late nineteenth-century anarchist thought which has arisen
because of what he leaves out; he excludes certain key figures. The
most serious omission is that of Reclus whose stature in this period was
second only to that of Kropotkin. To neglect Reclus is not only to
overlook an important influence on the anarchist movement and on
the thought of Kropotkin, but also to fail to achieve a more precise
view of the essential nature of European anarchist thought. A study of
Reclus sheds light on several important questions, for example on the
nature of the revolution which the anarchists envisaged, a matter of
central importance which has not received sufficient attention.

It is sometimes suggested that nineteenth-century European
anarchists were convinced of the possibility of an apocalyptic transformation of society, that they put their faith in a revolution which
could transform society totally and instantly and which would establish
a veritable heaven on earth. I shall show that Reclus (and also Kropotkin)
came to believe in precisely the opposite, that as the century progressed
he became remarkably insistent upon the necessity of a gradual or
evolutionary process as the key to movement in the direction of
revolution. The struggle for socialism involved a fundamental attack
upon the prejudices, fears and illusions which were the psychological
supports of the bourgeois social-economic and political order. Only in
relation to the extent to which the hold of these supports had been
loosened, could the revolution be expected to be successful.[26] On the
surface, it is not difficult to reconcile these views on evolution and
revolution with a Marxist interpretation of the movement of history.
However, from 1871 Reclus' attempt to develop a revolutionary strategy
without resort to the parliamentary system increasingly differentiated
him from the Marxists and called into existence an almost religious faith
in the power of consciousness. The consequences for theory and
practice will be examined in some detail in the course of the discussion.

A more accurate account of the anarchism of Reclus and Kropotkin also reveals those distortions which arise when the thought of Proudhon and Bakunin is fused with the anarchism which developed later in the century. Both Proudhon and Bakunin have been called the fathers of anarchism, and there is some justification for accepting the paternity of one or the other, or even both. However, to suggest fatherhood is not to claim that the children bear a strict resemblance. The mistake is to assume that Proudhon and Bakunin were also representative of the theory which they helped to conceive. There is some basis for holding that Proudhon's ideas were inspired by certain liberal values; it may be largely because his ideas have been confused with those of the anarchist movement that the thought of which Kropotkin is a representative has also been judged — unjustifiably — to be closely related to liberalism.[27] To a great extent it is because Bakunin's ideas have been similarly grafted onto the thought of the movement that the anarchist theory of revolution has been misunderstood, and that there has been a failure to see the importance of the 'scientific' direction which was introduced by Bakunin's spiritual descendants. In particular, the importance of Reclus' wide-ranging scientific research has been overlooked, and there is much yet to be learned about the significance of Kropotkin's *Modern Science and Anarchism*, his *Mutual Aid* and his *Ethics*, to mention the most obvious examples of the interaction of science and anarchism.[28]

It has not escaped the attention of recent investigators that there is no single anarchist theory, that what is labelled as such in fact comprises varieties of theories. While an attempt at classification was more or less present in the earliest studies, the new sensitivity to the many faces of anarchism has given it an urgency and vigour that was unknown in the last century. It is now maintained that philosophical anarchism has to be distinguished from militant forms, individualistic from communist. Perhaps the most authoritative categorisation was made by Irving Horowitz who isolated no less than eight distinct strands — utilitarian, peasant, anarcho-syndicalist, collectivist, conspiratorial, communist, individualist and pacifist.[29] This typology is a contribution in so far as it exhibits an awareness of the complexities of the problem, but it is unlikely that this approach can advance the case much further. Documentation of the differences between the varieties of anarchist thought will consist mainly in filling in details. There is a further danger that, in much the same way that the continuities of anarchism used to be the main focus, writers will now be inclined to look for the continuities within the different strands. Classification is frequently helpful, but tends towards distortion, as delineations are drawn more precisely than is warranted by historical reality. A close examination of anarchism strongly supports the view that a strict distinction between philosophical and militant or political anarchism, for example, is not valid.[30]

According to the nominal lexical definition, anarchy simply means 'without government'. A survey of the literature shows that those who have come to be considered as representatives of anarchism have as a common denominator their perceived hostility to government and more generally to the state. Since such hostility issues from quite different premises, however, comparisons, as they have been usually drawn, are not terribly useful. The mere fact that the term 'anarchism' has been employed to describe the thought of people such as Kropotkin and Reclus does not in itself reveal very much about the nature of their thought. 'Anarchism' was thrust upon those exhibiting 'anarchist' tendencies in post-Commune Europe, because to observers opposition to government was their most striking message. In the event, this reveals as much about the observers' views as it does about the observed. Nor does the fact that Reclus and Kropotkin used the term mean very much. Historically, it can be shown that they had little choice. Even more importantly, their use of it does not demonstrate in what way the nominal lexical definition is to be interpreted, what precisely we are to understand by 'without government'. In my view the central problem in coming to an understanding of late-nineteenth-century European anarchism has been the tendency to examine it primarily as an anarchist theory, rather than as a socialist theory which is also anarchist. I am calling for a reconciliation between social and political theory, and for a classificatory scheme which unites 'political' thinkers in the first place by their social theory and only secondarily by their political theory. In the following pages I offer what I hope will be a contribution to a re-examination of the question.

## Notes

1. See especially Jean Maitron, *Le Mouvement anarchiste en France*, 2 vols. (Paris, 1975); James Joll has written an interesting review of this work in the *Times Literary Supplement,* 10 Sept. 1976. See also Clara E. Lida, *Anarquismo y Revolución en la España del XIX* (Madrid, 1972).

2. For information on this period see the *Fonds Guillaume, AEN*; the *AFJ, IISG*; the *BFJ*; James Guillaume, *L'Internationale. Documents et Souvenirs (1864– 1878)*, 4 vols (Paris, 1905–10); Jacques Freymond (ed.), *La Première Internationale, Recueil de Documents*, 4 vols.(Geneva, 1962–71), vol. III.

3. *BFJ,* 30 April, 7 May 1876.

4. Elisée Reclus, 'A Propos de l'Anarchie' in *Le Travailleur*, Feb./Mar. 1878.

5. There are many files on this period at the Paris Police Archives; for information on the attentats see especially B a/138, B a/139, B a/140, B a/141, B a/142, B a/143. See also Maitron, *Le Mouvement anarchiste*, vol. I, p. 206 ff; James Joll, *The Anarchists* (London, 1964), p. 117 ff; Henri de Varennes, *De Ravachol à Caserio* (Paris, n.d.) and J.C. Longoni, *Four Patients of Dr Deibler* (London, 1970).

6. J. Garin, *L'Anarchie et les Anarchistes* (Paris, 1885), p. 167.

7. Ibid., p. 185.

8. Ibid., p. 280.

9. Ibid., p. 185 ff.

10. See, for example, Cesare Lombroso, *Les Anarchistes* (Paris, 1896; Italian, 1894); Félix Dubois, *Le Péril Anarchiste* (Paris, 1894). The same kind of approach was taken by a highly regarded social scientist who was also a sympathiser of anarchist ideals: A. Hamon, *Psychologie de l'Anarchiste-Socialiste* (Paris, 1895).

11. Ernest Alfred Vizetelly, *The Anarchists* (New York, 1972; originally 1911); E.V. Zenker, *Anarchism* (London, 1898).

12. Vizetelly, ibid., p. 3.

13. This tradition has continued in the introduction of recent books on anarchism; cf. Joll, *Anarchists*, p. 17 ff, and George Woodcock, *Anarchism* (London, 1963), p. 35 ff.

14. Paul Eltzbacher, *Anarchism* (London, 1960; originally 1900).

15. Vizetelly, *The Anarchists*, p. 10.

16. This pattern continues today, sometimes slightly modified. Cf. Woodcock, *Anarchism*; Joll, *Anarchists*; also R.B. Fowler, 'The Anarchist Tradition of Political Thought' in *The Western Political Quarterly*, Dec. 1972.

17. Michael Taylor, *Anarchy and Cooperation* (London, 1976), p. 138 ff has made a similar judgement.

18. The European anarchists tended to dismiss the native American anarchists, such as Tucker, although they did identify with immigrant anarchists in the United States – and here Johann Most and Emma Goldman featured prominently. But Most had little influence on the American anarchists and Goldman was misunderstood; these 'foreigners' are more correctly assigned a place in the European movement.

19. Cf. R.W.K. Paterson, *The Nihilistic Egoist, Max Stirner* (London, 1971).

20. Harry W. Laidler, *History of Socialism* (New York, 1934), p. 283, fn. 16.

21. Peter Kropotkin, 'Must We Occupy Ourselves with the Examination of the Ideal of a Future System?' in P.A. Kropotkin, *Selected Writings on Anarchism and Revolution*, ed. Martin A. Miller (Cambridge, Mass., 1970), p. 47.

22. *Le Révolté*, 21 Jan. 1882. See also the proceedings of the Congress of the Jura Federation of 1880 in which the theory of anarchist communism was officially adopted: *Le Révolté*, 17 Oct. 1880.

23. Joll, *Anarchists*.

24. Daniel Guérin, *Anarchism* (New York, 1970).

25. Emile Durkheim, *Socialism* (New York, Collier, 1962), p. 63.

26. These themes were already important in the thought of Bakunin, but they were only elaborated in the work of Kropotkin and Reclus. See especially Reclus' *L'Evolution, la Révolution, et l'Idéal anarchique* (Paris, 1898).

27. See, for example, Fowler, 'The Anarchist Tradition of Political Thought', especially pp. 745–7.

28. Peter Kropotkin, *Modern Science and Anarchism* (Russian, 1901); *Mutual Aid, A Factor of Evolution* (London, 1902); *Ethics* (London, 1924).

29. Irving Horowitz (ed.), *The Anarchists* (New York, 1964), Intro. This book is an anthology of the 'classics'; see Leonard Krimerman and Lewis Perry (eds), *Patterns of Anarchy* (Anchor, 1966) who present lesser known writings.

30. Martin A. Miller, *Kropotkin* (Chicago, 1976) suggests that this was the case with Kropotkin.

PART I

THE MAKING OF AN ANARCHIST: 1830–71

# 1 EARLY INFLUENCES AND WRITING

Jean-Jacques Elisée Reclus was the fourth of twelve children born to Jacques Reclus and Zéline Trigant. He came into the world on 15 March 1830 at Sainte-Foy-la-Grande, a small village in the department of the Gironde in southwest France.[1] At the time of Elisée's birth, Jacques Reclus was pastor in the neighbouring Montcaret and one of the teachers at the Protestant collège of Sainte-Foy; at the end of 1831 he left Sainte-Foy to become pastor to the farmers of Castétarbes and Orthez in the department of the Lower Pyrenees. Elisée was left behind with his maternal grandparents in Laroche, presumably because of his young age, but for some reason, he remained there until late 1838 when he rejoined his parents and brothers and sisters at Castétarbes.

As son of a pastor Elisée grew up in close contact with members of the Protestant church, and at the age of 18 he himself took up the study of theology, with a view to entering the ministry. This choice of career might appear unsurprising for the son of a pastor, and on the surface might indicate that Elisée had a good relationship with his father and was tempted to follow in his footsteps. Once we examine the evidence, however, we find that Elisée Reclus' childhood and youth, in fact his whole life, consisted in a struggle to overcome almost everything which his father, and more generally, religion had come to represent. His personal decision to join the church may be viewed both negatively and positively. It was a protest against what he believed was a shallow and ritualistic interpretation of religion, and, at the same time it was an act which was expressive of a desire to play a role in redirecting the church to a more vigorous pursuit of Christian ideals. Elisée changed his mind about becoming a pastor, and came to denounce all religion, though not the ideals of Christianity. His father played a dominant role in shaping the kind of person he was to become.

Pastor Reclus embodied a rigorous, Christian-inspired individuality and lived by the dictates of his conscience to the point where his family was subjected to material hardship. As a young man in Sainte-Foy, his natural abilities and theological training, as well as the social connections within his own and his wife's family, had placed him in a favourable position for advancement within the church hierarchy.[2] In 1831, at the age of 35 he was offered the presidency of the Consistoire. He decided not only to spurn the wishes of those who encouraged him to get ahead in the world, but also to attempt to get back to the roots of his Calvinism by leaving for the poorer department of the lower Pyrenees. His reliance upon donations from the farmers of Castétarbes and Orthez as his only source of income assured him of the independence from the state which he believed he needed in order to follow the Biblical message. The inflexibility of character which, on the one hand, could lead Pastor Reclus to make this praiseworthy attempt to re-establish his life in accordance with his religious principles, also tended to render him stern, authoritarian, and to his children at least rather awesome. Elisée later remembered that

> his powerful personality dominated absolutely every one of his friends, his congregation and all those who gravitated around him. It was impossible not to see him as a being apart, as the natural intermediary between each of his charges and that formidable world of the beyond where the Lord reigns surrounded by his angels. He represented the divinity; this was the first impression one had of him, an impression which gradually became transformed as it rendered him more human, but it left him, at least in the eyes of his son as the Ideal of the inflexible Conscience.[3]

The evidence suggests that the boy  Elisée had a most unsatisfactory relationship with his father; in fact it is clear that he found his father oppressive and suffered tremendously under the burden of his authoritarianism. His sister Louise remembered that his stay at Castétarbes had been a 'life of sadness and dread, of which he never spoke without bitterness'.[4] It is not difficult to understand why. The young Elisée, who showed himself to be a naturally friendly and out-going child, with a vivid imagination, inquisitive mind and remarkable sensitivity, had been tolerably happy up to the age of eight; he had lived with good-natured grandparents who placed little emphasis upon formal education and acted rather leniently towards his childhood pranks.[5] Thus, it was to be expected that he would find life more severe among his many brothers and sisters. However, a difficult situation was exacerbated by Pastor Reclus' austere character. Shortly after the family reunion, for example, Elisée was reprimanded by his father for having 'corrupted' Elie, his elder brother by three years, through encouraging him to explore the neighbouring countryside. The boy was astonished at his first encounter with paternal authority, and he demanded to know 'how he had done wrong',[6] For the father it was necessary to discipline a 'spoiled' child; for the son the father represented force and oppression which had to be endured in silent, though defiant, agony.

The tension which issued from Elisée's relationship with his father was partially alleviated by the tenderness which existed between him and his mother, whom he described as 'admirably zealous, but of another manner than her husband'.[7] Madame Reclus seems either to have shared her husband's religious fervour or to have abided by his decisions without complaint. However, she was no submissive wife; she showed a courage, independence of spirit, and physical and emotional endurance that was truly remarkable. As a fairly educated woman among poor peasants, she took it upon herself to found a school in Orthez; devotion to learning was, one suspects, mixed with a common-sense attitude towards the amelioration of the family's material condition which had suffered through the Pastor's intransigence. Elisée's first teacher was his mother, whose insistence upon excellence tended to haunt him when he first began to write and indeed was to remain with him throughout his life. His mother's influence can also be detected in his emphasis upon the importance of education for the revolutionary struggle.

Life could not have been easy for Madame Reclus, the wife of a poor pastor, mother of a large family and local school-teacher. Elisée recalled that this woman who devoted every minute of her life to her children ironically did not have the time to show them any real affection.[8] While he felt deprived of a certain amount of physical attention, he was, none the less, emotionally drawn to a mother who was quite successful in transmitting feelings of warmth and love. His many letters to her testify to his deep affection and enduring respect, as well as to a high degree of intimacy between them. The mother made it even clearer what it was about the father that was so oppressive. In a sense Elisée's life became a quest for that maternal love which he could never manage to experience in sufficiently satisfying quantities, even as, paradoxically, he was to show the uncompromising inflexibility characteristic of his father in his efforts to achieve it.

Pastor Reclus was the single most important figure in instilling into his son the scruples of his Calvinist background which were to re-emerge in new forms in later years. In fact, the father was far more successful than he could have imagined, or indeed have understood, for the boy Elisée very early became disturbed that a religion which could preach brotherhood and equality could also be so complacent when faced with the social reality of greed and inequality. As a mature man he recalled how, as a boy, he had attributed great significance to the idea of the heavenly father providing the 'daily bread'.

> It seemed to me that by a mysterious act a meal would descend
> from on high on all the tables of the world. I imagined that these
> words, repeated millions and millions of times, were a cry of human
> brotherhood, and that each, in uttering them, thought of all.[9]

Elisée came to sense the contradictions involved in his father's rejection
of organised religion for a literal adherence to the words, but not the
real meaning, of the Bible.[10] His subsequent categorical approach to the
salvation of men and women on earth  may be viewed as an attempt
to see Christian ideals fully realised.

Elisée's concern with the meaning of Christian brotherhood was
intensified during his experiences with the Moravian brothers in the
German Rhineland. Pastor Reclus had been led to believe that the
Moravians, who operated a school for German and foreign children in
Neuwied, would inculcate a true Christian spirit into his children, and
in spite of the family's poverty, Elie and his sister Susi attended the
school from 1840 to 1842 and Elisée from 1842 to 1844. The
Moravians, Elisée later wrote, were for the most part 'docile subjects,
with their lives regulated in advance by a disgusting ritual of childish
practices and conventional lies'.[11] The director of the school he described
as a cowardly and contemptible fellow who flattered the rich and
ridiculed the poor. But he seems to have felt that, in addition to the
discrimination which he suffered because of his poverty, he was also
victimised on account of his nationality. The description which he
has left of Elie's experiences at the hands of school comrades doubtlessly reflected his own fate. He wrote that Elie was beaten and called
names such as 'French frog' and 'froggie', each occasion being termed a
little 'Waterloo' and that the Moravian brothers encouraged the ill-
treatment.[12] The Moravians, we are led to believe, were preoccupied
with ritual, small-minded and nasty; men who had devoted their lives
to Christ had become totally un-Christian in their relations with their
students. It is not surprising that Elisée, who had already become sensitive to the religious 'failings' of his scrupulous father, could react so
negatively to the Moravians, who in comparison with his father, had
carried hypocrisy to an unprecedented degree. This disillusionment
with religion was accompanied by a growing interest in the 'social
question' which can be detected from 1844, the year in which Elisée
joined Elie at the Protestant collège of Sainte-Foy.

His lifelong friendship with Elie had begun in late 1838 when he had arrived at Castétarbes, but it did not develop in any meaningful way until the period 1844 to 1847 when the two boys were bosom pals at Sainte-Foy (where Elisée studied for the baccalauréat from 1844 to 1848).[13] At this age, from mid to late teens, they were already taking on the features of manhood, and the pair must have made an interesting contrast. Elisée was short and slender, with intense blue eyes, blond hair and an enthusiastic manner, while Elie was tall, broad, dark and sombre looking, with a tendency to be rather withdrawn and melancholic. It is worthy of note that Elie, who resembled Pastor Reclus in looks and personality, should have become a true inspiration for Elisée, to the point of assuming the role of father. The impression which emerges from the sources is that Elisée was deeply impressed by his elder brother.

At Sainte-Foy, Elisée remembered, Elie was possessed by a 'literary fervour' and most of his friends shared the enthusiasm. A good deal of attention was given to the 'social question', especially as represented in the works of Saint-Simon, Auguste Comte, Charles Fourier and Félicité de Lamennais.[14] A disrespectful attitude was adopted towards teachers who demanded devotion to their studies: 'Little matter, we said, since they were supposed to succeed in their various bourgeois careers, as property-owners, employees of the State, stock-holders with easy consciences.'[15] The boys lived at the home of their mother's sister at Sainte-Foy, and she and her husband were decidedly unsympathetic to the radical nature of their political attitudes. Made to answer for all their actions, they deeply resented the intrusion of the aunt and uncle into their affairs, and they reacted rebelliously to the advice of the uncle to seek 'wealth and honours' and to secure 'admiration of the hierarchy among men'. As far as the uncle was concerned, the activities of the two boys after 1851 were 'the abomination of desolation'.[16]

Although both Elisée and Elie were highly critical of religion as it was being presented to them, they chose, interestingly, not to abandon it, but rather to become more deeply involved. When in 1847 Elie began his theology studies at Geneva, the original home of Calvinism, Pastor Reclus was perplexed to say the least, not being able to understand how his son, who was completely 'outside grace', could study what theologians had to say without partaking of their faith.[17] He must have been doubly shocked when Elisée decided to take up the study of theology one year later at Montauban in the department of the Tarn-et-Garonne in southwest France. The spirit of proselytism which pervaded Elisée Reclus' whole career had struck deep roots at an early age. As he said in 1851, 'the very sight of a pulpit makes me palpitate, and I have rarely been happier than I was on that day when I preached at Montauban in front of two teachers, my brother and the empty benches'.[18] The years 1848 to 1849 marked a crucial stage in his development. In this period he was once again the companion and school comrade of Elie who had returned from Geneva to continue his theology studies at Montauban.

By early 1848 economic grievances were giving expression to the political unrest which was sweeping Western Europe. The brothers were soon casting anxious glances in the direction of Paris, eagerly awaiting 'the news of political battles'.[19] Though Louis Philippe had attempted to suppress radical movements, he had not been able to halt their growth in underground organisations, and under the cover of 'friendly' societies. The round of 'banquets' led by public figures such as Adolphe Thiers and Odillon Barrot which began in 1847, intensified the political climate and drew attention to the need for electoral and parliamentary reform. When the government banned the banquet planned for 22 February 1848, the barricades went up in Paris and did not come down when Louis Philippe tried appeasement by dismissing Guizot and his ministry. Deserted by the National Guard, the king was forced to abdicate on 24 February, and the Republic was success-fully proclaimed for the second time in French history. An Englishman who in 1852 was given French lessons by Elisée, remembered that his tutor 'often spoke of that marvellous dawn, stormy day, and most unhappy sunset'.[20] The excitement which was felt in 1848 remained at a peak in 1851 when he wrote:

> For eighteen years a hideous blast of interest and egoism crept over France. At last there arrived the Revolution of contempt, the throne disappeared, and the bourgeois began anew to celebrate the magnanimous people, the magnanimous people who would have been shot down if they had been defeated . . . That was a beautiful day when one saw a king pale at the approach of the people and look for an ill-smelling cellar in his splendid castle, a king who had felt that he would be able just once more to imprison the rioters.[21]

The political upheaval of 1848 was not restricted to France. On 12 January there was a popular uprising in Palermo, Sicily, against the abuses of Ferdinand II of Naples, and similar democratic agitation followed in other parts of Italy. The big popular demonstrations in Mannheim on 27 February were followed by uprisings throughout the German states and led to the convening of the Frankfurt Vorparlament.

Popular demonstrations in Vienna forced Metternich to resign on 13 March. The March Laws, which assured Hungary of virtual home rule, were a triumph for Louis Kossuth. In the same year there were also disturbances in Belgium and England and revolt in Switzerland. While there were strong nationalist overtones in many of the uprisings, from what Elisée wrote shortly after 1848, it can be gathered that he regarded them essentially as attempts of the people to emancipate themselves from all forms of oppression.[22] Similarly, his own feelings of local patriotism he tended to regard as a force to be used against oppression within France.[23] It is not surprising that he would react favourably to the movement for national liberation of the 1840s, for it was widely recognised to be linked with the struggle against autocracy. On 22 February 1848 Karl Marx had praised the rising (of 1846) at Cracow, Poland and had held it up as an example 'in identifying the cause of nationality with the cause of democracy and the enfranchisement of the oppressed class'.[24]

In the meantime the Reclus brothers were growing increasingly restless as theology students at Montauban which, they complained, was a town totally without intellectual stimulation.[25] They were beginning to become more decisive in their social and political views, and Elisée recalled that their attitudes and appearance were 'republican' and 'aggressive'.[26] They even decided to remove themselves from the direct tutelage of the theology teachers at Montauban, and with their friend Edouard Grimard they installed themselves in a place four kilometres away. The boys engaged in a voracious reading of a wide selection of writings and did not allow themselves to be obstructed by the day-to-day routine of seminary life.[27] Defiance of teachers finally led, in the spring of 1849, to their being advised to leave the college, when they made a trip to the Mediterranean[28] instead of attending a meeting at which some speakers from Paris were to address the students. Elisée later claimed that the prefect of the department had discriminated against them for their political beliefs and had put pressure on the doyen to expel them.[29] It is unlikely that the prefect would have intervened in such a matter, though it is possible that the doyen was anxious to rid himself of three trouble-makers and had indicated the prefect's dissatisfaction (or supposed dissatisfaction) to strengthen his case. Elie soon left for Strasbourg, interestingly once again, to resume his theology studies,[30] while Elisée spent some time in Orthez and Sainte-Foy before departing for Neuwied in the autumn of 1849 to take up a position — secured probably through the intercession of his father — as a teacher in, of all places, the school of the hated Moravian brothers.

Elisée's experiences at Neuwied re-affirmed his earlier impressions of the Moravians. While relations were considerably relaxed this time, they were generally superficial and carried no depth of feeling. He saw even more clearly that any religious faith which the brothers may have originally possessed now consisted in habit, that the name of God was no longer an inspiration, but only mentioned at the appointed times. His attitudes doubtlessly caused some degree of friction, and he wrote in a letter of 1850: 'If I appear a heretic to them, at least my heresy is dear and profound to me.'[31] Discontent with a position which was emotionally and intellectually unsatisfying, he resigned and set out in January 1851 to study at the University of Berlin.[32]

A letter which he wrote on 11 February suggests that his interests were becoming more terrestrial. While his attention continued to be directed towards theology, parental preferences and personal inclinations being difficult to dismiss, he seems to have attended courses in political economy and the history of diseases. He also followed a course in geography with the well-known Carl Ritter whose lectures sparked his imagination and were an important influence upon the development of his career as a geographer.[33] It is not unlikely that a growing interest in social and economic matters led him to make contact with German socialists, though we have no proof of this. At any rate, he was aware of socialist ideas then blossoming in Germany.[34] It was also in this period that he made what was to be his final decision on the question of whether he should become a minister. In a letter of April 1851 he wrote to his mother that, although he experienced great excitement at the idea of preaching to the faithful, the formalities which went with the life of the pastor would weigh heavily upon him, and it was for this reason that he was declaring: 'I do not wish to be, nor am I able, nor ought I to be a pastor.'[35] The year of interruption in his studies had put an end to all his hesitations in the matter, and he had resolved in a manner surprisingly reminiscent of his father, to spend the rest of his life heeding nothing but 'the cry of my conscience'.[36]

In 1851 Elisée Reclus was 21 years old. It was in this year that he set down the first known systematic account of his social and political ideas in the form of an essay entitled 'Développement de la Liberté dans le monde' (Development of Liberty in the World).[37] The essay was written as an exercise in self-clarification, and was soon laid aside and forgotten, until it was rediscovered many years later among some old papers and presented to Reclus in the final years of his life. There is some justification for considering this writing as a programme which was drawn up very early in life and which formed the basis of his subsequent theorising. Or, as seems far more likely to me, it was an essay written by a youth full of enthusiasm for revolutionary change who had not yet considered, and who could not yet have understood, the social-economic and political implications of what he wrote. There is no denying that the anarchist theory which he developed in the 1870s bears striking resemblances to his position in 1851. However, while it will be part of my aim to point to the continuities in Reclus' thought, I shall also show that the importance of such similarities as did exist between the position of 1851 and that of the 1870s should not be exaggerated. I shall return to this question in a later chapter, once I have discussed the development of his thought in greater detail. At this point I should like to examine the main themes of the 1851 essay.

The title 'Development of Liberty in the World' is misleading. While on a conscious level Reclus sets out to show that the quest for liberty is inherent in human beings, his notion of liberty quickly becomes subordinated to what he regards as the ultimate aim, love or that which appears to be its equivalent, universal brotherhood. 'For each particular man liberty is an end, but it is only a means to attain love, to attain universal brotherhood.' Reclus was saying that it was wrong to view liberty as an end in itself, since the pursuit of liberty for its own sake would lead to nothing but massive egoism. His concept of liberty was based upon an individual's coming to a consciousness not only of his own need for liberty, but also to a consciousness of the need for brotherly love. The Declaration of the Rights of Man erred because it had liberated (or at least had called for the liberation) of men *qua* citizens rather than men *qua* men, 'since it accords to the citizen the right to liberty in such a way that this liberty is not limited by love, but by duties'. Reclus rejected a negative liberty which posited one's fellows as posing restrictions upon the scope of one's actions, and expressed the notion of a positive liberty in which one's fellows provided the essential ingredients to find fulfilment as a naturally loving human being.

It might be said that the essay would have been more appropriately entitled 'Development of Love (or Brotherhood) in the World', since liberty was subordinated to love and brotherhood. However, we must understand that Reclus' interest in liberty arose not out of a concern with liberty as such, but out of a concern with liberty within the context of the struggle for a more just society. In particular, he was severely critical of pre-1848 'utopian' communism which threatened to limit rather than to increase liberty, and which maintained that people 'ought to become absorbed in the mass and to be no more than the innumerable arms of the polyp'. A person 'is not an accident, but a free being, necessary and active, who though united with his fellows, remains distinct from them'. Reclus was most insistent that communism had to free the individual at the same time as it guaranteed the well-being of all. People were perceived as forming a 'human association'; each member of the association must 'develop freely according to his means and his faculties, without being hindered in any way by the mass of his brothers', while the work of each person must contribute to the welfare of the whole association. This criticism of 'utopian' communism is important because it demonstrates important aspects of a central concern of the theory of anarchist communism which was to be formulated in the 1870s. This will become more apparent in a later chapter.

Reclus' notion of liberty merged with, and became an inseparable part of, his idea of equality. *Laissez-faire* liberalism, on the one side, and utopian communism on the other, gave rise to the establishment of a society totally alien to human needs; liberty without equality was the mistake of the former, just as equality without liberty was that of the latter. He would have agreed with the thesis that the fatal error which led to the development of utopian communism was the assumption that practice should be put at the service of theory, the notion that the ideas of major thinkers should constitute the blueprint for communist communities. In the first half of the nineteenth century there had been several famous attempts in the New World to establish communities based upon the ideas of Charles Fourier and Robert Owen; in 1850 Etienne Cabet set out to found his Icaria in Illinois. Reclus saw such endeavours as misguided, to say the least. Socialism, he said, was not to be found in books, not even in those of men such as Proudhon and Louis Blanc, but 'in the hearts of the people . . . in the hearts of those poor naive and artless peasants'. It was here, amid the needs and desires of ordinary people that the key to social advance was to be found.

History was viewed by Reclus as a struggle to achieve an equality that did not preclude, but rather enhanced liberty. Primitive society had been moved by selfish drives and egoisms and ignorance of anything else but martial values. Each stage in the rise and fall of civilisations, however, represented a step towards the wider dissemination of the idea of equality. Christianity, he saw as one of the most important. The development of feudalism with its order of institutionalised inequality had not been able to overcome the victory of Christianity, because the lord and his serf had continued to remain 'equal' at least in the sight of God. And the great French Revolution, with its ideals of liberty, equality and fraternity, had held out the promise of the kind of social order which he was convinced could and would be established. Writing in 1851, when reaction had successfully re-asserted itself throughout Europe, his optimism continued undaunted. While he believed that the movement of history was sometimes progressive, sometimes regressive, he insisted that the progressive elements were always stronger than the regressive, and therefore 'it is incontestable that humanity advances in the direction of progress'. Progress was closely linked to a growing consciousness of the value and potentialities of humanity, but the whole point of a consciousness was to prepare the way for a new reality. It was most likely he believed, that violence and revolution would be necessary to conquer the forces of habit, egoism and the past. 'Peaceful democracy is utopia', said the young man, whose childhood sensitivity to cruelty in the slaughterhouses of rural France had led to a lifelong practice of vegetarianism.[38]

The ultimate aim of revolution, as Reclus saw it, was the creation of a universal Republic. Even though he pronounced on the liberating effects of nationalist movements, he believed he was witnessing the beginnings of a new era in which nationalism would become a weakened and unnecessary force. Carried away with enthusiasm for the future of humanity, he declared that national hatreds were already on the wane and remarked that people were being regarded more for what they were than whence they happened to come. While France may have been viewed from police states, such as Prussia or Russia, as in some sense in the vanguard of revolution, he emphasised that French oppressors were indistinguishable from those of other countries. It was possible, therefore, for those who shared the common denominator of their oppression to look upon one another not as members of antagonistic groups, but as people united in their suffering and in their struggle. 'We democrats are united in spirit . . . with all you rejected peoples, with you oppressed of all nations, wretched of all climates, with you against your German oppressors, against your French oppressors.' 'Our destiny', said Reclus, 'is to arrive at that state of ideal perfection where nations no longer have any need to be under the tutelage of a government or any other nation. It is the absence of government; it is anarchy, the highest expression of order.'

There is a striking similarity between the final expression and the title of Belligarrique's journal which appeared in April and May of

1850: *L'Anarchie, c'est l'ordre* and *L'Anarchie, journal de l'ordre* (Anarchy is order; Anarchy, journal of order). Reclus was also acquainted with the writings of Proudhon and was no doubt familiar with his infamous *What is Property?* in which Proudhon had proclaimed 'I am an anarchist' and explained how 'society looks for order in anarchy'.[39] What Reclus might have been thinking when he used the term anarchy in 1851 and how this was related to his views in the 1870s will be taken up in a later chapter. At this point it is clear that he was one of the few who, in 1851, accepted the notion of anarchy in a positive sense.

Reclus' remarks in this period suggest a continuing belief in God, but he was nearer than he would have been prepared to admit to becoming an atheist. In his 1851 essay, the idea of God seems to have been superimposed upon an analysis of society and an attempt made to reconcile religious and radical political beliefs. 'It is then ridiculous to admit . . . that the hand of God directs the universe . . . All events proceed from the free development of man, all from irrevocable destiny . . . Man and God each have a real existence; let us therefore be neither fatalists nor atheists.' In this period, Christianity was regarded by Reclus even as a means by which the ideal of brotherly love might be inculcated into the hearts of all. In one passage it was declared that 'tomorrow is the great day of combat . . . the day when Jesus will come to reign over his enemies and impose upon them brotherhood and the adoration of his God'. In a later section he wrote of the 'Christian Republic', 'the day when all brothers of Jesus Christ are equal and free, when each person's conscience is the rule of religion, when there are neither priests nor shackles nor limits, but love only and forever!' There is understandable reluctance to dismiss God, even though he believed that people were — at any rate they could become — 'free' beings. There was a point where God was simply equated with love and liberty. God did not belong to this view of society and would soon be removed.

In the late summer of 1851 Elisée left Berlin to meet Elie in Strasbourg. Elie had successfully completed his theological studies, and had immediately resigned from the ministry rather than compromise himself by becoming a pastor.[40] At the beginning of September the brothers left Strasbourg with little more than 30 francs in their pockets and their dog at their heels. They spent the next 21 days making their way across France, living on bread and sleeping in the open air. They were continually under the suspicion of being 'false vagabonds', for it was less than three months before the *coup d'état* of Louis Napoleon and security was rigid. In late September they arrived among friends in Montauban, and some days later they were in Orthez with their parents.[41]

Elisée has recorded that, in the evening following the *coup d'état* of 2 December, the republicans of Orthez gathered around a Deputy and demanded resistance, but that when the Deputy pleaded with them not to act too hastily, Elie and a few others (including Elisée) decided to take the matter into their own hands. What support they won dwindled until they were reduced to a handful of friends outside the Hôtel de Ville.[42] Within the Reclus family it has been accepted as fact that Elisée and Elie were threatened with arrest, and this threat was documented by Elisée later in life.[43] There is no official record of any protest in Orthez following the *coup* and no report of orders to arrest the brothers. Whether the mayor managed to prevent things from amounting to anything big enough to be reported and merely un-officially indicated the possibility of arrest cannot be substantiated. For whatever reason, however, it was thought advisable that the brothers leave France, and Madame Reclus quickly raised the sum of money necessary to get her sons out of the country. Elisée and Elie, who had been already planning to go to England 'to continue their apprenticeship of life and their sociology studies', happily put their plans into execution.[44]

Elisée Reclus' early exposure to Christianity produced favourable impressions, but the hypocrisy which he experienced led to perplexing moments. A still somewhat vague notion of socialism provided him with a framework in which he might attempt to resolve those questions which he found most vexing. He rebelled against a religion which postulated that all people would be equal in a life after death and which at the same time sanctioned the existence of gross social-economic inequities on earth. Many years later, in 1884, he condemned Christians who called men 'brethren' and then proceeded to turn a blind eye upon the poor. 'The very life of humanity is but one long cry for that fraternal equity which still remains unattained.'[45] However, a rejection of traditional Christianity was not a rejection of Christian ideals. Reclus' whole life may be viewed as an attempt to fulfil the promises of brotherhood and equality, to create a Christian society without a God, an earthly brotherhood of equals, without fathers, spiritual or otherwise! (A rather extreme case of father hatred.) Anarchism itself became the struggle for the 'conquest of bread', the 'daily bread' which the Heavenly Father had failed to provide. In 1904, the year before his death, he conceded that in many respects it was right to emulate the Christian of the Bible. 'Thus, I ought to call no one "master", nor to say that I am the master of anyone; I ought to attempt to live in con-ditions of equality with everyone, Jew or Greek, property-owner or slave, millionaire or beggar, without making exceptions for alleged superiorities or presumed inferiorities.'[46] 'No one could be more in harmony with the spirit of early Christianity', said a lifelong friend, 'Jesus Christ would I believe, have regarded him as a brother.'[47] Elisée Reclus' religion had not been abandoned, so much as it had been redefined and redirected.

## Notes

1. For a copy of Reclus' birth certificate, see *Papiers ER, NAF* 22909. The most important sources for the early development of Reclus are Elisée Reclus, *Correspondance*, 3 vols. (Paris, 1911—25), especially vol. I; Paul Reclus, *Les Frères Elie et Elisée Reclus* (Paris, 1964); Max Nettlau, *Elisée Reclus: Anarchist und Gelehrter* (Berlin, 1928).

2. Elisée's godfather had been Jacques Drilholle, protestant pastor and president of the Consistoire of Sainte-Foy; see birth certificate. Cf. Elisée Reclus, *Elie Reclus, 1827—1904* (Paris, 1905), p. 7; also as 'Vie d'Elie Reclus' in Paul Reclus, *Les Frères*.

3. Reclus, *Elie Reclus*, p. 9. Although the word 'son' refers to Elie, the passage may also be taken as a description of Elisée's impressions.

4. *Corr.* I, p. 9.

5. Ibid., p. 8.

6. Ibid.

7. Reclus, *Elie Reclus*, p. 9.

8. Ibid.

9. Elisée Reclus, 'An Anarchist on Anarchy' in the *Contemporary Review*, May 1884, as pamphlet *An Anarchist on Anarchy* (Boston, 1884).

10. This has to be inferred from his later remarks on religion. See especially ibid.

11. Reclus, *Elie Reclus*, p. 11.

12. Ibid., p. 13.

13. Paul Reclus, 'Biographie d'Elisée Reclus' in Paul Reclus, *Les Frères*, p. 19. Elisée's 'Diplôme de Bachelier ès Lettres' was awarded on 5 Aug. 1848 by the doyen and teachers of the 'faculté des Lettres, Académie de Bordeaux'. For the document, see *Papiers ER, NAF* 22909.

14. Paul Reclus, 'Biographie', p. 19.

15. Reclus, *Elie Reclus*, p. 16.

16. *Corr.* I, pp. 15—16; Paul Reclus, 'A Few Recollections on the Brothers Elie and Elisée Reclus' in J. Ishill, *Elisée and Elie Reclus: In Memoriam* (Berkeley Heights, 1927), p. 8.

17. Reclus, *Elie Reclus*, p. 16. The year of Elie's stay in Geneva was a year of political turmoil in Switzerland. On 20 July 1847 the Liberals managed to get the Diet to order the dissolution of the Sonderbund of the seven Catholic cantons, and civil war ensued. Elie's letters to his family showed him to be uninterested in 'a political movement in which all the main characters were repugnant to him' (ibid., p. 17) and he preferred to research the origins and development of religion in its multifarious forms. Elie's personal problems, including his rejection as a suitor because, it has been said, of his poverty (Paul Reclus, 'A Few Recollections', p. 10), may have inclined him towards introspection and contributed to his aversion to the contemporary world.

18. Elisée to his mother, Apr. 1851, *Corr.* III, p. 2.

19. Reclus, *Elie Reclus*, p. 18.
20. Richard Heath, 'Elisée Reclus' in *The Humane Review*, Oct. 1905.
21. Elisée Reclus, 'Développement de la Liberté dans le monde', an essay written very likely in 1851. The manuscript was discovered by Reclus' sister, Louise, among old papers in Brussels (in the late 1890s or the early 1900s) and passed on to Clara Mesnil. When Reclus was approached, he commented: 'Oh! that silly thing!' (See the account by Clara Mesnil in the *NA, IISG*.) It was only after his death that any part of the essay was quoted in print. Jacques Mesnil quoted some parts of it in 1906 (*Les Temps Nouveaux*, 29 Sept.–1 Dec. 1906). and *Le Libertaire* published the entire essay in 1925 (28 Aug.–2 Oct.). The manuscript was not initially dated, and it was at the end of his life that Reclus wrote '1851 Montauban' at the head of it. *Le Libertaire* changed the date to 1850 because 'in 1851 Elisée Reclus was no longer at Montauban' and because the manuscript seemed 'to have been conceived after the revolutionary period of 1848' (*Le Libertaire*, 2 Oct. 1925). It is unlikely that Reclus would have mistaken the date, and while some parts of the essay seem to have been written in 1849, there are also similarities between the essay and a letter which Reclus wrote to his mother from Berlin in April 1851 (*Corr.* III, p. 1 ff). It is possible that the essay was composed sometime during the period 1849 to 1851 and completed in the few days of Reclus' stay in Montauban in the autumn of 1851. Cf. Nettlau, *Elisée Reclus*, pp. 8–9. For the original manuscript, see *Archief ER, IISG*.
22. Reclus, 'Développement'.
23. Ibid.
24. Quoted in Boris Nicolaevsky and Otto Maenchen-Helfen, *Karl Marx, Man and Fighter* (London, 1973), p. 148.
25. Reclus, *Elie Reclus*, p. 18.
26. Ibid., p. 20.
27. Ibid., p. 19.
28. For Elisée's excitement on seeing the Mediterranean for the first time, see Paul Reclus, 'A Few Recollections', pp. 24–5.
29. Elisée recorded; 'He [the doyen] sent for the three youths, and not without chagrin, officially transmitted the consilium abeundi . . . ', *Elie Reclus*, p. 20.
30. Ibid., pp. 20–21.
31. Elisée to his mother, n.d. (1850), *Corr.* I, p. 29.
32. On 1 Feb. 1851, Dr A. Twesten, Rector at the University, signed Reclus' certificate of acceptance. For the original document, see *Papiers ER, NAF* 22909.
33. Elisée to his mother, 11 Feb. 1851, *Corr.* I, p. 37. In the introduction to his translation of an essay of Carl Ritter in 1859, Reclus recalled Ritter's courses: 'De la Configuration des continents sur la surface du globe, et de leurs Fonctions dans l'histoire' in *La Revue Germanique*, Nov. 1859.
34. Although the entire German socialist movement, if there ever had been such a 'movement', had suffered under the reaction that followed the unrest of 1848, there were many individuals in Berlin who were interested in the 'social question'.
35. Elisée to his mother, Apr. 1851, *Corr.* III, p. 2.
36. Ibid., p. 1.
37. For the original manuscript, see *Archief ER, IISG*. A published (unedited) copy can be found in *Le Libertaire*, 28 Aug.–2 Oct. 1925. See above, n. 21.
38. Elisée Reclus, 'On Vegetarianism' in *The Humane Review*, Jan. 1901 (reprinted as a pamphlet by the Humanitarian League, London, 1901).
39. Pierre-Joseph Proudhon, *Qu'est-ce que la Propriété?* (Paris reprint, 1873), p. 212 ff.
40. Reclus, *Elie Reclus*, p. 21. The title of Elie's thesis was 'Le Principe d'Autorité'. Elisée described it as 'a beautifully original work for which he would

have been burned at the stake or hanged three or four centuries earlier' (ibid.).

41. Ibid., pp. 22–3.
42. Ibid., p. 23.
43. Ibid., Paul Reclus, 'Biographie', p. 23.
44. Reclus, *Elie Reclus*, pp. 23–4.
45. Reclus, 'An Anarchist on Anarchy'.
46. Reclus to Pastor Roth (Orthez), n.d. (1904), *Corr.* III, p. 285.
47. Heath, 'Elisée Reclus'.

# 2 THE QUEST FOR AN ALTERNATIVE LIFE-STYLE

The Reclus brothers arrived in London on 1 January 1852, on a cold and snowy night, as Elisée recalled many years later.[1] For Elisée, it was the first day of a five-year absence from France, and the beginning of an important phase in the development of his social and political thought, particularly his views on revolutionary practice. The first half of 1852 he spent in London, the second half on a farm south of Dublin. He lived from early 1853 until early 1856 on a plantation in Louisiana and from early 1856 until the summer of 1857 in Colombia. As many other political refugees from France after the *coup d'état*, he and his brother had arrived in London almost penniless. Elie has left a depressing description of one early lodging 'the smallest imaginable – a mere dressing-room over the doorlight' and has said that there were times when he walked around at night 'trying to find a sheltered corner on one of the bridges'.[2] Elisée had some difficulty in finding permanent employment in London, and seems to have been supported in large measure by Elie who was more fortunate.[3]

It is clear that the brothers, especially Elisée, perceived themselves as persecuted French republicans, tolerated, but not welcomed in London. Elisée wrote that

> the questioning eye of the mistress of the house rigorously surveyed the clothes of each intruder, especially if he had been born in France, that 'country of corruption and profane levity' . . . That was the period in which a Stuart Mill refused to receive a Pierre Leroux, in which *the Times* boasted of the superiority of the way Britain treated the refugees in comparison with continental practices: was it not better to allow them to die of hunger under the contempt of all than to place them in a prison from which they would one day be released as heroes or martyrs?[4]

Elisée, to a greater extent than Elie, saw his experiences in 'political terms' and quite deliberately and consciously set out to reflect upon their significance. I do not wish to pronounce upon the 'truth' of the persecution which he claims to have suffered, but I believe that he rather relished the thought of being singled out as an enemy of the *status quo*. We have already come across a number of incidences –

Neuwied, Montauban, Orthez after the *coup* — for which Elisée's claims
of political persecution cannot be substantiated by historical evidence.
While this does not necessarily mean that we should reject the claims, it
does at least introduce an element of uncertainty concerning the degree
of persecution. Throughout his life, he attempted to evoke the image of
a man who was the victim of social injustice, and he made several
references to the 'joy of suffering for a good cause'. His tendency to
'politicise' very likely led him to find evidence for persecution which
another less vigilant person might have overlooked.

There was not a great deal of personal contact between Elisée and
well-known revolutionaries in 1852. Still, in a letter of 2 March he told
his brother that he had spent his last shilling to attend a meeting
addressed by Louis Blanc and Pierre Leroux.[5] He may have become
better acquainted with Leroux whom Elie met at about this time[6] and
he may have met Ernest Coeurderoy[7] who had settled in London in
1851 after his expulsion from Switzerland. There is a strong possibility
that there was an introduction to the Russian exile Alexander Herzen.[8]
The evidence permits us to say nothing further. While it is difficult to
estimate the exact numbers of those who fled to London from the
continent after the revolutions of 1848, there is general agreement that
many refugees lived in anticipation of another rising of the people
against tyranny and, in the meantime, squabbled among themselves
about the relative merits of their own particular revolutionary theories.[9]
Elisée seems to have steered clear of sterile theoretical discussions, and
to have maintained a spectator's interest in political affairs.

In 1851 Reclus had judged nationalism to be declining, even while
he recognised the revolutionary potential of national liberation movements. In 1852 he believed that Napoleon III was playing something of
a revolutionary role in spite of himself by setting the forces of nationalism
in motion.[10] He seems to have adhered to the view that the heightened
nationalism as represented by Napoleon might lead to national
liberation, if it gave rise to a revolution which promoted a healthy self-
esteem among the people of France, along with the development of a
genuine respect for all peoples of the world. His faith that the will of
the people would not be subverted indefinitely remained intact, and as
was his wont throughout life, he emphasised those aspects of an unhappy
situation which seemed to him to contain the seeds of future progress.

> Yes, you are right, great things are being prepared; everything was
> badly begun . . . until today the life of love and liberty was not
> strong enough to transform society; but the governments are

making a tabula rasa of all our feeble beginnings, so that, when they are finished, we shall be able to begin everything again on a new scale.[11]

The extent of the reaction and the unlikelihood of immediate change after 1851 did not escape him, and since in the short run there was little to be done, he turned his eyes away from Europe in search of other possibilities. By the middle of 1852 he had obtained a position on a small farm some 30 kilometres south of Dublin, through the intercession of Elie who at this time was a tutor in an Irish home. In the autumn of the same year Elisée left Ireland for America.

The circumstances surrounding the departure are not clear, although we can isolate the major factors behind the decision to set out for America. First, Elisée was interested in organising some kind of agricultural experiment in the New World. A survey of his letters to Elie in the period from 1853 to 1857 reveals that a more or less general plan had probably been worked out by the brothers before Elisée left England.[12] Elie in particular was impressed by the ideas of Fourier,[13] and in spite of the reservations about utopian communism which Elisée had expressed in 1851, he was enthusiastic about establishing a community. In 1852 there was considerable support for such projects within the circles of political refugees in London. While there existed strong elements of a personal quest for an immediately realisable 'utopia', leaving for the New World did not always represent a total abandonment of the Old. There were persons who still hoped to set up in America the alternative societies which they envisaged would provide models for the (eventual) reorganisation of European society, but many refugees of 1848 simply hoped to find in America a place where they could express themselves more freely, after the nature and extent of the reaction in Europe had become clearer to them.[14]

Reclus' interest in geography provided him with another motive for undertaking the voyage to America, for he must have been excited at the prospects of exploring another part of the globe. As a boy, growing up in the country regions of southwest France, and as a student, he had shown a fascination with nature. In his first trip to the Mediterranean, which had been made in 1849, he had been overcome with excitement. 'When we saw the sea you were so moved', recalled Elie on his deathbed in 1904, 'that you bit me on the shoulder until the blood came.'[15] In a letter of 1852 to Elie he described his impression of the area around the River Shannon in Ireland,[16] and this impression was later recalled in the 1868 preface to his *La Terre*. Elisée insisted that the inspiration for his geography came not from an examination of textbooks, but from his own travels and experiences. The writing of his first major geographical work began

> not in the silence of my room, but in the open air. It was in Ireland, on the top of a small hill which overlooks the rapids of the Shannon ... It was there, in that charming spot, that I began to conceive the idea to tell the story of the phenomena of the Earth and, without delay, I sketched the plan of my work.[17]

As he wrote to his mother from New Orleans in 1855,

> to see the earth; for me that is to study it. The only truly serious study which I would undertake is that of geography, and I believe that it is much more worthwhile to observe nature herself than to imagine it from the back of one's study.[18]

While this motive was more personal, it was closely related to Reclus' *Weltanschauung*, even though at that time there was probably little consciousness of the relationship between his social and political theories and his approach to geography.

Many lasting impressions were formed by Reclus during his stay in the United States, and not surprisingly, the experiences which affected him most deeply were those associated with slavery. In his position as tutor on a plantation near New Orleans, he was confronted daily with the reality of institutionalised inequality; after he returned to France in 1857 many hours of writing were devoted to the question.[19] Although the members of the family with whom he lived in Louisiana were not harsh with their slaves and had even developed close relations with some of them, Reclus became troubled by the human debasement which he witnessed, and his rather sudden departure from the plantation in early 1856 was largely due to scruples about slavery. He felt a need, he said, to be a little hungry and to sleep by the side of the road; it grieved him to be forced, through the salary he received as family tutor 'to cheat the negroes who, by their sweat and blood, have more than earned the money which I put into my pocket'.[20] But looking back many years later, he said that he had fled perhaps because of the ensuing Civil War in which he, as an abolitionist, would have had to take sides against his friends.[21]

In Reclus' opinion there was only one solution to problems arising from slavery, the Blacks in America, race itself; that was the fusion of the races. He recognised the distinctive features and unique qualities of different nations, races and societies, but in contrast to people such as Gobineau,[22] he believed that the mixing of peoples would strengthen rather than weaken a race. Whereas Gobineau postulated that race was the all-important factor in human development and that the superior races were those which guarded their racial purity, Reclus countered that any nation which attempted such a course would be weakened. As early as 1851 he had claimed – with more than a trace of traditional French chauvinism – that the French had a greater instinct for sociability and were more 'advanced' in their social and political views precisely because they were a product of the mixture of the many peoples who had founded their country. 'And now it is France', he wrote, 'from which originates all those new ideas whose foreboding alone causes the old world to crack.'[23]

It is true that Reclus' encounter with slavery was emotionally very disturbing. However, his disgust for the institutions which led to the degradation of human beings was matched by the exhilaration which he experienced as he viewed the efforts to emancipate them.

> It is beautiful to see this relentless war of the press, of discussion, of conversation day and night, of all the moments against that elusive fantom of human freedom; every negro, every white who protests in exalted voice in favour of the rights of man, every word, every line in all the south affirms that man is the brother of man.[24]

In a letter from New Orleans he spoke of the 'most interesting ethnographic question of the century, that of the fusion of the races'. In France one observed the fusion of 'classes and principles', in America the fusion of riflemen. While the French dreamed of the brotherhood of souls, across the Atlantic the brotherhood of colours was being prepared by the 'brutal force of gravitation'.[25] Reclus was a person who enjoyed a good fight, and the nobility of the cause intensified his excitement.

Though the solution to social and political problems lay in the actions of people, there was a considerable degree of determinism in Reclus' analysis:

> Fortunately, each problem contains the key to its solution within itself, and indeed, it will not be due to the Americans if the mixture of races takes place, if negro, Indian and white end up by resembling each other, physically as well as morally, and blending

together in one nation.[26]

The process of the fusion of the races had already commenced. The planter had begun to assume the habits, character and language of the negro, and sexual intercourse between negro and White was producing a copper shade which characterised the typical American face.[27] From another perspective Reclus could also perceive the inevitability of the emancipation of the Blacks. The sheer weight of numbers was on their side: 'the *proportion of negroes and whites is constantly being displaced in favour of the former*'[28] (Reclus' emphasis). And from yet another angle, the slave-owners were undermining their position by invoking the principle of authority to support their claims. The attempt to place traditionally unquestioned authority on a rational basis would be self-defeating because, in the process, blind faith would be destroyed and this traditional authority weakened.[29] As the analysis of Reclus' thought in 1851 has already suggested, there was an element of tele-ological determinism which was fundamental to it. His experiences in America reinforced his conviction that progress could be only tem-porarily halted by the acts of people. As he wrote of developments in the United States in 1855:

> But the great progress is almost totally independent of their will. This progress has to follow the new relationships of man to the Earth and of races to races, because these new relationships have posed for humanity new questions which have to be resolved whether we like it or not.[30]

Reclus was severely critical of American institutions and the American way of life in general. 'You judge the United States well', he wrote to Elie, 'but not with enough severity. It is a great auction hall where everything is sold, slaves and owner into the bargain, votes and honour, the Bible and consciences. Everything belongs to the one who is richer.'[31] None the less, he recognised that profound questions were being raised in the United States, as well as the peculiar virtues of the Americans as they confronted those questions. In particular, it was with an indomitable energy and boldness that they had plunged themselves into an investigation of traditional 'lies'. The dissemination of the idea of the fundamental equality of all people was beginning to break through the obstacles placed in its path in the United States. 'All Yankees are the apostles of civilization.'[32] While admitting that the Americans were dealing with questions of fundamental importance, however, he was far from relinquishing the leading role of the French in revolutionary matters. The Americans remained country bumpkins in comparison with the French who would offer them brotherly guidance and provide them with a sophisticated framework in which they might be able to analyse and come to an understanding of social change.

> The education of the Americans resembles that which we give the pedants in France; they know the name of things. They talk of the blunt fact to the entire world and, later, we shall come to demonstrate the idea behind the fact. To use an anglosaxon comparison, they are putting the glasses on the table while waiting for us to fill them up.[33]

From early 1856 until he returned to France in the summer of 1857 Reclus travelled in Colombia, anxiously awaiting the arrival of Elie. He had been making preparations for some time. In a letter of 28 June 1855, he had written to his mother: 'Believe me, dear mother, the little colony that we are going to establish will be charming and my brother's family will be able to find happiness there.'[34] After Elie had returned to France and married his cousin Noémi, Elisée wrote to them both, urging them to join him.[35] In May 1856 he was promising his brother that, in their new abode, they would enjoy 'a certain freedom of action'.[36]

The efforts to establish a community in Colombia were without success.[37] There were several reasons for the failure. First, Elie did not arrive to complete the little group. Second, Elisée had very limited financial resources. Moreover, his relationship with the old Frenchman with whom he had intended to start the plantation turned out to be 'the most foolish episode of my life: precisely because the old man talked too much, was a lier, a busybody, bad-tempered . . . '[38] (He was reluctant to discontinue the relationship because, according to his letters, he felt a sense of responsibility both for the old man and for the project which they were undertaking.)[39] Furthermore, because the site which had been chosen for the little community was rather high up in the mountains, communications were difficult. Finally, in the winter of 1856 to 1857, Elisée became seriously ill with yellow fever. 'Instead of beginning by establishing a serious plantation at Sierra', he wrote in February 1857, 'we have allowed both time and money to run out, we have arrived in the mountains without a sou . . . '[40] In the same letter, his imagination and optimistic nature led him to flights of fancy:

> If we succeed half-way in our coffee plantation, if communications

become easier as a result of the invention of some new hydro-
locomotive, and it becomes possible to reach the delicious climate
of Sierra Nevada by passing through the tropical climate like a
hurricane, then we shall be able to have our town house at Paris
and our country house at Sierra Nevada. Is it not true that all the
forces of the air and water, of matter and science are working
together to bring us closer to this little earthly nest?[41]

Reclus may not have analysed his motives for returning to France.
In fact, his letters of early summer 1857 indicate little more than
excitement at the prospect of his forthcoming reunion with his family.
The attitudes expressed in these letters should be understood within the
context of the immediate longings of a young man separated from his
family for a number of years. The return to France represented much
more than a wish to be reunited with his family. The quest for a freer
way of life in Sierra Nevada was completely abandoned, and a project
of this nature was never again to be undertaken. To understand why
this was so, his experiences must be set within the context of the
evolution of his social and political thought.

In the 1850s Reclus believed in the inevitable progress of humanity
and in the historical value of humanity's accomplishments, both material
and cultural. These accomplishments were viewed not only as goods in
themselves, but were linked with the continuing evolution and dissemination of the ideas of liberty, equality and fraternity. However,
each move from 1852, London to Ireland, Ireland to Louisiana,
Louisiana to Colombia, had been in the direction of increasingly 'under-
developed' areas. From Europe it may have initially seemed desirable at
least to attempt to incorporate humanity's achievements (and none of its
evils) into an alternative society. His experiences in the New World
taught him that only with difficulty (if at all) could the accomplishments
of the advanced civilisations — that is those of Western Europe — be trans-
planted into the environment of more primitive societies.

Reclus was a man keenly interested in all facets of social, economic
and political development and concerned about all injustices. It would
have been difficult for him to turn his back on advanced societies and
to inhabit a little community, divorced from the realities and injustices
which he recognised continued to exist. He was outraged by the presence
of slavery in the southern United States and deeply moved by the
pernicious effects of the white invader on the native Indians of South
America. In 1856 he described the Indians who inhabited Sierra Nevada as

poor children, very sweet, who . . . observe everything with the un-
intelligent curiosity of the bird . . . It is said that they originally
lived on the plain; the barbarism of the Spanish drove them to look
for a refuge in these mountains . . . the woman is the slave of her
husband and every poor girl who does not find a master becomes the
rightful slave of the nearest rich man.[42]

He was struck by the similarity between the social system in the mountain
villages of Colombia and that of Europe: 'The social system of Europe
is duplicated here, but is incomparably simpler and freed of all the com-
plications which disguises it at home.'[43] His experiences in Colombia led
him to view the social injustices of Europe with greater clarity, but they
had also made him see the evils under which both Europeans and
Colombians suffered in more universal terms.

This sensitivity to the universal nature of the human condition was
accompanied by a growing awareness of the effects of the continuing
expansion of the European economic system, and he seems to have
gained a sharper vision of the struggle which would be needed in order
to bring the economy under democratic control. In answer to Elie's
description of corruption in France, he wrote:

Viewed from afar, the spectacle of this corruption has something
grandiose about it and provides a magnificent response to the
question of competition, such as it was posed in 1789. Everything
universalises, and when these gigantic companies, organised for
*profit*, extend over the entire society, one will at least know that it
is by joining together that great things are accomplished.[44]

The passage reveals not only an awakening consciousness to the nature
of the struggle against social injustice, but also an excitement at the
thought of the coming battle and a barely concealed desire to be a part
of it. For a man who so dearly loved the thick of battle, it is unlikely
that he would have remained content for very long in distant
Colombia, even if the colony had flourished, and indeed, setting up
such a colony would not have gone very far towards ameliorating
universal evils, and might even be said to have amounted to a tacit
acceptance of them. As early as 1855, while in Louisiana, he realised
that his plan to establish a colony in the mountains of South
America would be little more than a temporary respite from a world
dominated by Europe. 'Come', he coaxed Elie's wife, 'it will be
delicious. Later, when three or four years of paradise have tired you

out, it will be time to see the old world again.'[45]

Reclus' first book on geography, *Voyage à la Sierra-Nevada de Sainte-Marthe*, was published in 1861, and drew heavily upon his experiences in South America. In the 1880s it attracted the attention of a number of people interested in founding communities, among them the members of the Société Anonyme de Colonisation de la Sierra-Nevada which was very likely directly inspired by the book.[46] Beseeched by this society for advice, Reclus maintained that, while he had confidence in the initiative of the indigenous population and acclimatised foreigners, he did not believe that such a project directed from afar could be successful. At the same time he warned of technical difficulties, communications and climate.[47] As regards the possibilities for establishing a more just society through such communitarianism, Reclus' statements were quite categorically negative. Regardless of the high motives behind the experiments, it was *ipso facto* 'authoritarian' to believe people should be brought to establish their relations according to some preconceived plan, and it was a delusion to think that they could be brought to do so without resort to force. The communitarians could not help, so it seemed, but rely upon authoritarian principles to guide their activities, and so their experiments were doomed to failure from the very beginning.

> It is to live in conditions of equality and escape from the falsehoods and hypocrisies of a society of superiors and inferiors, that so many men and women have formed themselves into closed corporations and little worlds apart. America bounds in communities of this sort. But these societies, few of which prosper while many perish, are all ruled more or less by force; they carry within themselves the seeds of their own dissolution, and are reabsorbed by Nature's law of gravitation into the world which they have left.[48]

These negative attitudes towards communitarianism were based upon more than a mere calculation of probable success. Communitarianism had come to violate a fundamental principle, and it is here that we can perceive the significance of Reclus' experiences in the period from 1852 to 1857. Even if communitarian experiments were successful, he argued in 1884, even 'if man enjoyed in them the highest happiness of which his nature is capable', they would none the less, be 'obnoxious' in their 'selfish isolation' from the rest of humanity. The pleasures which communitarians sought were 'egotistical' and 'devotion to the cause of humanity' would draw back the best people, even in a successful community, into the 'great struggle'. Writing in 1884, at a time when the anarchists had become a separate group within the European socialist movement, Reclus emphasised how alien to him (and to his comrades) had become the desire to establish the 'ideal' community.

> As for us Anarchists, never will we separate ourselves from the world to build a little church, hidden in some vast wilderness. Here is the fighting ground, and we remain in the ranks, ready to give our help wherever it may be most needed.[49]

Not only was it impossible to shut oneself off from society; more importantly, a person was morally bound to remain as fully a part of it as possible.

The question of 'colonies' emerged in a new and more urgent form at the very end of the nineteenth century, after the movement which the anarchists had come to represent had been reduced to impotence. Rejected by the socialists who were rapidly assuming a parliamentary identity, some anarchists believed that the creation of anarchist (non-urban) communities throughout Europe would provide an opportunity to put their beliefs into practice, if only on a small scale. Reclus' response was decidedly negative. While he sympathised with the motives behind European experiments in communal living, he made it clear that he could not support the establishment of 'Icaries' outside the bourgeois world. On the one hand, he said in 1900, colonies — at home or abroad — had an incredibly slim chance of survival, as could be seen from experiments in France, Russia, the United States, Mexico and Brazil. The colonies failed because they were infected from their foundation by bourgeois institutions — legal marriage and paternity, subjection of women, private property, buying and selling and the use of money. While the enthusiasm of the members might hold the colony together for a while, dis-integration could not be avoided in the long run, even when there was no violent attack from outside. People continued to found colonies, he believed, because of their mistaken assumption that if they worked harder than their predecessors, they would be able to remove themselves from society, and not the values and prejudices which had formed part of that society. Reclus was saying that there had to be massive social change before a successful colony could be established. But, of course, by that time the conditions which led to the founding of colonies would no longer exist and there would be no need and presumably no desire for them.[50]

On the other hand, colonies had nothing at all to do with anarchism as Reclus understood it. Those comrades who were attracted to the idea of some paradise, he said, were suffering from the illusion that the anarchists constituted a 'party' outside society. That was not true. 'Our joy, our passion, is in putting into practice that which seems egalitarian and just to us, not only with regard to our comrades, but also with regard to all men . . . In our plan of existence and struggle, it is not the small chapel of comrades which interests us; it is the entire world.' Anarchists were, therefore, obliged to remain in the 'civilized world' and to continue their propaganda in the shops and factories, homes, army barracks and schools. Their enemies understood this very well, sneered Reclus. They were already saying that it would be very useful if all anarchists fled to some utopia, and were even suggesting that it might be advisable to provide assistance. Colonies formed no part of revolutionary agitation. They not only did not point the direction of the future, but even recalled the past. Their establishment was akin to the creation of monasteries in the Middle Ages.[51]

## Notes

1.  Elisée Reclus, *Elie Reclus, 1827–1904* (Paris, 1905), p. 24.
2.  Richard Heath, 'Elisée Reclus', in *The Humane Review*, Oct. 1905.
3.  The few letters of 1852 which have survived suggest that Elisée and Elie shared what money was available. See Elisée to Elie, n.d., *Correspondance*, 3 vols. (Paris, 1911–25), vol. I, pp. 54–5. Cf. Paul Reclus, 'Biographie d'Elisée Reclus', in *Les Frères Elie et Elisée Reclus* (Paris, 1964), p. 25.
4.  Reclus, *Elie Reclus*, p. 24. Cf. Leroux's impressions of life in London in the early 1850s in his *Quelques Pages de Vérité* (Paris, 1859), p. 47 ff.
5.  Elisée to Elie, 2 Mar. 1852, *Corr.* I, pp. 50–1.
6.  Elie Reclus, *La Commune de Paris au jour le jour 1871 (19 mars–28 mai)* (Paris, 1908), pp. 134–8. Elisée was acquainted with the ideas of Leroux at least by 1849; Reclus, *Elie Reclus*, p. 19. See Elisée's references to Leroux in his correspondence from Colombia; Elisée to Elie, n.d., *Corr.* I, p. 125 and Elisée to Elie, 1 Feb. 1857, *Corr.* I, p. 153.
7.  In a conversation with Max Nettlau in 1895, Elie said that he remembered Coeurderoy very well; Max Nettlau, *Elisée Reclus: Anarchist und Gelehrter* (Berlin, 1928), p. 54. Max Nettlau, *Der Vorfrühling der Anarchie* (Berlin, 1925), pp. 205–19, discusses the contributions to anarchism of Joseph Déjacque and Ernest Coeurderoy. See also his *Historie de l'Anarchie* (Paris, 1971), pp. 88–93.
8.  By 1855 Elie had come into contact with Herzen and Elisée had some appreciation of Herzen's approach to the theories of West European socialists. Elisée to Elie, n.d., *Corr.* I, p. 94.
9.  See the section, 'Refugee Politics' in David McLellan, *Karl Marx, His Life and Thought* (London, 1973), pp. 252–62. Cf. Elisée to Elie, 8 Mar. 1852, *Corr.* I, p. 53.
10.  Elisée to Elie, 8 Mar. 1852, *Corr.* I, p. 53.

11. Elisée to Elie, n.d. (1852), *Corr.* I, p. 55.

12. See correspondence in *Corr.* I, p. 71 ff.

13. Reclus, *Elie Reclus*, p. 26. Much of the inspiration for the Brook Farm Community, founded by New England intellectuals in 1832, had been derived from the ideas of Fourier. In the 1840s a number of colonies based on Fourierist principles had been founded under the guidance of Albert Brisbane in the United States. For a description of early experiments in communal living in the United States, see A.E. Bestor, *Backwoods Utopias* (Philadelphia–London, 1950).

14. Note, for example, the impressions of the German refugee, Carl Schurz, who left London for the United States in Sept. 1852; Carl Schurz, *Lebenserinnerungen* (Berlin, 1952), p. 296. After 1848 Herzen's disillusionment with revolutionary activity in Europe led him to study the possibility of achieving a more enlightened way of life in America. The refugees, he concluded, might well find a life of contentment in America, but, he warned: 'Their contentment will be poorer, more commonplace, more sapless than that which was dreamed of in the ideals of romantic Europe'. Quoted in G.D.H. Cole, *A Study of Socialist Thought*, 5 vols. (London, 1958 ff), vol. II, pp. 42–3.

15. Paul Reclus, 'A Few Recollections on the Brothers Elie and Elisée Reclus', in J. Ishill, *Elisée and Elie Reclus: In Memoriam* (Berkeley Heights, 1927), pp. 24–5.

16. Elisée to Elie, n.d. (1852), *Corr.* I, p. 65.

17. Elisée Reclus, *La Terre*, 2 vols. (Paris, 1868 and 1869), Preface to vol. I, pp. I–II.

18. Elisée to his mother, 13 Nov. 1855, *Corr.* I, p. 109.

19. See Elisée Reclus, articles in *La Revue des Deux Mondes*: 'De l'Esclavage aux Etats-Unis', 15 Dec. 1860, pp. 868–901 and 1 Jan. 1861, pp. 118–54; 'Les Noirs américains depuis la guerre', 15 Mar. 1863, pp. 364–94; 'Un écrit américain sur l'esclavage', 15 Mar. 1864, pp. 507–10; 'Deux années de la grande lutte américaine', 1 Oct. 1864, pp. 555–624; 'Le Coton et la crise américaine', 1 Jan. 1862, pp. 176–208. See also 'John Brown' in *La Coopération*, 14 July 1867.

20. Elisée to Elie, n.d. (1855), *Corr.* I, pp. 104–5.

21. Reclus to Clara Mesnil, 25 Oct. 1904, *Fonds ER, IFHS*. He had earlier indicated that the Fortier children, and especially the eldest, a girl of 14, were fond of him (Elisée to Elie, n.d. (1855), *Corr.* I, p. 102). In his 1904 letter to Clara Mesnil, he explained that the girl had been in love with him, but that he had felt only a brotherly affection for her.

22. Count Joseph-Arthur Gobineau published his *Essay on the Inequality of Human Races* in 1853. While it is not known what, if anything, Reclus knew of Gobineau's theories at that time, he subsequently studied them with a great deal of scrutiny. Reclus to De Gérando, 24 June 1883, *Corr.* II, p. 307.

23. Reclus, 'Développement'.

24. Elisée to Elie, n.d. (1855), *Corr.* I, p. 97.

25. Ibid., p. 96.

26. Elisée to Elie, n.d. (1855), *Corr.* I, p. 92. Cf. Ernest Coeurderoy's sketch of a socialist Europe reinvigorated by fusion with the Russians, *Hurrah! ou la Révolution par les Cosaques* (London, 1854). See also *Miscegenation: The Theory of the Blending of the Races, Applied to the American White Man and Negro* (New York, 1864).

27. Elisée to Elie, n.d. (1855), *Corr.* I, p. 92.

28. Elisée to Elie, n.d. (1855), *Corr.* I, p. 97.

29. Ibid., p. 96.

30. Elisée to Elie, n.d. (1855), *Corr.* I, p. 92.

31. Ibid., p. 91.

32. Ibid., pp. 92–3.

33. Ibid., p. 93.

34. Elisée to his mother, 28 June 1855, *Corr.* I, p. 87.

35. Elisée to Elie, n.d. (1855), *Corr.* I, p. 105.

36. Elisée to Elie, 5 May 1856, *Corr.* I, p. 117.

37. For Reclus' experiences in Colombia, see his *Voyage à la Sierra-Nevada de Sainte-Marthe* (Paris, 1861); *Corr.* I, especially pp. 112–67; 'La Nouvelle-Grenade, paysages de la nature tropicale' in *La Revue des Deux Mondes*, 1 Dec. 1859, pp. 624–62; 1 Feb. 1860, pp. 609–35; 15 Mar. 1860, pp. 419–52; 1 May 1860, pp. 50–83. See also Reclus to 'Société Anonyme de Colonisation de la Sierra-Nevada', 20 Feb. 1884 and Reclus to P. Gérance, 6 Mar. 1885 in *Papiers ER, NAF* 22917.

38. Elisée to Elie, 1 June 1857, *Corr.* I, p. 164.

39. Elisée to Elie, 1 Feb. 1857, *Corr.* I, p. 155 and Elisée to Elie, 1 June 1857, *Corr.* I, p. 164.

40. Elisée to Elie, 1 Feb. 1857, *Corr.* I, p. 153.

41. Ibid., pp. 154–5.

42. Elisée to his mother, 14 Oct. 1856, *Corr.* I, pp. 146–7.

43. Ibid., p. 147.

44. Elisée to Elie, 10 Mar. 1857, *Corr.* I, p. 161.

45. Elisée to Elie, n.d. (1855), *Corr.* I, p. 105.

46. See the copy of a circular put out by the 'Société Anonyme de Colonisation de la Sierra-Nevada', dated Paris, 1 Feb. 1884 and quoting from Reclus' book, in *Papiers ER, NAF* 22917.

47. Reclus to 'Société Anonyme de Colonisation de la Sierra-Nevada', 20 Feb. 1884, *Papiers ER, NAF* 22917. Cf. Reclus to Gérance, 6 Mar. 1885, *Papiers ER, NAF* 22917.

48. Reclus, 'An Anarchist on Anarchy'.

49. Ibid.

50. Elisée Reclus, 'Les Colonies anarchistes' in *Les Temps Nouveaux*, 7–13 July 1900.

51. Ibid.

# 3 THE SEARCH FOR POLITICAL EXPRESSION

The France to which Elisee Reclus returned in 1857 was dominated by Napoleon III. In spite of the limited scope for political expression, he was consoled to be reunited with Elie and to find himself 'in an atmosphere of art, science, life, which I did not experience for such long years'.[1] The pattern which his politics assumed in the years following his return was one of relative inactivity, but this was to be expected, given the political climate of the Second Empire and the practical non-existence of a European revolutionary movement. As the period of the 'liberal' Empire opened up opportunities for political activity, however, he became increasingly involved with a wide variety of political groups. Since there was no fixed and organised socialist movement until much later in the century, he was able to identify with revolutionaries of highly varying opinions without having to choose between a particular set of political theories. Doctrinaire socialist schools were only to develop from the early 1870s. What emerges clearly from a study of these years is Reclus' attempt to reconcile theory and practice in his own mind, to find expression for personal views within revolutionary groups of all kinds.

The close friendship between Elisée and Elie which had been interrupted in 1852 was resumed upon Elisée's return. On 14 December 1858 Elisée married (in a civil ceremony only) the mulatto Clarisse Brian of Sainte-Foy, offspring of a French sea captain and a Senegalese woman, and the couple took up residence with Elie and Noémi in Paris. This arrangement must have been rather pleasant, and there is nothing to indicate that it was anything less than fruitful for all concerned. In the beginning the financial support of the enlarged household seems to have fallen mostly on the shoulders of Elie who was working in the Crédit Mobilier, a bank founded by the brothers Isaac and Emile Péreire in 1852 to put some of the Saint-Simonian ideas into practice; Elisée soon began to contribute to the upkeep of the household by writing articles and reviews for various geographical journals. A series of articles based upon his observations in Colombia was enlarged and modified, and published as a book in 1861.[2] In the early 1860s Elisée also spent long periods out of Paris conducting research for a number of travel guides put out by the publishing firm Hachette, with which he was to have relations for over 30 years.

The brothers Reclus had some contact with republicans and socialists in these years. Elie's son Paul has said that there were visits to the notorious Auguste Blanqui, who was permitted to return to France after the amnesty of 1859, as well as to Proudhon.[3] Elie, as mentioned earlier, was interested in the work of the Fourierists.[4] However, since there was no 'movement' in which to participate at this time, the period was one in which there was a preoccupation with more personal concerns. None the less, even in these years, beneath the rhythm of daily routine we can detect a persistent and vital interest in the social question. Elisée continued to wage his own battle against slavery in the many hours of writing which he devoted to this question during the course of the American Civil War.[5] We may reasonably suspect that his marriage to a mulatto  was a political statement. Elie became restless at the Crédit Mobilier, whose business affairs were conducted little differently from that of the other banks, and in 1862 he left his position to write for the Russian journal *Dêlo*, directed by G.E. Blagosvetlov, and the newspaper *Russkoe Slovo*.[6] The Reclus brothers kept an anxious eye on political events in Europe.

Elisée remained strongly opposed to the principles upon which the Second Empire was based, but as in 1852, he could see that some of Napoleon's policies were breaking down the old order and thereby furthering the liberation of the peoples of Europe. His belief in national self-determination led him to the view that the struggle of the Italians against their Austrian oppressors represented a significant step in the direction of their liberty. Thus, in contrast to Proudhon,[7] he found himself among the many republicans who reacted favourably to Napoleon's decision to bring France into the Italian War against the wishes of his ministers, the clergy and the majority of the well-to-do. Travelling in Italy in 1860, he chanced to see King Victor Emmanuel and showed his familiar sparkle in his spontaneous expression of personal solidarity with the Italians in their struggle for national unification:

> I confess, to my shame perhaps, that when I saw him go past, that man excommunicated by the pope, enemy of Austria, betrayed at Villafranca, that stout hunter of men, whose name has become the keynote of policy for all of Italy, I believed I owed it to Italy herself to hum my *Evviva* too. The man is not much, but the Italians have made a principle of him. Through revolutionary esprit de corps I act with them.[8]

The progressively more liberal policies which were adopted within the Second Empire in the 1860s fostered a climate which was conducive to political debate and had the effect of releasing the forces for change within France. The motives behind Napoleon's changing policies have become the subject of considerable controversy among historians. There is some support for the view that Napoleon was led to an increasing liberalism largely out of a desire to retain the popular support which had begun to erode even in the 1850s. As early as 1857 there had been indications of a shift of public opinion away from the widespread support which he had enjoyed in the early years of the Empire. In the elections of that year the turnout at the polls had been considerably lower than in previous elections, and the republicans had made limited gains. The elections of 1863 gave a majority to opposition candidates in 18 out of the 22 largest towns in France, and eight republicans were elected in Paris. The following year Napoleon countered, not by becoming more repressive, but by initiating a series of reforms. The law of November 1849 which forbade concerted industrial action was removed from the Penal Code, and although organised trade unions remained illegal, there were positive signs that they would be tolerated. The effects of these and other such reforms upon the evolution of Reclus' political views were profound. Before I take up this question I shall trace his participation within the various strands of the burgeoning socialist movement which emerged in the relatively relaxed political atmosphere of the 1860s.

The single most important development for socialism was the founding of the First International. Napoleon did his part by subsidising the visit of the French workers to the London International Exhibition of 1862,[9] a visit which established contacts important to subsequent developments. In 1862 the London Trades Council extended a warm welcome to the French, and the latter sent a delegation to the mass meeting on Poland in London the following year.[10] Shortly after this meeting, George Odger, Secretary of the London Trades Council, drafted an address entitled 'To the Workman of France from the Workingman of England', proposing the foundation of an international association of workers. On 28 September 1864 a meeting was held in St Martin's Hall in London, and the International Working Men's Association (IWMA) was born. Henri Tolain, Charles Limousin and E.E. Fribourg, three of the Frenchmen who took part, were followers of Proudhon. Other French participants included Eugène Varlin who pursued a more trade-union-like approach.

While there is but scant documentation, it is fairly certain that Elisée

(and probably Elie) joined some of his countrymen of republican per-
suasion and enlisted himself in the Paris section of the IWMA in 1865 or
shortly after.[11] For Elisée, as for many others in this period, membership in the IWMA represented no more than a gesture of solidarity with
the aims of the association. In the early years of the IWMA's existence
he did not become deeply involved, and he was not well-informed about
the internal affairs of the association.[12] This lack of commitment may
have been largely due to poor relations with Tolain who had control of
the Paris section. It can be established that there were personal conflicts
between Elie and Tolain in 1865, for example.[13] Some republicans who
were dissatisfied with Tolain openly withdrew their support for the
Paris section, while simultaneously declaring their sympathies for the
avowed aims and principles of the International. In March 1865 Henri
Lefort made this point clear in an announcement in a newspaper with
which the Reclus brothers were closely associated.[14]

Elisée took a more active interest in the Paris IWMA, once Tolain's
influence had begun to wane. Tolain continued to be the spokesman
of the French at the congresses and conferences of the IWMA, but his
position was being steadily undermined in Paris through the efforts
of Varlin and Benoît Malon. On 11 June 1868, in the company of
Aristide Rey, Reclus made the acquaintance of Malon,[15] and became
more enthusiastic about the Paris section which seemed to him to be in
the hands of a new group of men.[16] The initial respect which arose
between Reclus and Malon grew into a close friendship. (Both Malon
and his companion Madame Champseix, the novelist who wrote under
the name of André-Léo, were among the handful of relatives and friends
who witnessed Reclus' second marriage held at Vascoeuil on 26 June
1870.)[17] It is almost certain that Reclus became a member of the Paris
Batignolles section of the IWMA in which Malon was a leading figure.[18]
The closer contact which he had with the Paris IWMA from mid-1868
led him to seek out the members of the General Council while he was
on a trip to London in the summer of 1869. On 6 July and 17 August
he took part as a 'visitor' in the meetings of the General Council.[19] He
met Karl Marx and was presented with a copy of the latter's
'Eighteenth Brumaire of Louis Bonaparte' especially dedicated and
dated 27 July 1869.[20] While their first meeting may have been in the
summer of 1869, there was some earlier contact between them.[21]

Marx was most insistent that *Das Kapital* be made available to a
French audience because, as he wrote on 1 May 1867, he considered
it 'of the greatest importance to emancipate the French from the
false views in which Proudhon buried them with his idealised lower

middle class'.[22] Negotiations began between Paris and London, and it
was hoped that Reclus and Moses Hess would undertake the translation
of the first volume of *Das Kapital* into French and publish the book in
France.[23] By 30 November 1867 Marx had already requested his
publisher to send Reclus a copy of his book and judged that Reclus
seemed to him to be the right person 'as French translator with German
co-operation'.[24] Negotiations broke down in January 1868, however,
when Reclus and Hess became unwilling merely to translate the book,
and wanted 'to shorten it and to modify it for the French public'.[25]
There was also some question about how much payment Reclus and
Hess should receive.[26] The discussion probably continued for another
year.[27] In October 1869 Charles Keller, a member of the Paris section
of the IWMA, undertook the task, but did not complete it, and in late
1871 Marx began to make arrangements with Joseph Roy. (The French
translation of *Das Kapital* finally appeared in 1875.)

By the time Reclus and Marx met in the summer of 1869, it was
unlikely that Reclus would continue with the translation. However,
Marx's remarks to Engels leave no doubt that the meeting was relaxed
and friendly.[28] There is no evidence of further contact between them
and no record of Marx's opinion of Reclus until 1876, just after the
death of Bakunin. By this time Reclus was becoming a prominent
figure in a rival revolutionary organisation, and Marx began to discredit
him. He alleged that both Elisée and Elie had been members of
Bakunin's 'secret' Alliance and referred mockingly to their religious
origins.[29] In 1877 Engels wrote to Wilhelm Liebknecht that Elisée was
'politically confused and impotent',[30] and Marx referred to the Reclus
brothers as the 'souls' of the (rival) Swiss revolutionary review *Le
Travailleur*.[31] Despite the differences which developed, Reclus continued
to have a high regard for Marx's contribution to socialist thought and
practice.[32]

During the years of the First International Elisée and Elie also
became involved in the co-operative movement.[33] Elie was one of the
24 founders of the co-operative credit society, La Société du Crédit au
Travail, which was established on 1 October 1863 and directed by J.P.
Béluze, the son-in-law and disciple of Etienne Cabet. Elie — and Elisée
to a lesser extent — helped to direct this association until it was liquidated
in December 1868. In 1864 the brothers were two of the founders of
the first Paris co-operative of the Rochdale type, L'Association générale
d'approvisionnement et de consommation, which was based upon the
Fourierist notion of the phalanstery. For a time Elie was director and
editor of the co-operativist journal *L'Association* which was published

(in Paris and Brussels) from November 1864 to July 1866. The Reclus brothers were also closely associated with another Paris journal, *La Coopération*, which appeared from September 1866 to June 1868.

Producers' co-operatives enjoyed a brief period of success in France after 1848. Much of their inspiration came from Louis Blanc who had preached his theories of state-subsidised producers' societies in his *Organisation du Travail* in 1839. Even after the June days of 1848, producers' co-operatives were given some support by the National Assembly, partly because it was thought that the promotion of co-operation would provide an alternative to the radical threat, and partly because it was the view of the Assembly that co-operation would prove itself inadequate as a means of industrial organisation. In the 1860s, however, governmental authorities generally began to adopt more positive attitudes towards co-operatives. By then the principles of co-operation had been endorsed by some liberal economists such as Léon Say and Léon Walras and were supported by republican politicians such as Jules Simon. It had come to be believed that co-operatives, whether of producers or consumers, could perform the useful function of giving the workers a stake in the existing society and thereby tying them more securely to it.

Elie's experiences with the Saint-Simonian Crédit Mobilier had been disappointing, and the founding of the Crédit au Travail represented a determination to overcome the Crédit Mobilier's 'bourgeois' short-comings, to make real headway in the emancipation of the working class. The underlying principles of every school of co-operation, according to Elie, were mutuality, independence and solidarity. Every type of social reformer, Fourier, Comte, Saint-Simon, Cabet, Proudhon, Louis Blanc, Pierre Leroux and Frédéric Bastiat (the last mentioned is not usually considered a social reformer), made important contributions, and while these men brought forward different and sometimes opposing views, at one time or another they all stumbled upon something of the truth. Elie believed that, through the co-operative movement, he and his companions were carrying out tasks which had been begun in 1792.[34] Elisée later said that an important aim of the Crédit au Travail had been 'to contribute in every way to a promotion of the relations between the republican bourgeoisie of good will and the world of the workers'.[35] The purpose of the society, as given by an historian of the movement was 'to credit the existing workers' associations, to assist in the formation of new co-operative societies, in the development and the publicity of the principles of mutuality and solidarity'.[36] Elie embraced with some enthusiasm a movement which held out the promise of change without violence, and he believed that co-operatives would 'strongly assist social evolution'.[37] It was perhaps this attitude that led 'the people of the International' to paint him as 'that anti-socialist and anti-revolutionary patriarch'.[38]

It is much more difficult to isolate Elisée's views on co-operatives in this period. The general impression is one of scepticism, to say the least; his support of such projects was largely motivated by his sentiments for Elie.[39] Even at this age (mid-thirties) there was a lingering over-responsiveness to his elder brother. He was not to make a firm decision upon the social and political function of co-operatives until the following decade when, as we shall see, he was quite explicitly negative.

Elisée Reclus was a man who was thorough in any investigation which he undertook, and he exhibited this same thoroughness in his search for political expression. Another avenue which he explored was that of Freemasonry. Until the mid-1860s the Freemasonry of the Second Empire had been more or less under the undisguised direction of Napoleon III who had personally selected the men at the head of its official organisations. From 1865 a number of factors combined to reduce this governmental control, and the lodges adopted a more liberal policy towards discussion of social and political matters, thereby attracting the attention of many young people interested in revolutionary change. Alongside the officially recognised organisations, however, there was a masonic-like organisation dedicated to the overthrow of the Empire and persecuted by the government. It was made up of groups which called themselves the Loge des Philadelphes (Lodge of the Philadelphians).

Reclus' interest in revolutionary politics led him to make contact with Freemasonry, very likely both forms, although it is difficult to trace his relations within it. Not only is the history of the organisation and activity of Freemasonry obscure;[40] there are, furthermore, nothing but scattered references to his participation. Even though the nineteenth-century masonic press claimed that he was a member, his involvement was so limited that his membership has been open to question.[41] A letter of 17 December 1894 leaves no doubt that he went through the ceremony of entrance into a masonic lodge. In the letter he stated that he had become a mason some 30 years earlier, but that he had had only a 'short experience' with the organisation.[42] A notice given by the editors of the anarchist paper *Les Temps Nouveaux* in 1896, which was very likely written according to information provided by Reclus, states that he had had nothing to do with the 'closed society' after 1866.[43] It may be concluded that he was a more or less active mason at least in the period from 1865 to 1866. Elie was a member of the lodge, La Renaissance, and it was through these connections that he managed to escape from Paris after the suppression of the Paris Commune.[44] There is also some evidence to suggest that both brothers were members of another lodge, Les Elus d'Hiram.[45]

Elisée and Elie may also have had some experience with the Lodge of the Philadelphians in London − or at least some of its members − as early as 1852. This lodge, which had been established at the end of 1850, was active among the French émigrés, although in practice anyone who spoke French was admitted. In any event, during their stay in London (1852), they met Alfred Talandier, who was to hold a high position in the lodge and who remained a friend for many years. In the late 1860s Elisée was on close terms with several Philadelphians, including Charles Bradlaugh and Louis Blanc. Later he claimed that, while he had been initially attracted to Freemasonry, it had not held his interest: 'On the contrary, it found itself then as it does today [1894], in a period of evolution, in which, having fallen into the hands of an haute bourgeoisie, so-called liberal, it does not have any aim other than to deliver to its members the conquest of political power and, by consequence, wealth.' This attitude did not prevent him from accepting the hospitality of a group of Freemasons in Brussels who in 1894 offered him the use of a hall where he might deliver geography lectures,[46] nor from addressing Freemasons on the subject of anarchy.[47]

After his flirtation with Freemasonry, Elisée was drawn to the circles of Freethinkers. In 1868 he had close relations with Agis comme tu penses (Do as you please),[48] a society which had been founded by French students and which included among its members figures such as Aristide Rey and Georges Clemenceau, as well as some groups of workers. The statutes of the society proclaimed the law of reason and science and rejected all religious ceremony at birth, marriage and death. Agis comme tu penses was 'an association whose law is science, which is based upon solidarity, and which has justice as its aim'.[49]

Reclus shared the desires of many others who considered participation within Freemasonry and Freethinking as opportunities to become acquainted with people of similar views, to discuss and to seek to clarify social and political issues. It is likely that he was attracted by the climate of intimacy and brotherhood as much as by the opportunity to air political views. His comments on a banquet which he attended in the summer of 1869 indicates how interconnected were his feelings about Freethinking, republicanism and socialism: 'We were there, one hundred and twenty men and women, all united, freethinkers, republicans, socialists, and were happy to find ourselves together.'[50] Reclus' experiences with the IWMA, co-operativism, Freemasonry, Freethinking all contributed to the development of his social and political views, and although he was quite aware of the gulfs which separated such different groups,[51] he did not feel that participation in one necessarily precluded activity in another.

The most important personal contact which Reclus made in the late 1860s was Michael Bakunin, the legendary antagonist of Karl Marx. Having made his famous escape from Siberia, Bakunin arrived in London in 1861, full of enthusiasm and undaunted by the reaction that had brought many a revolutionary to despair. As Herzen wrote of him:

> The European reaction did not exist for Bakunin; the bitter years from 1848 to 1858 did not exist for him either; of them he had but a brief, far-away, faint knowledge . . . the events of 1848, on the contrary, were all about him, near to his heart . . . they were all still ringing in his ears and hovering before his eyes.[52]

Marx gave Bakunin a warm welcome and on 4 November 1864 wrote to Engels: 'On the whole he is one of the few people whom after sixteen years I find not less, but more fully, developed.'[53] Reclus was immediately attracted to this gregarious rebel, gigantic in size and spirit, a man whose lust for action had led him to commit deeds of epic proportion and had resulted in his imprisonment in Siberia where he underwent severe physical and emotional hardship.

Bakunin may have become aware of the existence and interests of the Reclus brothers through their friends in England, Talandier or Herzen, for example. In any event, Bakunin, in an effort to recruit members for his International Brotherhood, which he had founded in Florence in 1864, sought out the Reclus when he was in Paris in November of that year.[54] Elisée and Elie are traditionally named among the members of the International Brotherhood.[55] In 1865, it is said, they also joined Bakunin's Italian Alliance of Social Democracy, which seems to have been virtually identical with the International Brotherhood.[56] Certainly Elisée, who travelled to Italy after the eruption of Mount Etna in Sicily,[57] went to Florence to visit Bakunin in April 1865 and was introduced to the local circle.[58] There is, furthermore, a sentence in Elisée's correspondence which may be considered a reference to the involvement of the brothers in Bakunin's societies.[59] It is likely that both were members of the International

Brotherhood and the Alliance of Social Democracy. However, because so little of the correspondence between Elisée (in this case Elisée was the more enthusiastic brother) and Bakunin has survived, it cannot be established with any certainty what part the brothers played in the web of secret societies founded — or supposed to have been founded — by Bakunin.[60]

While Elisée enjoyed Bakunin's confidence and had access to the intimate group around him, there is no detailed record concerning their relations until 1867 and then only in connection with the League of Peace and Freedom. Elisée had been among the first supporters of this League, which had been set up on the initiative of the former Saint-Simonian, Charles Lemmonier, and which aimed to combine peace talks with the question of European unity under republican government. The League, which was supported by a heterogeneous group, including members of the left, literary figures and radical politicians, held its first congress on 9 September 1867. Though Marx had dismissed the League as a 'futile gathering of impotent bourgeois ideologues',[61] the majority of the delegates at the Lausanne Congress of the IWMA in 1867 had decided to support the Geneva Congress of the League in its struggle against war. However, the final form of the address, delivered by James Guillaume to the Geneva Congress, contained a direct challenge to the political views of the League's middle-class sympathisers, and was as well a blow to the organisers who were anxious to obtain working-class support.

Although Elisée did not attend the 1867 Congress, he followed developments with great interest. He counselled Elie to accept the offer from the Central Committee of the League to act as French editor of the proposed journal *Les Etats Unis d'Europe* (The United States of Europe), and he was disappointed at Elie's wish to concentrate his attention on a newspaper in Saint-Etienne.[62] This difference of view represents changing, although never hostile, relations between Elisée and Elie and is a sign of the former's growing desire to become more deeply immersed in revolutionary politics. Elisée's enthusiasm was strengthened through correspondence with Bakunin who was a member of a committee charged with drawing up a draft programme to be presented at the League's 1868 congress.[63] Bakunin continually sought the opinions of his friends, and several letters were exchanged between Berne (where the meetings of the committee were held) and Paris. Alfred Naquet and Elisée insisted that the word 'republican' be inserted. 'Perhaps', wrote the latter, 'on the eve of the day when the masses cry out the word, it is fitting for us to say it under our breath.'[64]

Elisée was an enthusiastic participant at the Berne Congress of the League of Peace and Freedom which was held from 21 September to 25 September 1868,[65] and was disappointed at the negative reaction of the IWMA, as expressed at its recent Brussels Congress. The IWMA, which had been invited to send a delegation to the Berne Congress, had decided instead to nominate three of its members to point out to the League that there was no basis for its separate existence and to invite its members to join the IWMA.[66] Reclus clearly believed that the League was working in conjunction, not in competition, with the IWMA, and he attributed the unfriendly attitude of the IWMA to the efforts of the Proudhonists, with whom there had been some degree of friction. It was Reclus' contention that the Proudhonists, who had been defeated in Brussels on the question of collective ownership, were also chiefly responsible for the attitude of the IWMA towards the League.[67] The lack of grace and downright meddling of the Proudhonists he considered impertinent and childish, but agreed with Bakunin that it would be better to let the matter rest and to avoid a hostile encounter.[68]

At the Berne Congress of the League, Reclus was a member of a committee set up to study the 'social question' and to submit a report on the second day of the meetings. The committee failed to reach any agreement, refusing to adopt the programme in which Reclus (and Bakunin) supported 'as ideal "the equalisation of classes and individuals", understanding by that equality as the point of departure for all, in order that each person might follow his career without hindrance'.[69] Bakunin was so disgusted by the results of the vote — which left the question undecided — that he was ready to break away immediately. However, he was persuaded by Reclus and Aristide Rey who insisted on the value of remaining until the end and putting forth their opinions. Reclus was strongly motivated by the desire to clarify his own views which in the heat of debate were becoming more precise.[70] In fact, the Berne Congress had aroused in him an excitement which he had not experienced for many years. He described to Elie how deeply he had been drawn into the discussions:

My intention had been to write you a very detailed account of the Berne Congress. I had even drawn up three pages, which I have since lost; but impossible to continue my work because my role of spectator having, from the beginning, become that of an actor, I could not find the necessary time. Committee meetings, congress meetings, drafting of projects and redrafting followed without respite and until well into the night: at two or three o'clock the

conversations were still going on. At the end of the week I was
exhausted.[71]

Reclus' first public declaration of his political views was made on 24
September, on the fourth day of the congress. It was delivered within
the context of the question of federalism,[72] specifically in connection
with a resolution on the 'United States of Europe'.[73] He felt that it was
important to be explicit on the nature of the federation which they
desired. It should not merely be assumed that a United States of
Europe would represent an advance on what they had at present, and it
should not be overlooked that such unity might be won at the expense
of subservience to a gigantic centralised state. Moreover, he was
reluctant to envisage the creation of a united Europe as anything but a
small step on the way to the realisation of the ultimate aim of the
'federative republic of the entire world'. He was, therefore, insistent
that 'provisionally' be introduced into the resolution of the congress
so that it would read: 'The Congress is able to propose provisionally no
better example than the Swiss and American confederations.' He was
not satisfied with the bases of existing federations, and he was determined to specify the differences between any existing or immediately
realisable federation and the 'ideal' federation.

The revolutionary Carlo Gambuzzi had spoken of the removal of
countries themselves, said Reclus, without stipulating that the borders
between countries were artificial lines established by force, war and the
'cunning' of kings. A theory of federalism would be acceptable only
if it were an upward extension of administrative units into a federal
republic. Federalism would have to be based upon the needs and
wishes of the people who would themselves decide with whom to
federate, and if and when to alter any alliances already made. The
people of Alsace should have the right to determine whether or not
to join the Germans, and the Basques should be left to establish their
own relations with one another. Just as boundaries between countries
should be dependent upon the will of the people, so also should the
boundaries of the different provinces within a country be determined
by the will of those living within the provinces. In France, Germany
and even Switzerland, the existing provinces might be considered as
nothing less than the feudal possessions of dukes, counts and barons,
that is as relics of a bygone age.

Reclus demonstrated how the system of local units imposed from
above had been used as an effective tool of despotism, especially in
France. At every level there were representatives of the central

government – at those of the marshals (the military divisions), the prefects (the departments), the subprefects (the *arrondissements*), the mayors and local councillors (the communes). These functionaries, among whom was the parish priest, were servile towards their superiors and looked with scorn upon their subordinates, a technique of authority which was being skilfully used to enforce the will of the central authorities. At the bottom of the social scale came the citizen, who had little to say about how his affairs were run, who was compelled 'to obey and to pay his taxes'. Reclus was confident, none the less, that the powerful machinery of the centralised state could and would be overcome, and that the people would be able to establish the 'social Republic' upon its proper basis. He was much less precise on the question of the means to be used by the people to rid themselves of the yoke of despotism. He was also vague about how long this process would take, although he recognised that an integral part of this emancipation was the raising of the consciousness of people.

At this point Reclus had certain specific views about the nature of the 'social Republic' which he believed ought to be established. Basically, it would take the form of small groups or associations. What geographical relationship these would bear to existing communes would be entirely dependent upon the people involved. While each association would be completely independent and self-administering, the people of one, acting out of a sense of brotherly love rather than that of competition, would freely join those of another to form larger associations, and these would vary in size according to the needs of the people in different areas. Within any given group the people would decide whether they wished to associate with any other group and be free to withdraw from any association which they had already formed. The association would be constantly in a state of flux, changing according to the will of the people and taking on different forms in relation to the kind of work which had to be undertaken, whether, for example, the construction of a city quarter or a railroad came into question. Workers who were dissatisfied with living and working in one area should be free to work elsewhere. Work, as the most enriching human endeavour, was to occupy a central position in the society of tomorrow. Idlers and parasites would not feel comfortable there, and while permitted to co-exist with their brothers, would be given only a life of pure charity, tolerance and scorn.

With this organisation in mind, Reclus proposed to the congress the need for emphasising that the basis of future society rest upon 'the autonomy of productive associations and groups formed by these associations'. These words were suggested as an amendment to the original resolution which read 'the autonomy of the communes and the provinces', a wording which Bakunin had proposed and Reclus himself had supported a year earlier.[74] The amendment represented the attempt to introduce the all-important point that, in any discussion of freedom, what a person does is intimately related to where that person lives. At the same time, Reclus very likely felt that 'communes and provinces' too readily implied the retention of the existing boundaries and believed that 'productive associations' would avoid giving this impression. In later years he was to reject this concept as inadequate (all people in a community are not equally productive) and to return to the idea of the commune as the basic unit of society, emphasising that he meant a community of people, one that might only incidentally coincide with an existing administrative commune.

It is worth noting that this address at Berne in 1868 was Reclus' first elaboration of the principles of wide-ranging decentralisation. The ideas were not new, and one suspects that Bakunin was an important influence behind his advocacy of them.[75] However, a detailed discussion on this question cannot be found in Reclus' later writings, even though such ideas were to re-appear and to be given some prominence in the thought of his friend and fellow theoretician Peter Kropotkin. The disappearance of these concerns from Reclus' writings does not indicate a rejection of the underlying principles of decentralisation, but rather represents a reconsideration of the relative importance of such questions for the revolutionary struggle. As will become clear in later chapters, his determiñation to be 'scientific' led him to place an important emphasis upon the struggle to achieve a socialist society and to avoid detailed discussions on the nature of that society. He was to exchange a 'utopianism' in theory for a 'utopianism' in action.

Bakunin and Reclus had hoped to push the League of Peace and Freedom into a radical direction, but their failure to enlist the support of the IWMA weakened their position, and they were not able to convince fellow members to endorse an advanced social programme. They, along with their friends, including Aristide Rey, Giuseppe Fanelli and Albert Richard, were among the 18 who signed a statement declaring their secession from the League.[76] The immediate question to be faced by the group was the form which their political activity should assume. In opposition to Bakunin, who wished to take his 'brothers' directly into the IWMA, it was decided to found an 'open' international organisation.[77] Reclus seems to have been in favour of the decision, but it is not certain whether he attended the meetings

which were held in Geneva to discuss the founding of the new society,
the International Alliance of Socialist Democracy.[78] The Alliance
applied to the General Council of the IWMA for affiliation as a distinct
international body, and after being refused admission on this basis on
22 December 1868,[79] dissolved itself as an international organisation
and advised its sections to join those of the IWMA. As a 'non-international'
association the Alliance applied for admission to the IWMA, and as
requested by the General Council, revised a phrase in its statutes to read
'abolition' rather than 'equalisation . . . of classes'. The section of the
Alliance at Geneva was finally accepted by the General Council as a
section of the IWMA on 28 July 1869.[80]

Both Elisée and Elie Reclus are usually named in connection with
Bakunin's Alliance of Socialist Democracy.[81] Marx was convinced that
they were members of a secret Alliance which, it was claimed, Bakunin
continued to lead within the IWMA.[82] Regardless of possible membership in any of Bakunin's societies, secret or open, from 1869 to 1872
Elisée had very little contact with the group around Bakunin and
Elie even less. In fact, from late 1868 a strain was developing in the
relations between the brothers and Bakunin. The story, in so far as it
can be reconstructed, deals directly with Elie and only indirectly with
Elisée, but both were grouped together in Bakunin's estimation and
both considered guilty of the same offence, namely that of courting
the bourgeoisie. The first indication of a divergence of opinion can be
traced back to the autumn of 1868.

On 22 September of that year, while the Congress of the League of
Peace and Freedom was in session, a telegram arrived which carried the
news of the dethronement of Isabella and revolution in Spain. Among
the members of Bakunin's circle there was immediate talk of joining
the insurgents.[83] Fanelli, an Italian engineer, was entrusted with the
mission of broadening Bakunin's influence in Spain. It has been claimed
that Elisée went to Spain under Bakunin's orders and that he was
recalled.[84] Another account maintains that Elisée was unable, for un-
specified reasons, to travel to Spain and sent Elie instead.[85] Bakunin
did ask Elisée to undertake the task, but in the latter's own words, the
request was answered with 'a very categorical no'.[86] Elie did
eventually make a trip to Spain in the company of Aristide Rey, but
paid little attention to Bakunin's 'orders';[87] instead he met with
Spanish republicans, in particular with a friend, Fernando Garrido, a
leading Spanish Fourierist and the man who introduced co-operatives
into Spain. Disregarding the wishes of Fanelli, who considered him
morally obligated 'as a member of the Brotherhood' to help evangelise

Spain, Elie accompanied Garrido on a political tour of the country.
As he explained years later to Nettlau, he deeply resented Fanelli's
interference in his affairs and what he referred to as the Italian's
Machiavellianism towards the Spanish republicans.[88]

Bakunin's disappointment over Elie's 'non-revolutionary' activity in
Spain was exacerbated in early 1869. In the first edition of the
Mannheim newspaper *La Fraternité*, Elie was listed as one of its
collaborators. In the 20 February edition of the Swiss revolutionary
paper *L'Egalité* Bakunin characterised the Mannheim paper as 'a
new organ of bourgeois socialism'. Bakunin, who was by this time
well aware of Elie's activities in Spain, publicly expressed astonishment
at his decision to collaborate with La Rigaudière, the organiser of
*La Fraternité*.[89] Elisée came to his brother's defence and on 21
February wrote a letter to *L'Egalité*, stating his resentment at the
'mendacious assertion' which had appeared in *La Fraternité*. He claimed
that both he and his brother had been asked to contribute to the newspaper, but that they had refused.[90] On 10 March he wrote another letter
to *L'Egalité*, taking back the words 'mendacious assertion' and admitting
that Elie's reply to La Rigaudière had been 'evasive and dilatory'.[91] The
incident shows Elisée on the defensive and under pressure to assert his
revolutionary beliefs.

Shortly after this conflict, Bakunin saw yet another example of
what he considered Elie's 'bourgeois socialist' leanings in his support
of Madame Champseix. Elie was one of the four (the other three were
Louis Kneip, A. Davaud and the shoemaker Albert) who signed a
declaration in support of Champseix shortly after a long letter which
she wrote was published in the 13 March edition of *L'Egalité*.[92] In the
letter she had put forth ideas on a *rapprochement* of the different
democratic parties, views which were denounced in the same issue of
*L'Egalité*. A further letter from Champseix defending her point of view
and the letter of support were refused publication in *L'Egalité* on the
grounds of 'lack of space' in a note written almost certainly by
Bakunin.[93] The two letters, it was claimed, were

> inspired by the same spirit of conciliation *vis-à-vis* that good
> bourgeois class which devours us so calmly every day, as if it were
> the most natural and legitimate thing in the world, and [by the
> same spirit] of protestation against the tendencies of our paper,
> because, having raised the flag of the true politics of the
> proletariat, it does not wish to agree to any deals.[94]

The letter signed by Elie has not survived, and it is, therefore, impossible to establish the exact nature of his support of Champseix. He would, I believe, have defended his position by insisting upon her right to the opportunity to express her views. Bakunin was in no mood to be lenient with Elie, however, and he included Elisée as well on his list of conciliators of the bourgeoisie. In a manuscript of 1871 Bakunin wrote that the Reclus brothers and Champseix believed, at least in 1869, 'in the possibility of conciliating the interests of the bourgeoisie with that of the legitimate revindications of the proletariat. They also believed, like Mazzini, that the proletariat ought to join hands with the radical bourgeoisie.'[95]

Elisée and Elie were both 'bourgeois', as far as Bakunin was concerned, but their positions were not identical, as Bakunin's words would appear to indicate. The differences in their views during this period can be seen especially in their responses to Spain in 1868. It is important to note that Elie was as anxious to work for the republican cause in Spain, as Elisée was convinced that the whole project was a waste of time. Elisée attempted to discourage his brother from leaving for Spain, and advised him that there was plenty to do in Paris to prepare for the coming revolution in central Europe.[96] When Elie refused to heed these counsels, Elisée did nothing to encourage him in his 'compromising' with the moderates, and said that the republicans might as well at least have 'the merit of having been honest in battle', since they had no chance of success.[97] Elisée could not support Elie's efforts, not so much because he disliked his brother's approach to revolutionary matters, but because in the circumstances he believed that they were destined to bear little, if any, fruit.

On the Spanish question Elisée also differed from Bakunin. The refusal to make the trip was based upon more than personal considerations, as his attempt to discourage Elie from travelling there clearly indicates. His criticism of Bakunin is barely concealed in his statement that revolutionaries were too ready to believe that the great day had arrived and that this led to mistakes which slowed down the revolutionary process.[98] Contrary to Bakunin, he maintained that priority should be given to less spectacular activities in the advanced European countries. It may have been his opposition to Bakunin's plans for Spain which led to Elisée's detachment from the Alliance of Socialist Democracy formed after the Berne Congress of the League of Peace and Freedom.

Elisée's position *vis-à-vis* both Bakunin and Elie was based upon the premise that great dividends could be expected from working within centres of traditional revolutionary agitation. An examination of his correspondence of the late 1860s reveals that, as the 'liberal' Empire progressed, he lived in excited anticipation of wide-ranging revolutionary change. 'You are not unaware of how serious the circumstances are and in what political fever we are living', he wrote to Elie in the Autumn of 1867. 'The Empire is committing suicide, and Garibaldi is perhaps at Rome. Let us prepare ourselves for great things.'[99] The suicide was being committed through the series of liberal reforms of the 1860s which made the regime vulnerable to the venom of its republican critics. Elisée did not believe that a liberal Empire could survive for long, and he became steadily more enthusiastic as the restrictions on free speech were lifted and opportunities were opened up to spread revolutionary propaganda. A new law in 1868 brought an end to the strict administrative control of the press, and as a result, France was flooded with journals – among them *La Lanterne* of Henri Rochefort – giving voice to those opposed to the regime. He no doubt saw a great gain for the working class in such legislation as that which abolished article 1781 of the Civil Code, by which a master's word was final in a wages dispute. He eagerly attended the meetings which were held following the 25 May 1868 Law on the Freedom of Assembly. In 'coarse words pronounced by men without education, incorrect language, foolish remarks, passionate cries', he found the confirmation of his youthful belief in the power of the masses. 'Pressed one against the other, breathing an atmosphere of sweat and dust, they are there for hours in the hope of hearing a word of justice and liberty, small compensation for the miseries of each day.'[100] With great satisfaction he saw that most speakers respected their audience and that some of them earnestly spoke from their hearts or sought to back up their arguments with 'the solid discussion of facts'.

Although Reclus had supported Bakunin and had joined the International Brotherhood, he came to question the usefulness of secret societies in making progress towards the social revolution. While they might once have had certain advantages, their necessarily hierarchical structures and their separation from the people were serious weaknesses which condemned them in an age of 'free speech'. It was probably this view which had led him to support the foundation of an 'open' Alliance rather than what would have amounted to the continued existence of the (secret) Brotherhood inside the IWMA. He emphasised some years later that it was necessary for socialist theories to be developed within the context of full public discussion. 'To be sure, if our doctrine is . . . a secret doctrine, it will be stillborn.'[101]

In the relaxed political climate of the 1860s he chose not to engage in clandestine activities against the Empire, but to do what he could within the existing social-economic and political structure. While he sought the demise of Napoleon, he viewed the 'liberal' Empire as an advance on what had gone before.

Reclus' thought in this period is nicely summarised in a letter written by him to his brother-in-law Pierre Faure.[102] It contains traces of ideas expressed as early as 1851, but represents a fairly clear statement of his theory of Evolution and Revolution, which he was to formulate in the late 1870s and continually to revise until it appeared in its final written form in 1898.[103] According to this theory, it was more correct to say that the ultimate social revolution would be achieved through an inter-related process of evolution and revolution rather than through a single revolution. Evolution consisted in countless, small revolutions; a great outburst, on the other hand, or what was commonly called a revolution, represented a speeding up of the process of evolution and was a form of accelerated progress. At this time (1869) he was looking forward to the next large-scale revolution and claimed that its aim would be 'to ensure equality, to suppress the privilege of material life and intellectual life . . . to bring to an end the terrible antagonism between employers and wage-earners, between bourgeois, workers and peasants'.[104] There was no illusion that this revolution would bring equality overnight, that the struggle for the ideal would be over. 'Alas, no, but in working for our children, we take yet another step forward in the ruins, and perhaps in blood.'[105]

It is important to note that in 1869 Reclus was not willing to sit back and to wait for *a* revolution (much less *the* revolution) which, in any case, he did not believe would be the final answer to social problems. In sharp contrast to his later negative attitude towards the vote,[106] he was anxious to undermine the government by supporting the 'most revolutionary' candidate in the May/June 1869 elections. In the first round he gave his support to an old Fourierist, Cantagrel, in the second to the republican Henri Rochefort, who stood in opposition to the moderate Jules Favre. In Reclus' opinion, the victory of Thiers, Garnier-Pagès and Favre (moderate liberals) could not suppress the 30,000 'revolutionary' votes cast in favour of the opposition candidates. 'Those who have the most resolution, the most love of progress and justice, those whom the government detests the most, those are the zealots who have voted for Rochefort, for Raspail, for Alton-Shée.'[107] The tactic of supporting the most revolutionary candidates in elections was referred to as 'Negative

Voting' and he became very much attracted to the idea.[108]

By 1869 Reclus had come to the conclusion that revolutionary agitation could be effective if practised within the rules of the existing order and in certain circumstances could bear more fruit than a direct assault, Bakunin's suggestions notwithstanding. The task which loomed large was that of hastening the destruction of the Empire which was already well under way. In the long term he was working for the social revolution; in the meantime he was struggling for a regime in which there would be more channels through which to work for ever greater gains. It is not clear whether this was a completely conscious aim in 1869, but if his activities in 1870 to 1871 are any indication of where his views in 1869 were leading, he was working for the establishment of a Republic — a 'bourgeois' Republic which would represent an advance in the direction of the universal social Republic. At this point Reclus was a revolutionary socialist, and although there is no reason to believe that he had changed his earlier view on anarchy as the socialist goal,[109] he had not yet become an anarchist in the sense of working completely outside the parliamentary structure. After the Commune he became more selective in his choice of political agitation.

## Notes

1. Elisée to his mother, n.d. (1857?), *Correspondance*, 3 vols. (Paris, 1911– 25), vol. I, p. 172.
2. Reclus, *Voyage à la Sierra-Nevada de sainte-Marthe* (Paris, 1861).
3. Paul Reclus, 'A Few Recollections on the Brothers Elie and Elisée Reclus', in J. Ishill, *Elisée and Elie Reclus: In Memoriam* (Berkeley Heights, 1927), p. 17 and 'Biographie d'Elisée Reclus' in *Les Frères Elie et Elisée Reclus* (Paris, 1964), pp. 58–9.
4. Elisée Reclus, *Elie Reclus, 1827–1904* (Paris, 1905), p. 26.
5. See above, Chapter 2, n. 19.
6. Elisée to his mother, n.d. (1862), *Corr.* I, p. 217 and Elisée to Noémi Reclus, n.d. (1863), *Corr.* I, p. 230.
7. Proudhon exclaimed: 'What can he [Napoleon] do? Nothing, nothing, nothing.' George Woodcock, *Pierre-Joseph Proudhon, His Life and Work* (New York, 1972), p. 224.
8. Elisée to Mmes. Elie and Elisée Reclus, 12 or 13 Aug. 1860, *Corr.* III, p. 22.
9. See Elisée Reclus, *Londres Illustré. Guide Spécial pour l'Exposition de 1862* (Paris, 1862) which is an abridged edition of his *Guide de Voyageur à Londres et aux Environs* (Paris, 1860).
10. 'Well done, workers of London!' exclaimed Reclus. Letter to Noémi Reclus, n.d. (1863), *Corr.* I, p. 231.
11. It is difficult to establish the date of Reclus' membership in the IWMA. See police report of 27 Aug. 1874, *P.Po.* B a/1237; another of 2 Feb. 1879,

*AN* BB24 732. Cf. Kropotkin, 'Elisée Reclus' and E. Vaughan, 'The Criminal Record of Elisée Reclus' in Elisée Reclus, *An Anarchist on Anarchy* (Boston, 1884), p. 18.

12. Cf. Reclus' correspondence for the period, esp. letter to Elie, 11 June 1868 (see below, n. 15).

13. See the letter of 10 Feb. 1865 from Tolain to Lelubez in which Tolain attacks Elie Reclus: I. Tchernoff, *Le Parti Républicain au coup d'Etat et sous le Second Empire* (Paris, 1906), pp. 455–6.

14. *L'Association*, Apr. 1865.

15. Elisée to Elie, 11 June 1868, *Papiers ER, NAF* 22910. The letter is undated. However, on the day on which it was written Elie continued writing on the same piece of paper on which Elisée's letter had been written and dated it 11 June 1868. The published version of Elisée's letter (*Corr.* I, p. 289 ff) has been misdated 11 Oct. 1868.

16. Elisée to Elie, n.d. (Oct. 1868), *Corr.* I. p. 294.

17. See their signatures following the copy of the address delivered by Reclus and Fanny at their wedding: *Papiers ER, NAF* 22909.

18. Note Reclus' involvement in *La Republique des Travailleurs* organ of the Batignolles section, in early 1871. According to Jacques Rougerie, 'L'A.I.T. et le mouvement ouvrier à Paris pendant les événements de 1870–1871' in *International Review of Social History*, 1972, Parts 1–2, pp. 84–5 n, Reclus was a member of the Batignolles section.

19. *Documents of the First International*, 5 vols. (Moscow), vol. III, pp. 122, 143–6.

20. Karl Marx, *Chronik seines Lebens* (Frankfurt, 1971), p. 448.

21. Max Nettlau, *Elisée Reclus: Anarchist und Gelehrter* (Berlin, 1928), p. 95.

22. Marx to Ludwig Büchner, 1 May 1867, *Marx Engels Werke* (Berlin, 1956 ff), vol. 31, pp. 544–5. As early as Dec. 1862, Marx had been looking for a French translator. On 2 Jan. 1863 he wrote to Engels that Jenny Marx (who had been in Paris in late Dec. 1862) had met a 'certain Reclus' who wanted to undertake the work; Marx to Engels, 2 Jan. 1863, *MEW* 30, p. 306. According to the notes there and those in *Chronik*, p. 223, Jenny met Elie. Nettlau was aware of some talk that Marx had considered Elie as a possible translator of 'an economic composition' in the early 1860s; Nettlau, *Elisée Reclus*, p. 95 n. (See below, n. 23.) Marx's plan for what was to be his major work on economics went through a complicated series of modifications. The *Grundrisse*, manuscripts which were written from Oct. 1857 to Mar. 1858 (and published only in 1939) served him as a basis for the theories put forward in both the *Critique of Political Economy* (1859) and *Das Kapital* (1867 ff). The text which Marx was anxious to have translated into French in early 1863 was what was to be the first volume of *Das Kapital*.

23. *MEW* 31, p. 676, n. 443. Cf. *Chronik*, p. 264. The *MEW* and the *Chronik* contain notes about the letters from Schily, not their contents. The letters from Marx and Engels concerning the translation of *Das Kapital* in the *MEW* mention only the family name Reclus. According to the *Chronik*, originally put together in 1933 by the Marx-Engels-Lenin-Institute in Moscow, Elie was supposed to be the translator. However, the much later *MEW* of the Institute for Marxism-Leninism (which developed out of the earlier Marx-Engels-Lenin-Institute) names Elisée Reclus as the translator. Presumably, the Institute corrected or reinterpreted the material used in the *Chronik*. It can be established that it was Elisée whom Marx met in the summer of 1869. At this time Marx referred to him simply as Reclus. The *MEW*, which is a more recent and more comprehensive work than the *Chronik*, remains the more reliable source.

24. Marx to Victor Schily, 30 Nov. 1867, *MEW* 31, p. 573.

25. *MEW* 31, p. 727, n. 46.

26. Engels to Marx, 2 Feb. 1868, *MEW* 32, p. 28. Cf. Marx to Engels, 1 Feb. 1868, *MEW* 32, p. 26.

27. See Marx to Laura and Paul Lafargue, 11 Apr. 1868, *MEW* 32, p. 544, and p. 733, n. 109. Cf. *Chronik*, p. 267. See also Marx to Engels, 4 Aug. 1868, *MEW* 32, p. 131.

28. Marx to Engels, 18 Nov. 1869, *MEW* 32, p. 394: 'When Reclus was here, he also went to see L. B[lanc] and said to me after his visit. The little fellow shits in his pants from fright at the mere thought of having to return to France. He feels himself bedeviled here, no doubt as a "little big man" who has been removed from danger and – has, as he said directly to R[eclus], lost absolutely all faith in the French.'

29. Marx to Engels, 1 Aug. 1877, *MEW* 34, p. 65 and Marx to Wilhelm Bracke, 20 Nov. 1876, *MEW* 34, p. 225.

30. Engels to Wilhelm Liebknecht, 31 July 1877, *MEW* 34, p. 285.

31. Marx to Engels, 1 Aug. 1877, *MEW* 34, p. 65.

32. Preface by Elisée Reclus to F. Domela Nieuwenhuis, *Le Socialisme en Danger* (Paris, 1897), p. viii. Cf. Nieuwenhuis, pp. 46, 166–7.

33. For a history of co-operation in France and Elie's role within it, see Jean Gaumont, *Histoire Générale de la Coopération en France*, 2 vols. (Paris, 1924).

34. *L'Association, bulletin international des coopératives*, 17 June 1866.

35. Reclus, *Elie Reclus*, p. 28.

36. Gaumont, *Histoire Générale de la Coopération*, vol. I, p. 465. Cf. Guillaume de Greef, *Elogie d'Elie Reclus, Discours prononcé le 31 octobre à la séance de rentrée* (Brussels, 1904), p. 23. For the idea of internationalism in the co-operative movement, see Gaumont, vol. II, p. 619 ff. Cf. Lorenz Petersen to Hess, 4 May 1867, in Moses Hess, *Briefwechsel* (The Hague, 1959), pp. 547–9.

37. Reclus, *Elie Reclus*, pp. 27–8.

38. Elisée to Elie, 11 June 1868, *Papiers ER, NAF* 22910 (see above, n. 15).

39. Cf. Reclus to Alfred Dumesnil, n.d. (1868), *Corr.* I, p. 300.

40. See Boris I. Nicolaevsky, 'Secret Societies and the First International' in Milorad M. Drachkovitch (ed.), *The Revolutionary Internationals 1864–1943* (Stanford, 1966), p. 36 ff.

41. Jean Bossu, *Elisée Reclus* (Herblay, S. et O., n.d.), p. 18 n.

42. Reclus to Mlle. Rachel Goron, 17 Dec. 1894, *Autographes XIXème-XXème Siècles, NAF* 25101.

43. Elisée Reclus, *L'Anarchie* (Publications des Temps Nouveaux, no. 2, Paris, 1896), Notice Préliminaire.

44. Bossu, *Elisée Reclus*, p. 18 n. Léo Campion, *les anarchistes dans la F.M.* (Marseilles, 1969), pp. 87–91.

45. Campion, *les anarchistes dans la F.M.*, p. 91. The account is incorrect in so far as it implies that Elisée and Elie (and their brother Paul) were lifelong Freemasons.

46. See below, Chapter 10.

47. Reclus, *Anarchie* (address delivered at the *Loge des Amis Philanthropes* at Brussels in 1894).

48. Elisée to Elie, n.d. (1868), *Corr.* I, p. 314.

49. Quoted in Bossu, *Elisée Reclus*, p. 17.

50. Elisée to Noémi Reclus, n.d. (1869), *Corr.* I, pp. 294–5.

51. For example, see Elisée to Elie, n.d. (Oct. 1868), *Corr.* I, pp. 294–5.

52. Quoted in Woodcock, *Anarchism*, p. 147.

53. Marx to Engels, 4 Nov. 1864, *MEW* 31, p. 16.

54. Elie and Elisée provided Nettlau with information about their meeting with Bakunin in Paris. Nettlau, *Elisée Reclus*, p. 109.

55. Ibid., p. 108 ff and Nettlau, 'Elisée Reclus and Michael Bakunin' in Ishill, *Elisée and Elie Reclus*, p. 197 ff. Woodcock, *Anarchism*, p. 149, says Elisée 'later claimed that as early as the autumn of 1864 he and Bakunin were making plans for an International Brotherhood'.

56. Elisée is named as a member of the Alliance of Social Democracy in Guillaume, *Internationale*, vol. I, p. 77. Cf. Jean Maitron (ed.), *Dictionnaire Biographique du Mouvement Ouvrier français*, vol. VIII (Paris, 1970), pp. 299–300.

57. See Elisée Reclus, 'La Sicile et l'Eruption de l'Etna en 1865. Recit de Voyage' in *Le Tour du Monde* VIII, 1865, pp. 353–416 and *La Revue des Deux Mondes*, 1 July 1865, pp. 110–38.

58. See the comments of Angelo de Gubernatis, *Fibra, Pagine di Ricordi* (Rome, 1900), p. 238 ff.

59. Elisée to Elie, n.d. (Oct. 1868), *Corr. I, p. 293.*

60. Such a great deal of mystery surrounds the secret societies of Bakunin that there exists much controversy concerning their activities and even their existence. Cf. Max Nomad, 'The Anarchist Tradition' in Drachkovitch, *The Revolutionary Internationals*, pp. 65–6.

61. G.D.H. Cole, *A Study of Socialist Thought*, 5 vols. (London, 1958 ff), vol. II, p. 114. For Marx's comments, see *Documents of the First International*, vol. II, pp. 152–3.

62. Bakunin had suggested at the Central Committee meeting of 20 Oct. 1867 in Berne that Elie be asked to become the French editor of the proposed journal. See Elisée to Elie, n.d. (Oct. 1867), *Corr.* I, pp. 262–4, which includes a copy of the letter from Gustave Vogt requesting Elie to take up the position. Cf. Elisée to Elie, n.d. (Nov. 1867), *Corr.* I, pp. 265–6 and Elisée to Elie, n.d. (1867), *Corr.* I, pp. 267–8.

63. Guillaume, *Internationale*, vol. I, p. 78.

64. Elisée to Elie, n.d. (Oct. 1867), *Corr.* I, p. 264.

65. Elisée was not present at the 1867 Geneva meeting of the League of Peace and Freedom as claimed in Tchernoff, *Le Parti Républicain*, p. 468.

66. Freymond, *Première Internationale*, vol. I, p. 388 ff.

67. Elisée to Elie, n.d. (Oct. 1868), *Corr.* I, p. 280.

68. Ibid., p. 281.

69. Ibid., p. 282.

70. Ibid., p. 284.

71. Ibid., p. 279.

72. For Reclus' speech, see *Bulletin sténographique du deuxième Congrès de la Paix et de la Liberté. Stenographisches Bulletin des zweiten Friedens-und Freiheits-Kongresses*, 22–25 Sept. 1868 (Berne, 1868), pp. 235–8. See also Elisée to Elie, n.d. (Oct. 1868), *Corr.* I, p. 285.

73. For Gambuzzi's speech, see *deuxieme Congrès de la Paix et de la Liberte*, pp. 197–202.

74. Elisée to Elie, n.d. (Nov. 1867), *Corr.* I, p. 272.

75. Cf. the ideas in Bakunin's 1866 *Revolutionary Catechism* and in his *Organisation* which he had prepared for the International Brotherhood: Michael Bakunin, *Gesammelte Werke*, vol. III (Berlin, 1924), pp. 7 ff and 29 ff. Cf. also the ideas which he elaborated at the Berne Congress of the League of Peace and Freedom in *deuxième Congrès de la Paix et de la Liberté*, pp. 214–35 and in Guillaume, *Internationale*, vol. I, p. 78. See Bakunin's statement which was read out at the 1868 Brussels Congress of the IWMA in *Supplément au journal le Peuple Belge*, 22 Sept. 1868 and in Freymond, *Première Internationale*, vol. I, p. 391. See also Bakunin's 10 May 1872 letter to Lorenzo in Arthur Lehning (ed.), *Archives Bakounine*, vol. II (Leiden, 1965), pp. xxviii–xxx, especially p. xxix where

Bakunin states: 'Since 1868 . . . I have carried on at Geneva a crusade against the principle itself of authority and preached the abolition of States . . . '

76. For the statement and a fuller list of signatories, see Guillaume, *Internationale*, vol. I, pp. 75–6.

77. Nettlau, *Elisée Reclus*, p. 121 ff.

78. Nettlau's opinion that Reclus left almost immediately for Paris is based on a letter written by Reclus in Paris and dated 11 Oct. 1868. However, this letter has been misdated in the published correspondence. See above n. 15.

79. *Documents of the First International*, vol. III, pp. 300–301.

80. Freymond, *Première Internationale*, vol. I, p. 454.

81. Marx to Wilhelm Bracke, 20 Nov. 1876, *MEW* 34, p. 225; Engels to Wilhelm Liebknecht, 31 July 1877, *MEW* 34, p. 285. Guillaume, *Internationale*, vol. II, p. 344, says that the Alliance of Socialist Democracy was founded by Bakunin, Reclus and 'their friends'. Cf. Cole, *Study of Socialist Thought*, vol. II, p. 124. For the programme and rules of the Alliance (and Marx's comments), see *Documents of the First International*, vol. III, p. 273 ff and 379 ff. For an official list of 'Les Membres du Groupe Initiateur de Genève' (which does not include Reclus), see *Documents of the First International*, vol. III, pp. 276–7 and 382–3. Cf. Jacques Freymond, *Etudes et Documents sur la Première Internationale en Suisse* (Geneva, 1964), Appendix; Max Nettlau, *Michael Bakunin, Eine Biographie*, 3 vols. (London, 1898 ff), vol. II, p. 262 ff.

82. Marx to Wilhelm Bracke, 20 Nov. 1876, *MEW* 34, p. 225; Engels to Wilhelm Liebknecht, 31 July 1877, *MEW* 34, p. 285; 'Rapport Fait au Congrès de la Haye au Nom du Conseil Général, sur l'Alliance de la Démocratie Socialiste' in *Documents of the First International*, vol. III, p. 463 ff.

83. Elisée to Elie, n.d. (Oct. 1868), *Corr.* I, p. 294. Cf. Elisée to Elie, n.d. (Oct. 1868), *Corr.* I, p. 281.

84. Tchernoff, *Le Parti Republicain*, p. 479.

85. Gerald Brenan, *The Spanish Labyrinth* (Cambridge, 1962), p. 138.

86. Elisée to Elie, n.d. (Oct. 1868), *Corr.* I, p. 294.

87. Elisée wrote to Elie that, if he went to Spain, Carlo Gambuzzi would be one of his 'mandators'. Elisée to Elie, n.d. (1868), *Corr.* I, p. 293.

88. At Brussels in 1895 Elie discussed his feelings about the affair with Nettlau. Nettlau, *Elisée Reclus*, p. 130.

89. Bakunin's letter of 17 Feb. 1869 from Geneva in *L'Egalité*, 20 Feb. 1869; copy in Michel Bakounine, *Oeuvres*, vol. V (Paris, 1911), pp. 18–22.

90. Elisée's letter of 21 Feb. 1869 in *L'Egalité*, 27 Feb. 1869; *Oeuvres*, vol. V, p. 23. When the letter was written, Elisée was under a great personal strain. His wife was seriously ill; she died the following day, Feb. 22.

91. Elisée's letter of 10 Mar. 1869 in *L'Egalité*, 20 Mar. 1869; *Oeuvres*, vol. V, p. 24.

92. Champseix's letter of 2 Mar. 1869 in *L'Egalité*, 13 Mar. 1869; *Oeuvres*, vol. V, pp. 25–31.

93. *L'Egalité*, 27 Mar. 1869; *Oeuvres*, vol. V, pp. 34–5.

94. *L'Egalité*, 27 Mar. 1869; *Oeuvres*, vol. V, pp. 34–5.

95. Quoted in Nettlau, 'Elisée Reclus and Michael Bakunin', p. 201.

96. Elisée to Elie, n.d. (Oct. 1868), *Corr.* I, pp. 292–3; Elisée to Elie, n.d. (Oct. 1868), *Corr.* I, pp. 294–5.

97. Elisée to Elie, n.d. (autumn 1868), *Corr.* I, pp. 315–16.

98. Elisée to Elie, n.d. (autumn 1867), *Corr.* I, p. 267.

99. Elisée to Elie, n.d. (Oct. 1867), *Corr.* I, p. 262.

100. Reclus to Pierre Faure, n.d. (1869), *Corr.* III, pp. 62–3.

101. Reclus to De Gérando, 24 June 1883, *Corr.* II, p. 308.

102. Reclus to Faure, n.d. (1869), *Corr.* III, pp. 62–3.

103. Cf. Reclus' letter to the Congress of the Jura Federation of 1878 in *L'Avant-Garde*, 12 Aug. 1878; his *Evolution et Révolution* (Geneva, 1880); and his *l'Idéal Anarchique* (Paris, 1898).

104. Reclus to Faure, n.d. (1869), *Corr.* III, p. 64.

105. Ibid.

106. See his well-known letter on electoral abstentionism in *Le Révolté*, 11 Oct. 1885.

107. Reclus to Faure, n.d. (June 1869), *Corr.* III, p. 61.

108. Reclus to 'Mes biens chers amis' (Elie?), n.d. (1869?), *Papiers ER, NAF* 22910.

109. The 'political' activity could still be reconciled with his revolutionary beliefs. Reclus stated: 'If I write my little note on *Negative Voting* he [Pierre Faure] will believe that I am following his advice and letting myself be overtaken by the fever of ambition; but he will be a little deceived in thinking that I speak of things which do not comply with revolutionary fervour.' Ibid.

# 4 THE IMPACT OF WAR AND THE PARIS COMMUNE

Reclus' activities during the Franco-Prussian War can be baffling, and his conduct during the early days of the Commune is similarly difficult to explain. For a long time one of the fundamental tenets of his thought had consisted in a rejection of all boundaries between nations. However, under the impact of the events of 1870 to 1871 he took up arms in defence of his native land, and from January 1871 he became an advocate of 'a fight to the death' or what the French called *la guerre à outrance*. He not only co-operated with bourgeois republicans in this period, he was antagonistic to the activities of revolutionary agitators such as Blanqui and Charles Delescluze, and at one point declared that he would even support Thiers, the proven 'enemy' of the working class, if not of the Republic. In the 8 February 1871 elections he went so far as to offer himself as a candidate. One writer believed that Reclus 'remained a slave of national vanity for a long time'.[1] However, it can be shown that Reclus' primary objective during the Franco-Prussian War was not to defend his native land so much as to consolidate the newly established Third Republic and thereby to create an atmosphere which would be conducive to the development of the universal social Republic. His conduct during the Commune reflected the same underlying principle.

Napoleon III's *coup d'état* of 1851 had erected an insurmountable barrier between himself and the republican tradition, and regardless of the 1860s reforms, most republicans remained irreconciled to his 'liberal' Empire. Reclus shared the prevailing republican view that such democratic reforms as Napoleon had enacted were merely tactical necessities designed to stave off revolution rather than the product of any real sympathy for democracy. It is not difficult to see how he could come to this conclusion. In 1868 the new Press Law and the Law on the Freedom of Assembly had served to unleash the flow of republican hatred for the Empire. Napoleon's hand was forced in 1869 when the republicans, who had made increasing gains at every election, captured Paris and most of the big towns. The decree of 2 January 1870 appointed the new ministry of the former anti-Bonapartist Emile Ollivier and was followed by the new constitution which established a degree of cabinet responsibility to parliament. But

Napoleon's concessions to democracy through the liberal reforms were fairly successful in helping him to maintain his position, even if that position was being continually modified through the reforms. The 8 May 1870 plebiscite showed that there was overwhelming public support for the Empire, and despite opposition in the towns, it was recognised by many republicans and monarchists as a triumph for Napoleon. It seems that the Second Empire could only survive by becoming more democratic, although this very process of demo-cratisation was also a threat to its existence. Reclus later contended that the Empire had been cornered into a truce with democracy and that it viewed the war with Prussia as an opportunity to undo the recently enacted liberal reform.[2]

Reclus' initial reaction to the developments of early July 1870 and the official declaration of war by Napoleon III on 19 July is not known. When the Franco-Prussian War broke out, he may have been living with his brother-in-law Alfred Dumesnil at Vascoeuil where he and the English school-teacher Fanny L'Herminez had shortly before (26 June)[3] declared their marriage without religious or official ceremony in front of family and friends. There is evidence which indicates that he was in Paris on 4 September[4] for the proclamation of the Third Republic; in any event he was there shortly after and remained for the duration of the siege. As a resident of the fifth arrondissement he was enrolled in the 119th Battalion of the National Guard and assigned to guard duty around the fortifications of Paris.[5] While he joined the voluntary enlistment of a part of the National Guard for active duty in late October[6] and on 6 November came before the recruiting board,[7] there is no evidence that he took part in the active fighting.[8] Soon after the launching of the balloon post on 26 September, he was enlisted in the company of balloonists directed by the photographer Félix Nadar, but while he underwent a certain amount of training, he did not leave Paris in a balloon.[9]

Until early February 1871 Reclus' views reflected the general tenor of those which were to be found among certain groups of the International Working Men's Association in Paris. Although he had probably been a member of the IWMA from 1865, he had not been an active participant in the Paris section, partly because of some differences of opinion with the group around Tolain who had control of the section until 1868,[10] and partly because personal affairs and geographical pursuits (he was becoming a geographer of some renown) had kept him out of Paris for long periods during 1869 and the first half of 1870. From September 1870, however, residence in Paris brought him into closer contact with the Internationalists there.

As the siege drew on, many Internationalists came to associate with, if not to become members of, the Batignolles section of the Paris IWMA which was largely under the influence of Benoît Malon, the deputy-mayor of the seventeenth arrondissement.[11] Reclus was a close friend of Malon and of several of his companions, and he was probably one of the official members of the Batignolles section.[12] The Paris IWMA helped to set up the Vigilance Committees of the Twenty Arrondisse-ments in early September, but largely abandoned them and started on a period of 'reconstruction' of the IWMA sections from November. Fragmentary evidence suggests that, from this time on, the Paris IWMA was split into two opposing groups: those who continued to support the Vigilance Committees and to follow the 'old policy' and the majority — including Varlin, Malon, Léo Frankel, Reclus — who opted for the 'new policy'. From the beginning of January 1871, it seems, there were two rival central councils, with the majority belonging to the 'legitimate' (*vrai*) one.[13]

The response made by Reclus to the proclamation of the Republic echoed certain sentiments of the Address of the Paris IWMA to the German Workingmen drawn up on the night of 4 to 5 September. This suggested that the war against Napoleon III had been transformed into an assault against the French people and the Republic.[14] In the sense that the Prussians were enemies of the French Republic (and not only of France), Reclus felt compelled to defend it. It was the 'final irony', he declared, that the Prussians and Bonaparte, both enemies of the Republic, would impose war and peace upon it.[15] As early as September he did not have much hope of military victory;[16] his taking up of arms represented a gesture of support for the infant Republic. But what was the nature of this Republic and what did he think could be achieved by supporting it?

Reclus believed that although the revolutionary struggle was in many ways a continuation of the conflicts raised in 1789, it had entered a new phase. He complained that revolutionary journals of the time (such as *Le Réveil* and *La Marseillaise*) had not adjusted theory to the new practice, that the old vocabulary was still being used, as if the situation had not changed.[17] He believed that French workers were more sophisticated and far more shrewd than their forerunners in 1848. They could exchange their hopes of instant utopia for some concrete gains in the direction of a utopia by working within the existing order. Through securing their position within the Republic, they would initiate a period in which they would have more freedom to make further advances. The Republic of 4 September was no more than a 'suspension of arms between the parties'; it had been proclaimed by all 'as the means of supreme salvation' — 'through the instinct of preservation'. Revolutionaries would gain more by playing along with the old parties than by insisting upon the immediate establishment of a just society.

> Orleanists, legitimists, simply patriotic bourgeois have said to us: Dream now, guide us, triumph for us, and we shall see afterwards! Let us accept the dream and if we carry out our mandate well, if we save France, as we are requested, then the Republic will be secured and we shall have the joy to see open for our children an era of progress in justice and well being.[18]

This kind of reasoning led Reclus to dismiss charges of collaborating with the bourgeoisie. In his own view his approach to politics did not in any way contradict an unswerving loyalty to the revolutionary cause. He wrote to his brother-in-law Pierre Faure:

> Thus, Faure, my friend, I who am more revolutionary than you, I who am a frightful communist and an infamous atheist, I do not fear to see the bourgeois element in the economy: I would even accept Thiers . . . However, do not get the idea that I do not wish to keep up my propaganda for the social Revolution continuously and forever.[19]

These words should not be taken as an indication of unequivocal support of Thiers. Reclus was merely suggesting to Faure how far away his intentions were from undermining the existing Republic and the lengths to which he would go in order to consolidate it.[20] While Thiers had accepted no office in the new Republic, he had at least acquiesced in its existence. In Marx's *Eighteenth Brumaire*[21] Reclus had read that, in the Second Republic, 'Thiers had professed to Louis Philippe's family that "it was . . . wholly in accord with the tradition of their forefathers to recognise the republic for the moment and wait until events permitted the conversion of the presidential chair into a throne" '.[22] There seemed every reason to believe (as later events verified) that Thiers could be persuaded to tolerate the Republic. Reclus was aware that a Republic of a Thiers would be a very different affair than the social Republic, but he was convinced that it would be more acceptable than the Empire or a Restoration

under either Orleanists or Legitimists and would lead to a greater
freedom to pursue more socially-oriented policies.

The determination to consolidate the republican form of government was the over-riding consideration governing all Reclus' acts
during the siege and makes intelligible several curious episodes — for
example, his reaction to the 31 October uprising by those factions in
favour of *la guerre à outrance*. The uprising was provoked by the news
of the fall of Metz, the loss of Le Bourget and popular consternation at
the idea of possible peace negotiations with the Prussians. The IWMA
had refused to sanction the demonstration planned for 31 October and
had ruled that Internationalists who participated would be acting as
individuals,[23] not as members of the association. Reclus agreed with
the position of the IWMA — though not necessarily for the same
reasons — and divorced himself from Pierre Flourens, Blanqui and
Delescluze, all of whom still clung to the hope of military victory. A
letter of 6 November[24] to his wife Fanny reveals a satisfaction with
the government successes in the plebiscite of 3 November and the
municipal elections which followed, as well as a greater confidence
than ever before in 'the final maintenance of the Republic'. He hoped
that the Republic would make peace, for in this way it would be
securing its position. On 6 November he thought that it would
ultimately mean very little even if France did lose Alsace and
Lorraine, for if the Republic endured, Germany herself, along with
Alsace and Lorraine, would eventually enter 'the confederation of
free peoples'. No doubt nationalist pride was implicit within Reclus'
initial opposition to a peace imposed by Prussia. This 'bourgeois'
sentiment quickly gave way, even though his 'nationalism' persisted
in his obsession with the idea that the existence of the French
Republic was crucial to the establishment of a universal Republic.[25]

Reclus' political position in early 1871 can be judged from a review
of *La République des Travailleurs* (The Workers' Republic), the paper
launched by the Batignolles section of the Paris IWMA and which was
brought out in six issues from 10 January to 4 February.[26] The
programme put forward in the first issue was signed by several
revolutionaries, including Elisée and Elie Reclus, Malon and André-Léo
(Champseix). One of the unique features of the programme was its
almost 'anti-programmatic' tone. It did not claim to have found a
neat formula which might determine the course of the revolution. On
the contrary, such formulae would work themselves out only in the
course of struggle when theory and practice would be united.

It is in attaching ourselves to revolutionary principles, in studying them profoundly, in returning to them without cease, in applying [them] to real life on every occasion, in pointing out every violation of these principles in political and social deeds, it is by this constant elaboration, by this reciprocal penetration of the deed and the idea, that we shall arrive at unity, our only force but which would render us invincible if we knew how to acquire it.

The revolutionary struggle itself would determine the course of the revolution, provided that there was sufficient dedication within the ranks of those in revolt and given the presence of a will to victory, as well as a desire to think through the theoretical implications of action. The only, and supreme, precondition for the eventual establishment of the 'social' Republic was the defence and consolidation of the already existing 'political' Republic — which was accepted as a great advance.

While no precise definition of 'workers' was elaborated in the programme, the term was synonymous with 'people' and the 'disinherited'. The workers had a special role to play in the struggle both within France and against Germany. In the first instance, they would be the vanguard of this two-pronged struggle and become the mainstay of the existing 'Republic of liberty'. Having consolidated their position, they would play a major role in the founding of the 'Republic of egality'. The programme was an appeal to the Parisian people 'to work, to fight, to battle! with all your strength, with your whole heart, with your whole mind! because life or death, rebirth or decomposition are at the end of this trial'.

From early January, therefore, Reclus was moving steadily in the direction of *la guerre à outrance*. The 'Bulletin' section of the first issue of *La République des Travailleurs*, which he wrote on 6 January, provides an even clearer account of his position. 'We would like to speak of work, peace, liberty, justice', he began, 'but the war, the atrocious war, is there, with its hideous continuation of hatreds, massacres, destructions, infamies of every kind.' The majority of German soldiers, he believed, wanted peace and thousands of them were aware of their complicity in the 'crime' (of attacking the French Republic), but they had become the slaves of Bismarck and William, and were the enemies of the republican cause. Just as the German soldiers were at fault in so far as they acquiesced in the wishes of their masters instead of resisting them, so, too, the people of Paris were weak and wrong when they entrusted their fate to General Trochu and Jules Favre, as if these two men and their supporters at the Hôtel de

Ville embodied papal infallibility. The dictatorship of Trochu was no more capable of saving them than that of Napoleon had been; nor, for that matter, would a dictatorship of Flourens or Blanqui be any more effective. Everything that had been accomplished so far (from 4 September 1870) had been a result of 'public opinion alone' – the fortifications, requisitions, military engagements. According to Reclus, it was necessary that public opinion, or pressure from below, enter the councils of the government and inspire 'magnanimous resolutions, worthy of a people which claims to fight not only for the salvation of a city, but moreover, for that of the universal Republic'. The victory of Paris was also 'the salvation of the world', it was declared, and the people of Paris were enjoined to awaken to the great task which destiny had prepared for them. They were reminded that they were fighting not only for the existing French Republic, but also for the future German Republic.

> In the Reichstag of Berlin, the deputy Liebknecht has protested against the empire of William and his infamous victories. In the Parliament of Stuttgart, seven deputies, out of about a hundred, did not want their names to appear on the list of imperial lackeys. In the streets of Dresden, workers have torn up the bulletins announcing Prussian victories, knowing that every defeat of the French Republic is a disaster for the future German Republic.

An examination of Reclus' newspaper writing in early January suggests that, whether or not he believed a military victory was possible under the circumstances, he felt that he had no choice but to urge on his countrymen to ever greater feats of heroism in the name of the Republic.[27] As the Germans bombarded Paris, he pointed to the sympathy being extended to its beleaguered inhabitants by the outside world and to the courage and energy of the provincial armies. By late January he was more determined than ever to pursue a policy of *la guerre à outrance*, even though the bombardment, the failure of the 22 January uprising and the defeat of the provincial armies had made the possibility of achieving military victory even more remote. The major motivating factor is not difficult to isolate. The armistice signed by Favre on 28 January was proof that the Prussians would not, after all, negotiate with the French Republic, for it allowed three weeks for a newly elected National Assembly to meet at Bordeaux and to assume responsibility for the terms of peace.

In preparation for the elections of 8 February, the Batignolles section met with three other sections of the Paris IWMA, the Ternes, Grenelle and Vaugirard, on 1 February, and decided upon a list 'of fusion and conciliation' with the republican bourgeoisie.[28] On 3 February there appeared a list entitled 'four Committees' comprising the IWMA and three radical groups, the Alliance républicaine, the Défenseurs de la République and the Union républicaine.[29] On the following day the rival federal councils of the Paris IWMA held a joint meeting to come to agreement on a list of 'pure revolutionaries' to be supported 'without compromise with the bourgeoisie',[30] and, on 6 February, 'rectified' the IWMA's position concerning the four Committees.[31] Reclus, however, chose to abide by the principles under-lying the agreements between the four committees, and on 3 February, before the proposed meeting of the IWMA, he left Paris for the Lower Pyrenees where he hoped to stand as republican candidate – 'knowing that the position of deputy is morally of  the most perilous'.[32] His name appeared on at least two radical republican lists, those of the *Comité républicain radical du XIe arrondissement*[33] and the *Liste des candidats proposés par les Comités républicains radicaux de la Rive gauche et de la Rive droite.*[34]

In sharp contrast to his hostile reaction to those groups who had engineered the 31 October uprising, in February 1871 Reclus did not hesitate to take up the republican stand for *la guerre à outrance*, since he was convinced that the defeat of the republicans in the 8 February elections would mean the end of the Republic. The elections were, in reality, a plebiscite in favour of peace or war, and to side with the 'honourable' peace faction now largely meant to support the anti-republicans – the Legitimists, Orleanists and few Bonapartists who remained. 'Elisée thought', wrote Elie to Edouard Charton on 18 April 1871, 'that the triumph of Mr Thiers and the assembly would be the triumph of reaction and sooner or later the reversal of the Republic.'[35] This was the principle which guided Elisée's actions at the time of the February elections, as well as during the early days of the Commune.

Although the letters in which he had offered himself as candidate 'to the people of the lower Pyrenees' had arrived after the candidates had been decided, a short stay convinced Reclus that 'these Messieurs' would not have preferred his *guerre à outrance*, that 'a so-called "honourable" peace' would have been much more to their taste'.[36] (In fact, the Lower Pyrenees voted in a fairly moderate republican fashion in the elections of 8 February.) As he returned to Paris via Sainte-Foy where his wife was living, he was everywhere disappointed with the political attitudes of the French farmers, those of the richer peasants who had enthusiastically voted for the Legitimist-Orleanist-Bonapartist list,[37] as well as with the mass of peasants who seemed disappointed and annoyed that the Republic had not immediately disappeared with the electoral results.[38] After the election of a monarchist National Assembly, Reclus was determined to rescue whatever remained of the Republic and to prevent a royalist restoration. It was important, he wrote to Elie, to organise a 'Defenders of the Republic' committee in every town, with a representative in every village. Before returning to Paris, he continued to travel in the area around Sainte-Foy in defence of 'the cause of the Republic', although he was reluctant to follow his brother Paul's advice to begin a campaign in Orthez for the next elections to the National Assembly:

> I replied that when I had thought of standing as a candidate, I
> had reflected on the terrifying responsibility which deputies
> have to assume. But I do not know what the task of the future
> Chamber will be and, consequently, I am not able to consider
> keeping my candidature open on a permanent basis. I take
> back my liberty completely.[39]

A rather striking example of what has been termed Reclus' patriotism appears in a letter of this period to Nadar: 'Since all is lost, let us begin life again with a fresh start; let us act as if, waking up from a sleep of a hundred thousand years, we perceive that there is everything to win: fatherland, liberty, dignity, honour.'[40] To Reclus and many other republicans in this period, these words had revolutionary connotations; 'fatherland, liberty, dignity, honour' were identified with the French Republic which after 8 February was in grave danger of assault from the monarchist Assembly. When he said to Nadar, 'if exile or misery do not force me to leave France, I shall remain: here is my battlefield', he was reaffirming the decision which he had made in 1857 to press for social change from within France.

Before the outbreak of hostilities in 1870 Reclus had believed that there could be significant progress towards the social revolution through working from within — though not necessarily in co-operation with — a 'liberal' social and political order. It was therefore essential to protect civil liberties even while exploiting them in behalf of the revolutionary cause. His every move during the siege of Paris was motivated by his determination to see the consolidation of the new Republic and to contribute to a style of politics in which there would be more opportunity to work for the social Republic of the future. There is no evidence to indicate that he supported any French military undertaking directed at the German armies until after the proclamation of the Republic on 4 September. From this time he maintained that the people of Paris were struggling not only to defend the existing French Republic. In his view, they were fighting in behalf of the future German Republic and making progress towards the establishment of the future universal Republic. That the defence of the Republic — and not simply France — was his main concern is borne out by his favourable reaction in the autumn of 1870 to the possibility that Bismarck might negotiate with the infant Republic — thereby giving it recognition. In January 1871, as French military victory appeared less and less likely, Reclus became more emphatic that republicans make even greater sacrifices to avert the military defeat which, he believed, would spell the end of the Republic. At the end of January he came out decisively in support of the republican stand for *la guerre à outrance*, for he had become convinced that the defeat of the republicans in the 8 February elections would also amount to a death warrant for the Republic.

It is not known at what point Reclus returned to Paris.[41] He may have been present for the demonstrations of the National Guards which began around the Place de la Bastille on 24 February and continued until 26 February when the guns earlier placed in various artillery parks were taken to Montmartre.[42] The guns were removed out of the fear that they would fall into the hands of the Prussians when they entered Paris in their Triumphal Procession on 1 March. However, the reluctance of the National Guards to respond to government orders to disarm themselves led to bloodshed and the proclamation of the Commune on 18 March.

After Thiers had ordered the withdrawal of the government agencies from Paris to Versailles on 18 March, the 'moderate' Central Committee of the National Guard emerged as the only political force remaining in Paris. Unwilling to act without some kind of moral sanction, the Central Committee restricted its activities to carrying out essential services and arranged for elections to take place on 22 March. As early as 19 March Thiers had instructed the mayors of the twenty arrondissements, who varied in their political outlooks according to the districts they represented, to mediate with the 'insurgents'. Under the lead of the radical mayor of Montmartre (and Deputy), Clemenceau, a series of meetings took place between the Central Committee and the mayors and Deputies of Paris. On 20 March the Central Committee agreed to hand over the Hôtel de Ville to the mayors and to postpone the municipal elections until the Assembly in Versailles – through the intercession of the mayors – voted a municipal law for Paris. However, on the following day the Central Committee, under pressure from the Vigilance Committees of the Twenty Arrondissements, informed Clemenceau that it had decided not to hand over the Hôtel de Ville, although it would postpone the elections.

Thiers reacted by preparing the reorganisation of his military forces to meet the challenge from Paris, and the Central Committee, in turn, did its utmost to destroy the last vestiges of support for Thiers. The municipal buildings of the conservative Tirard in the second and even that of Clemenceau were occupied. At the same time there was mounting unrest among the moderate elements of Paris who had been less concerned about revolution than about the decisions of Versailles regarding the lifting of the moratorium on rents and promissory notes, decisions which meant economic ruin for a large sector of the lower middle class. This opposition to the more radical elements of Paris had led to the demonstrations of the 'friends of Order' on 21 March and the Massacre in the rue de la Paix the following day. Impatient at the lack of response from Versailles concerning municipal elections for Paris and encouraged by the sympathetic risings in centres such as Saint-Etienne, Le Creusot, Marseilles, Lyons and Toulouse, the Central Committee held the postponed elections forthwith.

The first days of the Commune found the IWMA bewildered by the nature of the political situation in Paris and indecisive about the position which it should take up *vis-à-vis* the proposed municipal elections. In a general meeting of the Paris IWMA on 23 March Frankel assured his comrades that the municipal council would represent nothing more than a 'supervisory council' in an association, and the decision was taken – albeit reluctantly by some – to support the Central Committee of the National Guard and to call for municipal elections. The IWMA manifesto issued the following day called for the 'communal revolution' which would ensure the 'independence' and the 'autonomy' of the Commune.[43]

Such an optimistic view of the Commune elections was not to be found in the statement of 25 March signed by Elisée Reclus, his brothers Elie and Paul, and F.D. Leblanc.[44] It resembled the statement issued also on 25 March by the Deputies, mayors and Central Committee[45] in its emphasis upon the avoidance of bloodshed and the consolidation of the republican form of government as the main aims of the elections to be held the following day. However, the Reclus brothers also charged the mayors and Central Committee with responsibility for the confusion which they believed threatened to lead to civil war. The people of Paris were beseeched to put an end to the struggle between their representatives and to pronounce their verdict with the vote. The Deputies, mayors and Central Committee, who had already compromised the Republic through their 'clumsiness', did not have the right to expose it to a 'street battle'. An example of the clumsiness of the representatives was their concern over legality, which had no place in 'full revolution'. The statement suggested that the 'authorities' were a brake on revolutionary change, but that to challenge them at this point would be to jeopardise whatever chances for survival the Republic continued to enjoy.

The conciliatory tone of the 25 March statement indicates that the focus of Reclus' activity at this time was not very different from that during the first siege. Throughout the entire period his aim was the preservation of the Republic, and he was ready to employ a policy of conciliation to achieve that end. This conclusion is also borne out by his association with the republican *Groupe de la Conciliation par l'action* (Group for Conciliation through Action), which chose him as a candidate in the sixth arrondissement in the by-elections to the Commune on 16 April (even though he was in prison at this time).[46] On 27 March, the day after the Commune elections, Reclus commented briefly in a letter to Alfred Dumesnil that he considered the 18 March to be 'the greatest date in the history of France, since 10 August'.[47] It represented both the triumph of the 'Workers' Republic' and the inauguration of the 'Communal Federation'. He referred to the birth of the Commune as 'a change of this scope' which 'has been able to take place almost peacefully'.[48] On 25 March he had expressed his disillusionment with the behaviour of public figures, but his words of 27 March show that he had not yet abandoned the electoral process as the way to social change.

Reclus' experiences within the Commune were cut short by his arrest on 4 April by the Versailles forces. With the co-operation of Bismarck, Thiers had managed to muster over 60,000 troops at Versailles by early April. A reconnaissance of 30 March by the Marquis de Gallifet was followed up by a strong attack on Courbevoie on 2 April which resulted in the seizure of the vital bridge at Neuilly. On the following day massed units of the Paris National Guard set out to march upon Versailles in three columns, Bergeret and Flourens heading on either side of Mont-Valérien towards the village of Rueil,

Eudes advancing via Meudon and Chaville, and Duval whose task was
to secure the left flank by an attack on the Châtillon Heights. Elisée
Reclus and his brother Paul were among the men installed by Duval on
the Châtillon plateau on the night of 3 April.[49] In the early hours of
the next morning, the Versailles troops counter-attacked, and Duval
was forced to surrender. Elisée was among the prisoners who witnessed
the brutal slaying of Duval and suffered the unspeakable indignities
of the march to Versailles and the trip to Brest.[50] Paul Reclus, who
had accompanied the battalion as a medical doctor, returned without
news of him. Through the help of Edouard Charton,[51] as well as
through the efforts of an American medical student Mary Putnam and
very likely the American Ambassador Washburne, the Reclus family
learned of his whereabouts.[52]

Reclus was imprisoned at the Fort de Quélern until the end of July
or the beginning of August when he was transferred to Tréberon. At
the end of October he was taken to Versailles, and on 15 November
he was sentenced by the Seventh Council of War sitting at Saint-
Germain-en-Laye to 'simple deportation', a decision which destined
him to a say at New Caledonia. Reclus was found guilty of having
carried and used arms in the 'insurrectional movement of Paris', but
innocent on the charge of wearing a uniform in the movement and,
significantly, also innocent on the charge of participating in 'an attempt
to destroy or to change the form of government'.[53]

French and English friends and scholars, who had commenced to
petition for Reclus' release before the trial, continued their efforts
after it. By 1871 he had become a well-known figure in international
geography circles. In the late 1850s and the 1860s several major
journals had accepted articles and book reviews from him, including
the *Bulletin de la Société de Géographie, Le Tour du Monde* and
*La Revue des Deux Mondes*. He wrote some of the travel guides
published as the *Guides Joanne*, and collaborated on several others.
His first important geographical work appeared as the two-volume
*La Terre*: volume I, *Les Continents* in 1868 and volume II, the
*L'Océan − L'Atmosphère − La Vie* in 1869. Another book, probably
the best known at this time, *Histoire d'un Ruisseau* (Story of a
Stream) was also published in 1869. At the time of Reclus' imprisonment, *La Terre* was being translated into English (a four-volume
edition which appeared in 1871 to 1873). The world of geography
took notice of his plight, the French earlier, though more cautiously,
than the English; it was not until after the decision of 15 November
1871 that the agitation began in earnest. Henry Woodward, a member

of the London Geological and Zoological Society and the editor of the English translation of *La Terre*, forwarded the first petition from London on 30 December.[54] In the meantime Reclus had been moved to Mont-Valérian and in December to the Maison de correction de Versailles. On 3 February 1872 the penalty was commuted to ten years exile from France. He was transferred from Versailles to Paris and then taken to Pontarlier where he spent four days before he finally set foot on Swiss soil on 14 March 1872.[55]

The year which Reclus spent in prison was largely spent in reflection. His prison letters, therefore, reveal certain key aspects of his character and personality, and these are worth considering in some detail before proceeding to the next chapter in which I shall examine the impact of the events of 1871 on his approach to politics.

The most striking theme running throughout the prison letters is Reclus' determination to do his duty and to act according to the dictates of his conscience. A letter of 8 January 1872 represents a kind of personal testament for the years 1870 to 1872. It brings to mind the young student at Berlin and is indicative of the priest-like attitude which accompanied his every activity.

> I have certainly suffered very much since my imprisonment and, earlier, during the Franco-Prussian War and the Commune, but ... my great consolation has been to have been able to act according to my conscience. More than once, I have had need to question the sense of duty, but I have not hesitated to obey, at the risk of compromising life or liberty. It is that which today gives me the satisfaction of having won the respect even of my political adversaries.[56]

Although there are occasional allusions to the uncertainty of the outcome of the case, the letters abound in examples of Reclus' refusal to compromise in order to obtain a release. In the latter part of July 1871 he received a letter from the secretary of the Paris Geography Society requesting some sort of statement or at least 'a phrase of allegiance in a private letter' which might be used to win support for him within the society, a request which was flatly refused.[57] On 19 October Reclus again showed a stubbornness, as well as more than a hint of a proud temperament, when Pastor Berth, a friend of his father, suggested appealing to Casimir Périer. 'Of course ... What I want is to be set at liberty as my comrades are, without condition, without promise that could be offensive to my dignity.' He wrote a declaration 'weighing every word. I explained what are in my opinion the legal reasons which ought to ensure my liberty, but naturally I did not stoop to ask for it.'[58]

A man who was determined to live according to his ideals, Reclus was also defiant in his attempt to live as 'normally' as he could even within the confines of a prison, and doggedly continued to carry on his intellectual pursuits.[59] In early June 1871 he commenced research on the *Sol et les Races* (Earth and the Ràces), which was probably incorporated into his later geographical work, and began 'a purely literary, little work' which was very likely the beginning of the *Histoire d'une Montagne* (Story of a Mountain). In July he was occupied with correcting the proofs to the second volume of the abridged edition of *La Terre*. In reply to a letter of the same month from Edouard Charton, editor of *Le Tour du Monde*, he submitted a plan for 'a kind of geographical Encyclopedia, separated into little instalments and costing three or four sous each'. In August there was favourable news from Emile Templier of Hachette, with whom there had been some disagreement. (It seems that Templier wanted to have nothing to do with him after his imprisonment.) Reclus wrote to Alfred Dumesnil on 20 August: 'If I remain in France – which is what I believe – I shall then be able to continue my work, and perhaps undertake great things which are still at the stage of dreams'[60] – a reference to his future multi-volume *La Nouvelle Géographie Universelle*.

The faith which Reclus showed in the revolutionary cause, his concern for the intellectual and moral welfare of other inmates and his personal stature as a man of note in the scientific and literary world placed him in an influential position among the other prisoners, especially during the sessions of the 'free mutual instruction' which was arranged at Quélern and undoubtedly at Trébéron. As early as April 1871, a prisoner at Quélern reported in a Belgian journal that Elisée Reclus

> is making a great contribution to rendering our sad stay more endurable with his daily discussions as interesting as they are instructive and always stressing the highest form of the idea of right and justice. He supports our republican faith, and several among us owe it to him that they will leave prison better than they were upon entering.[61]

At Quélern Reclus was in charge of the small prison library and spent some time giving English lessons and holding seminars. He himself took lessons in Flemish from the Belgian socialist, Victor Buurmans, who was a fellow prisoner.[62]

It seems that, in the months following his arrest and imprisonment, the authorities were rather embarrassed at having incarcerated so eminent a figure as Reclus and gave him every opportunity to express his 'regrets'. However, his influence among the other prisoners and his refusal to 'compromise' stiffened their resolve to deny him a pardon unless he professed his guilt.[63] In a report of 16 January 1872 from the Ministry of Justice it was declared that Reclus' ideas made it impossible for him to be given a commutation of sentence, much less a pardon, until a promise was elicited to keep out of political activity in the future. The commander of the subdivision of the Seine-et-Oise condemned him even more harshly and stated that there were no grounds for clemency, given the absence of any repentence. 'In these conditions, his knowledge and his intelligence only render him more dangerous.'[64]

Reclus' iron will was a great source of satisfaction, but as might be expected, the small triumphs were counterbalanced by black moments. It is clear that he was often disappointed with the behaviour and attitudes of some fellow inmates, who did not measure up to his own high ideals.[65] At the same time, at least on occasion, he became paranoid and depressed, as is revealed by his relations with Jules Simon. On 23 July 1871 Simon, who was on a routine visit to the prisons of Brest, asked to see Reclus and expressed a concern for his welfare. Reclus refused to meet him and later claimed that this deliberate slight had led Simon to have him transferred from Quélern to Tréberon. He believed that the authorities at Tréberon had been ordered by Simon 'to keep a sharp eye on my doings and to have me shut up in my room', and when he was treated kindly, he attributed his good fortune to the fact that the marine doctors and officers who were in charge at Tréberon (his brother Armand was an officer of the marines) had not taken any notice of Simon's words.[66] It seems that Reclus misjudged Simon. The latter had said that, in spite of Reclus' attitudes, he would provide some comfort for him,[67] and according to the available evidence, that is exactly what he did.[68] Some idea of Reclus' state of mind at this time can be gathered from the first pages of the *Histoire d'une Mongagne* which were written in prison. An alienated Reclus claimed that men whom he had called his friends (Templier, for example) turned against him when they saw him overtaken by misfortune. He saw humanity motivated by self-interest and possessed by uncontrolled passions, and it struck him as 'ghastly'. Many years later, when questioned about these lines, he answered that at the time, 'I felt around me the thick, almost impenetrable wall of the hate, the aversion of the entire world against the Commune and the Communards. Perhaps I braced myself and that movement suppressed my true nature.'[69]

The prison experiences were deeply distressing for Reclus, both emotionally and intellectually. He suffered when he perceived — or imagined — the intense hatred which was directed at the communards, and it pained him to see the 'weaknesses' of many of the communards who were unable to achieve a level of dignity and resignation when confronted with this hatred. At the same time, Reclus' reaction was one of surprising calm, as he attempted to relate to his friends and to conduct his professional career as normally as possible. In spite of all that had happened, he had not flinched from his decision to struggle for the overthrow of the existing social and political order. He was possessed of a determination and inflexibility of purpose born of a religious-like passion, a controlled emotionalism which was superbly suited to a revolutionary career. The efforts to work through the 'bourgeois' Republic had ended in catastrophe, but revolutionaries would prepare to strike again. Reclus reflected that a route other than through parliamentary institutions had to be found.

## Notes

1. Han Ryner, *Elisée Reclus (1830–1905)* (Paris, 1928), pp. 12–13. Cf. however, the observation in Paul Reclus, 'Biographie d'Elisée Reclus', in *Les Frères Elie et Elisée Reclus* (Paris, 1964), p. 65; ' . . . it is not as a patriot, it is as a revolutionary that Elisée took part in the war of 1870.' Cf. also Max Nettlau, *Elisée Reclus: Anarchist und Gelehrter* (Berlin, 1928), p. 138 ff.
2. Elisée Reclus, *Elie Reclus, 1827–1904* (Paris, 1905), p. 28.
3. See the address delivered by the couple in *Papiers ER, NAF* 22919.
4. Reclus was at Paris on 23 Aug. 1870. See the document 'Mon Testament' in ibid. However, on 29 Aug. he was at Sainte-Foy-la-Grande where he made arrangements for the care of Fanny and his two daughters in the event of his death. For the document, see ibid. According to a police report, Reclus (and his brothers Elie and Paul) took part in the 'invasion of the legislature . . . he broke windows and furniture'. The report contains inaccuracies and is not reliable in this kind of detail. Police report of 27 Aug. 1874, *P.Po.* B a/1237.
5. Cf. the reports of 16 Jan. 1872, *AN* BB24 732; *P.Po.* B a/1237.
6. Reclus to Fanny, 25 Oct. 1870, *Correspondance*, 3 vols. (Paris, 1911–25), vol. II, p. 8.
7. Reclus to Fanny, 6 Nov. 1870, *Corr. II*, p. 13.
8. The police report of 9 Jan. 1874, *P.Po.* B a/1237 states that Reclus 'did

duty on the ramparts'. See references in *Corr.* II, and in *Fonds ER*, 14 AS 232, *IFHS*.

9.  Balloons left Paris, but did not return. Reclus was still in Paris in Feb. 1871 when he left the city with a *laissez-passer*. Reclus to his sister Louise, 8 Feb. 1871, *Corr.* II, p. 14.

10.  See I. Tchernoff, *Le Parti Républicain au coup d'Etat et sous le Second Empire* (Paris, 1906), pp. 455–6. See also the announcement of Henri Lefort in *L'Association*, Apr. 1865.

11.  Jacques Rougerie, 'L'A.I.T. et le mouvement ouvrier à Paris pendant les événements de 1870–1871', *International Review of Social History*, 1972, p. 35.

12.  According to ibid., pp. 84–5 n, Reclus was a member of the Batignolles section.

13.  Ibid., p. 29 ff.

14.  For a copy of the IWMA address 'Au Peuple Allemand, à la Démocratie Socialiste de la Nation Allemande', see *Les Murailles Politiques Françaises* (Paris, 1873), p. 6. Cf. Reclus to Faure, n.d. (Sept. 1870), *Corr.* II, pp. 4–5.

15.  Reclus to Faure, n.d. (Sept. 1870), *Corr.* II, p. 4.

16.  Ibid., pp. 4–5. On 15 Oct. Reclus' confidence in a military victory was raised to a limited extent by his view (and that of many others, including the Germans) that there was a growing improbability of a bombardment. Reclus to Fanny, 15 Oct. 1870, *Corr.* II, p. 7.

17.  Reclus to Faure, n.d. (1870), *Corr.* II, p. 10.

18.  Ibid., pp. 10–11.

19.  Ibid., p. 11.

20.  Cf. the similarity of views in the 'Second Address of the General Council of the International on the Franco-Prussian War' written by Marx and endorsed on 9 Sept. 1870. *Karl Marx and Frederick Engels, Selected Works* (London, 1970), p. 269.

21.  On 27 July 1869, during a visit to London, Reclus had been presented with a personally signed copy of the 'Achtzehnten Brumaire' by Marx. *Chronik*, p. 448.

22.  Karl Marx, 'The Eighteenth Brumaire of Louis Napoleon' in *Selected Works*, p. 154.

23.  See Serraillier's report to the General Council meeting of 28 Feb. 1871 in *Documents of the First International*, vol. IV, p. 140.

24.  Reclus to Fanny, 6 Nov. 1870, *Corr.* II, pp. 12–13.

25.  In 1870 to 1871 Reclus' attitude was pro-Republic rather than anti-German. Cf. his comments on Elie's residence in 'beautiful' Zurich in Sept. 1871. One of the advantages of living in Zurich was the 'contact of two races'. Reclus to Alfred and Louise Dumesnil, 7 Sept. 1871, *Corr.* II, p. 65.

26.  Reclus sent a letter dated 4 Jan. 1871 to the editor of *Le Combat* announcing the appearance of *La République des Travailleurs* as 'a new organ of militant socialist democracy . . . founded by the Batignolles section of the "International" '. *Le Combat*, 11 Jan. 1871; clipping in *P.Po.* B a/1237.

27.  See Reclus' contributions to *La République des Travailleurs*, 10 Jan. and 13–22 Jan. 1871.

28.  *La République des Travailleurs*, 3 Feb. 1871.

29.  *Le Vengeur*, 3 Feb. 1871; *La République des Travailleurs*, 4 Feb. 1871.

30.  L. Dautry and L. Scheler, *Le Comité central républicain des vingt arrondissements de Paris* (Paris, 1960), p. 160 ff; *Documents of the First International*, vol. IV, pp. 141–2; Rougerie, 'A.I.T.', p. 41.

31.  *Le Mot d'Ordre*, 6 Feb. 1871.

32.  Reclus to Louise, 9 Feb. 1871, *Corr.* II, p. 14. Reclus never felt bound by party discipline, and it is unlikely that the agreements reached by the IWMA

on 4 Feb. would have led him to reverse his own decision to support the republican bourgeoisie. Before 4 Feb. there were already sharp differences of opinion, of which he must have been aware, concerning the appropriate IWMA attitudes towards the election. See *Documents of the First International*, vol. IV, pp. 141–2.

33. For a copy of the electoral placard, see *Murailles Politiques*, p. 873.

34. Nettlau, *Elisée Reclus*, p. 145.

35. Elie Reclus to Charton, 18 Apr. 1871, *Papiers Nadar, NAF* 25016.

36. Reclus to Louise, 9 Feb. 1871, *Corr.* II, p. 14.

37. Ibid., p. 15.

38. Reclus to Elie, n.d. (Feb. 1871), *Corr.* II, p. 18.

39. Ibid., pp. 18–19.

40. Reclus to Nadar, Feb. 1871, *Corr.* II, p. 16.

41. The earliest letter written by Reclus after his return to Paris, but before the Commune, is undated; Reclus to Elie's wife Noémi, *Corr.* II, p. 20.

42. Paul Ghio, *Etudes italiennes et sociales* (Paris, 1929), p. 200, attributes a statement of 26 Feb. (Ghio mistakenly wrote 25 Feb.) in *Le Cri du Peuple* to Reclus. The statement expressed wonder at the 'human sea' of demonstrators who would willingly die for their beliefs.

43. Rougerie, 'A.I.T.', pp. 52–3.

44. Firmin Maillard, *Affiches, professions de foi, documents officiels, clubs et comités pendant la Commune* (Paris, 1871), pp. 101–2; reprinted in *Le Cri du Peuple*, 26 Mar. 1871. Cf. the similarity of views in Elie's diary, published as *Commune de Paris*.

45. For a copy of the statement, see Maillard, pp. 99– 100 and Louise Michel, *La Commune* (Paris, 1898), p. 181.

46. For a copy of the electoral placard, see Maillard, pp. 186–8. Cf. police report of 27 Aug. 1874, *P.Po.* B a/1237.

47. Reclus to Alfred Dumesnil, 27 Mar. 1871, *Corr.* II, p. 23.

48. Ibid.

49. According to *Le Cri du Peuple*, 7 Apr. 1871, there were 500 men present at Châtillon.

50. For a description of the events of 4 Apr., see Reclus' *Evolution et Révolution* (1891), pp. 58–9; his letter concerning the death of Emile Victor Duval in P. Cattelain, *Memoires inédits du chef de la Sûreté sous la Commune* (Paris n.d., 1900), pp. 108–9 and *Corr.* II, pp. 27–8; his account as told to Kropotkin in *Les Temps Nouveaux*, 15 July 1905.

51. Elie Reclus to Charton, 18 Apr. 1871, *Papiers Nadar, NAF* 25016.

52. Paul Reclus, 'A Few Recollections on the Brothers Elie and Elisée Reclus', in J. Ishill, *Elisée and Elie Reclus: In Memoriam* (Berkeley Heights, 1927), pp. 18–20. According to this account (by Reclus' nephew), Washburne had taken particular interest in Reclus' articles on behalf of the North in the American Civil War. Cf. Charles Delfosse, *Elisée Reclus, Géographe* in the series *Hommes du Jour* (Brussels, n.d.).

53. *Dossier ER, AHG, 7e Conseil de Guerre Permanent, dossier* no. 46. For the impressions of Nadar, who spoke in Reclus' defence at the trial, see his 'Elisée Reclus' in Ishill, *Elisée and Elie Reclus*, pp. 109–10; *Les Temps Nouveaux, Supplément* no. 33, Dec. 1950. For the text of Elie's letter of 17 Nov. 1871 to Elisée, see Guillaume de Greef, *Eloges d'Elisée Reclus et de De Kellès-Krauz, Discours* (Ghent, 1906), pp. 54–5.

54. See the letter from F.D. Leblanc and a French translation of the petition, including the signatories, in *Le Courrier de l'Europe, Supplément* 20 Jan. 1872 and a supplementary list of signatories in ibid., 23 Mar. 1872; as newspaper clippings in *Papiers ER, NAF* 22909. See also the letter from Eugene

Oswald to the President of the French Republic on behalf of Reclus, London, 27 Dec. 1871 in *Papiers ER, NAF* 22909. Reclus expressed his gratitude to Oswald on 21 Mar. 1872; *Corr.* II, pp. 92—3.

55. See *Dossier ER, AHG*; official report from the Ministry of War to the Ministry of Justice, 8 Feb. 1872, *AN* BB24 732; Paris police report of 27 Oct. 1903, 'Bulletin de vérification aux Sommiers judiciaires', *P.Po.* B a/1237. The commutation of penalty was granted on 3 Feb. and not on 15 Feb. as frequently reported.

56. Reclus to Heath, 8 Jan. 1872, *Corr.* II, pp. 86—7.

57. Reclus to Fanny, July 1871, *Corr.* II, p. 53.

58. Reclus to Fanny, 20 Oct. 1871, quoted in Fanny to 'soeur aimée' (Louise Dumesnil?), 25 Oct. 1871, *Papiers ER, NAF* 22913. Reclus' letter was written in English; for a French translation, see *Corr.* II, pp. 68—9.

59. *Corr.* II, p. 40 ff.

60. Reclus to Alfred Dumesnil, 20 Aug. 1871, *Corr.* II, p. 61.

61. *La Liberté*, Apr. 1871; for a copy of the letter, see Michel, pp. 467—70.

62. Reclus to Fanny, 8 June 1871, *Corr.* II, pp. 40—1; cf. letter to Alfred and Louise Dumesnil, 15 June 1871, *Corr.* II, p. 44. See Reclus to Lòis Trigant, 17 May 1871 and to his mother, 20 May 1871, both in *Fonds ER*, 14 AS 232, *IFHS*.

63. Reclus was optimistic about the possibility of release. In August he learned that more than 900 of the 12,000 to 13,000 prisoners at Brest had been freed and that the only charge against him was that of having marched against the regular army. Reclus to Fanny, 3 Aug. 1871, *Corr.* II, pp. 55—6.

64. *AN* BB24 732.

65. Cf. Reclus to Kahn, n.d. (1878), *Archief ER, IISG*; Reclus to Buurmans, 20 Oct. 1871, *Corr.* II, p. 71.

66. Reclus to Fanny, 3 Aug. 1871, *Papiers ER, NAF* 22913; letter written in English, French translation in *Corr.* II, pp. 55—6.

67. Ibid.

68. See police report of 27 Aug. 1874, *P.Po.* B a/1237, which holds true in substance in spite of exaggerations. Cf. Reclus to Fanny, 3 Aug. 1871; Nettlau, *Elisée Reclus*, p. 165.

69. Reclus to Clara Mesnil, 23 July 1904, *Corr.* III, pp. 277—8.

# 5 FROM COMMUNARD TO ANARCHIST

Disillusionment with parliamentary politics was evident among radical republicans in France as far back as the bloody repression of June 1848. However, despite the mistrust and even hostility which was directed at parliamentary regimes, many radicals continued to believe that a popularly elected body would help bring about a greater degree of social justice. Up to 1870 it had been possible for the loosely organised International Working Men's Association to contain representatives of a variety of conflicting views; the role of the state was not yet the crucial issue it was to become. It was particularly from the mid-1870s that the controversy concerning the so-called 'role of the state' developed and contributed greatly to the separation of anarchism from the mainstream social-democratic movement in Europe. The details of Reclus' life fit into this pattern. His correspondence from early youth reveals how eagerly he had participated in the mid-nineteenth-century debate on the social question and how anxious he had been to find some expression for his views. An examination of these suggests many aspects fundamental to his later theories of anarchism, but none – including the final goal of anarchy – precluded some kind of accommodation to the parliamentary political system, even if conceived of as a temporary expedient. In the period immediately preceding 1871 there is every indication that he was becoming convinced that there were positive gains to be made within the existing order. There is no doubt that his experiences in 1870 to 1871 constituted the most important factor in redirecting the thrust of his revolutionary activities. While he was a self-professed revolutionary socialist up to 1871, it was only in the period following the Commune that he became implacably opposed to all party-political activity.

It might be expected that, as the years passed, Reclus would comment profusely on the political significance of the events of 1871. After all he was a noted scholar and a highly regarded anarchist theorist, who had participated in the Commune and who had suffered imprisonment and banishment as a result. But he was extremely reluctant to make any statement at all. Although he was the 'soul' of the Geneva based *Le Travailleur* (1877–8),[1] the paper which did so much to create the 'myth' of the Commune[2] did not carry anything on the subject from him. In a letter of 1877 he said that he had refused a request for an article on the Commune[3] because he was not qualified to write on it;[4] still, the following year he admitted that he was working on a piece entitled 'Experiences of a Prisoner'.[5] Save for a few brief comments written towards the end of his life, Reclus could not be coaxed, even by sympathetic friends and colleagues, to provide the analysis of the Commune it was clearly in his power to write. In 1905, for example, he said that he could not locate the 'personal impressions' which he had already written and that he could not find the necessary time to write another account.[6]

Reclus' silence on the Commune is so conspicuous that it arouses attention. He tried to justify his decision to write so little by pleading ignorance. 'I do not know the history of the Commune: I was so small an actor and spectator that that does not count. To improvise that which one does not know is a bad thing.'[7] But this is more of an excuse than a defence, precisely because he wrote prolifically and unhesitatingly on any subject which struck his fancy, and he was always especially interested in examining the significance of contemporary politics. There had been no event of comparable importance since the time of the Great French Revolution, as he himself had claimed from the very first days of the Commune. Moreover, there were many others who had been much less involved in the events of 1870 to 1871 who dared to speak out boldly. But here we may have a clue to explaining his silence. Reclus was a person whose attention to detail was mercilessly precise, even as he pronounced, with dramatic and sweeping strokes, on the coming social revolution. He would not relate his experiences exactly as they happened, for fear of damaging the memory of the Commune; since he could not bring himself deliberately to fabricate, he remained quiet. But it is possible to uncover at least the general lines of his critique.

One of the most striking features of Reclus' political outlook in the period following 1871 is the contrast between his violent rejection of the Third Republic which he had initially struggled so much to defend and his passionate devotion to the memory of the Commune. The Assembly of 'MM. the gunmen', he wrote shortly after he arrived in Switzerland, did not exist for him: '. . . I dissolved it. It is in spite of us that it holds together.'[8] While much of his correspondence from 1872 to 1874 deliberately avoided discussion of contemporary politics (partly because of a fear that it might fall into the hands of the police), his attitude oscillated from repugnance to an embittered curiosity. According to a letter of October 1873, he felt that political developments in France were leading to 'very sad days'. 'When the republicans lent their hands to the extermination of their own avant-garde, how could they have the naivety to count on their triumph?' he asked.[9] In their ruthless persecution of the communards, the republicans were slitting their own throats; they were turning away from the goals of the Third Republic, as Reclus had understood them in 1870 to 1871. On 4 July 1874 he told a friend:

> Should the centre triumph, the words of M. Laboulaye remain true: 'We have all marched under the flag of the Republic against the external enemy, why not march under the same flag against the internal enemy?' The internal enemy, what is it, if not every man of justice and truth.[10]

The internal enemies of the Third Republic were the very people who had struggled to create it in 1870 to 1871, those who had become the hated communards.

Nor did Reclus any longer show much sympathy for moderate left agitation in other spheres of political activity. The Labour Congress at Rome in April 1872 was labelled a 'Congress of would-be workers', and two delegates who were expelled, one for his views on strikes, the other for his views on secular education, were lauded as 'true workers'.[11] The report to Elie on the Congress of the League of Peace and Freedom at Lugano in September 1872 reveals the extent to which his whole political approach had changed from the Berne Congress of 1868 when he had been an enthusiastic participant.[12] In 1872 he was no more than a spectator, and Elie was sent a somewhat detailed but cynical account of the 'bourgeois' and 'mediocre' congress. Something in the words of the Englishman Hodgson Pratt was found to deserve praise, even though Elisée insisted that Pratt was himself unaware of the implications of his declaration: '. . . with bourgeois societies, one will never do anything; it is necessary not only to work for the workers, but also to work with them.Without their support, every work  is stillborn.'[13] In 1869 Reclus had believed that 'Negative Voting' could prove a useful revolutionary tactic; after 1871 there was no question of ever again participating in elections.[14] Henceforth the universal struggle for the liberation of humankind was to be carried on simultaneously against the social-economic order and against the political system.

The Commune, on the other hand, became a hallowed event. Reclus began his personal campaign to enshrine it on his very first day in Switzerland when he changed the 'horror' of an old lady friend for the Commune into 'respect'.[15] His principles of brotherhood were successfully put to the test as he lived and worked among the many communards who had fled to Switzerland following 1871 or who had chosen to live there after they had been sentenced to banishment from France. He remained faithful to the prison vow never to forget his fellow communards; he tirelessly worked among the refugees in Switzerland and, whenever possible, helped those who were in other parts of the world.[16] Loyalty to the memory of the Commune led to fully uncharacteristic behaviour when he broke off all relations with his brother-in-law and Radical Deputy, Germain Casse. In a letter of 12 May 1876 Reclus wrote to his unhappy sister, Julie Casse, who was anxious to patch up the family quarrel: '. . . your husband having disowned the Commune after he had taken part in it, I shall never be able to feel friendship for him'.[17] After his amnesty on 3 March 1879 Reclus publicly expressed his solidarity with those communards to whom the French government had refused to grant an amnesty. 'I would be a vile man, if my first words were not words of solidarity, respect and love for those, worse stricken than me, who still inhabit the jails or the prison of New Caledonia . . . Their cause is always mine, their honour is mine, and every insult which is addressed to them hurts me most deeply.' The letter was addressed to *La Solidarité*, the Society of Refugees of the Commune, and Reclus requested that it be passed on for publication in French newspapers.[18]

His was anything but an uncritical devotion to the memory of the Commune, however. In a police report of 20 December 1885 Reclus is reported to have warned his comrades in a private meeting of anarchists that to hasten into revolution too quickly would be to commit the mistakes of the Commune, and that such a repetition would set them back 20 years. When the next revolutionary opportunity presented itself, it would be necessary to seize the Bank of France and the big rail companies, get the economy going immediately and take up arms in defence of the revolution.[19] It was not until 1897 that he made a public declaration on these 'mistakes', and then only in a paltry few pages of an obscure work.[20] Even so, it is clear that he saw the reality of the Commune as much less than the grand affair it was supposed to have been, and in a couple of merciless strokes, he cut away at the legend which had become an important part of the ideology of the entire Left. The Commune's military organisation, he said, had been as bad as that under the 'lamentable' Trochu during the first siege, the proclamations as unclear, the disorder as great and the activity as ridiculous. While he believed that the 'improvised ministers' had remained honest in exercising power, they had not had the good sense and the will to assess the situation correctly and to act accordingly. They continued all the errors of official governments; they maintained the entire bureaucratic structure and simply brought in new faces; and every day they protected the supply of money which the Bank of France despatched to Versailles. The Commune elections brought to office men who, seized by the 'dizziness' of power and 'stupid routine', had dutifully followed the rules of the old political game. They had failed to comprehend the revolutionary movement which had carried them to the Hôtel de Ville. Hard words indeed!

The only other statement of any consequence was contained in the short account of the Commune in Reclus' *L'Homme et la Terre*, a six-volume work published posthumously by his nephew Paul.[21] Here it is stated that anyone with a notion of history could have had no doubt about the final outcome of the conflict in 1871. All those who acclaimed the Commune, the old campaigners of past revolutions, as well as the 'young enthusiasts infatuated with liberty', knew in advance that they were doomed to defeat. Paris had no chance of winning the struggle with Versailles so long as she was surrounded by German troops delighting in pillage, French troops who were aching to wreak vengeance upon their compatriots in compensation for their recent defeat at the hands of the Germans and the mass of the French people who were only too ready to pounce upon Paris, the traditional centre of revolutions.[22] These words evoke the Reclus of the period of the Commune, even if the pitch is somewhat altered. However, it is an exaggeration to suggest that the final outcome was expected by those who participated in the Commune. Any battle, however hopeless it appears, must contain some hope of success, even if it is merely a glimmer, and there surely was a glimmer. But it is also true that the fighter Reclus was not easily cornered, and that even the fading of that last glimmer of hope would not convince him to yield, but on the contrary, encourage him to respond more fiercely than ever. His psychological make-up calls to mind the tradition of the warriors who defied both life and death in Homer's *Iliad*.

In *L'Homme et la Terre* Reclus stated that, given the odds against them, the communards could not have been successful. Yet he was deeply disappointed with their record. The prospect of a pitiless repression was no excuse for not leaving behind great examples of revolutionary action and the first attempts at the creation of a society which was rid of famine and the scourge of money.[23] The principal factor in the failure of the Commune to accomplish even this much was 'precisely that of being a government and of substituting the force of circumstances for people'.[24] Reclus also seemed to be thinking of the Commune government when he wrote in 1873 that the bourgeois state had 'interfered' with the natural evolution towards communal property.[25] The analysis suggests that examples of great revolutionary action had not occurred because the revolutionary potential of the people had been stifled through the 'natural' functioning of power and the 'dizziness' of authority which were unavoidable accompaniments of all governments. A similar statement was made in 1880 when he claimed that the Paris Commune had been insurrectional below, but governmental above.[26] There are two difficulties with the analysis.

Reclus says that the very fact of being a government had condemned the Commune to impotence, but he also says that the Commune officials should have taken the initiative and proceeded systematically to destroy all state institutions and to suppress the obstacles which prevented the spontaneous groupings of citizens. He even declares that a few officials had progressed to the stage at which they understood that this should be their goal.[27] Is it reasonable to speak of what should be done by an institution which is supposed to be inherently incapable of carrying it out? Was Reclus, at the very end of his life and after decades of anarchist theorising, expressing a lingering doubt about the function of government? The second point which I wish to make is this. Reclus suggests that the Commune officials had held the revolutionary potential of the people in check or at least did not know how to release it. But he also says that the people did not want a social revolution. 'If the citizens had been inspired by a common will for social renovation, they would have imposed it upon their delegates, but they had only the preoccupation with defence: to fight well and to die well.'[28] In the final analysis, the people were responsible for the pattern which the Commune assumed. A more highly conscious people would not have reacted so naively, and would have compelled the Commune government to make greater effort towards the fulfilment of a revolutionary programme.

At a conscious level Reclus was saying that government was at fault; between the actions of the Paris provisional government, the Commune government and the Versailles government he had certainly witnessed the whole range of evils associated with the institution. In fact, however, the evils of government paled in comparison with the failures of the people who would have 'imposed' social change upon the Commune delegates, had they wanted it. In the first siege he had persuaded himself that he was part of a powerful movement for social justice, but as the months passed, he became steadily more disillusioned. When he heard the news of Favre's 28 January armistice, he did not react, as many other revolutionaries did, by accusing the government negotiators of treachery. Instead, he pointed to the people whom, in the course of the siege, he had come to consider ultimately responsible for the defeat.

> We are conquered, and conquered through our own fault! From 4 September our cause was just, but we are all the more culpable for not having been worthy of it because we allowed force to surpass right. Immense were the resources at our disposal, but also unbounded was our inertia, our cowardly routine, our blind confidence in some personnages of chance. Our fate was in our own hands, and if we had really wished it, the Republic would have come out of the battle triumphant. We preferred mealy mouthedly to hand over the care of our future to a little coterie of saviours, the sworn officials of the empire, and to the former aide de camp of Marshal Saint-Arnaud [Trochu].[29]

The weakness of a people without the necessary resolve to follow through on revolution and sufficiently naive to trust in their leaders. became ever clearer after the election of the Monarchist Assembly in February 1871 and especially as he observed the course of the Paris Commune.

The way in which Reclus chose to remember his initial response to the Commune can be gained from an account written by Kropotkin in 1882.

> 'I will never forget,' said a friend [Reclus] to us, 'those delightful moments of deliverance. I came down from my upper chamber in the Latin Quarter to join that immense open-air club which filled the boulevards from one end of Paris to the other. Everyone talked about public affairs; all mere personal preoccupations were forgotten; no more was thought of buying or selling; all felt ready, body and soul, to advance towards the future. Men of the middle-class even, carried away by the general enthusiasm, saw with joy a new world opened up. "If it is necessary to make social revolution", they said, "make it then. Put all things in common; we are ready

for it". All the elements of the revolution were there, it was only
necessary to set them to work. When I returned to my lodging at
night I said to myself, How fine is humanity after all, but no one
knew it; it has always been calumniated.'[30]

The account deviates substantially from the general thrust of Reclus'
views at the time. Since it was written years after the Commune, it is
possible that he merely romanticised his experiences. It is more likely
that the euphoria of the early days of the Commune had indeed led
him to glimpse the heights to which ordinary people might rise, and
to renew a revolutionary faith tested by the defeat of the first siege.
What followed on the euphoria quickly brought him down to earth.

> Then came the elections, the members of the Commune were
> named — and then little by little the ardor of devotion and the
> desire for action were extinguished. Everyone returned to his usual
> task, saying to himself, 'Now we have an honest government, let it
> act for us'.[31]

Within the experiences of 1870 to 1871 Reclus was able to perceive,
alternately with joy and with sadness, what people might become
and what they actually were. For a long time he had been aware that
there existed a wide gulf between the members of his ideal brotherhood of equals and the flesh and blood men and women who were to
be elevated to that lofty existence. However, it took the experiences
of 1870 to 1871 to demonstrate to him the real extent of that gulf.
The real culprits in the messy affair of the Commune were the people.
They were too weak even to attempt to live up to the demanding
requirements of a social order based upon liberty and equality.

Reclus was deeply shaken by the direction which the Commune
took, the glimpses of utopia, followed by confusion and weakness, a
pitiless repression, and a less than noble defeat. Publicly humiliated
and incensed by 'the thick, almost impenetrable wall of the hate, the
aversion of the entire world against the Commune and the
Communards',[32] he came back stronger than ever. The communards
he sought to draw together in their darkest hour; he longed to
participate in a collective and massive spirit of defiance which would
prove that the victory of bourgeoisie represented no more than a
temporary setback. Since the people were too weak to use the
bourgeois political machinery to advantage, another way to social
justice would be found. The struggle would be taken up anew, with

greater vigour and no compromises. The implications which he drew
from the events of 1870 to 1871, while he was still a prisoner, are
summarised in a letter written at Quélern on 28 August 1871, as the
anniversary of 4 September 1870 drew near. The terrible sufferings of
the previous year were not to have been in vain; the successes and
failures needed to be assessed and the lessons of the Commune had to
be learned.

> Frightful have been the misfortunes of every kind, and however,
> looking at things from a point of view completely general, we
> indeed have to say that we are fortunate, in the sense that all
> these things have taken place for the instruction of the world.
> Necessarily, each generation has to sacrifice itself for those that
> follow. Let us not complain then, if the terrible lesson of
> history which has been made at our expense ought to profit
> future republics.[33]

On 8 May 1872 Nadar was told: 'Everything miserable and horrible
that we have seen nonetheless contains something great in germ, and it
is that that it is important to see.'[34] Reclus had a grand vision of what
society might become, and people were the instruments with which to
create such a society. 'For my part', he wrote shortly after his release,
'I very much love my poor brothers in humanity who in general are
worth so little, but with them, through affection, through incessant
propaganda, one can develop such great things.'[35] It is not clear
which was the object of Reclus' love, his human brothers or his
idealised versions of them. In any event, the man whose faith in
the people was expressed so joyfully and eloquently also felt bitter
disappointment in their failure to make greater advances towards his
grand vision.

As already mentioned, Reclus was not pleased with the conduct of
some communards. In 1878 he confided to a friend that his
'Experiences of a Prisoner' could not be published for at least 20
years, for he was obliged to recount from time to time 'things of
which we are not proud'. These aspects he was unwilling to make
public right away because 'we are still in the period of struggle and
before the common enemy we stick together'.[36] In the first years
after the Commune, he explained later in life, the repression and
outrages experienced by the communards had united them, and he
had, therefore, not permitted himself to judge men who, in his
opinion 'had been little worthy of the cause defended by them'.[37]

He was deeply solicitous of the welfare of the communards, and yet reproachful. These attitudes do not indicate ambivalence. Rather he had assessed the communards and had found them lacking. His energetic support of them was in spite of them and represented an attempt to salvage what he could from the experience of the Commune for the revolutionary cause. Reclus was aware of the potential for revolutionary politics which existed in exploiting the memory of the Paris Commune; in fact it became his deliberate aim to contribute to its promotion as a central feature of revolutionary ideology. He was also fully cognizant of the fact that he was participating in the creation of a 'myth'.

The lesson of 1871 was that people, not governments, make revolutions, and that the consciousness of people had to be raised if victory was to be achieved. And it would be difficult to quarrel with this assessment. However, the belief that power corrupts is not a sufficient basis for denying the possibilities for progress which exist through the use of already established political institutions. There is no reason to suppose that an emphasis upon consciousness-raising should necessarily rule out simultaneous participation within the governmental process. As consciousness is raised, governments become less autonomous in their actions and increasingly subject to pressures from below. This inverse relationship between governments and people must result, theoretically, in full popular control. To this argument Reclus might have responded that governments would resist popular pressures and take measures which were counter-revolutionary; but did he not believe, in any case, that the movement of history contained both progress and regression and that progress was a function of the will of the people?

After 1871 Reclus was confronted with the problem of achieving social justice without resorting to the parliamentary system. No longer could he even look favourably upon co-operativism and trade unionism, although for a time he preferred to remain silent rather than to condemn workers as they struggled to better their lot. The anarchist way to socialism essentially assumed the form of intense and unrelenting propaganda against the bourgeois order. It involved the awakening of people's minds to the injustices which they could come to observe around them, and the revolt which would follow upon such recognition. All and any revolt against injustice was viewed positively; even vengeance, which was seen as an act of primitive justice and an inevitable response to injustice. Propaganda by the deed, as it came to be defined by the anarchists, had quite a number of serious ramifications, but it appealed to Reclus because it was a weapon that exposed the vulnerability of the state and raised the hope that the revolution could be effectively waged in an anarchist fashion. In opposition to Jean Grave and Peter Kropotkin, Reclus saw important revolutionary implications in 'la reprise individuelle' (individual recovery of the fruits of labour) or theft as it was less respectfully called, and positive gains in an acceptance of the principle. Even violence could be justified, and Reclus' philosophical defence of the attentats in the 1890s caused concern even among some anarchists. The suppression of the Paris Commune had represented a declaration of war, *la guerre à outrance.*

### Notes

1.   Marx called Elisée and Elie the 'souls' of *Le Travailleur*; Marx to Engels, 1 Aug. 1877, *MEW* 34, p. 65. He was wrong about the importance of Elie's contribution; see below, Chapter 6.

2.   David Stafford, *From Anarchism to Reformism, a Study of the Political Activities of Paul Brousse 1870–1890* (London, 1971), p. 302.

3.   The proposed article was intended for *La Commune, Almanach Socialiste pour 1877.*

4.   Reclus to Joukowsky, n.d. (1877), *Fonds ER*, 14 AS 232, *IFHS.*

5.   Reclus to Kahn, n.d. (1878), *Archief ER, IISG.*

6.   Reclus to Galleani, 15 May 1905, in *Correspondance*, 3 vols.(Paris, 1911–25), vol. III, pp. 318–19.

7.   Reclus to Joukowsky, n.d. (1877), *Fonds ER*, 14 AS 232, *IFHS.*

8.   Reclus to Noémi, 8 June 1872, *Corr.* II, p. 109.

9.   Reclus to De Gérando, Oct. 1873, *Fonds ER*, 14 AS 232, *IFHS.*

10.   Reclus to De Gérando, 4 July 1874, *Corr.* II, p. 156.

11.   Reclus to Elie, 29 Apr. 1872, *Corr.* II, pp. 101–2.

12.   See Reclus to Elie, n.d. (Oct. 1868), *Corr.* I, p. 279 ff; *deuxième Congrès de la Paix et de la Liberté*, p. 235 ff.

13.   Reclus to Elie, 23 Sept. 1872, *Corr.* II, p. 113 ff.

14.   In 1897 Reclus did admit that under unusual circumstances an anarchist might be able to justify or even to approve the use of the vote. Reclus to B.P. Van der Voo, Apr. 1897, *Corr.* III, p. 201. See below, Chapter 13.

15.   Notes written by Reclus on 14 Mar. 1872, *Papiers ER, NAF* 22913.

16.   See references to Reclus' efforts to help the communards and his continuing interest in their problems in Reclus to Louise, n.d. (Dec. 1875), *Corr.* II, pp. 175–6; Reclus to Nadar, 15 Sept. 1880, *Corr.* II, pp. 225–6; séance du 3 août 1874, Procès-verbaux des séances du Comité fédéral jurassien, *AEN*; Jura Federation circular of 13 Aug. 1874, *AFJ, IISG*; police report of 2 Feb. 1879, *P.Po.* B a/1237; James Guillaume, *L'Internationale. Documents et Souvenirs (1864–1878)*, 4 vols. (Paris, 1905–10), vol. III, p. 289.

17.   Reclus to his sister Julie, 12 May 1876, *Papiers ER, NAF* 22909.

18.   The amnesty of 3 Mar. 1879, distinguishing between a criminal hard-core element and the misled, but guilty, majority, provided for the return from exile or prison of all but approximately 1,000 communards. La Solidarité held a meeting at Geneva on 28 March to examine the law, and a public declaration

was signed in protest against the attempts of the French Government to weaken the solidarity of the communards. The declaration and Reclus' letter appeared as a leaflet; a copy can be found in *Archief ER, IISG*. The letter is reproduced in *Corr.* II, p. 209.

19. Police report of 20 Dec. 1885, *P.Po.* B a/1502.

20. *1871, Enquête sur la Commune de Paris* (Paris, 1897).

21. Elisée Reclus, *L'Homme et la Terre*, 6 vols. (Paris, 1905–8), vol. V, p. 246 ff.

22. Ibid., pp. 246–7.

23. Ibid., p. 247.

24. Ibid., pp. 247–8.

25. Elisée Reclus, 'Quelques Mots sur la Propriété' in *Almanach du Peuple pour 1873* (St Imier, 1873), p. 326.

26. *Le Révolté*, 17 Oct. 1880.

27. Reclus, *L'Homme et la Terre*, vol. V, p. 247.

28. Ibid.

29. *La République des Travailleurs*, 29 Jan.–5Feb. 1871.

30. The 'friend' is almost certainly Reclus. The anonymity may have been achieved at Reclus' own request or through an understanding between the two men who were close friends at the time of the writing. Peter Kropotkin, 'Revolutionary Government' in Roger N. Baldwin (ed.), *Kropotkin's Revolutionary Pamphlets* (New York, 1970), pp. 239–40. For the original essay, see 'Le Gouvernement pendant la Révolution' in *Le Révolté*, 2 Sept.– 14 Oct. 1882, republished in *Paroles d'un Révolté* (Paris, 1885), pp. 245–65. Cf. the statement of 21 Mar. in *Le Cri du Peuple* which Ghio attributes to Reclus.

31. Kropotkin, 'Revolutionary Government', p. 240. A passage of a letter written by Reclus in the same year records similar impressions; Reclus to Heath, 18 Feb. 1882, *Corr.* II, pp. 242–3.

32. Reclus to Clara Mesnil, 23 July 1904, *Corr.* III, p. 277.

33. Reclus to Fanny, 28 Aug. 1871, *Papiers ER, NAF* 22913.

34. Reclus to Nadar, 8 May 1872, *Autographes Félix et Paul Nadar, NAF* 24282.

35. Ibid.

36. Reclus to Kahn, n.d. (1878), *Archief ER, IISG*.

37. *Enquête*, p. 53.

PART II

ANARCHIST THEORY AND THE CHALLENGE OF
PRACTICE: 1871–94

# 6 DEFINING THE ANARCHIST POSITION

The formulation of the theory of anarchism can be traced to Switzerland in the latter part of the 1870s. It developed out of the debates of a small group of revolutionary socialists who had helped to establish a so-called federalist wing of the International Working Men's Association (IWMA) in 1872. After the Hague Congress of that year the IWMA had split into two groups, the federalist or 'anti-authoritarian' International which revolved around the Jura Federation in Switzerland and the less successful centralist International which followed Marx's call for the use of party-political action and tighter control of the IWMA General Council over the various sections. The term anarchist is used today to refer to the members of the federalist International and was sometimes used in a pejorative sense in the first half of the 1870s to specify those socialists who refused to engage in party-political action within the framework of the bourgeois order. But the term did not come to be deliberately adopted until 1876 and not on any scale until after the collapse of the federalist (anti-authoritarian) International in 1877.[1] While the acceptance of the fundamentals of anarchism by individuals was often decisive and clear, the movement towards the formal adoption of an anarchist programme was halting and uncertain. By the late 1870s, however, those socialists who were professing 'anarchist' principles were overtaken by events and compelled to define their position more precisely. Elisée Reclus played an important role in this process.

Reclus' first two years of exile in Switzerland were politically inactive. At Lugano he set up residence with his wife Fanny and two daughters by his first wife Clarisse; much of his time was spent in writing and conducting research for his geographical projects.[2] A police report of 9 January 1874 states that he was 'a very learned man, hard-working, with regular habits, but very much a dreamer, bizarre, obstinate in his ideas and with a belief in the realisation of universal brotherhood'.[3] In 1869 he had become estranged from Bakunin who, with some justification, had noted 'bourgeois' tendencies in his friend's approach to questions of revolutionary activity. However, his decisive stand against all collaboration with the bourgeois order following 1871 impressed Bakunin who wrote a friend about the 'excellent Elisée Reclus . . . with whom I get along

119

better and better. There is the model of a man — so pure, noble, simple, modest, self-forgetting. He is perhaps not so completely the devil of a fellow, as might be desired, but that is a question of temperament . . . He is a valuable, very reliable, very earnest, very sincere friend and completely one of ours.'[4] Reclus probably grew uneasy about his own lack of direct involvement in revolutionary politics, and on 2 June 1873 he wrote to the Belgian socialist Victor Buurmans: 'We are still living very much in retirement, watching pass at a distance . . . the great human comedy. Do not think, however, that we have become sceptics. No, we take very much to heart everything that happens on the world stage.'[5]

The role of spectator was soon to yield to that of actor. The turning point came shortly after Fanny died in child-birth on 14 February 1874. Fanny the English school-teacher who had joined Reclus in marriage just before the outbreak of the Franco-Prussian War had been a match for her husband in obstinacy, idealism and courage, and had been a constant source of comfort to him during the period of his imprisonment. The marriage ceremony itself had been a political statement. It had defied the authority of both church and state, and had taken the form of a simple declaration of two people in front of family and friends. Reclus had been deeply attached to Fanny, and her death was a great personal tragedy from which he never fully recovered.[6] In 1874, his personal life shattered, he turned his full attention to the revolutionary 'cause'. The psychological significance is obvious.

From the time of his arrival in Switzerland Reclus had had some contact with members of the federalist International, but the earliest surviving reference to any membership is contained in an August 1874 circular of the Jura Federation which mentioned him as a 'central' member, that is a member who did not belong to a specific section.[7] Some time before 17 April 1875 he joined the section at Vevey where he took up residence.[8] This section comprised a small, but enthusiastic group, whose prominent members besides Reclus were the carpenter Samuel Rossier, the cook Joseph Favre and Charles Perron who moved to Vevey in 1875 to work as a cartographer on *La Nouvelle Géographie Universelle*. The group showed a keen interest in the workers' movement of the area, and was continually making suggestions and contributing to the discussion in the Jura Federation's *Bulletin*. Under Reclus' influence it came to assume an organisational character which closely anticipated that of the anarchist groups of the later part of the nineteenth century. There was no central direction, and each individual member was encouraged

to act independently in all matters. Correspondence was addressed to
Reclus, not because he held any office, but because this constituted a
convenience for those wishing to contact the section.[9]

The more direct involvement of Reclus in Jura politics in the latter
half of the 1870s is reflected in the changing attitudes of the police
towards his activities. Their reports dated prior to 1875 claimed that
he was living a quiet life and that, in spite of his 'advanced' views,
he was not active in politics.[10] In a report of 21 June 1876 from the
French ambassador at Berne to the French Minister of Foreign Affairs,
it was pointed out that Reclus, who had been giving lectures (on
geography) at Geneva, 'conducted himself very well'.[11] According to
a police report of 14 May 1877, however, 'since his arrival in
Switzerland [he] has not ceased to give the most active assistance to
all the intrigues of the revolutionary party'.[12] In another, written two
years later, it was claimed that he was 'one of the most ardent
propagators' of the federalist International.[13] And it is true that
Reclus played a very important part not only in the elaboration of
anarchist theories, but also in building the necessary momentum to
sustain interest in a set of principles which were to become embodied
in a movement of some consequence in the years to come in Western
Europe.

There is some confusion among scholars and the general public
concerning European anarchism and its relation to socialism. In the
period following the Paris Commune two camps were created, that of
the anarchists and that of the other schools of socialism; these
'others' have encompassed everything from revolutionary Marxism to
the various forms of social democracy. The rift between the anarchists
and the 'others' has been perceived to be so deep that the former
continually risk being ejected from the camp site altogether. There
has been a tendency among scholars to regard the anarchists as
belonging to a species other than socialist, and to link them with
every conceivable belief or theory which expresses an anti-statist or
anti-government sentiment.[14] In this study I am concerned with the
development of anarchism within the context of European socialism,
and it is part of my aim to show that socialism continued to be an
important part of the essential nature of late nineteenth-century
European anarchism. However, once we specify that the present study
is about that form of anarchism which was also socialist, there arises
the thorny problem of what precisely constitutes the anarchist position
*vis-à-vis* other socialists.

As early as 1851 Reclus had proclaimed that anarchy was the

highest expression of order, but it is a mistake to assume that he was articulating the anarchist position which was only to develop in the 1870s. His self-proclaimed mid-century 'anarchism' was meant to convey what he and many others perceived as the goal of revolutionary activity. Anarchy represented a society 'without masters' of any kind, at the social-economic and political levels. But this was — and still is — the ultimate goal of all socialists. Marx's 'withering away of the state' and Lenin's 'communism' evoke similar images of a self-directing society in which authority imposed from above has been dispensed with. The present century's 'Socialism in One Country' was born of necessity, and is an aberration from the universalism — and stateless-ness — which has been an essential ingredient in socialism from its gradual emergence in the early nineteenth century. In a sense all socialists are anarchists, but our task is to uncover what it was that distinguished those who came to be known as the anarchists from the wider socialist movement. The perception of anarchy as the revolutionary goal is a necessary but not sufficient basis for defining the historic anarchist position. Witness the 1872 attempt of the General Council of the IWMA to reassure its recalcitrant sections that anarchy was the goal of all socialists.[15]

This attempt was made in response to demands for the immediate decentralisation of authority and decision-making within the IWMA. The General Council insisted that this would be ineffectual in winning the battle against the powerful bourgeois state, that only after the capture of political power would the repressive machinery of the bourgeois state yield to unexploitative administrative functions of government. Marx believed that authority had to be met with authority; some of his opponents disagreed, and to emphasise this point they called themselves the anti-authoritarians. These were a varied lot — the English trade unionists, for example, and the Belgian socialists who supported the federalist Jurassians and Italians out of a conviction that the General Council had no right to assume wide-ranging powers. The spectre which loomed large in the early 1870s was that of the tyranny of a General Council which was attempting to impose discipline upon IWMA members before the revolution and which threatened to remain firmly in the saddle following it. The anti-authoritarians rose up in protest, and at St Imier declared a commitment to the complete autonomy of the sections and refused to envisage any revolutionary government after the overthrow of bourgeois society.[16]

To be sure, resistance to Marxist 'authoritarianism' is contained within several varieties of socialism, as the history of the past 100 years amply demonstrates. Thus, while a non-authoritarian approach to the struggle for socialism is a necessary ingredient within late nineteenth-century European anarchism, it is also insufficient to constitute a definition of the historic anarchist position. One can be non-authoritarian, strive for a society 'without masters', and still engage in parliamentary politics, as several social democrats – Jean Jaurès and Léon Blum, to mention two prominent figures – bear witness. The factor which separated the European anarchists from all other socialist groups in the late nineteenth century was their decisive rejection of all activity within the framework of the bourgeois political order. It is not clear that the federalist objections to Marxism would have necessarily led to the development of anarchism, had there not existed an intense hostility to the bourgeois state, and specifically to party-political activity.

The relative importance of politics and economics had been a delicate issue from the inception of the IWMA, but in the 1860s there were few critics of bourgeois politics who could not be persuaded that party-political activities might be used 'as a means' to achieve a 'stateless' society.[17] Bakunin upset this balance with his 'anarchist' programme of 1868,[18] but the impact which this had upon the development of anarchism in the late 1870s should not be exaggerated. Bakunin remained a great source of inspiration for the anarchists; for a time, indeed, he had an influence upon most socialists – including Marx. But the anarchists did not emerge out of loyalty to Bakunin or to his ideas, which in any case would have been a most 'un-anarchist' way to proceed. When Bakunin 'retired' from politics in 1873, there did not exist a clearly articulated anarchist position. Only after his death in 1876 was the theory of anarchism formulated, and by people who had rejected important parts of his theories. Marx's paranoia over Bakunin's conspiracies led him to see the federalist International as the brainchild of Bakunin, but, given their relations, this was to be expected. The development of anarchism was more complex than the continuation of the legendary Bakuninist opposition to Marx, and much work remains to be done. Reclus, for example, was not moved at all by the Marx/Bakunin debate, but he became one of the leading theoreticians of the nineteenth-century anarchist movement. His post-1871 position did not represent the return of a wayward Bakuninist to the fold, but rather the commencement of a new stage in revolutionary politics.

The major factor in the emergence of an anarchist position in the 1870s may have had less connection with Marxism than with the distrust of bourgeois politics which had developed (with the help of the bourgeoisie) into a bitter hostility. In the case of Reclus his experiences in the period 1870 to 1871 played an important part in qualitatively changing the negative attitudes towards the bourgeois state which he shared with all radicals into the relentless hostility which became characteristic of the anarchists. Any contact whatsoever with the bourgeois order, or anything resembling it, came to be contaminating. His objections to the question of revolutionary government were also rooted in the 'lessons' of the Commune. If the revolution threw up a government, he said in 1878, that government would by nature cease to be revolutionary and become conservative. From a defender of the oppressed, it would in turn become an oppressor. Having helped to raise the consciousness of the people, it would work to emasculate them. It was essential for revolutionaries to remain among the people and not to separate from them, not even under the pretext of serving them.[19] Anarchists were revolutionaries who constantly sought a purification which they could never attain, but for which they must always strive. Reclus' friend Carlo Cafiero finally became insane, haunted by the notion that he might be enjoying more than his share of sunlight. Cafiero's madness demonstrates, in exaggerated form, the psychological propensity to seek purification from the bourgeois state which is implicit in the thought of many anarchists. This should not be dismissed as merely a peculiar feature of the psychology of the anarchists. There had to be objective historical conditions which contributed to the particular form which the propensity for purification assumed. After all, people are not born with an aversion towards the state. (These conditions may have varied from country to country, although it is likely that there were considerable elements of similarity.)

The anarchists' intransigent opposition to parliamentary politics had a peculiar effect upon their attempts to work out a theoretical basis for revolutionary action. Having rejected Marxist authoritarianism and bourgeois party-politics, they increasingly came to support a revolutionary strategy resting upon the precept of a 'natural' view of social progress. The notion that socialism (however defined) was somehow natural to humankind was one that pervaded the thought of countless revolutionaries — including both Marx and Bakunin — for many decades.[20] As Marxists justified the need to capture political power, the anarchists built upon these assumptions of a natural socialism. They were compelled to prove that, although some forms of propaganda might be useful, the development of a socialist society could not depend upon any 'political' action. It became a recurrent theme in Reclus' writings that, if the individual were allowed to make all decisions which affected him, society would develop naturally towards socialism, in much the same way that the child grows into an adult. The consequences of this view for the development of anarchist thought were profound, as the remaining chapters will show. For purposes of analysis, the examination of the relationship between anarchist social and political theory will also be reserved for later. Here I shall examine some general concepts developed by the anarchists in the 1870s, as they struggled to define themselves *vis-à-vis* the bourgeois state and *vis-à-vis* other socialists.

The participants at the 'anti-authoritarian' St Imier Congress of 1871 did not believe that their position represented a break with past policies of the IWMA. On the contrary they were convinced that they were enunciating more clearly what the International had stood for all along. A great deal of the ambiguity within the anarchism of the 1870s can be traced to their insistence that their theories were a logical extension of the principles of the IWMA, and that therefore their socialism not only did not require any special definition, but was the only legitimate form of socialism. The federalists' Geneva Congress of September 1873, to which all sections opposed to the General Council and its centralist 'deviation' were invited, was entitled the 'Sixth Congress of the International' to emphasise that the resolutions of the Hague Congress were not recognised and that they were carrying on the business of the IWMA begun in 1864. It took some time before the anarchists became clearly distinguished from the varied assortment of groups which comprised the federalist International. This process began especially in response to the public service theory of the state put forth by the Belgian socialist Caesar de Paepe.

At the Brussels Congress in September 1874 De Paepe argued that, even in post-revolutionary society, there would be a need to organise public services such as communications at the level of the local commune or the federation of communes. After the capture of power the administrative structure would have to be imposed by a 'collective dictatorship'. The opponents of the theory objected on principle to the whole notion of a dictatorship which would impose a structure upon a free society, or upon a society struggling to become so. It was essential, it was said, for individuals to be able to associate as they chose and for communes to be able to federate freely.[21] This

line of argument seems to have been followed by Reclus in the discussions which took place at the 1876 Lausanne anniversary reunion
in honour of the Paris Commune. Paul Brousse wrote that, on the
morning of 19 March 1876, Gustave Lefrançais and Nicholas
Joukowsky had defended the public service theory of the state, while
he himself and Reclus had attacked it.[22]

The federalist International embraced a range of organisations with
widely varying theoretical positions. However, until the mid-1870s it
had not been thought necessary to employ any labels other than those
such as collectivist, revolutionary, socialist or libertarian or for that
matter, to preach any doctrine other than the basic truths of
collectivised property, the abolition of the state and spontaneous
revolution. The debate over labels and doctrine began in 1876. By
that year the terms anarchist and anarchy were being used to refer
to certain groups and individuals, though not without strong
opposition from some of them. James Guillaume argued that it would
be extremely unwise to employ negative and ambiguous labels. He
also reminded the readers of the Jura Federation's *Bulletin* that there
was a collectivist theory, which had been formulated in the congresses
of the International, and that this was the theory which informed their
actions.[23]

As early as 1851 Reclus had employed 'anarchy' to refer to the
harmonious running of a stateless society based upon the principles of
justice, equality and brotherly love.[24] He is said to have called himself
an anarchist for the first time in public in his address to the Lausanne
anniversary reunion on 19 March 1876.[25] On 3 March 1877 he
delivered an address entitled 'Anarchy and the State' at St Imier,[26]
and in 1878 he defended the use of anarchy and anarchist on
etymological and practical grounds.[27] The terms conformed to
etymology and logic, he said — did not socialists strive to achieve
anarchy? — and they were also sufficiently uncommon in usage as to
be an aid in drawing attention to themselves. Moreover, there was
little point in a resistance to them, since they were already being
employed by friends, as well as by enemies. The fact of terminology
would not alter the essence of their message, he was saying.

The sources for the early stages in the formulation of Reclus'
anarchist theory are to be found in his address at St Imier on 3 March
1877 and in the revolutionary review *Le Travailleur* (1877–8),
particularly the programme of the review and two essays which were
published in it in early 1878.[28] These sources are also important for
an understanding of the development of European anarchist thought,

for they are among the first statements of any significance on its meaning.

In the address which he delivered at St Imier Reclus traced the different forms which the state had assumed from the earliest times: the theocratic, the monarchic, the aristocratic and the democratic. The last mentioned, he said, professed to be the government of the people by the people, but of course it was nothing of the kind. Were that the case, what he meant by anarchy would already have been realised. He was suggesting that the modern European state was part of an evolution and contained the seeds for future progress. While Kropotkin tended to see the European state as an artificial creation imposed upon an idealised medieval decentralisation, for Reclus it was one further embodiment of authority, though in a sense an advance upon the political institutions of the past. In the Middle Ages, Reclus had said in 1851, the Lord and the serf had remained equal in the sight of God; in the 1870s all men were equal under the law. The task of the anarchist was to make this theoretical equality of men a practical reality for both men and women.

Although Reclus' historical survey demonstrated that there had been real progress in the direction of anarchy, the state had to be abandoned completely if anarchy was to be achieved. The development towards a decentralised society was being held up by existing states whose tendency to centralise was by nature counter-revolutionary. Modern states had completely outlived their usefulness, though advocates tried to argue that states performed essential directing or policing functions.[29] The programme of *Le Travailleur*, which Reclus probably wrote, or at least closely supervised, saw the state as existing in several forms, political, juridical, religious, and as constituting a governmental machine which reflected the economic system and at the same time reinforced and protected it. Contrary to what has become the popular conception of the view of the anarchists, the state was not seen as the source of all evil. It was economic inequality which was isolated as 'the source of all oppression' while the state was judged to be 'the most powerful instrument of oppression' under which the working class suffered.[30] It was Reclus' belief that the workers were oppressed on two sides, and while the revolutionary struggle might be seen to be against the state, it was first and foremost against that which gave rise to the state, the social-economic system. The state was the weapon used by the bourgeois to guard their economic system. Should the revolutionary attempt to snatch the weapon away from his opponent, we might ask, or should he make an effort to destroy the weapon without first taking possession of it? The latter is the more tricky, but that is what the anarchists decided they would do.

Here is one anarchist who did not simply believe, in the so-called 'Bakuninist' tradition, that once the state had been abolished, people would automatically develop what was supposed to be their natural ability for friendly social and economic ço-operation. At St Imier Reclus specifically said that the removal of the state would not necessarily bring about a transformation of the social-economic order.[31] Even gaining control of the means of production would be insufficient to bring about a just society, unless this control was linked with a development of intellectual and physical faculties.[32] In the period of the 1870s the relationship between consciousness and social-economic equality tended to become blurred, as Reclus fully committed himself to the immediate struggle, the revolutionary overthrow of bourgeois society. The question of consciousness played a more prominent role as the century progressed.

The anarchist attack on the bourgeois state did not rule out the establishment of some form of government or co-ordinating body within an anarchist society. An anarchist 'government' is a contradiction in terms only if government figures are 'masters' rather than people performing a community service and subject, in fact as well as in theory, to the will of the people. Government structures would have to be centred on 'natural' communities and take shape from the bottom up, not from the top down as in bourgeois society. This was clear in Reclus' address to the 1868 Congress of the League of Peace and Freedom, and it was explicit in much of Kropotkin's writing. In 1877 Reclus continued to say that the law had to be replaced by 'free contract' and the constraint of the state by the 'free association of the forces of humanity'.[33] However, from the 1870s he had little interest in vigorously pursuing this general line of argument. He could not deny that some government (non-bourgeois) co-ordination would be useful, desirable and even necessary in the society of the future. Moreover, he could not object to the establishment of institutions which arose from the needs of the people and which were their creation. On the other hand, however, given his assessment of the existing circumstances, it was rather pointless to advocate immediate steps towards such a restructuring of society. Not only was there a need to concentrate efforts on ousting the bourgeoisie, but until people had reached a certain level of intellectual and moral development, they would be incapable of controlling those 'governments' which they created.

Reclus insisted that the conscious efforts of people were crucial to the eventual success of revolution, and that it was important to be selective in the choice of revolutionary means. Yet, he found it easier to say what these means were not, rather than what they were. All participation in parliamentary politics had been ruled out. But so had non-parliamentary activity such as involvement in co-operative enterprises. Elisée had joined Elie in the 1860s co-operative movement, but by the 1870s the former had fully shed the young brother image, along with his former ambivalence towards the value of co-operativism. In 1878 he stated that co-operative undertakings were so far from being the way to socialism that they were even counter-revolutionary. A successful co-operative enterprise meant that the association earned money, became a property-owner and was obliged to conform to the conditions of capital, in a word it became 'bourgeois' and separated from the people, entered 'the great brotherhood of the privileged'. From the point of view of the revolution, success was more fatal than failure, he argued. A failed co-operative would permit, even encourage, those who took part to renew their efforts within the revolutionary struggle, but success amounted to the integration into bourgeois society of potential revolutionaries who would be lost forever.[34] In politics and economics Reclus saw what amounted to 'iron' laws. Just as participation in bourgeois politics produced integration into the bourgeois political order, so too would participation in the bourgeois economy promote the bourgeois economic order. In his view, the liberal economists who advocated co-operativism as a means of ensuring the stability of the bourgeois system had been essentially correct in their analysis.

There was also no doubt as to which social class would constitute the agent of revolution. It could be none other than that composed of the worker and the peasant both of whom had a special cause for demoralisation, the contempt of physical labour which all members of society directed at them.[35] Reclus was saying, although he does not make himself clear, that the full equality which anarchism demanded would be accomplished through the emancipation of society's lowliest members because of their position within the social and political order. They were most deprived and therefore especially sensitive to the evils of inequality. Moreover, their liberation from inequality would necessarily mean the liberation of the whole of society from the evils of privilege. Reclus perceived an unbridgeable gulf between those who supported privilege/inequality on the one side and the promoters of equality on the other. In contrast to what he had advocated in 1870 to 1871, he pontificated that it was out of the

question to help the bourgeoisie as caste, because a caste believed itself
entitled to privilege and was a miniature of the state. The anarchists
were levellers, he insisted, and both the caste and the state, traditional
and legal inequalities would have to be abolished. For the same reasons,
it was a serious illusion to support the petite bourgeoisie, even if it
had legitimate cause for grievance.[36] Elsewhere he suggested that it
would be a dupery to await the emancipation of the workers through
a reconciliation with the bourgeoisie, since bourgeois society was
based upon private property, while the route to justice and liberty
consisted in an attack upon private property, not a support of it.[37]
Questions dealing with the social-economic order will be examined
in more detail in a later chapter.

The revolutionary, according to Reclus, had to pledge himself to a
life of incessant propaganda among the people, to help awaken in them
the great task which lay before them. Yet he was at a loss to say
precisely what could be done beyond spreading the word through the
press and popular meetings. He sensed the limitations of this strategy
when he said that it was better for anarchists to march directly
towards their goal even if this meant proceeding more slowly, than to
follow the 'circuitous ways' through parliamentary politics and co-
operatives which would cause them to lose sight of their goal.

> In remaining sincerely anarchists, enemies of the state in all its
> forms, we have the advantage of deceiving no one, and especially
> of not deceiving ourselves. Under the pretext of realising a small
> part of our programme, even with the chagrin of violating
> another part, we shall not be tempted to address ourselves to power
> or to try to take part in it too. We shall spare ourselves the scandal
> of those retractions which so many ambitious people and sceptics
> make and which trouble the conscience of the people so
> profoundly.[38]

Such idealism was, and remained, of paramount importance, but it was
not likely, by itself and over the long run, to prove emotionally
satisfying for a man of Reclus' spirited temperament and he was soon
to place his hopes in the revolutionary potential of propaganda by the
deed, a new approach to propaganda which was to strike terror in the
hearts of bourgeois everywhere.[39]

Reclus' refusal to work within the bourgeois political order was
final. The world was divided into bourgeois and anti-bourgeois, enemies
and friends. On the one hand, there were those who wanted to profit

from injustice and inequality and, on the other, those who struggled
for their own liberty and that of others.[40] As he declared in 1882,
there were only two principles at work, government and anarchy:

> There are socialists and there are socialists, it will be said, and
> among the different schools, which one will prevail? Of course, if
> one kept to appearances, there would be a great diversity of forms,
> but that is only an illusion. Fundamentally, there are only two
> principles present: on the one side, that of government, on the
> other, that of anarchy, authority and liberty ... All revolutionary
> acts are, by their very nature, essentially anarchical, whatever the
> power which seeks to profit from them.[41]

Unlike Bakunin, Kropotkin and Brousse, he believed that the post-1871
period represented a new stage in revolutionary politics. It was new
because of the war against governments, and also because of the
universal nature which the struggle for socialism had assumed. The
significant development of the 1870s, pronounced the programme of
*Le Travailleur*, was that the localised commune (Paris Commune) had
given way to a wider, working-class struggle. In every country, Italy,
Spain, Germany, Greece, Belgium, Switzerland, Russia, the workers
were responding to the great challenge. Regardless of their differing
strategies, all workers had the same aim: to emancipate themselves
from the employer. The questions of production and consumption were
the same all over the world; artificial boundaries, mountains and oceans
did not affect the situation of workers who were the exploited of
every country.[42] In a sense Marxist attempts to capture political power
were a recognition of the existence and importance of bourgeois states.
Anarchists, on the other hand, were revolutionaries who had assigned
the state to the dustbin of history. For Reclus this led to a relaxation
of his former French chauvinism, and stimulated him to seek universal
laws of human behaviour which denied the necessity of working
through existing states, even in order to destroy them — which was
essentially the Marxist position.

As one conscious of the 'newness' of the period, Reclus was not
anxious to immerse himself in 'old' politics, and he did not see a
value in working with elements which constituted an anarchist 'party'.
He chose to work among the motley Geneva group of French and
Russian exiles, communards, De Paepists and others, instead of
moving in the more sectarian circles of the Jurassians centred around
Guillaume in Neuchâtel. Reclus was a curiosity; the most anarchist

of the anarchists, who chose to be with non-anarchists and aroused the ire of those whose outlook was closest to his. And true to form, much of the hostility directed at Reclus in the 1870s came from people who were to become his closest associates in the years to come. This was especially true regarding his relations with Kropotkin.

When Kropotkin had left England for Switzerland in late 1876, he had been full of enthusiasm to renew his acquaintance with Guillaume and the Jura watch-makers who had impressed him so much on his first trip to Switzerland in 1872. His visit to Belgium, to 'spy out' the land for Brousse in early 1877 convinced him that he could accomplish nothing profitably there unless he remained at least a year. He returned to Switzerland in February 1877, with the intention of involving himself deeply in the revolutionary struggle, and he seems to have been captivated by a romanticised notion of working for a 'pure' anarchist party. He experienced some uneasiness on account of Reclus' 'learning', but became reassured upon meeting him. 'I liked him very much', Kropotkin wrote to Paul Robin, ' . . . I was pleasantly surprised to see a true socialist.'[43] However, as Kropotkin became beguiled by the vitality and 'extreme' position of Brousse, he adopted a narrowness of approach and chose to align himself with the Jurassians in opposition to Reclus and the Genevans. There were disagreements over the value of some projects connected with 'scientific' education which Reclus was anxious to pursue (see Chapter 7), and the dispute came to a head when the Genevans decided to bring out the review *Le Travailleur*.

This review was born out of the hopes aroused by the revival of the working-class movement in France. By 1876 the labour movement, which had collapsed with the defeat of the Commune, had begun to recover. A workers' delegation from France had been present at the Vienna International Exhibition in 1873 and another at Philadelphia in 1876. Also in 1876 the first Labour Congress was held in Paris, and although it represented moderate opinion, its very existence was considered significant. In the general elections of January 1876 a Republican majority was returned, and as republicans became more confident, agitation began for a general amnesty for the communards. These developments were taking place at about the same time as the myth of the Commune was being established. France was becoming more accessible to propaganda, and by early April the decision had been taken by the Geneva exiles to set up a review which would enjoy an open existence in Switzerland and which would be smuggled into France.

Nor was Reclus the only person to see the possibilities for revolutionary agitation in France. Brousse was planning to bring out *L'Avant-Garde* as an organ of the French Federation with which he had close contacts, and he saw a conspiracy against both the *Bulletin* and the proposed *L'Avant-Garde* in the motives behind the setting up of *Le Travailleur*. He wrote to Kropotkin about the dangers of collaborating with the men of such varying opinions who were behind it (the Jacobin Gambon, the anarchist Reclus and the De Paepist Lefrançais). The letter shows that Brousse was also concerned about what appeared to him to be the unlimited ambition of the Geneva group, and the consequent threat to his own powerful position in Berne. The 'friends' in Geneva were involved in the *Almanach* and were making plans for a socialist dictionary; 'now it is a question of a review; tomorrow it will be a question of a newspaper'.[44]

Kropotkin supported Brousse without reservation, and in a letter to Robin explained his version of the 'split' between the south (Geneva, Lausanne, Vevey) and the north (Neuchâtel, St Imier, Berne, La Chaux-de-Fonds). The leader in the south was Joukowsky, said Kropotkin, who made a lot of noise without doing anything. Behind him was Reclus who, it was claimed, did absolutely nothing and contributed only his name. Then there were the easily led Perron and Ralli. The only good word was reserved for the 'likeable' Kahn, who, alas, let himself be exploited. Because these people never came together with workers, it was explained, they began to scribble and to use up precious finances. Kropotkin refused to co-operate with the southern anarchists, and claimed that the Free Tribune section of *Le Travailleur* was only an 'open door' for the Jacobin friends of Joukowsky and Kahn. He maintained that the review was directed against the *Bulletin* and saw nothing open to question when in the same letter (29 April) he informed Robin that Brousse was planning a paper for clandestine distribution in France.[45] He later declared that *L'Avant-Garde* had been founded by Brousse (and himself) because the *Bulletin* had begun to become too 'insipid'.[46]

While the varied opinions expressed by the Geneva group on revolutionary matters had led to the northerners' suspicions, relations were exacerbated by the independent action of the group, its propensity to take the initiative in writing up propaganda, and disagreements over the use of funds. It is likely that Brousse's ambition and conviction that his was the true way to socialism – which contributed to his poor relations with Guillaume – were largely responsible for his hostility towards the Geneva group. At the same time Brousse's natural enthusiasm and thirst for action, which inclined him to resent the cautious and conciliatory manner of Guillaume,[47] also played a role in his animosity towards the more reflective and eclectic approach of the Genevans. Kropotkin himself, anxious to belong to a 'party of pure anarchy', showed a narrowness of outlook and a disquieting readiness to repeat gossip for which there was little or no foundation. 'As for me', he wrote to Robin, 'I rally openly to the Jurassians of the north, party of pure anarchy, of agitation in the milieu of the workers, of action.' He was attracted to this group, he said, because they had an 'intimate relationship' and represented a 'compact party with a well determined programme'.[48]

As might be expected, Reclus handled the affair in an exasperatingly tolerant manner. He preferred – for the sake of the cause for which they all worked – to say nothing. But beneath the calm exterior he was highly critical of his fellow revolutionaries. Two years earlier, in 1875, Bakunin had remarked on the 'heroic patience and perseverence' of the Jurassians and the Belgian socialists, but Reclus had responded by expressing his concern about their very weak spirit of cohesion, and their whims rather than their will to see the struggle through.[49] This negative opinion was no doubt reaffirmed by the squabbles in the Jura, although it did not lead him to modify his behaviour. He stubbornly went his way, refusing to submit to 'authority', but neither also refraining from any kind of attack. When Champseix complained in April 1877 of the ill-treatment which Benoît Malon was receiving at the hands of Guillaume and asked him publicly to defend Malon, he remained silent.[50] And yet, as exasperating as Reclus could be in his martyrdom, he was also touchingly innocent in his childlike glee at signs of mended quarrels. At about the time of Champseix's letter, he wrote joyfully that he had seen Brousse and Guillaume who appeared to be experiencing better relations. 'No rivalries, no gossiping!' he exclaimed, 'that is indispensable. "Oil! oil!" as Nadar used to say to me when we went up in a balloon . . . '[51]

Reclus managed to avoid direct confrontation with the Jurassians, as well as with non-anarchist groups, even as he maintained the intensity of his anarchism. When De Paepe wondered whether he would be a suitable collaborator for the proposed *Socialisme Progressif*,[52] Malon replied that he did not think he would do it, even if he were asked directly, because he was 'an out and out anarchist, the most anarchist of the editors of the *Travailleur*, and a great friend of the Jurasso-Italian enragés'.[53] A notice in *Le Travailleur* announced the appearance of the *Socialisme Progressif* as a review of the statist school of socialism, but none the less, as marking a contribution to the continuing discussion on the social question. 'Our duty, as revolutionary anarchists, is no less to welcome this socialist organ of free and courteous discussion. It is up to the readers to study it and to judge with full knowledge of the facts.'[54] In a similar spirit *Le Travailleur* was said to be devoted to study. All questions would be raised and all solutions examined; the discussion would be frank and the criticism fair. Serene in its detachment, the review proclaimed that the question of self-esteem did not exist for revolutionaries whose cause was that of the workers of the entire world.[55] As far as Brousse and Kropotkin were concerned, *Le Travailleur* left much to be desired. They were much more in tune with the programme of the French Federation in *L'Avant-Garde* which stated that the first task of the people was to rise up spontaneously and bring about the overthrow of the state by violent revolution.[56]

The ninth annual Congress of the (federalist) International was held at Verviers from 6 September to 8 September 1877, and its aim was to decide on the policy to be followed at the International Socialist Congress, due to take place at Ghent from 9 September to 16 September. By this time the anarchists had become a strong, self-conscious group within the Jura Federation. At Verviers the intransigents, Brousse, Andreas Costa and Garcia Viñas, managed to silence the more conciliatory-minded delegates represented by Guillaume,[57] and at Ghent the anarchist policies led to a rejection of the proposed Pact of Solidarity between all socialists.[58] Reclus' position on the proposed pact is not known. In principle he was doubtlessly in favour of co-operation, though a fear of compromising the anarchist position would have led him to react cautiously to any formal agreements. In any event, the defeat of the Pact of Solidarity led to the virtual isolation of the anarchists within the European socialist movement.

The Verviers Congress was the last annual Congress of the International. Having failed to establish a popular base and having lost much support through the crisis in the watch-making industry, the Jura anarchists were faced with a rapidly declining movement in 1878. The *Bulletin* had to close down for lack of funds in March and shortly afterwards Guillaume himself departed for France. An announcement in the April—May issue of *Le Travailleur* indicated that it, too, was in financial difficulty. This was the final issue to appear, for in a joint meeting at Neuchâtel on 9 June it was decided that *L'Avant-Garde* would carry on the work of *Le Travailleur*. At the meeting there were indications of a relaxation in the hostility towards state socialists and signs that some 'anarchists' were becoming less strongly opposed to working within the bourgeois system![59] At a Federal Congress held at Fribourg from 3 August to 5 August of that year, the intransigent Brousse even questioned the advisability of abstention from electoral activity.[60]

The collapse of the federalist International softened the rigidity of the 'pure' anarchists and led to a breakdown in the personal hostility directed against Reclus. He was present at Neuchâtel on 9 June 1878 and described the meeting as a 'gathering of friends. We were about fifteen, full of good will with respect to one another.'[61] There was even some personal contact between Reclus and Brousse in 1878. The latter had been living at Vevey for some weeks when he was arrested by the Swiss authorities on 26 December and charged with responsibility for the allegedly subversive nature of some of the articles in *L'Avant-Garde*.[62] Reclus and Brousse's friend, Natalie Landsberg, were the only two persons permitted to see the incarcerated revolutionary in the weeks following his arrest. Reclus' general support and defence of Brousse is suggested by a letter of 18 January 1879 from Kropotkin to Robin, [63] and his trips to Lausanne, where Fauquiez, Brousse's lawyer, lived, in February and March must have been in connection with the proceedings.[64] He was in the Pyrenees at the time of the trial in April, and on 4 May formally expressed his thanks to Fauquiez for his sympathetic handling of the case.[65] Brousse succumbed to this energetic concern for his welfare, and in late 1879 he was hoping to obtain Reclus' collaboration on a newspaper project.[66] Brousse's arrest and trial had provided Reclus with the opportunity to extend his friendship to a fellow revolutionary and to show the power of solidarity. It was a pattern of action which was to be repeated throughout his life.

A closer understanding was also growing between Reclus and Kropotkin. Early in 1879 the latter reported to Robin that relations with the *Travailleur* group were improving.[67] He made some rather mild sarcastic remarks, but these were reserved for Lefrançais and Joukowsky, not Reclus. Moreover, by this time Kropotkin was evolving a more philosophical view of anarchism and the social revolution. How far this evolution was taking place under the influence of Reclus' ideas would be difficult to evaluate with any certainty. When Kropotkin decided to bring out a new anarchist paper, however, it was to be 'moderate in tone but revolutionary in substance'.[68] The paper was called *Le Révolté*, and it appeared from 22 February 1879, at the very point when the anarchist movement appeared to have fizzled out. In these circumstances the unexpected success of the paper was truly astonishing, for it quickly reached a circulation far greater than that of any other paper of the Jura anarchists.[69] Reclus began almost immediately to contribute to the financial support of *Le Révolté*,[70] and an address which he delivered on behalf of the abolition of capital punishment was published as a pamphlet by the press.[71] A few disconcerted revolutionaries in the Swiss Jura had been responsible for the elaboration of the anarchist position, but finally, just when many anarchists were changing their minds on the value of working outside the bourgeois political order, their message began striking a more responsive chord. The group around *Le Révolté* were heartened by these signs of support, and began to renew their efforts to refine their theories. In 1880, before all organisational ties had completely died away, the theory of anarchist communism was officially adopted by the Congress of the Jura Federation at La Chaux-de-Fonds.[72]

The major innovation of anarchist communism was the manner of the distribution of the fruits of labour in post-revolutionary society. According to collectivist theory in the Bakuninist tradition, distribution would be based on labour; according to the new theory, the fruits of labour would be distributed according to need. The first mention of the term 'anarchist communism' was made in a pamphlet signed by François Dumartheray on behalf of a group of refugees from Lyons during the year 1876. Entitled *Aux travailleurs manuels, partisans de l'action politique* (To manual workers, supporters of political action), it was the third in a series of pamphlets advocating electoral abstention. Another was promised in which the theory of anarchist communism would be given an exact definition, though this has never been traced and very likely was never published. In the same year, 1876, the theory of anarchist communism was being propagated among the Italian sections of the International by Errico Malatesta, Carlo Cafiero and Costa. These men were instrumental in persuading the Italians to accept it at the Federal Congress of Florence in the autumn, and in December the *Bulletin* carried a report signed by Malatesta and Cafiero.

Reclus is said to have been one of the first to accept the theory of anarchist communism. On 26 May 1927 the 85-year-old Dumartheray recounted to Max Nettlau that the address delivered by Reclus at Lausanne on the afternoon of 19 March 1876 was 'a completely anarchist communist speech'.[73] Moreover, Reclus' relations with, and influence among, the refugees of Geneva have led to the belief that

he collaborated in the writing of Dumartheray's pamphlet of 1876.[74]
We can be certain not only that he was among the first to accept the
principles of anarchist communism, but that he was active in the
formulation of the theory and in its promotion. Even the wording of
the 1876 report of Malatesta and Cafiero parallels passages from his
writings.

> The Italian Federation considers collective property of the products
> of labour as the necessary complement of the collectivist programme,
> the *co-operation of all for the satisfaction of the needs of each*
> being the sole rule of production and consumption which
> corresponds to the principle of solidarity.[75]

Reclus also probably played a prominent role in convincing Kropotkin
of the merits of the theory. The latter had been reluctant to endorse it,
because he had been preoccupied with the practical difficulties of dis-
tributing scarce resources after a revolution which he personally
expected within a few years.[76] In 1879, at the Congress of the Jura
Federation, he had relented somewhat by proposing the adoption of
communism as an aim, with collectivism as the transition stage. One
year later, however, at La Chaux-de-Fonds, he put forward the case
for anarchist communism, suggesting that the theory came closer to
expressing anarchist aims.

Kropotkin's statement was supported by Reclus. The products of
labour, Reclus said, could not be apportioned strictly according to
labour, for they were the result of the combined efforts of all people,
the existing generations, as well as those which had preceded them.
Therefore, it would be right for each individual to draw from the
common stock, with no principle to guide his actions other than 'that
which grows out of the solidarity of interests and the mutual respect
of his associates'. He assured his comrades that there was no   reason
to fear the problem of scarce resources, for there would be plenty for
all when the loss of products through commercial wastage and private
appropriation came to an end. No mention was made of individual
needs. Cafiero, who spoke later, stressed the slogan 'From each
according to his abilities, to each according to his needs'. Reclus
preferred to say that distribution would be regulated according to the
principle of solidarity, rather than that of individual needs.[77] This is
an important point which is not usually emphasised in studies dealing
with the theory of anarchist communism. For Reclus, need was a
rather crude measure of what any individual ought to take from the

common stock. It was also indicative of a *mentalité* which continued to be egotistical and primitive. Solidarity, or a consideration of the fulfilment of one's own needs within the context of the needs of others, on the other hand, represented a harmony between the individual and society, and consequently a higher level of humanity.

From the late 1870s until the mid-1890s the movement dedicated to the realisation of anarchist ideals assumed a character that was broadly different from that of the earlier movement which had revolved around the IWMA. For a few years the Jura Federation continued to hold congresses and reunions, and there was the famous Anarchist Congress at London in 1881. However, after 1882 the movement came to consist in small groups scattered throughout Europe which maintained only informal contacts with each other and with sympathetic elements in other parts of the world. The evidence suggests that these groups did not meet regularly, experienced a continually changing membership, did not keep records, and as a matter of principle did not recognise any leaders. In 1883 Emile Gautier described them as 'simple meeting places where friends meet every week to talk to each other about things which interest them. Most of the time, however, one sees only new faces, with the exception of a small nucleus of four or five faithful.'[78] There was no office in the anarchist group, no fixed membership fee, and the autonomy which the group claimed was, in reality, the autonomy of the individual to act as he saw fit. The 1870s had been years of transition from a formal organisational structure to an ever greater decentralisation of decision-making within the groups. In the 1880s and especially in the early 1890s, the individual became both judge and jury, as well as executioner. In aim all socialists sought a state of anarchy, a future society in which people would no longer be subject to any 'masters', social-economic or political. Those socialists who became known as the anarchists also insisted upon an anarchist revolutionary strategy.

## Notes

1.  See especially D. Stafford, *From Anarchism to Reformism, A Study of the Political Activities of Paul Brousse, 1870–1890* (London, 1971), p. 12 ff.

2.  Reclus initially hoped to find 'a calm and orderly life of work' (Reclus to his mother, 15 Mar. 1872, in *Correspondance*, 3 vols. (Paris, 1911–25), vol. II, p. 90) and was determined to 'create a new existence, to enter into a new life' (Reclus to Eugene Oswald, 21 Mar. 1872, *Corr.* II, p. 93). See also Reclus to Buurmans, 19 May 1872, *Corr.* II, pp. 107–8.

3. Police report of 9 Jan. 1874, *P.Po.* B a/1237.
4. Max Nettlau, *Michael Bakunin, Eine Biographie*, 3 vols. (London, 1898 ff), vol. III, p. 739; *Elisee Reclus: Anarchist and Gelehrter* (Berlin, 1928), pp. 172–3; 'Elisée Reclus and Michael Bakunin', in J. Ishill, *Elisée and Elie Reclus: in Memoriam* (Berkeley Heights, 1927), p. 202. Reclus and Bakunin visited each other several times in 1872 and 1873, and were on very good terms. See also James Guillaume, *L'Internationale. Documents et Souvenirs (1864–1878)*, 4 vols. (Paris, 1905–10), Vol. II, p. 279. Elisée to Elie, 29 Apr. 1872, *Corr.* II, p. 102.
5. Reclus to Buurmans, 2 June 1873, *Corr.* II, pp. 129–30.
6. See correspondence in *Corr.* II; *Fonds ER*, 14 AS 232, *IFHS*; *Papiers ER, NAF* 22913. See esp. Reclus to Buurmans, 17 Feb. 1878, *Corr.* II, p. 199. Cf. Paul Reclus, 'A Few Recollections on the Brothers Elie and Elisée Reclus', in Ishill, *Elisée and Elie Reclus*, p. 12.
7. *AFJ. IISG.* Cf. Guillaume, *Internationale*, vol. III, p. 196.
8. Reclus to Bakunin, 17 Apr. 1875, *Corr.* II, p. 170. The Vevey section had originally been attached to the Fédération Romande, but was reconstituted under the name of La Rénovation des bords du Leman and affiliated to the Jura Federation in Aug. 1874. See *Séance du 13 août 1874, PV du CFJ, AEN*; circular dated 28 Sept. 1874 of the propaganda section of the federal committee announcing the formation of the new section at Vevey in *AFJ, IISG*. The name was changed to the Section de Vevey; see report of May 1878 from the section to the Federal Committee of the Jura sections in *AFJ, IISG*.
9. See the report in *AFJ, IISG*. The report was in response to a circular of 14 Apr. 1878 which had requested information about the nature of the membership and the policies of all the sections.
10. Police reports of 9 Jan. 1874 and 8 Feb. 1874 in *P.Po.* B a/1237.
11. *AN* BB24 732.
12. *P.Po.* B a/1237.
13. Police report of 2 Feb. 1879, *P.Po.* B a/1237.
14. See above, Introduction.
15. *Documents of the First International*, vol. V, p. 407.
16. For the proceedings of the St Imier Congress of 15 to 16 Sept. 1872, see Freymond, *Première Internationale*, vol. III, p. 3 ff. Cf. *Mémoire de la Fédération jurassienne* (Sonvilier, 1873).
17. Consider the debates on this question within the IWMA in the 1860s.
18. See *Supplément au journal le Peuple Belge*, 22 Sept. 1868 and Freymond, *Première Internationale*, vol. I, p. 391.
19. Elisée Reclus,'L'Evolution légale et l'anarchie' in *Le Travailleur*, Jan./Feb. 1878.
20. Both Marx and Bakunin rejected a transcendental philosophy for a materialism which situated people in the realm of the existing order; materialism was tied to a conception of history in which progress was measured in terms of actualising natural potentialities. See especially Karl Marx, *Economic and Philosophic Manuscripts of 1844*, ed. Dirk J. Struik (London, 1970) and Michael Bakunin, *God and the State* (Dover, 1970).
21. For the proceedings of the Brussels Congress of 7 to 13 Sept. 1874, see Freymond, *Première Internationale*, vol. IV, p. 251 ff.
22. Guillaume, *Internationale*, vol. IV, p. 202.
23. Joseph Favre and Benoît Malon adopted the terms in a 'lettre addressée au meeting d l'Internationale, réuni à Lausanne, le 18 Mars 1876'. See Guillaume's comments in *BFJ*, 30 Apr., 7 May 1876. The section of Lausanne wrote a letter of protest at Guillaume's criticism of Malon and Favre which the *Bulletin* did not wish to publish. There arose the question of the right of the editorial committee

to criticise or to suppress members' views. An enquiry among the sections found that eight were against the publication of the letter, two were in favour, while four did not reply. Vevey was of the opinion that the *Bulletin* did not have the right to suppress the publication of any articles, letters or remarks. While agreeing that the editorial committee might discuss the issues, Vevey hoped that both sides would observe the courtesy and reasonableness which should prevail among socialists of all shades of opinion. *BFJ*, 25 May and 29 June 1876; Nettlau, *Elisée Reclus*, p. 189.

24. See above, Chapter 1.

25. Cf. Nettlau, *Elisée Reclus*, p. 189; *Histoire de l'Anarchie* (Paris, 1971), p. 140; Paul Reclus, 'Biographie d'Elisée Reclus', in *Les Frères Elie et Elisée Reclus* (Paris, 1964), p. 57; Ryner, *Elisée Reclus*, p. 16; J. Bossu, *Elisée Reclus* (Herblay, S. et O., n.d.), p. 42; note in *Corr.* II, p. 171.

26. *BFJ*, 11 Mar. 1877.

27. *Le Travailleur*, Jan./Feb. 1878.

28. *Le Travailleur*, Jan./Feb. and Feb./Mar. 1878.

29. *BFJ*, 11 Mar. 1877.

30. The programme of *Le Travailleur* appeared as a leaflet at the end of April and was reprinted in the first issue in May 1877.

31. *BFJ*, 11 Mar. 1877.

32. *Le Travailleur*, May 1877.

33. *BFJ*, 11 Mar. 1877.

34. *Le Travailleur*, Jan./Feb. 1878.

35. Ibid.

36. Ibid.

37. *BFJ*, 8 Aug. 1875.

38. *Le Travailleur*, Jan./Feb. 1878.

39. See below, Chapter 10.

40. Reclus to De Gérando, 25 May 1877, *Corr.* II, p. 188.

41. *Le Révolté*, 21 Jan. 1882.

42. *Le Travailleur*, May 1877.

43. Kropotkin to Robin, 16 Feb. 1877, *NA, IISG*.

44. Brousse to Kropotkin, 6 Apr. 1877, Guillaume, *Internationale*, vol. IV, p. 180.

45. Kropotkin to Robin, 29 Apr. 1877, *NA, IISG*.

46. Kropotkin to Emile Darnaud, 6 June 1891, as mentioned in Darnaud to Gross, 20 Jan. 1891, *Fonds Jacques Gross, IISG*.

47. See Stafford, passim.

48. Kropotkin to Robin, 29 Apr. 1877, *NA, IISG*.

49. Bakunin to Reclus, 15 Feb. 1875 in Nettlau, 'Elisée Reclus and Michael Bakunin', p. 203 ff; Reclus to Bakunin, 17 Apr. 1875, *Corr.* II, pp. 170–71.

50. Champseix to Reclus, 2 Apr. 1877, *Papiers ER, NAF* 22914.

51. Reclus to Kahn, n.d. (1877?), *Archief ER, IISG*.

52. De Paepe to Malon, 6 Nov. 1877, *La Revue Socialiste*, July 1913.

53. Malon to De Paepe, 3 Dec. 1877, *La Revue Socialiste*, Nov. 1908.

54. *Le Travailleur*, Jan./Feb. 1878.

55. *Le Travailleur*, May 1877. *Le Travailleur*, which appeared monthly from May 1877 to April 1878 was a well-written review, thoughtful and non-violent in tone. It had an editorial committee of four, Reclus, Oelsnitz, Perron and Joukowsky. From November 1877, on Reclus' initiative, the names of the members of the editorial committee were replaced by a list of collaborators, among whom were Arthur Arnould, Klementz, Metchnikoff, Ralli and Elie Reclus, as well as those formerly listed as editors. Although Rodolphe Kahn's name did not appear on the list, he played an important part in managing the

affairs of the review. Reclus exerted some influence over content and succeeded, with the co-operation of Kahn, in keeping within tolerable limits (or in disguising) the differences of opinion which arose. (See correspondence Reclus to Kahn in *Archief ER, IISG.*) Most of the articles concentrated on a critique of contemporary events and a large portion of the journal was devoted to correspondence from different countries. There were few theoretically oriented articles, and those which were printed were written by Reclus. When Lefrançais insisted on objecting to one of these, his remarks were carried, followed immediately by Reclus' reply to them.

56. *L'Avant-Garde*, 2 June 1877.

57. For the proceedings of the Verviers Congress, see Freymond, *Première Internationale*, vol. IV, p. 515 ff.

58. For the proceedings of the International Socialist Congress at Ghent, see ibid., p. 555 ff.

59. *Séance du 12 juin 1878, PV du CFJ, AEN, L'Avant-Garde*, 29 July 1878.

60. *L'Avant-Garde*, 12 Aug. 1878.

61. Elisée to Elie, 10 June (1878), *Papiers ER, NAF* 22911.

62. For an account of Brousse's arrest and trial, see Stafford, p. 126 ff.

63. 'Reclus is taking an active part in the Brousse affair', wrote Kropotkin to Robin, 18 Jan. 1879, *NA, IISG.*

64. See the reference to the trips in Reclus' account book, *Fonds ER*, 14 AS 232, *IFHS.*

65. Reclus to Fauquiez, 4 May 1879, *Fonds ER*, 14 AS 232, *IFHS*; reprinted in *Grütlin* (Lausanne) on 13 Sept. 1912. The letter was written from Stromstadt in Sweden.

66. Stafford, p. 144.

67. Kropotkin to Robin, 18 Jan. 1879, *NA, IISG.*

68. Peter Kropotkin, *Memoirs of a Revolutionist* (New York, 1971), p. 418.

69. According to ibid., 600 had been the limit of sales of any edition of previous papers. The first number of *Le Révolté* was printed up in 2,000 copies which were all sold in a few days. In another place Kropotkin said that 3,000 were printed up and 2,000 sold; Kropotkin to Darnaud, 6 June 1891, as mentioned in Darnaud to Gross, 20 Jan. 1891, *Fonds Jacques Gross, IISG.*

70. See Reclus' account book in *Fonds ER*, 14 AS 232, *IFHS.* From May 1879 Reclus began to contribute to *Le Révolté* on a more or less regular basis. It is likely that he was asked to help set up *Le Révolté*, and that he refused. In early 1879 he showed little enthusiasm for any newspaper project. In January he told Kropotkin that he would only consider bringing out *Le Travailleur* again if he could raise 1,000 or 2,000 francs in advance. There was also some question of who would edit any newspaper that the *Travailleur* group would take part in publishing. Reclus was of the opinion that Lefrançais was the only man for the job, but found him 'an obstinate fellow'. (Kropotkin to Robin, 18 Jan. 1879, *NA, IISG.*) Under these circumstances he was not likely to find Kropotkin's proposal to launch a paper on 23 francs a very exciting prospect.

71. Elisée Reclus, *La Peine de Mort, Conférence faite à une réunion convoquée par l'association ouvrière à Lausanne* (Geneva, 1879). After the printer had approached Kropotkin (about April) to say that he could not print any more issues of *Le Révolté* for fear of losing government contracts, it was decided to take up the daring suggestion of Dumartheray to start their own printing press. See Kropotkin, *Memoirs of a Revolutionist* (New York, 1971), pp. 420–21.

72. For the proceedings of the meeting, see *Le Révolté*, 17 Oct. 1880.

73. Nettlau, *Elisée Reclus*, p. 189.

74. George Woodcock and Ivan Avakumović, *The Anarchist Prince, Peter Kropotkin* (New York, 1971), p. 317; Clara E. Lida, *Anarquismo y Revolución en la España del XIX* (Madrid, 1972), p. 243.

75. *BFJ*, 3 Dec. 1876.

76. *Le Révolté*, 18 Oct. 1879.

77. *Le Révolté*, 17 Oct. 1880.

78. *Procès des Anarchistes devant la police correctionnelle et la Cour d'Appel de Lyon* (Lyons, 1883), p. 10.

# 7 ANARCHISM, GEOGRAPHY AND SCIENCE

The victory of Marxism as the dominant socialist theory was firmly
established in the 1890s, and as a result Marxist pretensions to a
theory of 'scientific socialism' have been fairly successfully entrenched
within left-wing thought and practice. The anarchists have been
generally relegated to a utopian tradition which seriously mis-
represents the nature and extent of their commitment to a
scientific understanding of social change and revolution. It is a mark
of the decisiveness of the Marxist victory that this could happen,
since it is also a well-known fact that the leading theoreticians of the
late nineteenth-century anarchist movement were men of science;
Elisée Reclus was a famous geographer and Peter Kropotkin, despite
his uneasiness about scholarship, made important contributions to
geography, geology and sociology. Anarchism, no less than Marxism,
was a product of the society in which the anarchists lived, a society
which was moving away from a certainty based upon religion and
philosophy, but which was intent upon establishing a certainty for
its views by looking to science. From the 1870s, in a world of
increasingly sophisticated socialist theorising, the anarchists too felt
compelled to legitimate their position by attempting to anchor their
theory of socialism in science. Reclus played a pivotal role in the
process through which anarchism became 'scientific'.

Reclus' career as a professional geographer and the development
of his political thought are closely interrelated. Chapter 2 outlined
how his awakening interest in geography could be traced to the year
in which he recorded his first views on socialism, and how geography
and politics combined to enrich his experience in the period 1852 to
1857. Just as the post-Commune period represented a turning point
in the evolution of his political thought, it also marked the beginning
of his lifelong project *La Nouvelle Géographie Universelle*. The
publication of *La Terre* in 1868 had established him as a geographer
of some promise, but it was only following 1871 that he fully
committed himself to his monumental universal geography, which was
to win for him a permanent place in the history of geography. The
parallel between his geography and politics becomes even more
striking, for he conceived the idea for *La Nouvelle Géographie
Universelle* while in prison, at about the same time as he began to

develop his anarchism. In the summer of 1871 he drew up a plan of a 'kind of geographical Encyclopedia, separated into small instalments and costing three or four sous each'.[1] It requires little imagination to form some idea of the immensity of the work involved, once one has learned that *La Nouvelle Géographie Universelle* comprised 19 volumes which appeared regularly, one each year, from 1876 to 1894 and that each volume, prior to its appearance as a book, was published, as planned, in weekly instalments. Methodical and systematic, Reclus was a disciplined worker who pursued his task doggedly and with a religious fervour. His insights were conveyed in colourful and powerful images which give his pages a warm and poetical tone.

*La Terre* was described by Reclus as a 'sort of preface' to the larger work which, as the title suggests, he believed to be both new and universal. *La Nouvelle Géographie Universelle* departed from conventional studies in its subject, scope and intended readership. He refused to confine himself to a geographical tradition which cited longitudes and latitudes, and enumerated the towns, villages, political and administrative divisions. What he did was to devote himself to a study of people's changing relationships with one another and with their environment, to what has become known as 'human geography'. Studying people in their environment from geographical, as well as from historical, biological and sociological perspectives, he sought to trace the development of institutions, as well as to examine such questions as the origins of languages and race relationships. He was not content to concentrate upon a small part of the earth, but was most eager to deal with the whole of it. There was need for a new and universal geography, he declared, because of the considerable progress in the scientific conquest of the earth. Vast regions had become part of the known world, and the laws 'which all terrestrial phenomena obey' had been scrutinised with the most rigorous precision. Geography had to be brought up to date. It was not sufficient that universal scientific laws be communicated to the world of scholarship; he deliberately set out to write for the general reader.[2]

His epistemological assumptions were largely in the positivist tradition. Part of the original attraction of geography had consisted in the relative ease with which it yielded to first-hand observation, and he entertained a disdain for those who would presume to contribute to the discipline from the isolation of the study.[3] Scientific method was tied to a close scrutiny of the existing order, and all concepts and generalisations had to be derived from observable facts. He perceived the entire earth as an historically and spatially inter-related system which was subject to discoverable laws. Human beings were an integral part of a natural process; to understand the nature of people, whence they came and whither they were going, it was essential to investigate the natural process of which they were a part. Reclus had become attracted to Carl Ritter's geography lectures in 1851 precisely because within the lecture hall the great geographer had managed to rescue geography from the dull monotony of textbooks. Ritter's lectures, he recorded, were of a 'marvellous clarity' and he 'treated the most grandiose subjects in a language of almost child-like simplicity'. In contrast to Ritter's written work in which he felt himself obliged to be 'academic', his lectures sketched 'les grands faits' (the main facts).[4] Here is Reclus' inspiration, and here is the clue to his approach to both politics and geography; to uncover and to transmit to his readers *les grands faits*.

As a geographer Reclus was preoccupied with the spatial dimension of human existence, and this led him to return continually to the question of boundaries between states. In 1868 he was carried away by his enthusiasm for 'natural' rather than artificial boundaries to the point where he was almost prepared to lay down a blueprint for the decentralised society of the future.[5] In his 1870 support for the French Third Republic he showed a generous disregard for French fortunes by subordinating the fate of Alsace and Lorraine to that of the maintenance of the Republic. What matter, he reasoned, whether these became French or German since, ultimately, they would be part of the universal social Republic.[6] (The assumption was that Alsace and Lorraine would want to be part of a universal Republic.) There was in this no relaxation of the conviction expressed in 1868 that these territories should have the sole right of determining whether they would associate with German or French groups in a 'free' federation. That Reclus was thinking along these lines for other areas of France in the period 1870 to 1871 is confirmed by an 1877 letter[7] in which he claimed that he did not understand what right the French had to keep Nice, if the people of Nice preferred to join Italy. The same principle held for every other city or town of French territory. During the Franco-Prussian War, he continued, he had written part of an article on the question 'to affirm that the strict duty of France was to restore Nice to its autonomy'.[8]

In his youth and into the 1860s Reclus had hoped that nationalism would be a force to liberate subject peoples. In the post-1871 period he began to see another side to the question of nationalism and to perceive with some horror that the spirit of nationalism might be

evoked 'artificially' and used to rally subject peoples against neighbouring peoples. While he was still in prison, he began to fear the
consequences of the growth of this perversion of nationalism and to
lament the considerable hatred which he saw building up between the
French and German people.[9] These fears were intensified when the
religious struggle in Turkey led to the intervention of the Russians,
ostensibly on behalf of their fellow Slavs and orthodox Christians. In
late 1876 he wrote a letter to the Jura Federation's *Bulletin*
suggesting that the forthcoming congress at Berne discuss the attitude
of the International towards the Eastern War which he believed was
more terrible than the Franco-Prussian War.[10] Even if the Internationalists were unwilling to soil themselves with the world of
politics, it was necessary to be able to comment on the event. To
separate themselves completely from contemporary society, to be
unaware of its political crimes in order not to become involved in
specific crimes committed against the workers would be to fall into
a sort of 'mysticism'. The Vevey section arranged for Joukowsky to
deliver a paper on the Eastern question on 29 January (a repetition
of one given earlier at Neuchâtel), and both Reclus and Joukowsky
presented addresses on 3 and 4 March at St Imier and La Chaux-
de-Fonds respectively.[11] In the February–March 1878 issue of *Le
Travailleur* Reclus attempted to demonstrate the importance of the
Russo-Turkish War.

Two major facts coloured Reclus' analysis of the impact of the
'new' nationalism upon the formation of the European states; the
emergence of a centralised Russia and the dominance of Germany. The
movement of centralisation in the East fitted into the pattern of
French unification and more recently German and Italian unification,
and it would lead to Slavic unity.[12] He believed that the immense force
of 'patriotism of race' and the 'brotherhood' of language had played
an important role in the consolidation of the German and Italian
'empires' and would enlarge the domains of Russia.[13] But he was also
convinced that this Slavic unity would not be the product of the
coming together of 'free' peoples; it would be brought into existence
by the 'will of the masters'. Moreover, Slavic unity was itself a mis-
nomer, because 'Slavs or no Slavs, all those whose geographical
position can enclose them within the framework of the new
boundaries will at once have to obey and to show themselves grateful'.[14]
Reclus was saying that the 'natural' feelings of co-operation among
those who shared certain features of their life were being ruthlessly
harnessed to serve those in power. 'National' unity in Russia, as

elsewhere, would only be accomplished through the repression of
'truc' nationalities. It will be noted that he refused to acknowledge
the national status of the European states, and preferred to speak of
empires (granted Germany was also an empire in name). In the case of
Italy, this would appear to be a reversal of his pre-1871 position,
although there would be some justification in arguing that he was
responding to a different set of circumstances.

Reclus saw that the Russian victories in the East did not threaten
the power of Germany. Bismarck's country remained supreme; without German support, or at least acquiescence, no country, including
Russia, dared advance her territory or go to war. Part of the difficulty
currently (1878) being experienced by England was due to the hold
which Germany had on England's allies, Austria–Hungary, for
example. However, the geographer Reclus was not content to rest his
case here. In addition to German aggressiveness, England was doomed
because of problems arising out of the very nature of the far-flung
British Empire, scattered as it was around the globe. Absence of
geographical cohesion was a fatal flaw, for it would quickly become
impossible to secure the various parts of the Empire in the face of
serious challenges (internal or external). In early 1878, before the
Concert of Europe in May of that year, at a time when England
appeared to be at the height of power and prestige, Reclus prophesied
the decline of the British Empire. The future, he forecast, lay at
least for a time with the centralised military states, Germany and
Russia in particular. The power of these was increasing at the rate
by which that of England diminished.[15]

In the world of the great states, Reclus continued to stress the
importance of the principle of national self-determination, and he
did not flinch when he saw how the principle was being used by the
new generation of leaders. However, he had become far more critical
than he had been in the years prior to 1871. No longer was he willing
to support any nationalist movement, even when it emerged from
below. In May 1877 he suggested that love of race and common
language were not in themselves sufficient to unite people in a
universal brotherhood. This could only be accomplished by means of a
higher moral, according to right and duty. To gain his support a
movement for national unity would necessarily have to view its
liberation within the wider context of the universal struggle for
justice.[16] Writing to Buurmans in February 1878,[17] he agreed whole-
heartedly that the extinction of the Flemish communes had been one
of the great evils perpetrated by men. There was no doubt that the

communes were free 'in right . . . it is for them to group themselves as they wish with other communes, Flemish or Dutch, of the south or of the north'. However, he continued, all rights were inter-related. The Flemings were making the mistake of restricting themselves to fighting for one right, their language, without relating their particular predicament to 'human right'. This was a great tragedy, for the 'nationalism' of some Flemings had led them to identify with the German empire and to view Bismarck as the great champion of nationality. This wing of the movement, which even contemplated abandoning Flemish as their literary language for high German, was facilitating German expansion. In words which by 1940 were to prove prophetic, Reclus wrote:

> The Prussian soldiers will take back their 'natural frontiers' as far as Lille and Saint-Omer and Pas-de-Calais, and in their turn, they will face the English as neighbours. These events of the future I see in advance with regret because, more than any other peoples, the Germans represent discipline, – that is to say death.

A positivist approach, as Reclus understood it, called for an analysis which corresponded to observable tendencies in reality, and he was startlingly precise in his accounts of developments in late nineteenth-century Europe, as well as in his estimation of the future course of society and politics. But a positivist framework in the Comtean tradition amounted to a recognition of laws to which people were more or less obliged to submit, in order to maintain the harmony of the existing pattern of development. It is here that Reclus departed most decisively from that tradition. He seems to have seen the existence of two sets of laws; one which flowed inexorably from the logic of the existing institutional framework, and another which flowed from human nature and which was continually threatening to burst through the institutional bounds which contained it. For Reclus, positivism represented both an investigation of the laws which contributed to the maintenance of the existing social-economic and political order, and a search for those laws which challenged that order. After the disappointment of 1871 he looked increasingly to science for reassurance of the triumph of the universal social Republic. In 1875 he pointed to the 'great scientific movement of the epoch' in an attempt to comfort a dejected Bakunin who was brooding over the fact that there appeared to be no revolutionary instinct in the masses. Even if the spirit which Bakunin called the great French civilisation were to disappear, he said, there would be the more important guides in the Darwinian theory of evolution, the study of the conservation of forces and comparative sociology.[18]

The notion of a progressive evolution was a fundamental part of Reclus' conception of the movement of history. In both their biological and social characters, people tended to move from the simple to the complex, and it was more or less assumed that the movement, unless it were diverted from its course (by 'unnatural' institutions), would give rise to a higher level of humanity.

> But whether it is a question of small or large groups of the human species, it is always through solidarity, through the association of spontaneous, co-ordinated forces that all progress is made . . . The historian, the judge who evokes the centuries and who makes them march before us in an infinite procession, shows us how the law of the blind and brutal struggle for existence, so extolled by the adorers of success, is subordinated to a second law, that of the grouping of weak individualities into organisms more and more developed, learning to defend themselves against the enemy forces, to recognise the resources of their environment, even to create new ones. We know that, if our descendents are to reach their high destiny of science and liberty, they will owe it to their coming together more and more intimately, to the incessant collaboration, to this mutual aid from which brotherhood grows little by little.[19]

Progress came through the intensification of the 'natural' inclination of human beings to co-operate with one another, that is through mutual aid. Related to this was a parallel intellectual development represented by a growing awareness of the bonds between all human beings. The seeds of instinctual co-operation were flowering into a more fully developed and conscious co-operation.[20] Reclus also believed that the growth in consciousness would in turn facilitate the development of morality, for the assumption was that a knowledge of how people did act 'naturally' was also a knowledge of how people ought to act.

Anarchists are almost without exception taken to have rejected the theory of the struggle for existence in favour of a theory of mutual aid which they are supposed to have believed was the determining factor in the survival of the species. This has contributed to an interpretation in which people of the stature of Reclus and Kropotkin have taken on characteristics of saintliness, exaggerated even for those whose life was devoted, admittedly, to the promotion of brotherly love. It has also led to much confusion on the question of the logic by which men renowned for their benevolence could accept, even condone, violence of the most extreme kind. But co-operation and violence are not at all mutually exclusive, and it is their complementarity that is the clue to explaining Reclus' position on mutual aid. As indicated in the above-mentioned letter to Bakunin, Reclus believed that Darwin's theory of evolution was evidence in support of the eventual success of the revolutionary cause. In a statement made some three decades later he left no doubt that Darwin had had a profound effect upon his thinking. 'In the history of the world all the armies of a Napoleon are not worth so much as a word of a Darwin, fruit of a life of work and thought.'[21] Reclus explicitly rejected the popular notion that the theory of the survival of the fittest and natural selection was supportive of the maintenance of the bourgeois system.[22]

In a passage which fairly pulsates with defiance he declared that the theory provided ammunition for revolutionaries, and moreover that it quite rightly referred to the natural superiority of the stronger — the working class.

> We ought to congratulate ourselves that the question is thus simplified, for it is much the nearer to its solution. Force reigns, say the advocates of social inequality! Yes, it is force which reigns! proclaims modern industry louder and louder in its brutal perfection. But may not the speech of economists and traders be taken up by revolutionists? The law of the strongest will not always and necessarily operate for the benefit of commerce. 'Might surpasses right', said Bismarck, quoting from many others; but it is possible to make ready for the day when might will be at the service of right.[23]

By the very fact of their having to band together in a 'collective defence'[24] against the bourgeoisie, the working class necessarily had to co-operate, and this co-operation would make them invincible. 'What can isolated individuals, however strong in money, intelligence and cunning, do against the associated masses?'[25] Mutual aid pointed the direction of the future. It was not simply desirable; it was necessary, natural and morally and intellectually superior to the primitive notion of competition which informed the actions of the bourgeoisie.

Denied any part in the moral and intellectual development of the human race, and propelled by the law of competition, the bourgeoisie were relegated to the status of a more primitive species, and in accordance with the law of natural selection they belonged to a world which would soon become the past.[26]

Mutual aid was beginning to make itself felt, but before it could become the dominant social value, it would have to break through the bonds of bourgeois society which held it in check. Reclus believed that he was being realistic when he concluded that the workers would have to fight for their liberation.[27] To be sure, the competitive nature of capitalism fore-ordained that the bourgeois would find it difficult to respond effectively to serious threats from a unified working class, and it is true that Reclus insisted that little effort would be required to unseat them.[28] None the less, it could not be expected that the bourgeois would yield to their own extinction as a class without a fight; this would run contrary to the natural order of things which demanded the presence of the survival instinct. It was also inconceivable that the working class, once victorious, would revert to the primitive law of competition employed by the bourgeoisie. In the very act of freeing themselves, workers had to develop their instincts for co-operation, and this would bring about a fundamental change in their nature. There was no better established fact, said Reclus, than that 'the external form of the society has to change in proportion to the internal pressure'.[29]

This notion of the internal giving birth to the external form of society, that is the moral and intellectual orientation shaping the institutional framework, also appears in a slightly different formulation throughout Reclus' writings. In an essay which he wrote in the 1870s he declared: 'Do not forget that the ideal of a society is always realised.'[30] The idea is also contained in a statement written in 1892: 'The first of the laws of history is that society models itself upon its ideal.'[31] For Reclus it was desirable and necessary to model society upon the anarchist ideal which was not 'human nature as we find it in ourselves', but rather the 'noble form of self-gratification, namely gratifying ourselves in the general good'.[32] The appeal of mutual aid lay in the self-fulfilment which derived from acting in the interests of all. This was the ideal which had to be fostered if workers were ever to build and sustain a socialist society. This did not mean that practice was a direct response to theory. Reclus insisted that there was an interaction: 'The deed grows out of the idea, and the idea out of the deed. It is an everlasting carambolage.'[33] It might be

suggested that the anarchists were imposing their ideal upon an unsus-
pecting society. This would have appeared preposterous to Reclus, for
whom anarchism was the science of the struggle of people attempting
to fulfil their natural potentialities. Far from imposing anything, he
himself believed that he was merely assisting a natural process.

It was somewhat perplexing for Reclus to be confronted with the
popularly held belief that anarchism was peculiar to 'backward' areas.
He also objected to the notion that all countries were equally susceptible to the growth of anarchism. Bakunin, he argued, had become
an anarchist at Paris, and though he had attracted to his ideas a large
number of Russians, none of them had remained anarchists after his
death. While Kropotkin had many contacts with Russian exiles in
England, all of them were more or less constitutionalists. The
countries in which anarchists were the most numerous were those

> where the spirits have for a long time been liberated from
> religious and monarchical prejudices, where revolutionary
> precedents have loosened the faith in the established order, where
> the practice of communal franchises has better accustomed men
> to dispense with a master, where disinterested study developed
> thinkers outside every coterie.[34]

The anarchist ideal was more highly developed in the consciousness of
people in those areas of the world where education had led to a
greater emancipation from religious and political prejudices. The
adepts of anarchy were to be found primarily in France, then in
Catalonia, Northern Italy, London, among the Germans in the
United States, in the Spanish American republics and in Australia.
It was not a question of race which determined the tendency towards
anarchism: '. . . education is everything'.[35]

The United States was not included in Reclus' list. He mentioned
only the Germans living there, and he was thinking especially of those
German anarchists around Johann Most's *Freiheit* in New York.[36] The
individualist school which flourished around Benjamin Tucker in the
United States he must have considered egotistical, and therefore
regressive rather than progressive. 'The only resemblance between
individualist anarchists and us', wrote Reclus, 'is that of a name.'[37] He
probably attributed the 'backwardness' of the Americans to their
education which had not emancipated them from the bourgeois bias
towards property. At any rate, he saw that the revolutionary
potential of the great American strike, which paralysed the country in

1877 and extended to Canada, had remained untapped; workers had concentrated their attention upon trade-union-like demands, higher wages and better working conditions within the framework of the bourgeois state.[38]

Reclus felt that science could help men and women come to an understanding of their world, as it existed and as it might be. However, science was not elevated above the status of a tool, for it was the human conscience which was the final authority as to what was right and wrong. 'I fight for that which I know to be the good cause', he wrote, 'because in that way I conform to my sense of justice.'[39] 'I am far from believing in progress as an axiom', he said, but all persons of principle had no choice but to fight and to suffer for it.[40] It was not a question of hope, but a question of conscience. 'It matters little whether we succeed or not; at least we shall have been the interpreters of the interior voice.'[41] Such statements might indicate that science was a façade for the arbitrariness of instinct. Reclus' notion of conscience should not be dismissed too lightly. Science itself was a method of explaining reality, and the reality about human beings was their position within a natural order, their conscience an integral part of this order. Presumably, if a person followed his conscience — that is, acted in good faith — no fault could be found with his actions, except perhaps to lament any of their unfortunate effects. Presumably also, if a person committed lamentable acts in spite of acting in accordance with his conscience, this would be an indication of his low level of moral and intellectual development.[42]

Within the schema of Reclus' evolution of the human species, a primitive being reacting blindly to the demands of the environment became gradually transformed into a being reacting in full consciousness to the demands of the environment. In an important sense both were in tune with nature. The primitive had only rudiments of a conscience and must be judged within the context of what could be reasonably expected. The more developed the conscience, the harsher the judgement. This did not mean that an individual would be subject to continual surveillance by his fellows, for these, not being in full possession of the facts, would be able to deliver only an opinion. The real judge was the individual who could never escape the merciless demands of the 'interior voice'. 'Do what you please!' (Fais ce que veux!) was the message of 'our great ancestor Rabelais' which Reclus passed on to comrades querying how an anarchist should conduct himself.[43] So long as a person followed his conscience, to do what he wanted to do was to do what was right. Reclus' whole system revolved around a faith in the human conscience or more precisely in what it could become.

While the conscience was the guide to right conduct, the successful execution of the decree issued by the conscience was a function of the human will. 'It is in each  person, in his interior tribunal, in his conscience and in his will that is to be found the spur of destiny.'[44] In a sense the entire course of human history was the history of the struggle of wills. Russia and Germany were unified under the 'will of the masters'; the revolutionary struggle consisted in the imposition of the will of the people in a spirit of brotherhood. And as people progressed to a higher level of humanity, and as their conscience became more developed, their will became all the more forceful. Like the conscience, the will was an integral part of human nature, and its potential power was formidable. It was this conviction which sustained Reclus in the belief that the great states could and would be conquered.[45] The belief, however, did not carry with it the strain of inevitability which characterised so much of his thought in the 1850s. As he wrote to Bakunin in 1875, he was very uneasy about the 'definitive result'; not for a long time, he said, had he believed in the inevitability of progress.[46] While Reclus could perceive the existence of a natural evolutionary process, he also came to see that the successful outcome of the revolutionary cause depended upon the efforts of human beings. Progress was not a foregone conclusion.

For people of good will, to make an effort to resist the movement of history was not to thwart historical development, but on the contrary to fulfil it, to actualise potentialities, to bring about a natural order. Reclus attempted to explain the natural order represented by anarchy as an organic unity similar in nature to a living body. The relationship between the individual and society was compared to that between the cell and the body, each of which had independent existences, if at the same time they were totally dependent upon each other. He was careful to distinguish his view of a society which did not impose restraints upon the individual from that of classic liberalism by insisting that in the social-economic sphere anarchists were collectivists.[47] The study of sociology had provided the anarchists with two primordial facts, he said; that one person is interdependent with every other person and perishes in isolation, and that social progress is accomplished through the thrust of individual wills. To conform to the first law was to become collectivist, to the second, anarchist. To be true to their nature, that is to be free, people must conform to both laws. This submission to the laws of nature he viewed, paradoxically, as a liberation, and he sharply differentiated it from the forced obedience to the laws of the state, against which the anarchists were in 'permanent revolt'.[48] Anarchy, wrote Reclus, was a ' "Life without masters", for society as well as for the individual, social accord, arising not from authority and obedience, from the law and its penal sanctions, but from the free association of individuals and groups, conforming to the needs and interests of all and of each.'[49] Anarchists could be so confident that anarchy was a theoretically possible human condition, because it represented the fulfilment of laws which were immanent in human nature.

The whole of Reclus' thought is permeated with the notion that it is important to resist, even when the situation appears hopeless. We saw this attitude fully apparent in the experiences of 1870 to 1871. It is also clear in his approach to the German question. In the period following the Paris Commune he shared the prevailing concerns among many anarchists regarding the possibility of an outbreak of another war between France and Germany. In a letter of 1887 he declared that, given the state of the world, war was to be expected.[50] For Reclus, to be able to see the future course of history was not to become resigned to it. He adopted an intransigent anti-militarism to the point where the Paris police became alarmed and were sure that he was preparing a 'seditious movement whose aim is to thwart the efforts of the French armies at the moment of a Franco-German war'.[51] By no means had he relaxed his thirst for war against the bourgeois state; the struggle for socialism remained a universal war of workers (and peasants) against the bourgeoisie. His anti-militarism was based not upon a philosophical pacificism, but upon the conviction that war between peoples directed by 'nation-states' was a factor in the regression of the human race and would, there-fore, slow down the revolutionary impulse.

In this regard he differed from his friend Jacques Gross who argued that there might be great advantages in a war, namely the 'mixing of the races'. In what way, Reclus asked, had the war of Tongking changed the Annamites into Frenchmen? In what way since the war of 1870 were the French and Germans any closer? The Franco-Prussian War had not led to the weakening of property or to the *rapprochement* of peoples; in fact, he suggested, the war had tended to strengthen property and to lead people away from a reconciliation.[52] Understandably, he could not support a war which divided the working class, when his life was dedicated to bringing them together. On this question Reclus also differed from Kropotkin whose obsession with the possibility of a European war was evident from early 1887.[53] In January of that year Kropotkin declared that war was on the point of breaking out, insisted that German armies would attack France no later than the spring and advocated that the German attack be resisted by declaring revolutionary communes.[54] This was an approach in the revolutionary tradition of the Paris Commune, and in view of Reclus' negative feelings about the virtues of such activity, we would not expect him to have been sympathetic to it. He was probably showing his impatience at Kropotkin's proposed strategy when he wrote to Gross that the discussion on war was diversionary, because it had distracted them from the social question.[55]

As a scientist who was committed to an understanding of general laws of development, Reclus could not be content merely to insist that the will of the people could and would radically alter the nature of the existing social-economic and political system. There had to be tangible evidence to suggest that such opposition had occurred in the past, and there had to be a pattern of behaviour which could be expected in the future. If science were to serve Reclus, it had to help him uncover the laws of social change. He believed that he had found them in his theory of Evolution and Revolution. The earliest mature statement of this was contained in an address which he delivered at Geneva in 1880. The address was an elaboration of a letter which he had written to the Fribourg Congress of the Jura Federation in 1878 and it drew together a number of thoughts which can be traced back at least to 1869. Evolution and Revolution became a leitmotiv in Reclus' thought, and almost everything which he wrote from the 1870s was related to it. His address of 1880 was published as a pamphlet entitled *Evolution et Révolution*, the first of six editions. In the course of the following years it appeared in several foreign languages, and finally the theme was expanded to book length and the results published in 1898.[56]

Reclus' argument was simple and forceful. It was wrong, he said, to assume that evolution and revolution were alternative approaches to social change, for social change was accomplished through an inter-related process of evolution and revolution. Evolution represented a period of preparation in which there was a development in ideas and morals, sometimes social change at a modest level. This evolution, although essentially revolutionary in nature, could not be expected to make significant progress toward the establishment of a socialist society, because change was constantly being opposed by established

interests. The pressure on the existing order could not be resisted indefinitely, however, and the resolution came in the form of physical
shocks or what were also known as revolutions. In this way revolution
followed logically and naturally upon evolution. Social change,
according to Reclus, was achieved through a repeated series of
evolution and revolution, and it did not really matter whether one
preferred to consider this process essentially evolutionary or
revolutionary, for the gradual and the accelerated had become aspects
of the same phenomenon. He also liked to think of the process in
terms of 'permanent revolution'.[57] The implications for revolutionary
practice were staggering, as we shall see in the chapters which follow.

As Reclus attempted to come to terms with personal and political
tragedy in the 1870s, the idea that the hour of revolution had passed,
but would return in an ever more forceful form was comforting to him.
His views on the question may have been clarified in an exchange of
letters which he had with Bakunin in mid-decade. This correspondence
also indicates the change of direction and pace which was being introduced into European anarchism. Reclus explained to Bakunin that the
evolution which was taking place was a 'normal evolution'; the flood of
the revolution had returned to its bed without having done great
damage. Although there were unpleasant times ahead, at least the
experience would be 'conclusive and complete'.[58] Bakunin, however,
was incapable of adopting such a Stoic attitude, and while he agreed
with the analysis, he found it extremely unsettling. He was alarmed
by what he saw as the dangers of the evolution, and he bemoaned the
'MacMahon-Bonapartist dictatorship in France, that of Bismarck in
the rest of Europe'.[59] At one point he even accused Reclus of not
being affected by events in France.[60] Bakunin, whose revolutionary
inspiration had come from the upheavals of mid-century Europe, could
not understand Reclus' controlled enthusiasm. While the latter looked
to science for the answers to the questions posed by the human condition, and thereby set the pace for future anarchist thought, the
former looked to the past and found a modicum of comfort in the anti-
clerical movements of the latter part of 1875.

Bakunin died at Berne on 1 July 1876, and the funeral which was
held on 3 July brought together many leading revolutionaries. Reclus'
graveside speech emphasised Bakunin's personal qualities, the vigour of
his intelligence and his tireless activity in the revolutionary struggle.[61]
After the funeral he became a principal member of the international
committee set up to collect and edit the great revolutionary's
manuscripts. For Reclus, Bakunin had embodied the spirit of revolt

which underlay all social progress, and his death represented the end of an era of revolutionary activity via the barricades. The future lay with science, with an instinctual revolt which was becoming more and more conscious.

The view of social change developed by Reclus had wide-ranging implications for the nature of the anarchist society. Anarchy was an ideal for the distant future, he said.[62] Theoretically, there could never be fixed and permanent institutions, because any institutions which would arise would also be subject to continual change, in order to meet changing needs.[63] Moreover, the anarchists of his own day were at a relatively low level of development, and thus they were not qualified to say how people who in the distant future would have evolved to a higher level of humanity, ought to go about organising their world. Reclus was attempting to come to terms with the demands of science and to avoid the age-old trap of utopianism. His scientific search for the universal brotherhood had led him to admit that the more he learned about human nature, the less certain he was about the kind of society for which he worked. It must have been uncomfortable at times to be caught between science and utopia.

Anarchists, it is frequently said, believed in an apocalyptic revolution which would transform the world totally and instantly, and which would establish a veritable heaven on earth. So far as Reclus was concerned, nothing could be further from the truth. And it is likely that more anarchists than Reclus have been misread on the question. Granted, it appears fairly certain that in the latter part of the 1870s there continued to be enthusiastic anarchists, even people like Kropotkin, who felt that an apocalyptic revolution was imminent. While such a belief never entirely died, it was considerably weakened. Even the popularity of Reclus' pamphlet on Evolution and Revolution would indicate a break with the traditional 'Bakuninist' notion of revolution. It cannot be doubted that Reclus was an important influence not only upon Kropotkin but upon the movement as a whole. In 1905 Kropotkin attributed to all anarchists ideas which were practically identical with those which Reclus had been formulating for decades. 'In common with most socialists, the anarchists recognise that, like all evolution in nature, the slow evolution of society is followed from time to time by periods of accelerated evolution which are called revolutions; and they think that the era of revolutions is not yet closed.'[64]

Reclus continued to elaborate and to refine his theories until his death in 1905, but the essentials of his thought remained as they had been laid down in the 1870s. By 1880 his theory of Evolution and Revolution had established a pattern for social change which represented a natural 'unfolding' of the potentialities of men and women. This process could not be forced, though Reclus clearly preferred to think that it might, and should, be guided and even hastened. As a 'conscious anarchist', that is one who had arrived at a consciousness of the anarchist position, he thus found it necessary to formulate a revolutionary strategy. In view of the nature of anarchist theory, especially its rejection of any organisational structure which denied individual autonomy and its hostility to all political processes connected with the bourgeois state, the development of a revolutionary strategy was not easy. Reclus came to develop a position in which both education and violence followed logically upon his theory of evolution and revolution.

### Notes

1.   Reclus to Alfred Dumesnil, 23 July 1871, *Correspondance*, 3 vols. (Paris, 1911–25), vol. II, p. 51.

2.   *La Nouvelle Géographie Universelle*, vol. I (Paris, 1876), 'Avertissement'.

3.   See ibid., and the passages cited above, Chapter 2.

4.   Carl Ritter, 'De la Configuration des continents sur la surface du globe', translated and with an introduction by Elisée Reclus, *La Revue Germanique*, Nov. 1859, p. 242.

5.   See above, Chapter 3.

6.   See above, Chapter 4.

7.   Reclus to De Gérando, 1 Aug. 1877, *Fonds ER*, 14 AS 232, *IFHS*.

8.   Further evidence of this line of thought can be found in 1876. On 2 Sept. 1876 Reclus participated alongside Schwitzguébel and Brousse at a meeting in Berne organised in protest against the attempts to arrange a German celebration of the anniversary of the French capitulation at Sedan. Reclus' address concentrated on the 'free formation' of nationalities. See *BFJ*, 10 Sept. 1876; J. Guillaume, *L'Internationale. Documents et Souvenirs (1864–78)*. 4 vols. (Paris, 1905–10), vol. IV, p. 79.

9.   Reclus to Fanny, 28 Aug. 1871, *Papiers ER, NAF* 22913.

10.  *BFJ*, 15 Oct. 1876.

11.  *BFJ*, 4 Feb. and 11 Mar. 1877.

12.  *Le Travailleur*, Feb./Mar. 1878.

13.  Reclus to De Gérando, 25 May 1877, p. 187.

14.  *Le Travailleur*, Feb./Mar. 1878.

15.  Ibid.

16.  Reclus to De Gérando, 25 May 1877, p. 188.

17.  Reclus to Buurmans, 17 Feb. 1878, *Corr.* II, p. 196 ff.

18.  Reclus to Bakunin, 17 Apr. 1875, *Corr.* II, pp. 170–1. See Bakunin to Reclus, 15 Feb. 1875 in Nettlau, 'Elisée Reclus and Michael Bakunin', in J. Ishill, *Elisée and Elie Reclus: In Memoriam* (Berkeley Heights, 1927), p. 203 ff.

19,  Elisée Reclus, Preface to Leon Metchnikoff, *La Civilisation et les Grands Fleuves Historiques* (Paris, 1889), p. XXVII.

20. See esp. Reclus, *l'Idéal Anarchique*, p. 44 ff.
21. Reclus to unnamed person, 18 July 1892, *Corr.* III, p. 122.
22. Reclus, *Evolution et Révolution* (1884), p. 24 ff.
23. Ibid., pp. 25–6 (English from London 1885 edition).
24. Reclus to Heath, n.d. (1884), *Corr.* II, p. 324.
25. Reclus, *Evolution et Révolution* (1884), p. 26 (English from London, 1885 edition).
26. See esp. Reclus' remarks in his 'Pages de Sociologie préhistorique' in *L'Humanité Nouvelle*, Feb. 1898. Cf. his *L'Homme et la Terre*, vol. V, p. 134 ff.
27. See, for example, Reclus to Faure, n.d. (1869), *Corr.* III, pp. 62–3; his letter of 1878 to the Congress of the Jura Federation in *L'Avant-Garde*, 12 Aug. 1878; his *Evolution et Révolution* (Geneva, 1880).
28. Reclus, *Evolution et Révolution* (Geneva, 1884), pp. 26–7.
29. Reclus, *Evolution et Révolution* (1880), p. 10.
30. Elisée Reclus, 'L'Avenir de nos enfants' in *La Commune, Almanach Socialiste pour 1877* (Geneva, 1877).
31. Reclus' preface to Peter Kropotkin, *La Conquête du Pain* (Paris, 1892).
32. Reclus to Heath, 14 Aug. 1903, *Corr.* III, p. 263.
33. Reclus to Darnaud, 21 Jan. 1891, mentioned in Darnaud to Gross, 6 Feb. 1891, *Fonds Jacques Gross, IISG*.
34. Reclus to Georges Renard, 2 June 1888, *Corr.* II, pp. 441–2.
35. Ibid., p. 442.
36. See Pierre Ramus' recollections on Johann Most's enthusiastic reception of Reclus in the late 1880s; Ramus, pp. 124–5.
37. Reclus to Renard, 27 Dec. 1895, *Corr.* III, p. 192.
38. See Elisée Reclus, 'La Grève d'Amérique' in *Le Travailleur*, Sept. 1877; reprinted in *BFJ*, 20 and 28 Oct. and 4 Nov. 1877.
39. Reclus to Buurmans, 25 Apr. 1878, *Corr.* II, pp. 202–3.
40. Reclus to Fauquiez, 4 May 1879, *Fonds ER*, 14 AS 232, *IFHS*.
41. Reclus to Buurmans, 25 Apr. 1878, p. 203.
42. See especially the discussion below, Chapters 9 and 10.
43. See, for example, *Le Travailleur*, Jan./Feb. 1878; Reclus to Auguste Rouveyrolles, 9 July 1890, *Corr.* III, p. 82.
44. Reclus to unnamed person, 18 July 1892, *Corr.* III, p. 122.
45. *Le Travailleur*, Feb./Mar. 1878.
46. Reclus to Bakunin, 17 Apr. 1875, *Corr.* II, p. 170.
47. *Le Travailleur*, Feb./Mar. 1878.
48. Ibid.
49. Reclus to unnamed person, 18 July 1892, *Corr.* III, p. 122.
50. Reclus to Gross, 12 Jan. 1887, *Papiers Gross, Dépôt du CIRA, 1964, BPU*, Geneva. The greater part of this letter has been reproduced, but without date, in *Corr.* II, pp. 410–11.
51. Report of 8 Dec. 1887, *P.Po.* B a/75. Reclus was closely identified with the anti-militarist point of view, and at a meeting in 1892 the anarchist Denéchère is supposed to have said that Reclus would give 100 francs to any conscript desiring to escape across the border to avoid the exigencies of the military law. See police report of 13 Nov. 1892, *P.Po.* B a/77.
52. Reclus to Gross, 12 Jan. 1887, *Papiers Gross, Dépôt du CIRA*.
53. George Bernard Shaw said of Kropotkin: 'His only weakness was a habit of prophesying war within the next fortnight. And it came true in the end.' Quoted in George Woodcock and Ivan Avakumović, *The Anarchist Prince, Peter Kropotkin* (London, 1971), p. 225.
54. *Le Révolté*, 1–7 and 8–14 Jan. 1887; Woodcock and Avakumović, p. 225.
55. Reclus to Gross, 12 Jan. 1887, *Papiers Gross, Dépôt du CIRA*.

56. Reclus, *l'Idéal Anarchique*.

57. Reclus to the Congress of the Jura Federation, *L'Avant-Garde*, 12 Aug. 1878.

58. Reclus to Bakunin, 8 Feb. 1875, *Corr.* II, p. 169.

59. Bakunin to Reclus, 15 Feb. 1875 in Nettlau, 'Elisée Reclus and Michael Bakunin', p. 203 ff.

60. See reference in Reclus to Bakunin, 8 Feb. 1875, *Corr.* II, p. 169.

61. *BFJ*, 9 July 1876. Graveside speeches were also delivered by Schwitzguébel, Joukowsky, Guillaume, Carlo Salvioni, Brousse and a German workman called Betsien. After the Geneva Congress of 1873 Bakunin had decided to retire from the Jura Federation and to devote his attention to his memoirs. Reclus had encouraged him to write and had replied favourably to Bakunin's request to help polish up his literary style; see Reclus to Bakunin, 8 Feb. 1875, *Corr.* II, p. 168. Reclus published a section of Bakunin's manuscripts on the Paris Commune in *Le Travailleur*, April/May 1878, and in 1882 he and Cafiero published part of another manuscript, the most widely read of Bakunin's writings, which they entitled *Dieu et l'Etat*.

62. Reclus to the Congress of the Jura Federation, *L'Avant-Garde*, 12 Aug. 1878; cf. *Le Travailleur*, Jan./Feb. 1878.

63. Reclus to the Congress of the Jura Federation, *L'Avant-Garde*, 12 Aug. 1878.

64. *Encyclopaedia Britannica*, 1905.

# 8 REVOLUTIONARY STRATEGY

In the course of the 1870s ideological positions within the European socialist movement became sharply defined. During this process the anarchists became ever more isolated until they emerged as a distinct group with a fairly coherent philosophical outlook, but lacking a plan of action. The effectiveness of modern means of repression at the disposal of governments, as demonstrated in 1871, had placed severe limitations upon the value of the tradition of the barricades. The anarchists had also dismissed any possibility for political activity, Marxist or otherwise, within the framework of a parliamentary system. Anarchist theory did not, however, preclude some sort of activity which might accelerate the revolutionary process. The role of the revolutionary anarchist became, and remained, essentially that of informing and stimulating the people to action. From the perspective of the good bourgeois, however, anarchist propaganda became a weapon which overshadowed anything contained in the arsenal of the Marxists. The flexibility of the anarchist notion of propaganda allowed it to range from a chat with a fellow, to the writing of a newspaper article, to acts of violence against life and property. For Reclus, all forms of propaganda had their place, and all were scientifically valid.

The 1870s were a period in which anarchist theory was being formulated. It was also a time in which Reclus tended to be out of tune, and out of favour, with other anarchists. Much of the hostility directed against him can be traced to clashes of personality, but underlying these clashes were fundamental differences regarding the nature of revolution and revolutionary practice. While Kropotkin and Brousse emphasised revolutionary tradition and continued to place their hopes in imminent revolution, Reclus believed that the period following 1871 was a new stage in the revolutionary struggle. In 1878 he said that the way to anarchy would be very long; how long no one could tell.[1] In the early 1880s he continued to refer to the 'great revolution'[2] and to the 'next revolution',[3] but in accordance with his theory of evolution and revolution, such an event would represent one of an unknown number of future revolutions. Since the 1870s were a period of evolution, it was important that revolutionaries concentrate their efforts on helping the masses prepare

for the 'next' revolution. This preparation was basically emancipation
from prejudice, ignorance, and the past, and it constituted a process
which would loosen the emotional and intellectual supports of the
bourgeois system. It amounted to what we today would call consciousness-raising. The anarchist's role was perceived to be that of
providing propaganda. It is worth noting that, in the terms of the late
nineteenth century, propaganda did not carry the pejorative connotations which have come to be attached to it in the present century.
For Reclus propaganda was simply information, communication, the
'facts'.

The preparation which took place in a period of evolution, Reclus
reasoned, was crucial to the success of the revolution which would
follow upon it. In the 1870s, therefore, a time of evolution, he was
led to place an important emphasis upon education. In December 1876
the Vevey section of the Jura Federation inserted in the *Bulletin* a
circular concerning 'scientific socialist education'. Three questions
were presented for the sections of the Jura Federation to discuss:
(1) which existing textbooks might be recommended to friends and
sympathetic teachers, (2) which books might be selected from
among revolutionary socialist literature and which needed to be
produced at any price and (3) which measures had to be taken to assure
their children a truly scientific education outside all religious, national
and political influence.[4] The assumption underlying the proposal was
that the existing educational system promoted the values of the
bourgeois order, and therefore that that order could be challenged
through weakening the educational system. This is perfectly true,
and Reclus was shrewd enough to see the possibilities for revolutionary
activity through education at a time when his comrades were decidedly
unsympathetic to the idea. He believed that there were teachers in
the educational system who would be prepared, or who could be
persuaded, to use texts which were favourably disposed to the
revolutionary point of view. It is important to note, however, that he
did not see this as constituting an alternative indoctrination, but
rather as a way of liberating people from all indoctrination. In his view
socialist education would be *ipso facto* 'scientific'; it would present the
facts not through the eyes of the bourgeois, and not even through the
eyes of the revolutionaries, but as they really were. At least this was
the goal of science, as Reclus understood it.[5]

There was hardly any response to the circular on education put out
by the Vevey section. At first Kropotkin was rather enthusiastic, partly
because he hoped that the project would dovetail with his friend Robin's

plans to bring out a series of children's books.[6] He became impatient when he realised that Reclus was thinking along the lines of bringing out a third series of Guillaume's *Esquisses historiques* (Historical Sketches) and a collection of chansons.[7] His reply to Reclus came in the form of a letter from the section of La Chaux-de-Fonds — where he was active — which maintained that the education of children had to be subordinated to the struggle for the social revolution. In an open letter to La Chaux-de-Fonds in the *Bulletin* on 4 March 1877,[8] Vevey expressed its agreement, and went on to emphasise that its members were not under the illusion that an 'integral and rational' education — or 'scientific' education as opposed to bourgeois in-doctrination — could be given within the existing society. None the less, this did not mean that nothing at all could be done to establish more control over education. It was a question which Vevey was deter-mined to pursue because it was believed that education was an 'indispensable weapon in the battle which we have undertaken against the old society'. Vevey pointed to the excellent *Esquisses historiques*, and proposed that this work be used as a model for an elementary work in each particular 'science'. The second project in the pattern might be the *Esquisses géographiques*, the plan of which had already been sketched. The aims of the geography project would be to expose the laws regulating the planet, to study the species inhabiting it, the races 'which quarrel over it and whose common property it is'. It would represent a scientific argument in support of the universal brotherhood. The Vevey section responded favourably to the proposal of La Chaux-de-Fonds to publish a history of popular movements, but thought that for the moment it would be better to concentrate their efforts on a collection of songs and revolutionary poems which could be more easily put together.

Vevey's letter made it clear that lack of support was not going to deter Reclus from proceeding with plans. At their above-mentioned conferences on the Eastern Question on 3 and 4 March he and Joukowsky outlined plans for the publication of the third series of the *Esquisses historiques* and the proposed *Esquisses géographiques*, collected money to help towards the costs and aroused a certain amount of enthusiasm.[9] By 29 March Kropotkin, who had remained silent on the question of the *Esquisses historiques*, either because it was too late to do much about it or for fear of offending Guillaume, expressed irritation at the plan to bring out the geography project.[10] The work, he explained to Robin, would use up precious funds which could be more fruitfully spent on some sort of socialist review. Expressing fears

about the varied views of the Geneva group, he went on to complain
that a proposal to publish a socialist dictionary had been welcomed in
Geneva. Such a project, he said, should only be entrusted to people who
shared the same beliefs and who knew how to work. He suggested that
a social-economic résumé might be drawn up for use as a guide, but he
doubted that any precautionary measure would be effective against the
threat posed by the Genevans.[11]

In 1876 and 1877 there were substantial differences between Reclus
and Kropotkin, the two men who were to become the leading
theoreticians of the late nineteenth-century European anarchist movement. These were more than mere differences in temperament, and
went deeper than questions of judgement. The heart of the problem
was a serious divergence in their views concerning a scientific basis for
anarchism. Reclus was convinced that anarchism was the truth and
that science was the impartial judge which would pronounce it so
and suggest how it could be promoted. Therefore, it did not matter if
people of different political persuasions joined in the investigation
(although this might be trying at times),[12] for in the end the truth
would win out. Kropotkin had already engaged in fruitful scientific
endeavours in Siberia, but there was a distinct strain of anti-intellec-
tualism which surfaced in his personal relations with Reclus, and which
was to linger in his political writings. While Reclus was anxious to
explore the whole gamut of alternatives in search of the truth,
Kropotkin was convinced that it was already embodied in the policies
put forward by the Jura Federation and feared lest it be lost amid
the eclecticism of the Genevans. Kropotkin's anarchism, at least in
the 1870s, was a matter of faith, jealously guarded by the high priests
of the 'pure' anarchist party. Reclus' was also based upon faith, but
it would become the property of the entire world, once people had
become attached to the principles of science. He not only had faith
in the truth of his anarchism; he also had faith that science would
prove him right.

Reclus may have been willing to overlook the shortcomings of the
all-too-human Kropotkin, but he was bitterly disappointed at the
lack of support which led to the abandonment of his plans for the
*Esquisses historiques* and the *Esquisses géographiques*. His stinging
retort was contained in 'L'Avenir de nos enfants' (The Future of our
Children) which he wrote for *La Commune, Almanach Socialiste pour
1877*. The article commenced: 'Egoists that we are. In our vows of
revolution, it is rare that we think of others as we do ourselves. We
expose the griefs of the workers, especially those of the men, because

men are the strongest.' Socialists, he pleaded, 'think about the
future of our children still more than the amelioration of our situation.
Do not forget that we belong more to the world of the past than to the
future society.' The education of the existing generation, the old
ideas, the remains of prejudices had determined that anarchists were
still the enemies of their own cause. It was essential to save the
children from the evils of bourgeois education, to learn to teach them
so that they would develop 'in the most perfect physical and moral
health'. The task of revolutionaries was to strive towards the creation
of a free society by helping to create free individuals.[13]

These discussions on the role of education took place at about
the same time as the Jura movement was rapidly facing disintegration.
The anarchists' prospects in Switzerland were far from good, as police
harassment and the failure to establish a popular base encouraged
many of their number — Brousse and Costa, for example — to find an
outlet for their energies in some form of municipal or parliamentary
socialism. With no hope of a successful wide-ranging revolution, the
core which persisted generally restricted its activities to spreading the
word, mainly through the press and via addresses to the initiated. For
men whose aim was to foment universal social revolution, the scope
for action was exceedingly narrow, and in fact it looked as though
they might be reduced to a small band of impotent ideologues totally
out of touch with the demands of modern society and politics. As
early as 1875 Reclus had written to Bakunin about the very weak
spirit of cohesion among his fellow revolutionaries and their whims
rather than their will to see the struggle through.[14] He spent part of
the period from 1878 to 1879 in despondency over his own and his
companions' inability, or unwillingness, to establish an anarchist
movement. Frustrated by his own helplessness, he longed to suffer
for the cause and lavished praise upon those revolutionaries
struggling against Tsarist autocracy or languishing in Russian prisons.[15]
Even as he was beginning to lose hope, however, his fighting spirit was
re-asserting itself. His approach to revolutionary questions became
even more extreme, and we have an excellent record of his position
as it evolved in the next two years. It is contained within the proceedings of the last Congress of the Jura Federation which took place at
Lausanne on 4 June 1882.

Perhaps the most surprising statements which Reclus made at
Lausanne were within the context of the discussion on 'integral'
education. He warned his comrades that the necessary precondition
for such education was the abolition of property, that so long as

society was divided into classes, workers and employers, efforts to establish integral education would only be diversionary. Klementz asked whether it was wise to wait until the morrow of the revolution and suggested that anarchists take an interest in vocational education. For example, they might persuade the trade associations to agitate at the level of the commune for the establishment of facilities. Reclus became incensed, and insisted that it was absolutely wrong to have anything to do with the state or the commune, to ask anything of authority under whatever form. If the trade associations succeeded in convincing the communes to establish vocational education, the most intelligent pupils would be developed into 'little tyrants', good foremen who would become the enemies of workers and socialists. If socialists demanded anything of the state and the commune, they would wake up one day to find themselves Deputies.[16] The socialist's task was to demonstrate by propaganda 'all the evil sides of the society'.[17] At the informal gathering following the congress, he spoke again on the subject:

> It is only in a free society, based upon solidarity and economic equality with the most complete individual liberty, that one can obtain the real results of integral instruction, because . . . instruction, that is life, is the perpetual development of the individual from the physical and moral points of view . . . in a solidary and free society, which we shall only reach through revolution.[18]

In the 1870s Reclus had been interested in improving education, and he even thought that it might be possible to build up what would amount to a counter-educational system. His statements in 1882 were not in conflict with what he had said earlier, but they indicate that he was no longer interested in pursuing the question of education, even though other anarchists appeared to have become more sympathetic to the idea of working through the educational system. As the Jura movement declined, the last vestiges of his 'moderate' approach to revolution were abandoned. His emphasis in 1882 was upon revolt; significant changes in education could only take place in a society liberated from bourgeois control. In coming to this view he was influenced by Kropotkin. But his position was also a logical extension of what he had said in the late 1870s. Working within the bourgeois educational system, along with parliamentary politics and co-operativism, had come to be seen as a 'circuitous' route, to be avoided by anarchists as they struggled for the achievement of the just society. He was not to return to an emphasis upon education until the 1890s.

On the question of trade associations, the same logic was followed. Some members of the Federation pointed to the advantages of working within trade associations, and there was a feeling that anarchists might even help to organise them. Reclus retorted that it was not possible to create such organisations without catering to the often very narrow ideas and prejudices of the workers who would be involved in them. Socialists would necessarily have to become opportunists and run the risk of compromising their beliefs in return for the co-operation of the trade associations: 'We shall not be able to unfurl our socialist flag; we shall be obliged to work on a plane which is not ours.' On the other hand, he relented, revolutionaries might infiltrate the already established organisations with the intention of fighting against 'the old ways'. Within these groups it was necessary to agitate for the emancipation of the workers, not to concern themselves with the future of the corporation.[19] Reclus' arguments were forceful, and the Congress registered its approval by passing resolutions in support of his position on both education and trade associations.

> The Congress is of the opinion that without the abolition of private property and the State, its gendarme, agitation for integral education can only be illusory. The Congress, recognising the great usefulness of every workers' organisation insofar as it is an oppositional force, declares its solidarity with every strike and every struggle on the economic terrain.[20]

Reclus' energetic participation in the discussions at Lausanne in 1882 is rather surprising, in view of his customary|reluctance in the post-Commune period, to take a prominent role (for ideological reasons?) in public debate.[21] Behind his arguments one senses an urgency to clarify issues while the organisation remained more or less intact. It was at his instigation that it was decided to plan a further meeting of all interested socialist revolutionaries, to coincide with the international music festival to be held at Geneva in August of 1882.[22] This meeting, which was the last international gathering of anarchists to take place for many years, was held from 13 to 14 August, and was attended by the Jurassians, several Frenchmen and one delegate from Italy.[23] The manifesto which was drawn up emphasised the definitive separation: 'Between us anarchists and every political party, conservative or moderate, whether it fights against every liberty or grants it by doses, the scission is complete . . . ' The groups were to be absolutely autonomous 'in the means which will seem to them the most efficacious'.[24] At the Lyons trial of anarchists in January 1883, one of the defendants declared that Reclus had drafted this manifesto.[25] At a later date, Tscherkesoff made a similar statement, claiming that Reclus had composed the draft and that others (among them Dumartheray) had edited it.[26]

Socialist revolutionaries of all shades of opinion can usually agree on what they are against; there is also a fair amount of agreement on goals. The question which divides them most decisively is that of the means to be used to achieve these goals. For Reclus it threatened to become a particularly acute problem. In an effort to avoid 'circuitous' ways he had exhausted just about every possible avenue for agitation within the bourgeois order. And, as discussed in Chapter 2, he also refused to vacate that order for some anarchist 'colony' either in Europe or in the New World. He was not entirely cornered, however. He found a way whereby what he believed to be significant revolutionary activity could take place, without working within the system, but also without making an exit. This was through propaganda by the deed.

The notion of propaganda by the deed can be traced to some Italian anarchists in the 1870s. It began to gain recognition in anarchist circles in other parts of Europe after the famous Benevento affair of April 1877 when Cafiero and Malatesta provoked an uprising among the peasants of southern Italy in which tax records were burned and the deposition of Victor Emmanuel declared. The strategy was outlined by one of Malatesta's comrades who described how a small group of armed men could 'move about in the countryside as long as possible, preaching war, inciting to social brigandage, occupying the small communes and then leaving them after having performed there those revolutionary acts that were possible and advancing to those localities where our presence would be manifested most usefully'.[27] For some anarchists, propaganda by the deed came to be accepted as a suitable alternative to the word in educating the masses (especially when many were not able or had no time or desire to read), to stimulate them to action and to draw them into the movement.

In August 1877 an article entitled 'Propaganda by the Deed' appeared in the *Bulletin*. It was written by Brousse, with the support of Kropotkin. Traditional forms of propaganda, discussion and personal contact, it was explained, were inherently limited in their ability to reach the masses; these, it was argued, must henceforth be supplemented by deeds. The Paris Commune was offered as a powerful example of what ordinary people might achieve, by way of spreading the anarchist message, but even more modest performances, such as the demonstrations which were being held around that time at Berne, were thought immensely worthy of emulation.[28] Anarchist ideas had to be spread not only by speech and by the pen, Kropotkin insisted in 1879, but also and especially by action.[29] What precisely was meant by propaganda by the deed was not clear. It would have been well within anarchist principles to have provided a forum for the discussion of the moral and political implications of specific kinds of deeds which might be used as propaganda, and the failure to do so must be seen partly as a reflection of the existing state of anarchist revolutionary practice. Anarchists continued to think in terms of the uprising at Benevento; they did not foresee that propaganda by the deed might be used by individuals as a theoretical justification for acts of political terrorism, as was to happen in the years to come. There is some basis for arguing this case for the anarchists in general, but it is less satisfactorily applied to Reclus. Thus, as we shall see in Chapter 10, he reacted positively and with some enthusiasm to the terrorism of the early 1890s. The roots of his position can be traced back to the 1870s.

The shift in emphasis of the Russian revolutionary movement from the peaceful activities of the Narodniks (Populists) to the terrorism of Narodnaya Volya (People's Will) had an important impact upon Reclus. On 7 December 1878 he declared: 'In order to give birth to the new society of peace, joy and love, it is necessary that young people not be afraid to die.'[30] In July of the following year he wrote to Elie that the Russian nihilists were 'the salt of the earth. Their devotion to duty, their contempt of death, their spirit of solidarity, their tranquillity of soul amaze me, and I turn red when I compare myself to them.'[31] He had close contact with a number of Russian exiles in Switzerland, including Ralli, Joukowsky and Kropotkin, and he probably met the infamous Vera Zasúlitch who made her way to Switzerland in the spring of 1878.[32] He was also heartened by the actions of people such as Klementz who were encouraged by the struggle to return to Russia and who were prepared to suffer imprisonment for their beliefs. The Jura movement might be in decline, but at least there was a revolutionary spark, and it appeared all the stronger because it glowed in Russia, the darkest corner of the civilised world. In 1878, for the first time in almost a decade, Reclus made a statement which came out decisively in favour of force. If justice were the human ideal, anarchists would demand it for all, but if, however, it were true that only force governed society, then anarchists would use it against their enemies.[33]

Propaganda by the deed was officially recognised for the first time at the London (Black) International Congress of 14 to 20 July 1881, which even went so far as to advocate a study of the new technical and chemical sciences from the point of view of their revolutionary value.[34] However, there is some evidence to indicate that the anarchist programme reached at London may have been largely the work of a private meeting the year before. According to a police report, Reclus, Kropotkin and Pierre Martin were among the 32 'political agitators' who met at Vevey on 12 September 1880, just prior to the Congress of La Chaux-de-Fonds, for the purpose of discussing revolutionary tactics. A number of resolutions were drawn up, bearing a remarkable resemblance to those which were to be passed in London in 1881. In some places even the wording of both sets of resolutions are identical. According to the police report, the Vevey meeting called for:

1. Total destruction by force of existing institutions.

2. Necessity to make every possible effort to propagate by deeds the revolutionary idea and the spirit of revolt.

3. Departure from legality in order to carry out the action on the plane of illegality, which is the only way leading to revolution.

4. Since the technical and chemical sciences have already rendered services to the revolutionary cause, it is necessary to recommend to organisations and to individuals who make up the groups to give great weight to the study and the application of these sciences as a means of attack and defence.

5. The autonomy of the groups and individuals is accepted, but in order to maintain unity of action, each group has the right to correspond directly with other groups, and to facilitate these relations, a central bureau of international information will be created.[35]

This programme, as well as that of London the following year, declared all-out war upon the existing state, in particular singling out the deed as an effective means in the revolutionary struggle.

Unfortunately the above-mentioned police report is not dated, and the possibility exists that the whole affair was invented by a police agent after he had had access to the proceedings of the London Congress. There is a strong probability, however, that the report is valid and that the Vevey programme was adopted with minor modifications at London. Reclus did not travel to London, but as a member of the group around the new *Révolté* journal (launched by Kropotkin in 1879), he had signed a statement authorising Kropotkin as delegate.[36] There is nothing to indicate that he disagreed with the London resolutions. On the contrary, the record of his participation at the Lausanne Congress the following year shows that he supported them. The 1882 Congress of the Jura Federation may, in fact, be taken as confirming the conclusions reached at London. 'The Congress recognises the urgency of every means of action, the spoken and written word and the deed, [and] recommends that all comrades become zealously involved in an incessant propaganda, especially among our brothers, the peasants.'[37]

By 1882 propaganda by the deed was becoming identified with any act of revolt, even when the act was not performed consciously to elicit support for the anarchist cause.[38] On 24 March 1882 the young unemployed Fournier shot an employer whom he considered responsible for the crisis in the weaving industry at Roanne in France. From August of the same year there was extensive terrorist activity by the *Bande Noire* (Black Band) directed against the mine owners of Montceau-les-Mines in the Lyons areas. Fournier had not acted under the banner of anarchism, but none the less *Le Révolté* referred to his act as 'propaganda by the deed, the most fecund, the most popular'.[39] The terrorism of the *Bande Noire* was likewise considered an event of 'immense significance, and hence the consequences from the socialist-revolutionary point of view, are inestimable'.[40] There is little question that the root of such revolt was the unrest caused by a French economy which had been experiencing stagnation from 1873. The anarchists regarded the revolt as representing a desire for social justice among the masses and as an indication of the presence of a revolutionary spirit.

Despite the uneasiness which may well bave been experienced by some anarchists, the very nature of anarchist theory as the intellectual expression of the acts of the masses demanded accommodation to incidents of revolt. The Lyons trial of 1883 provides an important example of how anarchists played this role to the extent of becoming identified as instigators and justifiers of terrorism. It is not difficult to imagine how the Lyons authorities could conclude that the 'moral solidarity' provided by the anarchists was instrumental to, if not the root cause of, social revolt in their area. In any event, in an effort to bring terrorism under control, they arrested and brought to trial 65 anarchists, including such prominent figures as Kropotkin and Emile

Gautier, on the charge of alleged membership in an international organisation whose goal was the destruction of the bourgeois state.[41] Kropotkin did little to distinguish his position from that of the bombers when he declared: 'I have said that when a party is put in the position of having to use dynamite, it ought to use it, as, for example, in Russia where the people [as a force] would have disappeared, if they had not used the means put at their disposal by science.'[42]

Shortly after the Lyons trial a placard was posted up around Paris. It was signed by the *groupe parisien de propagande anarchiste* (Paris group of anarchist propaganda) and printed by the *Révolté* press, at that time under the supervision of Reclus who assumed responsibility for the paper when Kropotkin was sent to prison. 'Yes', the placard read, 'we are guilty of proceeding with the practice of our theories by all means, by the word, by the pen, BY THE DEED – that is to say by revolutionary acts whatever they may be.' With an anticipation of things to come, the text continued: 'Yes, we acknowledge them loudly. We claim them as ours. We glory in them.'[43] This placard represents a noticeable psychological adjustment to the implications of propaganda by the deed. In a word, some anarchists had turned from opportunistic approval to open acceptance and advocacy of terror. The rebel Kropotkin languished in prison, but the trial had brought him and the anarchists a good deal of notoriety. In keeping with the mood Reclus decided upon *Paroles d'un Révolté* (Words of a Rebel) as the title of a collection of Kropotkin's essays which he published in 1885.

Once Reclus had begun to consider the revolutionary implications of violent acts originating with the people, he also began to inject a more positive note into his theorising on the question of violence and revolutionary strategy. In a letter of 18 February 1883 he insisted that it was perfectly just to arm oneself in self-defence. So long as one acted within one's rights, a 'defence armed with a right' should not be equated with gratuitous violence.[44]

> If it is true, as I believe it is, that the product of a common work ought to be common property, it is not a call to violence to demand one's share. If it is true, as I believe it is, that no one has the right to deprive another man of his freedom, he who rebels is completely within his rights.[45]

Reclus saw that revolution would be violent, but maintained that the word 'violent', if pursued to its original meaning, really only meant 'strong'. The people had to put force at the service of justice and good-ness; it was a question of being strong.[46] Acts of social revolt were greeted with enthusiasm; they demonstrated the indefatigable energy of the human spirit and showed how revolution could be waged without resort to the bourgeois state. Governments had failed to check social evils and to impart justice, and this proved that 'free' men had to impose justice upon society.[47]

It was to be hoped, said Reclus, that the force necessary to over-throw bourgeois society would stop short of vengeance, for the cause of justice would not be served if one set of oppressors were replaced by another. Anarchists did not condemn people to destruction, however rich and powerful they might be. The institutions which produced such malevolent beings were the object of their attack.[48] None the less, he did not imagine that acts of vengeance could be eliminated, and he saw them as 'inevitable incidents of a period of violent changes . . . a fatal and necessary outcome' of unjust relations between people.[49] When the individual perceived that the governmental apparatus set up to demand his rights was in collusion with the bourgeoisie, would he not claim his ancient right to personal vengeance?

> In a word, if whole classes and populations are unfairly used, and have no hope of finding in the society to which they belong a redresser of abuses, is it not certain that they will resume their inherent right of vengeance and execute it without pity? Is not this indeed a law of Nature, a consequence of the physical law of shock and counter-shock? . . . Oppression has always been answered with violence.[50]

Explaining his view of revolution in June 1883, Reclus admitted that it would be made by those who had something to gain by it, but declared that he preferred to say: 'It will develop by the natural accommodation of men to their normal milieu.'[51]

In past revolutions, explained Reclus in *Evolution et Révolution*, people had groped towards a vague idea and not elaborated a definite aim. However, day by day they were becoming more conscious of the need to establish a society based upon justice.

> What the worker felt yesterday, he knows today, and each new experience teaches him to know it better. And are not the peasants, who cannot raise enough to keep body and soul together from their morsel of ground, and the yet more numerous class who do not

possess a clod of their own, are not all these beginning to comprehend that the soil ought to belong to the men who cultivate it?
They have always instinctively felt this, now they know it, and are
preparing to assert their claim in plain language.[52]

Instinct was giving way to consciousness of purpose, and it was
accompanied by a growing solidarity among the rebels. 'Isolated, the
rebels are doomed to death, but their example is not lost, and other
malcontents rise after them. They form a league and from defeat to
defeat, they finally arrive at victory.'[53] Revolutionaries, because of
their superior education, were able to formulate the ideas, but the
theories which they brought forward were based upon a study of the
deeds of the mass of the people.

> It is not they [the revolutionaries] who experience the joy of
> transforming ideas and passions into deeds. The Revolution is
> always made below. For those above there is a struggle between
> ideas and personal affinities; for those below, they are at one;
> there is where there is an immense superiority of force.[54]

Reclus' theories maintained that as a person reached a higher level
of development, the instinctual gave way to the conscious. Yet the
more conscious a person became, the farther removed he appeared to
be from the scene of the battle. Within the larger social context, the
revolutionary strategy was elaborated by the people as they struggled
to establish the just society. As a theoretician Reclus had to discover
what this strategy was, and to suggest how it might be improved. He
was an interpreter, a spectator. It was not his business to condemn
theft and violence, for example. His task was to show how they
fitted in with the people's revolutionary strategy.

Reclus' widely acknowledged fanaticism did not transform him into
a fire-eating radical, however. As an internationally renowned
geographer who was preoccupied with the coming of the universal
brotherhood, he appeared eccentric maybe, and even naive, but
hardly dangerous. To an extent, his scholarship provided a kind of
license denied to more ordinary comrades. For example, the French
authorities kept a close watch on his activities after 1872, but they
were reluctant to prosecute him without hard evidence. He was not
brought to trial at Lyons in 1883, even though he boldly declared that
he would co-operate in his own arrest[55] and in spite of the fact that
the prosecution considered that relations with him constituted evidence

against the accused.[56] Gautier declared at the proceedings that the
prosecution was afraid to arrest the famous geographer, lest not only
anarchists and radicals, but the whole of Europe rise up in protest.
Kropotkin was also a scholar, but at the same time an exile, persecuted
and foreign.[57] A similar reluctance to arrest Reclus was evident in 1894.
For his admirers, love and goodness and tolerance appeared to exude
from Reclus' very being. Even support of violence was attributed to an
over-abundance of goodness.[58] As he grew older, his reputation became
almost mythical, and was heightened by the flowing white hair and
beard of the sage. For anyone who cherishes this image there is
plenty of evidence to substantiate it. We have already noted the
generosity with which he responded in the late 1870s to his detractor
Brousse. Let us also look at the evidence for his subsequent relations
with Kropotkin, the man who had joined Brousse's pure anarchist
party.

At their first meeting in February 1877, Reclus had offered to introduce Kropotkin to the Swiss Geographical Society.[59] As noted above,
there quickly came to be little room for collaboration. As relations
improved, however, the two drew closer and Kropotkin was admitted
into the society on 13 January 1880.[60] At about this time Reclus invited
him to help prepare the sixth volume of *La Nouvelle Géographie
Universelle* which was devoted to a study of Siberia,[61] and Kropotkin
and his wife Sophie moved from Geneva to Clarens where Reclus had
been living from early 1879.[62] On 9 April Reclus wrote to the *Journal
de Genève* in support of his 'colleague and friend' whose lack of
official papers was causing the Genevan authorities some concern.
Kropotkin looked back kindly on his stay at Clarens and remarked that
it was in this period that he 'worked out the foundation of nearly all
that I wrote later on'.[63] After his expulsion from Switzerland in August
1881, Kropotkin went to live in Thonon in the vicinity of Lyons, but
his newly found friendship became even stronger.

In December 1882 Reclus hastened from Clarens to Thonon to be
at Kropotkin's side when he was arrested by the Lyons authorities.[64]
During the three years of Kropotkin's imprisonment, from 1883 to
1886, Reclus provided both moral and financial support.[65] When
*Le Révolté* began to suffer under the administration of a comrade
rather too fond of the nearby wine shop, he approached Jean Grave and
persuaded him to travel to Geneva.[66] Kropotkin wrote in his *Memoirs*:
'For the first year we had to rely entirely upon ourselves; but gradually
Elisée Reclus took a greater interest in the work, and finally gave more
life than ever to the paper after my arrest.'[67] Grave has left no doubt

that Reclus contributed money as well as interest. By the time Grave had arrived in Geneva, Reclus was paying for the printer as well as the comrade who had been in charge of the administration.[68] In addition to these expenses (since the latter continued in some capacity), he assured Grave of 80 francs every month.[69] The personal account book kept by Reclus from 1875[70] reveals that he was contributing to the support of *Le Révolté* from May 1879 and that he was paying out especially generous amounts – sometimes under the heading of Kropotkin, Herzig and Dumartheray, as well as that of *Le Révolté* – from the end of 1880. From the spring of 1883 contributions were entered into the book under these headings as well as those of Sophie, Grave and Clairvaux (where the anarchists condemned at the Lyons trial were imprisoned). The entries were usually made in sums of 100 francs, sometimes 200, but occasionally amounted to over 500 in one month; this pattern continued until about 1887.[71] (From time to time financial help was given to a number of other friends as well as to various relatives.)

Small wonder that in anarchist folklore Reclus and Kropotkin have emerged as close friends and allies in the struggle for a just society, and that the hostility directed by Kropotkin at Reclus has faded to insignificance. However, the severe strains which existed between them in the 1870s did not disappear. In the late 1880s, the Paris police were convinced that some sort of schism was about to take place. Kropotkin had been exiled from France after his release from Clairvaux in early 1886, and went to live in England. It seems that in late 1887, through the intercession of Sophie, he was attempting to impose some sort of discipline or at least direction upon the anarchist groups. The Paris police were highly imaginative in their speculations, but it is likely that the rumours which they picked up contained some truth. A police report of 8 December 1887[72] noted that Kropotkin was complaining about the state of stagnation of the groups, and some months earlier the imperious Sophie had travelled to Paris to set things in order. She was 'very irritated' with Grave who had monopolised *Le Révolté*; she was cool towards Elisée and considered Elie a bourgeois. The report suggests that Sophie wished to get *Le Révolté* more fully under the guidance of her husband and that she was encouraged and aided in this endeavour by Kropotkin's followers in the Paris groups. It was a struggle for the control of the paper which would give Kropotkin a mouthpiece in France. There was even some talk of bringing out a rival paper, and although 'the burning question' was that of money, its creation was considered possible.

For Kropotkin, England could never take the place of France, the land of revolution. He had helped Andreas Costa and Jules Guesde to create the first anarchist groups at Paris in the winter of 1877 to 1878,[73] and it is well known that he referred to *Le Révolté* as his 'child'. He seems to have taken it for granted that he would resume control over the paper when his stay at Clairvaux had come to an end. In April 1886, three months after his release from prison, he was contemplating the future of the paper and the energies which he would have to devote to it. 'For my child, the *Révolté*', he wrote to William Morris, 'I see with some anxiousness that we shall soon be compelled to make it appear weekly, and that I shall be bound to give it some two days, or more every week, instead of every fortnight.'[74] In the meantime, *Le Révolté* was under the administrative control of Jean Grave, whose temperament can be gathered from his nickname, 'the Pope of the rue Mouffetard' — the home of both *Le Révolté* and Grave. A shoemaker by trade, he occupied a place of some importance in the French anarchist movement, especially from 1885 when *Le Révolté* was transferred to Paris to avoid increasing harassment from the Swiss authorities.[75] Grave may have been attempting to assert his own position in September 1887 when he launched *La Révolte* to replace *Le Révolté*.

Something was happening in 1888 that upset Reclus, and his remarks on what he called the 'affair' at this time may have referred to an attempt either by Kropotkin or, more indirectly, by his followers to wrest *La Révolte* from Grave. 'The affair is disastrous', he wrote to Gross, '1. because it prevents us from spending our money usefully. 2. because it prohibits us from making recommendations in the future.' The letter, which is unpublished, but unfortunately has been edited, breaks off at this point and then continues: 'You tell me what has to be done. There will only be half an evil if good solidarity is maintained between comrades and if we recover from it better comrades and better friends.'[76] In any event, Kropotkin did not gain greater control over *La Révolte*, and became reconciled to working through the London-based anarchist journal *Freedom*, which he had helped to found in 1886. Understandably, Grave continued to be somewhat suspicious. When he was asked in late 1892 why Kropotkin no longer contributed articles, he replied: 'Because I corrected his articles 2 or 3 times. Should there be pontiffs here, yes of no?'[77] But Kropotkin's fiery soul succumbed somewhat more easily to Reclus who wrote the preface for his friend's *La Conquête du Pain* (The Conquest of Bread),[78] and read and corrected the proofs of the book.[79]

The strains between Kropotkin and Reclus were kept under control because of the latter's determined efforts to present a united front. Moreover, it became increasingly difficult for Kropotkin to adopt a hostile attitude. There was no one to fill the role of Brousse with whom he had allied himself in the 1870s, and even if there were, it would have been difficult to turn against one to whom he had become so heavily indebted. Furthermore, Kropotkin's years in prison had lost him some ground to Reclus, whose stature in anarchist and scholarly circles had grown steadily. For whatever reasons, solidarity won the day, despite those serious differences on revolutionary practice, science and war which we have already examined. As we shall see in the next two chapters, that solidarity also stood the test of the irreconcilable positions adopted by the two men on the question of theft, and the less obvious but important differences which arose over political terrorism.

Solidarity represented a peculiar type of influence which Reclus exercised over both Kropotkin and Grave. 'Pope' Grave could be decisively relieved of his infallibility with the mildest reprieve from Reclus. In 1891, for example, Grave was about to condemn the new syndicalist paper, *Le Pot à Colle*. Before pronouncing an order of excommunication against another paper, said Reclus, he would wait, or rather 'I would not make personal remarks against papers any more than against individuals.' The guiding principle was to take advantage of those articles which were good and to disregard the bad. 'Let us concern ourselves with our own affairs and let the others manage for themselves.'[80] There must have been many occasions on which Grave became exasperated by Reclus' axiom, 'We do not have to make ourselves the judges of anyone.'[81] This will become even more apparent in the next chapter. The point to remember is that Reclus set out to stress the common front; for a long time, he even avoided direct criticism of rival socialist theories. His mockery was reserved for the representatives of the bourgeois order.

To emphasise Reclus' natural goodness is to run the risk of denying the importance of the overwhelming evidence in support of him as a fighter. It might be suggested that there were two sides to the man, and that they existed in tension. I do not take this position. There were no schizophrenic tendencies within his personality. He was a fighter from the first to the last. 'I am a fighting cock', he once announced to a friend.[82] His personal behaviour was consciously regulated by the principle: solidarity against the enemy and a fight to the finish. Struggle and co-operation were complementary features of his social and political theory, and they also became complementary aspects of his personal behaviour. He chipped away at his character as a sculptor at a piece of marble. 'I still have my faults and my weaknesses, but I also have my sincere kindnesses, my high desires, my interior ideal. I am always working at the sculpture of the effigy of the hero which I dream of and which is the better me.'[83] An amazing example of the persistence of the human will, responding to the demands of an indefatigable conscience. The very essence of the revolutionary process. Since the individual was a microcosm of society, to change the individual was to contribute to the establishment of the new society. Solidarity was no blind sentiment; it was Reclus' revolutionary strategy. The theoretician, who interpreted the acts of the masses, was not, after all, removed from the scene of the battle. Or was he?

## Notes

1. *Le Travailleur*, Jan./Feb. 1878.
2. Reclus, *Evolution et Révolution* (1880), p. 25.
3. *Le Révolté*, 10 June 1882.
4. *BFJ*, 10 Dec. 1876.
5. See below, Part III.
6. Kropotkin to Robin, 11 Feb. 1877, *NA, IISG*.
7. Kropotkin to Robin, 27 Feb. 1877, *NA, IISG*.
8. *BFJ*, 4 Mar. 1877; the letter is addressed, according to the *BFJ*, to the Fédération ouvrière du district de Courtelary'. See *BFJ*, 11 Mar. 1877 where this error is acknowledged.
9. Guillaume expressed his thanks in the *Bulletin* on 11 Mar. 1877. The fund created by Reclus and Joukowsky would facilitate the publication of the third series of the *Esquisses historiques*, which had been interrupted because of difficulties with a Brussels publisher. Cf. James Guillaume, *L'Internationale Documents et Souvenirs (1864–1878)*, 4 vols. (Paris, 1905–10), vol. IV, pp. 148–9.
10. Kropotkin to Robin, 29 Mar. 1877, *NA, IISG*.
11. Ibid.
12. For example, Reclus' experience with *Le Travailleur* seems to have been at least partly responsible for his initial lack of enthusiasm for *Le Révolté*. He thought that Lefrançais was a good person to edit a paper, but found him an 'obstinate fellow'. Kropotkin to Robin, 18 Jan. 1879, *NA, IISG*.
13. Elisée Reclus, 'L'Avenir de nos enfants' in *La Commune, Almanach Socialiste pour 1877* (Geneva 1877).
14. Reclus to Bakunin, 17 Apr. 1875, *Correspondance*, 3 vols. (Paris, 1911–25), vol. II, p. 170.
15. Reclus was experiencing a period of reflection; see, for example, his letters in *Corr.* II, pp. 202–23.
16. *Le Révolté*, 10 June 1882.
17. *Le Révolté*, 24 June 1882.
18. *Le Révolté*, 8 July 1882.

19. *Le Révolté*, 24 June 1882.

20. *Le Révolté*, 24 June 1882.

21. Throughout the 1870s Reclus did not attend any congresses of the International, although he never ceased to show an interest in developments, and to pass along questions for discussion. At the 1875 Vevey Congress, the Vevey section was represented by two minor members, while Reclus remained 'among the people' and participated in the 'popular assembly' which Vevey had arranged to coincide with the Congress. Reclus was proposed as a delegate to the 1876 Berne Congress, but replied that 'pressing business' prevented him from undertaking the task and requested that his name be withdrawn (*BFJ*, 15 Oct. 1876). Although he had withdrawn his name, two sections voted for him; *séance du 19 octobre 1876, PV du CFJ, AEN*.

22. *Le Révolté*, 10 June 1882. All socialist revolutionaries were invited, those who were intending to make the trip and those who could be tempted to do so.

23. Among the French there were twelve delegates from Lyons, three from Saint-Etienne, three from Vienne, one from Villefranche, one from Bordeaux, one from Cette and two from Paris. Herzig to Kropotkin, 21 Aug. 1882, cited in *Procès des Anarchistes*, p. 129.

24. *Le Révolté*, 19 Aug. 1882. The last international congress of the anarchists for many years enthusiastically applauded the delegate from Cette who made the intriguing statement: 'We are united because we are divided.'

25. The statement was made by Jules Trenta on 9 Jan. 1883. *Le Temps*, 10 Jan. 1883; newspaper clippings in *P.Po.* B a/394.

26. Max Nettlau, *Elisée Reclus, Anarchist und Gelehrter* (Berlin, 1928), p. 221.

27. Quoted in James Joll, *The Anarchists* (London, 1964), p. 121.

28. 'La propagande par le fait' in *BFJ*, 5 Aug. 1877.

29. *Le Révolté*, 1 Nov. 1879.

30. Reclus to Mlle. de Gérando, 7 Dec. 1878, *Corr.* II, pp. 210–11.

31. Reclus to Elie, 20 July 1878, *Corr.* II, p. 214.

32. Kropotkin met Vera Zasúlitch in Geneva in the autumn of 1878. George Woodcock and Ivan Avakumović, *The Anarchist Prince, Peter Kropotkin* (London, 1971), p. 167.

33. Reclus to the Congress of the Jura Federation, *L'Avante-Garde*, 12 Aug. 1878.

34. At the London Congress there were 31 delegates representing 56 federations and 46 sections or groups without ties to federations. According to *La Révolution Sociale*, 24 July 1881, delegates came from Germany, America, England, Belgium, Egypt, Spain, France, Holland, Italy, Russia, Serbia, Switzerland and Turkey. For the proceedings of the Congress, see *Le Révolté*, 23 July 1881.

35. *AN* F7 12504.

36. The statement was signed by C. Thomachot, Dumartheray, Reclus and Charles Perron. Nettlau, *Elisée Reclus*, p. 218.

37. *Le Révolté*, 8 July 1882.

38. In Reclus' view, even enemies of the anarchists were engaged in making incessant propaganda on their behalf. See his *Anarchist*.

39. *Le Révolté*, 1 Apr. 1882.

40. *Le Révolté*, 2 Sept. 1882.

41. See *Procès des Anarchistes*.

42. Ibid., p. 29.

43. Police reports of 28 Jan. and 17 Feb. 1883, *P.Po.* B a/1502, contain copies of the placard. On 28 Oct. 1882, *Le Révolté* had published the placard of

the Justiciers du Peuple which advocated burning the furniture of property owners whose harshness singled them out.

44. Reclus to Heath, 18 Feb. 1883, *Corr.* II, p. 279.

45. Ibid.

46. Reclus to Heath, 10 Jan. 1885, *Fonds ER*, 14 AS 232, *IFHS.*

47. Reclus, *Anarchist*, p. 9.

48. Ibid., p. 14.

49. Ibid.

50. Ibid.

51. Reclus to De Gérando, 24 June 1883, *Corr.* II, p. 307.

52. Reclus, *Evolution et Révolution* (1884), pp. 9–10 (English from London 1885 edition). Cf. Reclus, *Anarchist*, p. 14.

53. *Le Révolté*, 21 Jan. 1882.

54. Reclus to De Gérando, 24 June 1883, *Corr.* II, p. 308.

55. Reclus to Rigot, 24 Dec. 1882, *Corr.* II, pp. 266–7. Cf. the police report of 28 Dec. 1882, *P.Po.* B a/1237. The letter was reproduced in *La Justice* and *L'Intransigeant* on 28 Dec. 1882.

56. For example, excerpts of letters from Reclus to Jean Ricard were read out in court. See the report of the proceedings of the trial on 9 Jan. in *Le Temps*, 10 Jan. 1883.

57. *Procès des Anarchistes*, p. 84.

58. See, for example, Jean Grave, *Quarante Ans de Propagande Anarchiste* (Paris, 1973; originally 1930), p. 223. Cf. Hamon, Dubois, Lombroso.

59. Kropotkin to Robin, 11 Feb. 1877, *NA, IISG.*

60. Marc Vuilleumier, 'Elisée Reclus et Genève' in *Musée de Genève*, Apr. 1971, p. 11.

61. In 1879 the Ukrainian Michael Dragomanoff, whom Reclus had met through the Geneva exiles, helped prepare the sections on Russia of vol. V. *La Nouvelle Géographie Universelle*, vol. V, p. 919.

62. Kropotkin, *Memoirs of a Revolutionist* (New York, 1971), p. 424; *La Nouvelle Géographie Universelle*, vol. VI, p. 918.

63. Kropotkin, *Memoirs*, p. 424.

64. Ibid., p. 450.

65. Ibid. See also correspondence Reclus to Kropotkin, in *Corr.* II, and *Fonds ER*, 14 AS 232. Kropotkin was sentenced to five years, but served only three.

66. Grave, *Quarante Ans*, pp. 194–5.

67. Kropotkin, *Memoirs*, p. 423.

68. Grave, *Quarante Ans*, p. 194.

69. Ibid., pp. 195 and 197.

70. *Fonds ER*, 14 AS 232, *IFHS.*

71. While the contributions continued in the late 1880s and the early 1890s, they decreased in frequency and in quantity. From 1887 there are records of large payments to Reclus' daughter Jeannie, who was left with three children when her husband Louis Cuisinier died that year. Payments were also made, but less frequently, to Reclus' daughter Magali and her husband Paul Régnier.

72. *P.Po.* B a/75 and B a/1237.

73. Kropotkin, *Memoirs*, pp. 406–7.

74. Kropotkin to Morris, 11 Apr. 1886, Morris Papers VIII, BM Add. MS. 45, 345.

75. For an account of the series of searches ordered by the government authorities, see J. Langhard, *Die Anarchistische Bewegung in der Schweiz* (Berlin, 1903), p. 148 ff.

76. Reclus to Gross, 17 Sept. 1888, *Fonds ER*, 14 AS 232, *IFHS*.
77. Police report of 12 Oct. 1892, *P.Po.* B a/77.
78. Peter Kropotkin, *La Conquête du Pain* (Paris, 1892).
79. See the correspondence of Reclus to Louise in *Papiers ER, NAF* 22912.
80. Reclus to Grave, 2 Nov. 1891, *Fonds ER*, 14 AS 232, *IFHS*.
81. Grave, *Quarante Ans*, p. 223.
82. Richard Heath, 'Elisée Reclus', *Humane Review*, Oct. 1905.
83. Reclus to Clara Mesnil, 25 Oct. 1904, *Corr.* III, p. 292.

# 9 PROPERTY AND THEFT

In Elisée Reclus' society of the future there would be communism in
production and distribution, and the principle of solidarity would
prevail. In the meantime, however, he perceived himself as a scientist
whose task was to uncover the laws of social-economic development.
As a revolutionary he attempted to make clear that what happened
historically was not necessarily in tune with nature, and that men and
women would best fulfil their potentialities as human beings by
challenging capitalism and establishing a communist society. But it
was not merely a question of a search for fulfilment. Capitalism was
pathological to human society. Allowed to proceed on its 'normal'
course, it would destroy achievements already attained, and reduce
the majority of people to slaves, before destroying itself. Reclus'
conclusions were decisive. The institution of private property was
the heart of the capitalist system, and since, he also reasoned, all
property was theft, to 'steal it back' was a revolutionary act. Among
the *Le Révolté* anarchists he and his nephew Paul stood almost alone
in their support of individuals who took possession of the 'common
property' from those who had 'wrongfully' appropriated it. His
position on property and theft flowed logically from his theories; he
could not, and would not, condemn the anarchist 'thief' short of denying
the validity of his own arguments.

The post-Commune years were, according to Reclus, a period in
which consciousness of oppression was increasing. In addition to
changing perceptions among those who were to make the revolution,
there was also an evolution in the objective fortunes of the
bourgeoisie. In 1875 he wrote to Bakunin of the 'normal' evolution
which was taking place in France. It was the bourgeoisie in its
'abstract state' which would reign, without religious trappings and
old symbols and would, therefore, so much the better reveal its true
value.[1] The Republic would survive in France under the form of
bourgeois domination, because there was no longer any need of an
instrument such as Napoleon.[2] The bourgeoisie had won their battle
with the aristocracy, though at the very moment of their triumph,
they also became more vulnerable, because they would no longer be
able to hide behind the traditional authority represented by the church
and aristocracy. Reclus could take heart even in the fact of bourgeois

domination, because the question between capital and labour was
becoming simplified.[3] The Vevey section of the Jura Federation sought
to emphasise this point, and in 1875 criticised those members of the
(federalist) International who were allowing the debate on the social
question to be diverted into a detailed and outdated discussion on the
evils of the clergy and aristocracy. Revolutionaries had a duty to
'acquaint all workers with the boldness of the bourgeois reaction'.[4]
The struggle to wrest social-economic power from the 'masters' was
what revolution was about; only after the destruction of the bourgeois
economy could people proceed to the construction of a society based
upon the principles of communism.

A hitherto neglected letter (or rather part of a letter), which can be
traced to the year 1887, provides a valuable insight into Reclus'
attitudes towards the relations between capital and labour. The letter
was apparently addressed to the Italian Oscar Bertoia and contains
Reclus' comments on a brochure written by Bertoia.[5] 'Your thesis',
wrote Reclus, 'is the following: The activity of workers under one or
several masters accustoms them to communism in production which is
followed by communism in consumption.' The thesis contained
serious flaws, he argued. Within a capitalist system industrial production
was a form of slavery, and as such could never lead in the opposite
direction, to freedom. While slavery might accustom workers to a
communal effort in production, the relationship collapsed as soon as
the fetters of the slave were loosened. Each freed slave took refuge
in his little garden, cultivated it and lived apart from his former comrades. (Was he thinking of the relationships between Negroes before
and after the American Civil War?) Large-scale industrial production
under capitalism did not promote association, but rendered it odious
and disrupted society itself. It exploited the possibilities for profit
within communal production and at the same time discouraged the
natural tendencies of people to want to co-operate. The bodies of
people were brought together, but their wills were broken. Under
capitalism the worker was brutalised both physically and morally
through the use of an excessive division of labour. How could poor
devils, occupied in a simple, mindless task, 14 hours a day, 320 days
a year, 40 years of their lives, slaves of the machine, be on their way
to 'libertarian communism'? The capitalists had succeeded in pushing
the principle of the division of labour to such an extreme that even
the scientists working in industry had been reduced to assembly-line
figures. Reclus personally knew one chemist who had been
employed to do the same scientific experiment for five years; there

were German scientists who worked alone all day, testing substances in a dark room. People who worked in industry performed mindless tasks, but worst of all they were also deprived of the knowledge of how their work fitted in with that of others.

Brutalisation was the inevitable consequence of capitalism, explained Reclus in his writings on social-economic development. As the capitalist became ever more subject to the mounting pressures of competition, he would be compelled to introduce new and more efficient machines. This would result in a continual simplifying of work procedures, as well as rising unemployment, which in turn would give the employer increasing power. He would be able to reduce salaries, sort out trouble-makers and employ the most docile. If the French worker thought too much, was too independent, he was replaced by a German. The German who ate too much might lose his position to a Chinese.[6] Nor were these developments restricted to the towns and cities. The cultivation of the earth was also being gradually transformed into an industry and day by day the old routines were being discarded and the 'method of chance' was yielding to scientific procedures.[7]

> By the normal development of economic laws, it is the fate of small property to be devoured by the large. The plots of soil owned by the peasant are destined to round off the large domains, in the same way as the small workshops are an inevitable prey for the powerful manufacturers and as the big financiers enrich themselves from the ruin of the petty speculators.[8]

For those who might be sceptical, Reclus pointed to the instances of large-scale agricultural exploitation in the United States, and to the proposals of the English to import American agricultural techniques.[9] Even the French peasant, the most tenacious of all, would not be able to hold out indefinitely.

> The peasant owner of a patch of ground may be in possession of what is left as is the artisan and the petit bourgeois. The moment is coming when it will be impossible for him to compete with the systematic exploiting of the soil by the capitalists and the machine, and that day there will no longer be anything left for him to do but to become a beggar.[10]

The laws which flowed inexorably from the processes inherent in capitalism led to competition both at the level of capital and at that of

labour. Among the capitalists there would develop increasing concen-
tration of economic power until it rested in the hands of a mighty few.
Among the workers there would arise the great hordes scrambling for
the crumbs which the mighty deigned to distribute to them. The
peasants and factory workers would share the same fate, 'working
when the employers are interested in giving it to them, always obliged
to lie under a thousand forms, soon humbly asking to be hired, soon
even extending their hands to beg a miserly pitance'.[11] To allow
capitalism to develop in accordance with the laws which governed
it would be to participate in the establishment of a world in which
the many would have become enslaved to the few. Ultimately, the
very success of capitalism would be its own demise, for the laws
governing its continuing expansion doomed it to collapse. Efforts to
increase production and to keep the work force to a minimum would
lead to mass unemployment and an inability to sell products.[12] But,
as we shall see shortly, simply to wait for the end would prove suicidal
for the workers and for society as a whole.

That Reclus was in general agreement with the arguments of *Das
Kapital* is clear, and there is little doubt that he was deeply influenced
by them. Before 1871, as noted above, his relations with Marx were
good, and it was in this period that he became familiar with Marx's
ideas. While both men were intent on presenting their views
'scientifically', Reclus was the less concerned about injecting a moralistic
tone into his work (that is not to say that Marx was not moralistic), and
he seems to have done so deliberately. He wrote of the capitalist's greed
and the miseries of the masses, and equated capitalism with injustice
and communism with justice. His religious roots are evident in such
statements as the following made in 1884. ' . . . One capital fact
dominates the history of man – that every kindred and people yearns
after justice. The very life of humanity is but one long cry for that
fraternal equity which still remains unattained.'[13] He pointed to the
injustices of a capitalist system which allowed those with ready money,
or those with more intelligence or cunning or luck, to control the lives
of honest men.[14]

Marxian economics were based upon the British experience. In
France, the land of peasants, Reclus' interest was understandably
focused upon the significance of capitalism for agriculture, and his
contribution to the debate on the economy came in the form of an
emphasis upon capitalist development in the countryside. His early
years in the Gironde and the Lower Pyrenees had made him particularly sensitive to the problems involved in extending democracy to

traditional rural France. In 1866 he had expressed a concern about the
political views of the peasants, their strong identification with the
Napoleonic regime and their lack of participation within the newly
emerging workers' movement. In that year he and Champseix were
the two founders of the Sunday paper, *L'Agriculteur*, which sought
to attract the interest of the peasants by appealing to them in terms
which they could readily understand.[15] At a General Council meeting
of the IWMA at London in July 1869, Reclus stated that the French
peasants knew very little about world developments. Not only did
they not attend the IWMA congresses; they did not even know that
they were held.[16] In the elections of February 1871, it will be noted,
he chose to offer himself as a candidate in the Lower Pyrenees, and
he engaged in Republican propaganda there and in the Gironde before
his return to Paris.[17]

Reclus believed that it was a serious mistake for revolutionaries to
single out urban workers as *the* agent of revolution. Far from being
shielded from the laws of capitalist development, he argued, peasants
too would eventually succumb to them. But the hope for the future
of humankind lay in this very defeat, because, in the struggle for
survival against the threat of capitalism, the traditional isolation of
the peasant would give way to solidarity. Agricultural associations
formed for the purpose of defence would compel the peasants to
adopt progressive attitudes and new institutions. This development he
perceived to have already begun to take place in England. There was
hardly ever a word said about this subject at the meetings of the
revolutionaries, he complained in 1873, but 'this association of the
workers of the land is perhaps the greatest development of the
century'.[18] Peasants and factory workers together comprised the
'true proletarians'.[19] With the expansion of capitalism all workers,
whether their workplace was the field or the factory, were, or were
becoming, dependent for their work upon the 'goodwill of a master'.[20]

With some dismay, Reclus saw that revolutionaries, through their
dogmatic concern for the urban proletariat, and their consequent
neglect of the peasants, were playing into the hands of the capitalists
who counted on what they believed to be the undying hatred between
peasant and factory worker to safeguard their own power and
money.[21] The peasants, too, had to be drawn into the movement
for communism. Henceforth, as all workers struggled to gain control
of the means of production (the land and the factory), they would
recognise that they had a common enemy, and that their interests,
far from being in opposition, were identical.[22] His conception of the

'people' was that of the disinherited, or those about to be disinherited, in both field and factory. Like Marx, he felt that the petits bourgeois were also bound to disappear and that most of them would become members of the working class. He might have used his arguments on the inexorable processes within capitalism to support an appeal to the petits bourgeois. However, he feared that too deep an involvement with the vociferous and politically active craftsmen and shopkeepers might lead to the development of a revolutionary programme based upon the needs of the petits bourgeois rather than upon those of humankind.

The 'people' signified factory workers and peasants, but it is difficult not to conclude that, for Reclus, the mention of people conjured up images of peasants and of his own early experiences among them. 'It is absolutely necessary to join the people; we ought to make use of the examples of the Russian youth.'[23] He wrote two pamphlets specifically designed to stimulate ideas about and among the peasants; *Ouvrier, prends la machine, Prends la terre, paysan!* (1880) (Worker, take the machine! Take the land, peasant!) and the popular *A mon Frère, le paysan* (1893) (To my Brother, the peasant). It was not the aim of the socialist, he said, to take the land out of the hands of the peasant who had cultivated it so lovingly, but, on the contrary, to ensure that he would maintain, or re-acquire, control over it. The socialist was presented as an elder brother, attempting to protect the interests of the peasants by driving out the large landowner who enriched himself by exploiting the labour of others.

> Thus we shall take the land, yes, we shall take it, but away from those who hold it without working it, in order to return it to those who do work it . . . That which you cultivate, my brother, is yours, and we shall help you keep it by all means in our power; but that which you do not cultivate belongs to a comrade. Make room for him.[24]

The peasant was warned of the cunning of his common enemy, the seigneur (read capitalist) and the state, and he was advised that he would gain a great advantage in warding off the enemy by living in common with his neighbours, as was practised in the Zadrougas or 'group of friends', in the *mir* (commune) or little 'universe' as in Russia. Under such a system, there would be no need to divide the collective property into innumerable little plots of land, nor would it be necessary to drive the cows into different enclosures in the evening. Everyone would work together, happy to be in peace with his brothers, and in times of emergency each would come to the aid of the other.[25] 'The commune is, at the same time, the property of all and of each.'[26]

Capitalist production by its very nature divided people; it could not bring them together. 'It is only through liberty that we achieve liberty', Reclus explained to Bertoia.[27] However, there was no turning round for humankind; 'Whether we wish it or not, we shall pass through the rolling-mill of [capitalist] large-scale industry.' But to know the future was not to submit to it; 'Alas, yes, but we shall rebel.'[28] Capitalism — according to the laws governing its expansion — was destined to extinction. But to await its end was not only to prolong suffering under its evils; it was to commit mental suicide by enslavement, for the capitalist process tended to destroy people morally and intellectually, making them unfit to attain or even to accommodate themselves to a liberated society. By attacking the social-economic system, people would hasten its fall and at the same time keep alive the spirit of revolt without which there could be no progress in the direction of freedom. As he explained in a colourful passage elsewhere:

> For if capital retains force on its side, we shall all be the slaves of its machinery, mere cartilages connecting iron cogs with steel and iron shafts. If new spoils, managed by partners only responsible to their cash books, are ceaselessly added to the savings already amassed in bankers' coffers, then it will be vain to cry for pity, no one will hear your complaints. The tiger may renounce his victim, but bankers' books pronounce judgments without appeal. From the terrible mechanism whose merciless work is recorded in the figures on its silent pages, men and nations come forth ground to powder. If capital carries the day, it will be time to weep for our golden age; in that hour we may look behind us and see like a dying light, love and joy and hope — all the earth had held of sweet and good. Humanity will have ceased to live.[29]

Whatever the outcome in the struggle between capital and labour, the scientific method would be applied in industrial and agricultural production. And the scientific method, by its very nature, led inevitably to the disappearance of individual workers and the emergence of groups of workers. The question was whether they would come together under the cudgel of a master, or whether they would associate freely to produce a common work.[30] The more deeply committed Reclus became to science and the scientific method, the more closely he tied progress to scientific achievement. With his political interest in the peasants and his professional interest in geography, he became quite keen to explore the possibilities for the application of science to agriculture. In 1873, for example, he was already suggesting how the combined efforts of scientists might work wonders on a river basin. The geographer and the meteorologist might provide information on probable temperatures and barometric pressures. The geologist and the chemist might together work out the most favourable mixture of soil, while the hydrologist might suggest effective approaches to irrigation. The engineer would be responsible for building canals, bridges and whatever other machines were thought necessary. The agronomists would take care of the soil, the sowing and the planting. It would also be necessary to obtain the services of the statistician, the economist and the industrialists in charge of transport, in order to ensure that production and consumption patterns were in harmony and in the best interests of society.[31] (An updated Saint-Simon?)

Unlike Proudhon, who lamented the demise of the small proprietor and whose theories were designed to create a world in which he would survive, Reclus marched confidently into a future in which the small proprietor would have no place. He declared that for certain types of production the labour of the isolated individual became absurd in comparison with the work of the machine, and advocated the replacement of the single artisan by a group of comrades who would work in friendly co-operation, taking advantage of the assistance provided by the machine and the latest scientific methods.[32] Through machines people would learn to subdue nature and to solve the age-old problem of scarce resources. 'It is very pleasing that one man, employed at the service of the machines can provide enough products for a hundred other persons.'[33] It was in the best interests of society, he said, 'to develop indefinitely the power of humanity through machines, and thus to augment in increasing proportion the resources which humanity possesses'.[34] Twentieth-century science is frequently associated with a technology which has taken on a momentum of its own, and which is almost beyond the reach of people. Reclus would have insisted that science has possibilities for good and evil, and that science in itself is nothing, that its 'power' is derived from the will of the people who control it. I do not believe that he would have changed his mind, had he been able to foresee the atrocities committed in our own day by means of, or in the name of, science.

Capitalism threatened to destroy humankind, but it also provided the groundwork for the establishment of the universal brotherhood. All potential victims would have to co-operate in order to survive, and through co-operative efforts would develop resources within themselves which would change their nature and hence re-direct the course of history. With the destruction of capitalism and the success of communism, bourgeois competition would be replaced by co-operation as the dominant social value. Aggression (but not acts of self-defence) would become less and less acceptable. Greed would steadily decline. The principle of solidarity would ensure that needs would be satisfied within the context of a consideration of the needs of all and society's capacity to provide. Reclus did not discuss the nature of work in a communist society, but the logic of his arguments would support a reduction in the work day, making unemployment a thing of the past. Division of labour would persist, and it would have been helpful, had he elaborated his views on this. Again we may allow ourselves the liberty of drawing inferences. In contrast to a capitalist society where goods are made for profit, not for people, a communist society would not unmercifully exploit the principle of division of labour. Moreover, with the reduced working day, each individual would have to contribute a lesser amount of time and energy to monotonous activity. In a society in which the individual was consciously working for the good of all and in which his contribution to the final product was not being appropriated by a particular class, it would be less oppressive, and perhaps even rewarding, to submit to the necessary monotony. Finally, with the continuing improvement in machinery, there would be less and less necessary labour time; theoretically, it would eventually disappear altogether!

Reclus never made it clear whether classes would be 'abolished' in the communist society, as Marx claimed, or whether, as Bakunin contended, they would be 'equalised'. The evidence suggests that he tended towards Bakunin's position. At the 1868 Congress of the League of Peace and Freedom, he and Bakunin supported 'as ideal "the equalisation of classes and individuals," understanding by that equality as the point of departure for all, in order that each person might follow his career without hindrance'.[35] For Reclus, revolution would doubtlessly abolish those classes deriving out of bourgeois society, but I do not believe that he objected to the rise of non-exploitative classes. Individuals of similar temperaments and attributes would perform certain social functions within a communist society, and would come to be distinguished as a 'natural' group. The aim of

revolution was not to make everyone the same, but to make all people
equal, to confer equal status upon, and provide equal rewards (non-
monetary, of course) for, all contributors to the common product.
While Kropotkin (and to an extent Marx) was intrigued by the notion
that the working day should be divided into so much physical and
mental labour, Reclus was more eager to assure each person the
absolute liberty to decide the nature of his own working day. So long
as there was no prejudice in favour of particular tasks, and so long
as each considered the well-being of all, there was no reason why an
individual should not make his contribution in any way he pleased.
Reclus did not feel, as Kropotkin did, that there was any special
virtue in manual labour. To each his own. 'Fundamentally', he wrote,
'anarchy is nothing but perfect tolerance, the absolute acknowledgement of the liberty of others.'[36]

Late nineteenth-century European anarchists employed the term
anarchist communism to refer to the principles of the future society
which they wished to establish. Etymologically, the term is redundant.
Communism in production and distribution would necessarily have to
constitute a society that was anarchist, that is a society 'without
masters'; the same held true in reverse. Reclus said that an anarchist
was necessarily a communist;[37] he might also have said that a
communist was necessarily an anarchist. In spite of the awkwardness
of 'anarchist communism', Reclus and Kropotkin considered it important, for practical considerations, to extend their seal of approval.
'Anarchist' was needed to avoid confusion with those varieties of
communism which had developed authoritarian structures, and
'communism' helped to remind those who would pay heed that the
people branded as anarchists were out to destroy the bourgeois social-
economic system. Reclus and Kropotkin were striving for the establishment of a society in which the social-economic system was communist,
in which the dominant social value was co-operation, and in which
government structures would arise and be controlled from below. The
bourgeois state, with its artificial boundaries and its complex of
bourgeois social-economic and political relations, would have entirely
disappeared.

It is easy to see why Reclus could never accept Proudhon's mutualist
position which advocated individual production and consumption and
which enhanced rather than abolished private property. According to
Proudhon's theories, mutualist society would develop out of a system
of national credit set up to enable small property-owners and workers
to free themselves from the shackles of debt and the wage system, and

to pursue their various careers as independent landowners and crafts-men in a spirit of justice and equality. Mutualism never promised to make any fundamental changes in the existing social-economic structure. It would rather re-order it, so that each individual would be given a 'fair' share. But Proudhon's 'anarchy' would not have abolished the market, merely the existing form of government. It was the market and private property which Reclus aimed to destroy, along with the government which policed it. That is why he so vehemently, and to the applause of the collectivists, attacked the views of the mutualist Charles Beslay at a meeting at Vevey in 1875, [38] and why in 1877 he insisted that the destruction of government would not necessarily destroy the bourgeois social-economic system.[39] There is some justification for holding that Proudhon's ideas bear a relation to liberalism; it is largely because these ideas have been confused with those of the anarchist movement that the theory represented by Reclus and Kropotkin has also been judged − unjustifiably − to be closely related to *laissez-faire* liberalism.

Like most socialists Reclus seized upon private property as the basis of the capitalist system, and insisted that the abolition of the one represented the abolition of the other. In 1875 he said that private property had come about as the result of robbery and exploitation, that justice and liberty could only be achieved through the collectivisation of property.[40] His 1880 arguments in support of communist distribution were based upon the view that the products of labour were the result of the collective effort of people in the past and in the present. No one worked alone, nor was it possible to isolate parts of the common work. It followed that all goods belonged to all people and that it was wrong (immoral!) for an individual (or group of individuals) to appropriate that which belonged to all. Property was theft, he agreed with Proudhon, but, in contrast to Proudhon, he did not restrict the label to that portion of the wealth which the capitalist claimed. Absolutely all forms of property were considered as theft; to claim ownership of any amount of goods or money was to become a 'thief'. From this perspective, there was little difference between work within the context of bourgeois society and what the law termed as theft, because both activities resulted in the appropriation of wealth. Furthermore, Reclus insisted, to recover extra-legally the 'stolen' goods was perfectly just. To Kropotkin and Grave this was an astonishing position to take, and for once, there was no room for reconciling the differences. This became particularly clear in the late 1880s, in the discussion which arose over the question of *la reprise individuelle* or individual recovery of the products of labour.

This question began to assume importance in early 1887 when Clément Duval, a member of the anarchist group entitled *La Panthère des Batignolles* (The Panther of the Batignolles), appeared before the Assize Court of the Seine on the charges of stealing jewellery and injuring a policeman. On 24 October 1886, a few days after the robbery had been committed, Duval had written to *Le Révolté*, explaining the circumstances behind an earlier theft for which he had been condemned to one year in prison. The letter and his statements at the trial in 1887 revealed that Duval considered theft to be no more than the restitution of the products of labour which had been produced by the collectivity and appropriated by the few. He became a hero in many anarchist circles and went off bravely to serve his sentence of twenty years hard labour. There was definitely some uneasiness among the *Le Révolté* anarchists. In 1885 the paper had claimed that there was little difference between a bourgeois and a thief who 'is not a rebel, nor even a victim', but only 'the product of society'.[41] It published Duval's 1886 letter without, however, compromising the paper. After Duval had vehemently presented himself in court as an anarchist of some conscience, *Le Révolté* was carried along with the enthusiasm in many anarchist circles, and gave its support to Duval, even if with a degree of ambiguity.[42] Reclus' personal approach to the question raised by Duval was sympathetic from the beginning.

Because there was no reason to doubt the man's sincerity, he said in 1887 to a sceptical friend, there was no choice but to take Duval at his word. In that case, as far as the facts were concerned, it had been known in advance that, in an abandoned house, there was a useless fortune which might be put to good use to feed the poor. Duval had, therefore, taken the money, even reproaching a companion who had been unnecessarily destructive, and later when he had been attacked by a policeman, he defended himself. 'Knowing, especially in a practical way, that property is collective, he took his part of it, not for himself alone but for others, and he defended his right as a man when he was attacked.' How, he asked, did this action differ from the deeds of those traditionally beloved redressers of wrongs who took from the rich and gave to the poor? An individual who took property stolen from the people by the few did right, if he acted in a spirit of justice and solidarity. While he himself adopted a different course of action, by nature, habit and personal tendency, he did not have the right to expect others to follow that particular pattern of behaviour.[43] A few years later he advised Grave to revise views concerning theft in an article written under the 'prejudice of the state'. Otherwise, he would be attacking 'our friends the nihilists of Kharkof' and reducing to 'smugglers' those whom Proudhon had said accomplished 'not only a right, but even a duty'.[44]

In 1889 the case of the militant anarchist Pini brought the discussion to a crisis in anarchist circles. Pini, an Italian who had founded the group *Intransigenti* (Intransigents) at Paris two years earlier, carried out a number of thefts there and in the countryside. *La Révolte* described him as a man of 'very few needs, living simply, even in poverty and with austerity', who stole 'for propaganda'.[45] Grave's misgivings were growing, however, and his position became hardened in relation to that of Reclus who relentlessly pursued the anarchist right to 'theft'.

In a letter of 19 August 1889, almost certainly written to Grave, Reclus followed the implacable logic of his theories.

1. Does the collectivity of workers have the right of recovery over the products of its work? Yes, a thousand times yes. This recovery is the revolution and without it everything is to be done.

2. Does a part of the workers have the right to partial recovery of the collective products? Without any doubt. When the revolution cannot be made in its entirety, one makes it at least so far as one is able.

3. Does the isolated individual have the right to a personal recovery of his part of the collective property? How can it be doubted? Since the collective property is appropriated by a few, why would he acknowledge this property in detail, when he does not recognise it in toto? He has the absolute right, therefore, to take – to steal, one says in common language. – It is very necessary that the new moral develop in this respect, that it enter into the spirits and into the mores.[46]

These were the truths which should guide anarchists in judging the worth of revolutionary acts. It was impossible to formulate rules to cover all cases, as religion and authority had attempted. As far as the individual was concerned, there was no law except the counsel of his own conscience, and the morality of an act was determined by the extent to which the individual had followed this guide. While it was true that the consequences led one to form opinions, Pini's case 'does

not prejudice anything, neither for nor against'. If this 'thief' was in
effect a 'redresser of wrongs', a man who sought justice, who rendered
to labour that which belonged to it, who had ridden himself of former
prejudices to make his 'little revolution' within the measure of his
'little power . . . we ought sincerely to commend him and to comprehend the great example that he gives us'. If, on the other hand, he was
a simple 'exploiter of the work of others', and if he lowered himself
on account of pride and sloth to pretending to defend the rights of
work, he would be recognised for what he was; his boastings would
never save him from the scorn of his comrades.

Reclus had settled in Switzerland as an exiled communard, but
though he was amnestied in 1879 he remained there until the autumn
of 1890, when he returned to France. He stayed for a short while
with his widowed daughter Jeannie at Nanterre, spent much of the
following year travelling, and in the autumn of 1891 settled at Sevres.
It was at this time that Grave, serving a six months sentence at
Sainte-Pélagie for press offences, left the administration of *La Révolte*
in the hands of Reclus' nephew Paul. A controversial article 'Travail
et Vol' (Work and Theft) written by Paul was published in the 21–27
November issue. 'I protest against this pretence that there is an honest
means of earning a livelihood, work, and a dishonest one, theft or
swindle . . . ' When Grave complained, Elisée replied that the article
was one of two which were intended as food for thought. While he
understood Grave's agitation, he did not share it. It was not a bad
thing to be reminded that they themselves, 'moralists and moralisers',
also lived from 'theft and pillage' and that personally 'we all have to
cleanse ourselves'. He himself regarded these observations not as an
insult, but as a subject for meditation. 'In the society of injustice and
caprice in which we live, we are, in spite of ourselves, supportive of all
the evil which occurs . . . '[47] It was guilt by association, and Reclus was
quite prepared to include himself. 'Thieves, we are all thieves', he wrote
to the perplexed Grave, 'and I am the worst, working for an editor and
striving to obtain a salary that is ten times, twenty times the ordinary
pay of an honest man. Everything is theft.'

In an attempt to make his position clear, Reclus sent to Grave a
short article which he was asking Paul to publish in *La Révolte*.[48]
In the article Reclus thanked the author of 'Travail et Vol' for his
remarks and strongly supported them. It was true, he said, that they
lived in a society in which everything was based upon inequality and
monopoly and in which money alone bought bread. According to the
prevailing social-economic conditions, therefore, all people without

exception were obliged to live from thievery. 'Like the raging wolves we argue about the daily pitance at the expense of the weakest. Each morsel of bread which we eat is snatched from other poor people and carries a stain of blood.' The important point was that it was outside this frightful social state that they were orienting their lives, and in accounting for the miseries and shame to which an individual might be reduced, they were searching above all to shorten this hideous period of 'mess' and corruption which preceded the advent of a harmonious society. What was generally referred to as theft had always taken place, but a different attitude now accompanied the act. The thieves had come to see that they had a right to the booty. For Reclus, they had become rebels of a higher order. It was one further step in the progress towards the creation of a society where all robbery — the legal and the extra-legal — would come to an end, where no person would be forced to degrade himself in order to obtain his daily bread.

Grave was not alone in objecting to Paul's article. Kropotkin also sent Elisée a letter putting forth objections similar to those of Grave and promising an article on the question.[49] Kropotkin's article, 'Encore la Morale' (Morals Again), which appeared in three parts in December 1891,[50] showed that he was unable — or not prepared — to consider theft in terms other than in those in which it was viewed by the mass of society. The people did not understand theft in the name of equality, deceit in the name of liberty and distribution of stolen money to the wretched in the name of solidarity. Such 'jokes' might find listeners in the anarchist groups, but the people had too much good sense to follow these 'digressions'. Theft, deceit and lies were characteristic of the bourgeois society, and revolution would not be brought about through perpetuating existing evils. Kropotkin's advice concerning the guide to action was the well-known dictum which he preached in his pamphlet *Anarchist Morality*: 'Treat others as you would like them to treat you under similar circumstances.'[51] According to this principle, theft would be wrong, whatever the motives of the individual. It was admitted that under unusual circumstances, there were strong arguments in favour of abandoning the principle — for example, in the cases of Sophie Perovskaya and her comrades who killed the Tzar and those Russian terrorists who had to steal from the rich in order to survive. However, and Kropotkin was most emphatic on this point, 'if such an act is to produce a deep impression upon men's minds, *the right must be conquered*, (Kropotkin's emphasis).[52] This statement meant that those who would practice retribution must be so pure of heart as to leave no doubt about the morality of the deed.

It was almost as if, for Kropotkin, the final judge of morality was the people. Reclus, on the other hand, would have maintained that the individual had to follow his conscience. In contrast to Kropotkin he would have said something like the following: 'Treat others as you would like them to treat you under similar circumstances, unless they are your enemies, whom you should always attack.' He conformed to the pre-Christian maxim of 'an eye for an eye, a tooth for a tooth', and saw it as representing legitimate personal and collective defence. To the charge that this was a primitive way of proceeding, Reclus would have replied that the only thing which was primitive about the maxim was the way in which primitives practised it. Primitives generally allowed a legitimate right of defence to descend to acts of vengeance which a more conscious (more highly developed) person avoided.[53] When Reclus responded with kindness to the hostility of such people as Brousse and Kropotkin, he was not 'turning the other cheek'. Brousse and Kropotkin were not the enemy, in spite of how they might act; the real enemy was the bourgeoisie.

Grave shared Kropotkin's views on theft and never did understand the position taken by Reclus whom he preferred to see as an overly tolerant, impractical visionary who could find plenty of excuses for thieves.[54] He also tended to shift the blame for the disagreements to Paul, about whom he expressed serious misgivings, in particular Paul's alleged adoption of the position 'to understand is to pardon'.[55] When Grave appealed from Sainte-Pélagie, Reclus replied that, of course, the position was of an 'unseasonable naivety', but that Paul's article made a contribution to the on-going discussion.[56] Grave refused to accept the full import of Reclus' own views on theft, for he pleaded with him to take over responsibility for the paper, an invitation which was categorically refused; 'With the comings and goings, the hitches, the shortages of money, that is to ask me completely to change my style of life and my work. That appears to me to be chimerical. I cannot do it.'[57] In contrast to those anarchists who openly advocated theft,[58] Reclus was simply urging Grave to open up the columns of *La Révolte* to a discussion of the different sides of the question, but Grave insisted that this would be tantamount to condoning the practice. The few thieves (property-owners), he believed, would be joined by an increasing number, making it more difficult to bring about a trans-formation of society.[59] Reclus wrote to him that some of the facts could be explained by 'misunderstandings and misapprehensions', but that it was not worth the effort to linger over explanation.[60] He admitted that there was much to discuss, but insisted that propaganda had to be kept free of prejudice and quibbling.[61]

It may have been the question of theft which helped Reclus to clarify his views on the logical distinction of ends and means. Here we gain a tremendous insight into the nature of the evolution of his thought and locate the root of the disagreements over *la reprise individuelle*. In a letter of 21 May 1893 Reclus explicitly stated that 'the end justifies the means'.[62] The letter dealt with Grave's new book *La Société mourante et l'Anarchie* (The Dying Society and Anarchy). Reclus pointed to what he saw as a contradiction between the chapter title 'How the means are derived from the principles' and Grave's disapproval of the Jesuit maxim, the end justifies the means. Whereas Grave assumed that the means determined the nature of the end, Reclus maintained that the means were only the instruments, the tools. Just as hands could indifferently serve good or ill, the means could be used to contribute to progress or regression. The comrade who lied to save a friend did well to lie. The revolutionary who stole to serve the needs of his friends might 'calmly and without regret allow himself to qualify as a thief'. The man who killed to defend the weak was a 'murderer with honourable intentions'. 'Yes, "the end justifies the means!" ' Those who merely called themselves anarchists, in order to justify lies and theft and murder did not employ the Jesuit principle at all. The principle which guided their actions was 'the pretext justifies the means'. The moral worth of this principle won them the justly deserved aversion which was directed at them. It was the logical and moral worth of the means, not the means themselves, which was derived from the principles.[63]

Reclus' support of the anarchist 'thief' was final. There was no logical reason why an individual should not immediately reject bourgeois morality for a communist morality which derived from the needs of human beings, not the social-economic system. Was it not important that each person, so far as possible, attempt to conduct his relations in accordance with his moral and intellectual evolution? How else would revolution come about? It was to be expected, there-fore, that changing social values would be translated into social realities. Those observers — anarchists too — who reacted negatively to the emergence of the anarchist redresser of wrongs were suffering under the prejudices of the past. As a man who had spent two decades lamenting the dangers of 'circuitous' routes to social justice, Reclus could also appreciate the boldness and directness of the individual recovery of the property 'stolen' from the people. Finally, every person possessed that right of individual autonomy, the right to interpret the dictates of the interior voice and to act accordingly. The 'thief' could not be condemned without destroying the basis of Reclus' social and political theory.

## Notes

1. Reclus to Bakunin, 8 Feb. 1875, *Correspondance*, 3 vols. (Paris, 1911–25), vol. II, p. 169.
2. Reclus to Bakunin, 17 Apr. 1875, *Corr.* II, p. 171.
3. Ibid.
4. *BFJ*, 7 Mar. 1875.
5. In *Archief ER, IISG,* there are two letters in one envelope. One is Bertoia to Reclus, 20 Oct. 1887; the other is not dated and contains no greeting, but the internal evidence of both letters suggests that the second is a letter from Reclus to Bertoia, 15 Oct. 1887. The envelope which contains the two letters is addressed to Max Nettlau and postmarked 19 June 1897, and the sender indicated is Jacques Gross.
6. Elisée Reclus, *Ouvrier, prends la machine! Prends la terre, paysan!* (Geneva, 1880), p. 7. This pamphlet first appeared as an article in *Le Révolté*, 24 Jan. 1880.
7. Elisée Reclus, 'sur la Propriété', p. 327; *Ouvrier*, pp. 7–8.
8. Reclus, *Ouvrier*, p. 4.
9. Ibid., p. 7.
10. Ibid., pp. 7–8.
11. Elisée Reclus, *A mon Frère, le paysan* (Geneva, 1893), p. 10.
12. Ibid., p. 14.
13. Reclus, *Anarchist*, p. 4.
14. Ibid., p. 9.
15. See 'Tous les Démocrates', extract from *L'Agriculteur*, n.d. (1886), at *BN*.
16. General Council meeting of 13 July 1869; *Documents of the First International*, vol. III, p. 122.
17. See above, Chapter 4.
18. Reclus, 'sur la Propriété', p. 325.
19. Reclus, *Ouvrier*, p. 3.
20. Ibid., pp. 2–3.
21. Ibid.
22. Reclus, 'sur la Propriété', p. 325.
23. *Le Révolté*, 24 June 1882. The statement was made at the Congress of the Jura Federation at Lausanne. When Reclus mentioned that there already existed brochures for the people of the countryside, Klementz replied that the articles and brochures were written in too theoretical and difficult a style to appeal to the peasants. Reclus later made an effort to reach them through his *A mon Frère, le paysan*. In 1892 he was making plans to bring out a collection of chansons to be used as propaganda among the peasants.
24. Reclus, *A mon Frère*, p. 6.
25. Ibid., pp. 7–9.
26. Ibid., p. 9.
27. Reclus to Bertoia, n.d., 15 Oct. 1887, *Archief ER, IISG*.
28. Ibid.
29. Reclus, *Evolution et Révolution* (1884), pp. 27–8 (English from London,

1885 edition).

30. Reclus, 'sur la Propriété', p. 327.
31. Ibid., p. 328.
32. Reclus to Bertoia, n.d., 15 Oct. 1887, *Archief ER, IISG.* Cf. his *Evolution et Révolution* (1880), p. 13 ff.
33. Reclus, *Ouvrier*, p. 7.
34. Reclus to an editor of *La Vie Naturelle*, 6 Feb. 1897, *Corr.* III, pp. 197–8. (*La Vie Naturelle*, Dec. 1911.)
35. Elisée to Elie, n.d. (Oct. 1868), *Corr.* I, p. 282.
36. Reclus to Renard, 2 June 1888, *Corr.* II, p. 445.
37. Reclus to Heath, 4 Nov. 1887, *Corr.* II, p. 428.
38. *BFJ*, 8 Aug. 1875.
39. *BFJ*, 11 Mar. 1877.
40. *BFJ*, 8 Aug. 1875.
41. *Le Révolté*, 21 June–4 July and 2–15 Aug. 1885.
42. *Le Révolté*, 5–11 Feb. 1887.
43. Reclus to Heath, n.d. (1887), *Corr.* II, pp. 414–15.
44. Reclus to Grave, 2 Nov. 1891, *Fonds ER*, 14 AS 232, *IFHS*.
45. *La Révolte*, 23–29 Nov. 1889.
46. The original can be found in *P.Po.* B a/1237.
47. Reclus to Grave, 29 Nov. 1891, *Corr.* III, pp. 96–7.
48. *La Révolte*, 28 Nov.–4 Dec. 1891; *Corr.* III, pp. 97–8.
49. Reclus to Grave, 29 Nov. 1891; *Corr.* III, p. 98.
50. *La Révolte*, 5–11, 12–18 and 19–25 Dec. 1891.
51. Peter Kropotkin, *Anarchist Morality* (*Freedom* Pamphlet, 1892) in Kropotkin's *Revolutionary Pamphlets*, p. 80 ff, especially 97.
52. Kropotkin, *Anarchist Morality* in *Revolutionary Pamphlets*, p. 101.
53. Reclus to Pastor Roth, n.d. (1904), *Corr.* III, pp. 285–6.
54. Jean Grave, *Quarante Ans de Propagande Anarchiste* (Paris, 1973), p. 223.
55. Cf. ibid., p. 247.
56. Reclus to Grave, 2 Nov. 1891, *Fonds ER*, 14 AS 232, *IFHS*; cf. Reclus to Grave, 21 Nov. 1891, ibid., and Grave, *Quarante Ans*, p. 222.
57. Reclus to Grave, 21 Nov. 1891, *Fonds ER*, 14 AS 232, *IFHS*.
58. See, for example, *Ca Ira*, 16 Sept. 1888. In response to the line of *Ca Ira* which extolled the virtues of thievery, Reclus wrote to Gross that he had shown his chagrin to Constant Martin by refusing to contribute a sou to the paper. Reclus to Gross, 2 Nov. 1888, *Papiers Gross, Depôt du CIRA 1964, BPU*, Geneva. An edited copy of the letter exists in *Fonds ER*, 14 AS 232, *IFHS*; in this copy Constant Martin has been replaced by C.
59. Grave, *Quarante Ans*, p. 223.
60. Reclus to Grave, 21 Nov. 1891, *Fonds ER*, 14 AS 232, *IFHS*.
61. Reclus to Grave, 22 Nov. 1891, *Fonds ER*, 14 AS 232, *IFHS*.
62. Reclus to Grave, 21 May 1893, *Corr.* III, pp. 139–140.
63. Cf. Octave Mirbeau's opinion: 'What I find unique in your book is that it is impossible to pick up a fault in logic; it is full of clarity.' Grave, *Quarante Ans*, p. 253.

# 10 ANARCHISM AND TERROR

Anarchist intellectuals deliberately fostered an identification of themselves as 'le parti des révoltés' — the party of the rebels — especially from 1879 when they brought out a journal called *Le Révolté*. Significantly, it replaced earlier ones entitled *Le Travailleur* and *L'Avant-Garde*. Propaganda by the deed, as it developed under the aegis of Reclus, came to be based upon a number of convictions: that all revolt against oppression was in itself progressive, that the transformation from blind and spontaneous responses to injustice into 'conscious' and calculated revolt represented significant advances, and that decisions to commit specific acts of revolt had to rest with the people. What this amounted to was a strict insistence upon individual autonomy, the right of the individual to act as he saw fit. In accordance with this framework for action some self-professed anarchists adopted a belief in the efficacy of violent acts, and these were to increase in number and intensity until they reached crisis proportions. Reclus stood firm on the issue, even as fellow theoreticians faltered when faced with the reality of the attentats which terrorised Europe in the 1890s.

The implications of the anarchist position on propaganda by the deed were becoming clear as early as 1878, the year in which there was a number of sensational attacks on European authorities and heads of state. In February Vera Zasúlitch shot at the chief of the St Petersburg police, Trepov, in protest over his treatment of the 'go to the people' movement. Two attempts were made to kill the German emperor, in May and June respectively; in October someone tried to assassinate Alfonso XII of Spain; and in November King Umberto of Italy was attacked. These events were generally linked with the anarchists. The Swiss authorities suppressed *L'Avant-Garde* for what they claimed to be its extreme views, arrested the editor (Brousse) and brought him to trial.[1] The anarchist response to the events of 1878, however, was quite ambivalent. For example, *L'Avant-Garde* had made some effort to distinguish the individual acts of the assassin from the collective deeds of 'conscious' anarchists such as those at Benevento in 1877. The suggestion was also made that assassination was of limited propaganda value, although the feeling persisted that under certain conditions it could lead to revolution.[2]

Anarchists were more decisive in their interpretation of the terrorism of the Russian Narodnaya Volya which was struggling against the impossible odds of Tsarist autocracy. Sophie Perovskaya, one of the five who were executed for their part in the assassination of Tsar Alexander II in March 1881, became a true inspiration. Kropotkin wrote: 'By the attitude of the crowd she understood that she had dealt a mortal blow to the autocracy. And she read in the sad looks which were directed sympathetically towards her that by her death she was dealing an even more terrible blow from which the autocracy will never recover.'[3] It is hardly surprising that such un-qualified approval could be given to the Russian revolutionaries. Throughout Western Europe there was an awareness of the extent of Tsarist oppression, so that even liberals might in all conscience extend their sympathies. In so far as Russia provided specific lessons for the anarchists, it is clear that these largely consisted in a re-affirmation of the importance of spontaneous acts of revolt within the context of propaganda by the deed. In spite of the enthusiasm with which anarchists might be expected to greet Russian revolutionary events their lack of anxiety over what constituted legitimate acts of revolt in Russia may be taken to indicate that the ambivalence of 1878 was gradually abating. Many anarchists must have been thinking of Russia in July 1881, four months after the assassination of Tsar Alexander II, when the famous London International Congress advocated a study of the technical and chemical sciences from the point of view of their revolutionary value.[4]

Propaganda by the deed demanded that theoreticians be prepared to submit to the revolutionary course mapped out by the people as they struggled to create a socialist society, and moreover, that they take it as their task to discover the revolutionary significance of all acts of social revolt — even provide a sense of legitimacy for them. Increasingly there occurred incidents which were the work of individuals who had absorbed sufficient anarchist theory to be able to translate (or justify) specific grievances in terms of an ideological hatred of the whole bourgeois order. An example of this had taken place as early as 1881 when Emile Florian went to Reims with the intention of killing Léon Gambetta, the noted Radical supporter of the French Republic. Failing to find the opportunity, he decided to attack the first bourgeois he met and shot (unsuccessfully) at a Dr Meymar. Brought to trial and found guilty, Florian greeted his sentence of 20 years hard labour with the cry, 'Long live the social revolution!' *Le Révolté* referred to his action on a number of

occasions and made some effort to place him in the tradition of
propaganda by the deed. In late 1883 the 17-year-old Paul-Marie
Curien travelled to Paris to kill the Prime Minister Jules Ferry, and
ended up pointing his revolver at an usher in the Chamber of Deputies.
A more consciously anarchist act was that of Louis Chaves in 1884.
Dismissed from his position as a gardener in a convent near Marseilles,
Chaves returned and killed the Mother Superior and injured the
assistant director. Explaining his behaviour in a letter to an anarchist
paper, he declared: 'It is not with words, nor with paper that we
shall change the existing situation.'[5] Two years later, on 5 March 1886,
Charles Gallo threw a bottle of Prussic acid from an upper gallery of
the Paris stock exchange and shot at the panic-stricken brokers and
employers. At his trial in June he provoked the court until the proceedings were adjourned, and he was dragged out, screaming 'Death
to the bourgeois magistrature!' and 'Long live anarchy!' Later he
expressed his regret only at not having succeeded in killing anyone
and professed that he had wished to accomplish an act of 'propaganda
by the deed of the anarchist doctrines'.[6]

The Paris explosions of March 1892 initiated a period of terror
which continued, principally in France, for over two years. The first
explosion of any consequence went off on 11 March, and caused considerable damage to a property on the boulevard St Germain. *La
Révolte* commented that this incident had re-established the
significance of dynamite which had been rather belittled in the few
minor explosions which had preceded 11 March.[7] There was a further
explosion at the Lobau barracks on 15 March and the biggest bomb to
date went off on 27 March in the apartment house inhabited by the
Deputy Bulot who had demanded the death penalty for the anarchists
implicated in the disturbances of 1 May 1891. A man known as
Ravachol was arrested and tried for these explosions, and condemned
to 20 years hard labour. He was then taken to Montbrison where he
was charged with a number of crimes committed in the period between
1886 and 1891. He admitted guilt to two of them: the desecration of
the tomb of the comtesse de la Rochetaillée at Terrenoire on the
night of 14 to 15 May 1891 and the robbery and killing of the 92-
year-old hermit of Chambles, Jacques Brunel, on 18 June of the same
year. The French establishment was somewhat startled when Ravachol
refused to recognise himself as a mere criminal, and insisted on
presenting himself as an anarchist redresser of wrongs, claiming that
he had killed and robbed, first to satisfy personal needs and then to
come to the aid of the anarchist cause. The verdict of death he greeted

with 'Long live anarchy!' and on 11 July 1892, he marched to the
guillotine, singing an anti-clerical song.

From this point onwards there was no shortage of aspiring terrorists,
and some souls were able to achieve a glorious end to an otherwise
miserable life. The young shoemaker Léon-Jules Léauthier is
remembered among anarchists for his words, 'I shall not strike an
innocent if I strike the first bourgeois I meet', and he earned himself a
place in history by seriously injuring the Serbian Minister Georgewitch
on 12 November 1893 with his (shoemaker's) paring knife. On 9
December Auguste Vaillant threw a bomb from the gallery of the
Chamber of Deputies, injuring several Deputies, some of them seriously,
as well as a number of spectators, an usher and himself. Although no
one was killed, Vaillant was condemned to death. He became an
anarchist martyr, having neither stolen nor killed, but only having
attacked a 'corrupt' Chamber severely discredited by the recent Panama
scandal. On 12 February 1894, one week after the execution of
Vaillant, Emile Henry blew up the Cafe Terminus (of the Saint-Lazare
Station), injuring 20 people, one of whom later died of his injuries.
Henry, sometimes known as the Saint-Just of Anarchy, expressed his
regret at the failure of the explosion to claim more victims; his aim
had been to kill, not to injure. 'There are no innocents', he cried. The
attentats reached a climax with the killing of President Sadi Carnot,
highest symbol of the bourgeois Republic, by the young Italian Santo
Caserio at Lyons on 24 June 1894.

It is not accurate, however, to view the period of the attentats as
merely the story of the handful of individuals who were driven by
their own wretched existence and inspired by anarchist theory to
express their anger through acts of violence against the political order.
Besides the few 'success' stories, the records show that there was a
considerable number of political dynamiters whose explosions were
not serious enough to warrant lasting attention. In addition, there were
numerous instances of threatening letters sent anonymously to
property-owners, warning them to expect an explosion and sometimes
informing them that they should vacate the property by such and
such an hour, in order to escape personal injury. In the Paris Police
Archives there are several boxes of documents dealing with the
explosions of the 1880s and 1890s; the vast majority of these
documents concern the period 1892 to 1894. There are also three
boxes which contain 'threatening letters' passed on by their recipients
to the police in the year 1892. (One suspects that many more were discarded upon receipt.)[8] The more sensational attentats were committed

amid general excitement, panic in bourgeois circles, approval (or at least no disapproval) in the anarchist press, and even extreme enthusiasm in some papers. Pictures of Ravachol were produced and distributed, as if they were images of a saint, and his deeds were celebrated in song. For one anarchist he was seen as 'a sort of violent Christ'.[9]

As early as 1885 at least some observers considered the 'anarchist party . . . a manifestation expressive of the state of spirits in the working class milieu'.[10] It is quite understandable how the attentats of the 1890s led the French establishment to believe that just about every anarchist, from the theoretician to the bomber, was guilty of crimes against the French state. In an 1895 analysis by a criminal lawyer Garraud, the anarchists represented a division of labour in which each person contributed to the destruction of society according to his temperament and abilities. Some anarchists were 'practiciens', those who propagated the doctrine by means of the deed, that is by theft, burning and assassination. At their side were the frequently gifted intellectuals who diffused the anarchist idea through newspapers, brochures, songs and pictures. Then there were the anarchist 'door-to-door salesmen' who could be found selling newspapers and so on in the working-class districts and in general inciting rebellion in every corner of the land.[11] Of course, Garraud's analysis was simplistic, but it sensed important elements of the underlying logic of anarchist theory.

It was a logic which some theoreticians were loath to admit. Approval had been given to certain acts of violence in the 1880s, though the enormous scale of the terror of the 1890s caught some of them unprepared. It was not until after Ravachol's appearance in court that *La Révolte* gave a hesitatingly favourable appraisal, suggesting that a distinction should be made between his earlier crimes and the Paris explosions.[12] Only after the death sentence had been passed did the paper come out in open support of him.[13] It was easier to applaud the efforts of angry, unemployed persons seeking redress for immediate grievances than to sanction the acts of bombers who were professing to be carrying out what the intellectuals appeared to be advocating in theory.

Kropotkin was genuinely troubled lest innocent people should become victims, and he wrote a letter intended for publication in *La Révolte* denouncing an explosion which had killed and maimed a large number of people in Spain. These initial waverings were met with the help of arguments put forward by Jean Grave who reported how he explained to Kropotkin that there was no basis on which to condemn

the wretched, as they struggled to overcome their miserable existence.[14]
There is reason to suspect that Kropotkin underwent a fair amount of
soul-searching in choosing to refrain from a condemnation of terrorism,
and we catch a glimpse of his agonising in comments to a friend concerning his regrets over the assassination of the Austrian empress
Elizabeth in 1898.[15] The explanation of terrorism offered by Kropotkin
depicted the bombers as mental and emotional cripples, victims of a
vicious society, and it echoed significant elements of the sentiments of
many non-anarchist intellectuals. 'In fact', Kropotkin declared, '*we* have
not suffered from the persecutions as they the workers, suffered; we
who, in our houses, seclude ourselves from the cry and sight of human
sufferings, *we are no judges* of those who live in the midst of all this
suffering . . . Personally I hate these explosions, but I cannot stand as a
judge to condemn those who are driven to despair . . . '[16] Such a
response was hardly consistent with his 1880 eulogy of the 'lonely
sentinel' whose courage and integrity were crucial to the success of the
revolutionary struggle.[17] 'So long as contempt for human life shall be
taught to men', he wrote in 1898, 'and so long as they will be told
that it is good to kill for what one believes to be beneficial for mankind — new and newer victims will be added, even though the rulers
should guillotine all those who take sides with the poor.'[18]

The hesitancy of Kropotkin (humanness or weakness depending on
one's view) was compensated by the determination of Reclus (courage
or fanaticism) to admit the implications of a theoretical position and
to approve action carried to its logical conclusion. He refused to condemn acts which were the result of 'horrible forces, the consequences
of inevitable passions, the explosion of a rudimentary justice',[19] and he
insisted that anger had its 'raison d'être . . . its day and its hour'.[20]
Within this analysis Ravachol had arisen above the status of a mere
victim; he had become a primitive lover of justice, striving for what
he believed was right, an inevitable phenomenon in the progress towards
justice. 'I admire . . . his courage', wrote Reclus, 'his kindness, his
grandeur of soul, the generosity with which he pardons his enemies, in
truth his denunciators. I know few men who surpass him in nobleness.'[21]
'It goes without saying that I regard every revolt against oppression as a
just and good act.'[22]

|Through his sociological and historical studies Reclus had been led to
expect violence as a natural part of social change, even as 'a law of
Nature, a consequence of the physical law of shock and counter-
shock'.[23] Confronted with what he believed to be manifestations and
verifications of his theories, once again he did not flinch. It was not

difficult to imagine, he said, how a man calling himself an anarchist could be brought to commit acts of violence against individuals. It was easy to single out a name which symbolised the detestation of the social order. Too many injustices, infamies, individual and collective cruelties were taking place every day to be astounded at the germination of a whole crop of hatred.[24] To take sides against the wretched in their struggle to liberate themselves would be tantamount to justifying, in an indirect manner, the whole oppressive system.[25] There was no doubt that every person had the right to raise his hand against an evil society.[26] Reclus differentiated himself from those anarchists who advocated revolt for its own sake. In order for an act of revolt to interest him, it had to be of a 'universal character', that is it had to be committed in the name of the happiness of the entire human race.[27] While the consequences of a particular act in terms of individual suffering might be lamentable, progress was secured, none the less, if the consciousness of a common humanity had been raised. It took a while for some of his friends to comprehend the full significance of this position.

In 1900 the son of an English friend wrote to Reclus that his support of violence indicated that he was no longer Tolstoyan. Reclus must have smiled as he replied that he was far from being Tolstoyan, and that he believed in the use of force to protect the weak. 'I see a cat that is tortured, a child that is beaten, a woman who is mistreated, and if I am strong enough to prevent it, I prevent it.' This was a duty which he had towards all the weak, and fulfilment of it would ensure that henceforth that they would be respected.[28] He did not linger over such questions as who would make the decisions to use force and who would decide when it should stop. As a conscious and rational being, he was prepared to resort to force when he felt it to be necessary, and would stop at the point at which he judged that it was about to turn to vengeance − and reaction.[29] 'To be very strong and to make use of force, in order to raise the question of love is the normal conduct of the anarchist.'[30]

This position supported an autonomy for each and every individual. It was the intention behind the act, and not the act itself, which was subject to moral scrutiny. Even then, there was no absolute moral standard to apply, for each individual might only be assessed in accordance with his own level of moral and intellectual development. Reclus would have reluctantly conceded that, theoretically, such a judgement might be given, if it were possible to ascertain both the individual's intentions and his level of development. However, he would emphasise that, in practice, it would be possible to give only an opinion, because one could never be certain that the facts were complete. Moreover, the question of morality would always be separate from that of behaviour. Two individuals at precisely the same level might act very differently, and yet both be responding equally to the call of their consciences. The individual had to evolve in his or her own particular way, not in conformity with some pre-established pattern. Reclus' catechism was crystallised in the period of attentats and summed up in a letter to a friend:

1. Let us not judge, not as the Bible says, 'in order that we may not be judged,' but because we do not know the motives and we may entirely deceive ourselves.
2. Let us not moralise. Because we do not have any right to substitute ourselves in this way for others and to give ourselves in example. To each to follow his own evolution.
3. Let us not preach, so much so that we do not have sufficient data to know, to see in advance.
4. Let us not interfere before the organism begins to grow of itself. Let us not force the flower to open out: it will open well by itself if the life penetrates it.[31]

Yet Reclus tended to insist upon the superiority of the 'reasoned argument', even as he explained or justified the use of violence. When he first heard of the March 1892 explosions, he maintained that they would never be attributed to conscious anarchists, that is anarchists 'who ponder their words and acts, who feel responsible for their conduct towards the entire humanity'. Bombs which went off haphazardly to destroy staircases were not arguments. They were not even weapons used wittingly, since it could happen that they worked in reverse, against the slave and not the master. 'Let us simply carry on our propaganda; the bombings will not prevent us from being heard.'[32] The cynic might be inclined to view this insistence upon the natural superiority of the argument as evidence of an ambivalence about violence, or perhaps even a sop to his friends in the world of bourgeois scholarship. This would misrepresent Reclus' views on violence. Not once did he say that violence was desirable in itself, only that it was inevitable. To suggest that violence is inevitable, even to welcome it as indicative of (or productive of) a higher degree of consciousness is not to advocate its use (although the dynamiters might have interpreted it this way). Reclus' hope for the future lay in the raising of consciousness which in turn would tend towards the elimination of violence. The more conscious the anarchist became the less instinctual was his behaviour; and the more sensitive he grew to the fact of a common human nature, the less likely he would be to resort to violence. In fact, the conscious anarchist was expected to attempt the impossible, to live his life as if the society of the future had already been established. Solidarity itself, as Reclus attempted to show, ought to be the predominant feature of his behaviour; anarchists ought 'to carry the light with them, to make our cause glow as an actual revelation of justice'.[33] Ravachol might call himself an anarchist and he might inspire hymns of praise, but he remained a 'primitive rebel' wielding a crude weapon. This did not detract from his nobleness nor from the essential morality which guided his actions.

Even though Reclus placed his faith in a growing solidarity and even though he was certain that the reasoned argument would be steadily recognised as the superior weapon, his theories did not preclude the use of violence by conscious anarchists. Means were neutral in themselves, and so there could be no question as to whether the use of dynamite was immoral; it was its low rate of accuracy which condemned it, its inability to discriminate between victims. In the recent bombings, he said in 1892, passion and chance had played a greater role than self-sacrifice and science. Moreover, while explosions might indicate a greater degree of awareness and serve to further the cause among the uncommitted, there was also the risk of the inefficient use of revolutionary energy in the event of wide-ranging repression. Indeed, the explosions of 1892 had furnished the social order with some temporary advantages against the anarchists, though to be sure these were quickly lost (he sighed with relief and a snicker) as the bourgeois, driven to panic, committed one stupidity after another.[34] Reclus' analysis certainly begs one or two questions. With science on their side, was it not possible eventually to fashion weapons out of dynamite which would be so accurate as to leave no room for error, and could there not arise a situation so threatening to the good of society that even a highly conscious anarchist would decide that the use of violence was in the common defence? He would have replied that in all questions the anarchist should follow his conscience.

Such concerns about the wisdom of using dynamite never had a significant impact upon the thrust of the anarchist movement. And as the upholder of strict individual autonomy Reclus would never have sought to redirect the movement. It is sometimes pointed out that he wrote a letter condemning the explosions, and specifically Emile Henry's attentat at the Café Terminus. Such a letter signed 'Elisée

Reclus' appeared in *Le Travail* on 13 February 1894 and was reprinted in other papers.[35] However, Reclus publicly denied responsibility for the letter and claimed that it was a forgery.[36] (It is likely that some sympathiser of anarchist ideals decided to use Reclus' name in order to provide moral weight to an appeal to end the violence which he believed was harming the movement.) The refusal to condemn was interpreted as approval by the popular press and by the terrorists, so much so that some sympathisers of the theories of Reclus and Kropotkin became alarmed at the 'wrong' impression which was being fostered on the issue of terrorism.[37] In the analysis of one such social scientist of the time, the 'true' anarchists were depicted as members of an exclusive club; they were rebels against injustice, lovers of liberty, altruistic, sensitive and intelligent, while the terrorists who acted in their name were a small minority with imperfectly formed brains.[38]

*La Révolte* continued to maintain a central position in the anarchist movement, but it was compelled to make room for the scurrilous *Le Père Peinard* which appeared in 1889. In the 1890s there arose a whole flock of anarchist papers. In 1893, for example, there were some 17 in France, many appearing on the occasion of the *attentats* and lasting for only a few issues. Sneering at the timidity of *La Révolte*'s rather old-fashioned position, the more extreme openly advocated terrorism and provided information for would-be dynamiters.

While the French authorities might execute a Ravachol, they were also convinced that such a figure could not have been transformed from criminal into hero without fairly extensive support from leading anarchists, and, furthermore, that the execution of one Ravachol did not prevent another from emerging. Certain that the only way to spare society the experience of a Ravachol was to cleanse it of the anarchists, and fired with a new enthusiasm following Vaillant's *attentat*, the Chamber of Deputies passed a series of laws which became the infamous *lois scélérates* (wicked laws). Such legislation was necessary because the activites of the anarchists could only with the greatest difficulty be subsumed under the relevant sections of the Penal Code. In the 1883 Lyons trial the anarchists had been charged with membership in an International Association; the nature of this International was anything but clear in 1883, and in 1894 it was thoroughly bewildering. It was common knowledge that the anarchists constituted 'a sort of' association, and that their *entente* (understanding) was to destroy the bourgeois order with every possible means. Also it was known that those who carried out the *attentats* were inspired by anarchist theory or what they understood of it. It became necessary, explained criminal lawyer Garraud 'to enlarge the traditional notion of the term "association" and to base criminal charges upon "entente" '.[39]

Under the first of the new laws, it became a crime even to apologise for criminal acts; another was directed against 'associations of mal-factors', defining them by intent rather than by action; after Carnot's death a third was passed forbidding acts of anarchist propaganda 'by any means whatsoever'. These laws have frequently been considered harsh, unreasonable and even ridiculous. Certainly they reveal the help-lessness of the French state when confronted with a determined effort to exploit its various 'freedoms'. French liberals of the period were anxious to defend themselves against charges of illiberalism, and attempted — unconvincingly — to justify the restrictions on the basic freedoms of its citizens. As Garraud put it: '. . . the propaganda that the law condemns and punishes is not propaganda for the idea and by the idea — anarchy is not a crime — it is the application of anarchy, that is to say the brutal solution of the social problem by theft, burning, murder.'[40] Here it is suggested that the promotion of anarchism through reason and argument was not a crime. However, even if the masses could be persuaded, through peaceful means, to accept the anarchist ideal, this very success would amount to the end of the bourgeois state. The French legal system, even as it strived to preserve the *status quo*, was revealing its Achilles Heel, its various liberal freedoms, as Reclus had perceived many years before. The liberal order could come to terms with the dynamiters only by becoming less liberal. Reclus could not have been surprised at this retreat from freedom, for he fully expected the bourgeoisie to go to any lengths to resist their extinction as a class.

From December 1893 the police armed with the new powers carried out wide-scale searches and made numerous arrests. Most of the anarchist papers came to an end by the early days of March 1894, *La Révolte* expiring on 10 March. Many anarchist activists, including Reclus' nephew Paul, escaped arrest only by leaving France. Reclus himself was high on the list of suspects. On 1 January 1894 a police search was carried out at Bourg-la-Reine, where he was living at the time. The effort uncovered a large cache of anarchist literature, collections of revolutionary and anarchist songs and poems, correspon-dence in French, English, Italian and German and various notes. The report concluded that while he had contact with individual anarchists, there was not sufficient evidence to link him directly with the 'malfactors', since the search had failed to uncover any explosives.[41]

Although the evidence against him was at least as firm as that against many of the other anarchists who were indicted in this period, there was a reluctance to arrest him without more compelling evidence. Once again, Reclus was shielded by his reputation as a scholar, for the government did not wish to weaken its case against the anarchists by causing a public (even international) outcry in defence of a man who less than two years previously had been awarded a gold medal by the Paris Geographical Society.[42]

The fear that Reclus could command a large following was justified by events in Brussels from early January 1894. At a meeting of the Governing Council of the Free University of Brussels on 16 July 1892, it had been decided, on the initiative of the Rector, to nominate Reclus Fellow of the Faculty of Sciences, at the same time authorising him to give a course in comparative geography at the University's School of Social Science.[43] Reclus accepted the nomination, but asked to postpone the course until the first weeks of 1894 when *La Nouvelle Géographie Universelle* would have been completed.[44] In December 1893 he informed the Governing Council that he would be prepared to commence the course at the beginning of the new term in early March. However, the members of the Council became uneasy about reports of recent events in France, especially the links which were being drawn between terrorism and the family Reclus. The decision was taken to postpone the course indefinitely, in order to avoid 'demonstrations, sympathetic or hostile, inspired by excitable strangers' at the lectures.[45] This information was communicated to Reclus in a letter of 6 January 1894, but not before Belgian and French newspapers had carried reports of the rumours of the Free University's reaction. By this time considerable resentment was building up. All kinds of student societies – convinced that the postponement effectively meant suppression – presented protests to the Council and sent letters of sympathy to Reclus. Student agitation won the support of politicians and scholars, as well as that of some members of the faculty. By 21 January a Protest Committee had been formed.[46] The agitation became violent and led to the expulsion of students and teachers, the resignation of the Rector who had sided with the students, and the closing of the university for weeks.[47]

With some amusement,[48] Reclus found himself a *cause célèbre*, and decided to act out the role which the fates had prepared for him. He accepted a request from the President of the University Circle of Brussels (a body of students and former students) to give the course on geography in spite of the administration's decision,[49] and on 2 March

he presented his first lecture to an enthusiastic audience[50] in a large
hall put at his disposal by the Freemason Loge des Amis Philanthrophes
de Bruxelles (Lodge of Philanthropic Friends of Brussels). The disturbances over the postponement of the course brought to a climax a series
of differences within the university, and at an assembly of 12 March the
decision was taken to found a new university.[51] Reclus continued his
lectures in improvised surroundings until the opening of the New
University of Brussels which was able to offer a limited number of
courses in the 1894 to 1895 academic year. As if to confirm any fears
which the French police may have had concerning his support in the
scholarly world, the Royal Geographical Society of London recognised
his achievements by awarding him their gold medal for 1894.[52]

Reclus' spirits were raised as the anarchists went about cleansing
society of social injustice, as the police attempted to rid society of the
anarchists, and as the popular press buzzed with the debate on the
latest anarchist exploits. On 23 April 1892 he wrote enthusiastically to
his sister Louise: 'It truly seems to me that the desire to learn and to
know is becoming general; it is even piercing those filthy papers
whose sole mission is to plead for the employer's coffer!' While
having avoided bourgeois reporters seeking interviews, he experienced
'the joy of having to speak frequently with people passionately fond
of the truth'.[53] He took care of much of the negotiations with Stock
for the publication of Kropotkin's *La Conquête du Pain*, read the
proofs, and on 19 April joyfully reported that only after a few months,
the book was already going into the second edition. That morning he
had also entered into discussions with Stock concerning the publication
of Bakunin's *Oeuvres choisies*.[54] On 27 April he wrote to Nadar that,
even though Grave was in prison and there was a shortage of funds to
run *La Révolte*, 'we live from day to day, happy and confident,
listening to the great blast of the revolution which is advancing'.[55] The
next month he was planning to bring out a collection of chansons to
be used as propaganda among the peasants. While the peasants did not
care for learned brochures, he explained to Gross, they loved the
chanson, understood it and were imbued with it.[56] It was in this
period that he wrote the well-known pamphlet, *A mon Frère, le paysan*
(To my Brother, the peasant).

There was a side to Reclus which delighted in mocking authority.
It is not difficult to imagine the defiant chuckles with which in his
youth he had composed an ode to the 1848ers who had successfully
toppled Louis Philippe: 'That was a beautiful day when one saw a king
pale at the approach of the people and look for an ill-smelling cellar in

his splendid castle . . . '[57] He remained convinced of the precarious basis
of the relationship between the rulers and the ruled, and it was an
important part of his message to attack the myths which sustained the
bourgeois order. In the 1870s he became uncharacteristically serious,
partly because of the uncertainty of revolutionary success following
the repression of the Paris Commune, and partly because he was
deeply involved in working out a scientific basis for his social and
political views. Armed with more fully elaborated theories, and
possessed of an indomitable spirit, he became more optimistic as well
as more openly, even boyishly, defiant of authority. An example of his
readiness to undermine the position of the 'high and mighty' comes
from late 1882, at the time of Kropotkin's arrest on the charges of
having some connection with an international organisation forbidden
by the Defaure Law of 1872.

In response to the arrest, Reclus wrote a provocative letter to Rigot,
the examining magistrate at Lyons on 24 December 1882.[58] He stated
that he had read (in the *Lyon Républicain*) that, according to the pre-
liminary investigation, the two leaders and organisers of the international anarchists were Elisée Reclus and Prince Kropotkin and that
he himself did not share his friend's fate simply because French law
did not allow for his apprehension outside the country. But, he
declared, Monsieur Rigot was well aware that he had only recently
spent two months in France. Moreover, he had attended the funeral
of Kropotkin's brother-in-law Ananieff, the day following Kropotkin's
arrest and had said a few words over the grave.[59] The officers, who
had been stationed immediately behind him and who had repeated his
name, would only have had to invite him to follow. The letter closed,
daring Rigot to make an arrest: 'But, it matters little whether I reside
in France or in Switzerland . . . Let me know the place, the day and
the hour. At the appointed moment, I shall knock on the door of the
prison which has been designated.' A similar letter was written to the
Belgian paper *La Réforme* after he had arrived in Brussels in March
1894. In this letter he remarked that on 19 March *La Réforme* had
carried reports that the newspapers were demanding his arrest. If an
order for his arrest were issued, he said, he would prevail upon himself
to leave the 'serious business' which had called him to Brussels.

Abandoning my work as soon as possible, I shall go to present
myself before the judges, not to give the satisfaction to the eager
letter-writers, but out of a sense of duty and respect for my convictions. It is not that I am attracted to prison, but even in prison I

can worthily live out a life which I know to be honourable.[60]

It was a game of 'Catch me if you can', and he clearly felt that he was on a winning streak. The jeers should be taken for what they were, a mischievous delight in belittling the authority of a French state already disillusioned by a persecution which was beyond its comprehension and, moreover, uncertain as to the most suitable attitude to adopt towards the eccentric geographer. On 17 July 1894 Reclus reported to a friend that he had been so openly watched and followed that he had to conclude that the exercise was a sham.[61] He had no intention of submitting to arrest, however, and when the pressure became too intense, he allowed himself to be whisked away to a country retreat where for a few days he worked away quietly. (The retreat, so the story goes, was the home of a young man who happened to be the director of a Flanders prison.)[62]

While Reclus had written the appropriately indignant letters to the university officials and had mockingly signed himself Fellow of the Free University,[63] he was obviously revelling in the excitement aroused on his behalf at Paris and at Brussels. 'I am not able to feel offended; but I have made up my mind to find it very funny, and that it is in effect. I can say that I have had my good dose of experiences in my life.'[64] With science on his side, and with the various manifestations of social progress all around him, his 1870s uncertainty had evaporated to almost nothing. Anarchist ideas would continue to take hold in society, whatever steps might be taken by the authorities, whether they closed down the anarchist press or arrested the more prominent spokesmen.[65]

There was no limit as to what Reclus would tolerate, so long as the intentions were 'good', and he even delighted in the idea that he himself was not immune to the just anger of the oppressed. At the beginning of the period of the attentats, he wrote that he was prepared to pardon in advance any wretch who might take him for an oppressor and strike him a mortal blow.[66] At about the same time, he had the opportunity to respond to a lesser attack, the looting of his library. Nadar recounted the story of how Reclus dealt with this 'restitution' of the common property. 'My poor, dear friend! Your books . . . ' 'Well! What of my books? I read all that they had to say to me, and now they are going to be of use to others . . . Moreover, since I did not give them, they did well to take them.' To the astonishment of Nadar, Reclus made these statements, smiling and rubbing his hands briskly in the best of spirits.[67]

Reclus' good humour and his renewed faith in the prospects for
social justice were not merely a response to immediate events; otherwise, he would in all probability have become despondent when the
anarchist movement came to an abrupt end with the Procès des Trente
(Trial of the Thirty) in 1894. As we shall see, his optimism continued
in full force. The attentats were seen by him as a particular stage in
social progress, and therefore their end was also the commencement of
a further, and more advanced, stage in the battle against the bourgeois
order. The passion and instinct of 'primitive' rebels were giving way
to the intellect and consciousness of 'sophisticated' rebels (anarchists)
who would all the more thoroughly carry out the work begun by their
brave predecessors. Part III of this study is a portrait of Reclus the
scholar who becomes physically and emotionally detached from the
European socialist movement, but who insists, at the turn of the
century, that anarchism has not been defeated, but on the contrary,
that it is stronger than ever. Significant signs of progress are perceived
in the globalisation of politics and economics, in the worldwide
network of communications, and above all, in the growing commitment to the principles of science.

## Notes

1. See above, Chapter 6.
2. For Brousse's position, see David Stafford, *From Anarchism to Reformism,
A Study of the Political Activities of Paul Brousse 1870–1890* (London, 1971),
p. 122 ff.
3. Quoted in George Woodcock and Ivan Avakumović, *The Anarchist Prince,
Peter Kropotkin* (London, 1971), p. 343.
4. For the proceedings of the congress, see *Le Révolté*, 23 July 1881.
5. *L'Hydre Anarchiste*, 9 Mar. 1884. Chaves fired at the police who came to
arrest him, but was killed by one of them. *Le Droit Social* (16–23 May 1885)
opened up a subscription to purchase a revolver to avenge him.
6. Jean Maitron, *Le Mouvement Anarchiste en France*, 2 vols. (Paris, 1975),
vol. I, p. 212.
7. *La Révolte*, 19–25 Mar. 1892.
8. For the documents collected under the heading *Explosions*, see B a/66,
B a/67, B a/136, B a/139, B a/140, B a/141, B a/142, B a/143; see also B a/508,
B a/509, B a /510 entitled *Lettres de menaces, 1892*. In addition, the Paris Police
Archives contain many files on general anarchist activities, as well as on the
more prominent individuals within the movement.
9. Victor Barrucand in *L'En Dehors*, 24 July 1892; quoted in Maitron,
*Mouvement Anarchiste*, Vol. I, p. 224.
10. J. Garin, *L'Anarchie et les Anarchistes* (Paris, 1885), p. 1.
11. R. Garraud, *L'Anarchie et la Répression* (Paris, 1895), pp. 17–18. Cf.
P. Fabrequettes, *De la complicité intellectuelle et des délits d'opinion. De la
provocation et de l'opologie criminelles. De la propagande anarchiste* (Paris,

1894–1895).

12. *La Révolte*, 23–30 Apr. 1892.

13. See *La Révolte*, 7–14 May 1892 for an article by Octave Mirbeau and 1–7 July 1892 for 'Déclarations de Ravachol'.

14. Jean Grave, *Quarante Ans de Propagande Anarchiste* (Paris, 1973), pp. 296–7.

15. Kropotkin to Brandes, *Freedom*, Oct. 1898; Martin A. Miller, *Kropotkin* (Chicago, 1976), p. 174.

16. Quoted in Woodcock and Avakumović, *Anarchist Prince*, p. 248.

17. Peter Kropotkin, 'The Spirit of Revolt' in *Revolutionary Pamphlets*, p. 39.

18. Kropotkin to Brandes, *Freedom*, Oct. 1898.

19. Reclus to Heath, n.d., *Correspondance*, 3 vols. (Paris, 1911–25), vol. II, p. 425.

20. Reclus to Lilly Zibelin-Wilmerding, 7 June 1892, *Corr.* III, p. 118.

21. Reclus to Sempre Avanti, 28 June 1892, *Corr.* III, p. 120.

22. Reclus to Zibelin-Wilmerding, 7 June 1892, *Corr.* III, p. 118.

23. Reclus, *Anarchist*, p. 14.

24. Reclus to Roorda van Eysinga, 25 Mar. 1892, *Corr.* III, p. 108.

25. Reclus to Heath, n.d., *Corr.* II, p. 425.

26. Reclus to Roorda van Eysinga, 5 May 1894, *Corr.* III, p. 164.

27. Ibid.

28. Reclus to Karl Heath, 31 Mar. 1900, *Corr.* III, p. 218.

29. Ibid., pp. 218–19.

30. Ibid., p. 219.

31. Reclus to Roorda van Eysinga, June 1892, *Corr.* III, pp. 119–20.

32. Reclus to Roorda van Eysinga, 25 Mar. 1892, *Corr.* III, pp. 108–9.

33. Reclus to Roorda van Eysinga, 9 Apr. 1892, *Corr.* III, p. 111.

34. Ibid., p. 112.

35. See, for example, *Le Radical*, 30 Mar. 1894; *l'Eclair*, 28 Apr. 1894; also, Félix Dubois, *Le Péril Anarchiste* (Paris, 1894), p. 181.

36. Reclus to *l'Eclair*, 2 May 1894; *Corr.* III, p. 163. See also Reclus to Gross, 3 Sept. 1896, *Papiers Gross, Dépôt du CIRA 1964, BPU*, Geneva, where Reclus mentions in passing that he had in his possession 'an extremely precious letter of Emile Henry setting forth his ideas in response to a letter of Malatesta'.

37. See, for example, Hamon, Dubois, Lombroso. Jehan-Préval, *Anarchie et Nihilisme* (Paris, 1892) was so anxious to extricate Reclus from association with the bombers that he may have fabricated reports on his reactions to terrorism; cf. pp. 89, 95–6 and 235.

38. A. Hamon, *Psychologie de L'Anarchiste-Socialiste* (Paris, 1895).

39. Garraud, p. 38. Cf. Robert Jousseaume, *Etude sur les lois contre les menées anarchistes et sur les modifications que ces lois ont apportées à la législation pénale* (Paris, 1895).

40. Garraud, p. 78.

41. See the police report of the search in *P.Po.* B a/1237. Another was carried out at Reclus' home in Sevres on 10 Jan. 1894; see the account in *L'Intransigeant*, 12 Jan. 1894. Searches were also made at the homes of Reclus' relations in Algeria, and reports were filed on the Reclus family and newspaper clippings collected; see esp. *P.Po.* B a/1237.

42. Reclus to Louise, n.d. (Feb. 1892), *Corr.* III, p. 103.

43. Governing Council to Reclus, 28 July 1892, *Papiers ER, NAF* 22915.

44. Reclus to Governing Council, 1 Aug. 1892, *Corr.* III, p. 125.

45. Governing Council to Reclus, 6 Jan. 1894, *Papiers ER, NAF* 22915. On 5 Jan. Reclus had sent a letter to the Governing Council requesting information *Corr.* III, pp. 152–3.

46. University Circle to Reclus, 21 Jan. 1894, *Papiers ER, NAF* 22915.

47. See 'Notes et documents relatifs à l'Université Nouvelle de Bruxelles', *Papiers ER, NAF* 22915; newspaper clippings in *P.Po.* B a/1237; Hem Day, *Elisée Reclus en Belgique, sa Vie, son Activité, 1894–1905* (Paris-Brussels, 1956); Bernard Lazare, 'A School of Liberty' in *Liberty*, 30 Nov. 1895; De Greef, *Eloges d'Elisée Reclus*, p. 34 ff.

48. Reclus to Perron, 6 Jan. 1894, *Corr.* III, p. 154.

49. Reclus to President of the University Circle, n.d. (Jan. 1894?), *Corr.* III, pp. 154–5.

50. See Reclus' comments to Joukowsky, 4 Mar. 1894, *Corr.* III, pp. 159–60.

51. Bernard Lazare, 'A School of Liberty' in J. Ishill, *Elisée and Elie Reclus: In Memoriam* (Berkeley Heights, 1927).

52. See the announcement of the award in *The Geographical Journal* (London), May 1894.

53. Reclus to Louise, 23 Apr. 1892, *Corr.* III, p. 114. Cf. report in *Le Temps*, Apr. 1892; clipping in *AN* F7 12504.

54. Reclus to Zibelin-Wilmerding, *Corr.* III, p. 113. See also the correspondence of Reclus to Louise in *Papiers ER, NAF* 22912.

55. Reclus to Nadar, 27 Apr. 1892, *Corr.* III, p. 115.

56. Reclus to Gross, 10 May 1892, *Corr.* III, pp. 116–17.

57. Reclus, 'Développement'.

58. Reclus to Rigot, 24 Dec. 1883, *Corr.* II, pp. 266–7. Cf. the police report of 28 Dec. 1882, *P.Po.* B a/1237.

59. According to Kropotkin, *Memoirs*, p. 450, Ananieff died late on 21 Dec. and the arrest took place in the early hours of 22 Dec. Reclus' letter to Nadar of 19 Dec. (*Corr.* II, p. 263 ff) which mentions the death of Ananieff is misdated; it must have been written on 22 or 23 Dec. Reclus was notified by telegraph of Ananieff's death and Kropotkin's arrest, and left Clarens for Thonon right away (Kropotkin, *Memoirs*, p. 450). The funeral took place on 23 Dec. and Reclus was back in Clarens on 24 Dec.

60. Reclus to *La Réforme*, Mar. 1894, *Corr.* III, p. 161.

61. Reclus to Roorda van Eysinga, 17 July 1894, *Corr.* III, p. 169.

62. Paul Reclus, 'Biographie', p. 145.

63. Reclus to Governing Council, 13 Jan. 1894, *Corr.* III, pp. 155–6.

64. Reclus to Perron, 6 Jan. 1894, *Corr.* III, p. 154.

65. Reclus to Gross, n.d. (Mar. 1894), *Fonds ER*, 14 AS 232, *IFHS*.

66. Reclus to Roorda van Eysinga, 25 Mar. 1892, *Corr.* III, p. 108.

67. Félix Nadar, 'Elisée Reclus', in *Les Temps Nouveaux*, Dec. 1905.

PART III

ANARCHIST AND TEACHER: 1894–1905

# 11 ANARCHISM AND THE SOCIALIST MOVEMENT

The anarchists received suprisingly lenient sentences at their trial in 1894, and pardons were granted at the inauguration of President Faure in 1895. However, from this time there was a general feeling among anarchists that times had changed, and the movement assumed a new direction and decidedly different character. Individual anarchists, instead of re-activating the groups which had been in existence up to 1894, began to infiltrate the syndicalist movement which had been winning recruits from the early 1890s and which was now gaining momentum under the dynamic leadership of Fernand Pelloutier. The major development in the wider socialist movement was the Second International founded in 1889. But Reclus remained decidedly distant from anarcho-syndicalism, and he openly condemned the Second International. Indeed, a curious thing happened. The more positive he became about social progress, the more negative he became in his critique of various forms of revolutionary strategy. As he ruthlessly pursued the logic of his theories, the man who was celebrated for his tolerance became ever more unyielding in his demands for perfection in the revolutionary struggle.

Reclus' apparent lack of interest in anarcho-syndicalism is at first sight rather puzzling, and since he said nothing explicitly, we can only surmise what his views were. A central concern would have been the movement's perception of the syndicat as the ideal unit of liberated society. It should be remembered that in 1868 he had publicly endorsed a programme whereby the future society would be based upon producers' associations. This was in conformity with Bakuninist collectivism. However, he reformulated his position on the role of producers' associations at least by 1880 when he defended the theory of anarchist communism at the Congress of the Jura Federation in La Chaux-de-Fonds. It was at his instigation that the Congress passed the resolution that the 'natural' commune or community (as opposed to the existing administrative commune) was to be the basic unit of the 'free' society.[1] Reclus could not help but view anarcho-syndicalism sympathetically, as part of the larger struggle against the bourgeois order. Similarly, in the 1870s he had perceived significant signs of progress in the varied efforts of the European working class, trade unionism in England, working-class parliamentary electioneering in

225

Germany, Holland and Denmark, 'revolutionism' in Spain, Italy, a part of Switzerland and especially France.[2] James Guillaume, the noted revolutionary socialist who became a keen anarcho-syndicalist said that, just before his death, Reclus expressed approval of the anarcho-syndicalist movement.[3] Reclus was with the syndicalists in spirit, even though he could not agree with them on the fundamentals of their programme. He was far more critical in his attitude toward the Second International.

Anarchists had attended the two rival socialist congresses which marked the birth of the Second International in 1889. However, their admission became a major issue when the socialists united at the Brussels Congress of 1891. At the Zurich Congress in 1893 anarchists claimed that they too were socialists, but were expelled amid noisy protests. After this experience, the members of the Second International passed a resolution to the effect that only socialists who professed the necessity of political action (within the context of parliamentary politics) should be admitted to future congresses. It is likely that Reclus took an interest in these events, but it would be misleading to suggest that he was supportive of anarchist membership in the Second International, even though he was present for the final battle at the London Congress of 1896. His unenthusiastic attitude towards the question of admission to the Second International is clearly indicated in the letters which he wrote from England to his sister Louise.[4] In one letter he spoke of the congress 'in which, however, I did not take part' and went on to say that he had dropped by to meet the 'anarchist elements'.[5]

About two months before the opening of the London Congress and in anticipation of their expulsion, the anarchists had arranged to hold a meeting on 28 July in the Holborn Town Hall. This meeting happened to take place on the evening of the day on which the anarchists were expelled and the timing won them much publicity and a good deal of sympathy from the more liberal-minded members of the congress, including such figures as Keir Hardie and Tom Mann. Reclus' address was simple and to the point. Far from engaging in a battle with rival socialists, he welcomed all delegates to the congress, hastening to add in his inimical way, that 'as Anarchists and Communists we cannot agree with their belief in government and laws'. It was a mistake for socialists to attempt to bring about revolution through the legal system because, as history showed, law did not promote social change, but was a brake upon it. The prime factor in human history was the *idea*; 'when an idea grows revolution must come; it is impossible to

stop it, it comes, it comes'. As for the vindication of the anarchist
position, he pointed to the remarkable cohesion which anarchists maintained as they dispensed with laws, regulations, congresses, binding
resolutions. 'All over the world we arrive at the same conclusions and
always co-operate. There is always a wonderful unity in thoughts,
sentiments, and the desire and determination to be free.'[6] If Reclus
attended the 'anarchist conference' which was held at St Martin's
Hall, the birthplace of the First International back in 1864, he did
not take an active part in the proceedings.[7]

That Reclus was in disagreement with those socialists who adopted
the parliamentary route to revolution was fairly clear, but only rarely
did he focus attention upon the differences between anarchists and
other socialists. In the 1890s, however, European socialists were increasing their support at the polls and they were moving into a position
which was heavily contributing to the acceptance of the parliamentary
system by the working class. Since, according to Reclus, socialists
were thereby also seriously undermining the revolutionary struggle, he
felt that it was time to make his objections explicit. If there were no
revolutionary uprising within the immediate future, he wrote in
1898, parliamentary socialists would become enmeshed in the web of
bourgeois politics and lose sight of the ultimate objective.[8] Even sincere
socialists, who were conscious of the hazards of the parliamentary arena,
were deluding themselves in their efforts to remain true to their ideals
by means of a rigorous programme. As the years passed, the sense of
the words would change and each person would come to view the programme from a different perspective, until, finally, the most clearly
stated declaration would take on no more than a symbolic significance
and become a simple document of history. The words would necessarily
become symbolic as socialists resorted to the franchise, for in the
process of winning votes they would have to play upon the prejudices
of the unliberated crowd, would have to flatter clericals, liberals,
patriots, even employers; socialist principles would be compromised
until they were shorn of their original meaning. Such was the inevitable
course whereby socialist leaders would gradually become transformed
into bourgeois.[9] The consequence would be fatal and could not be
denied; it had to be pointed out as a danger to those revolutionaries
who were apt to plunge themselves unthinkingly into the political
mêlée.[10]

On the other hand, in the event of a sudden revolution there was
another danger, the establishment of a dictatorship. The revolutionary
government which was being advocated by some as the transition stage

to the socialist society would, in all likelihood, give rise to despotism. This would happen if the revolution were premature, if it took place before the people had passed through an evolutionary process in which their political consciousness had been awakened. The socialists of the Second International would betray their own cause, despite whatever good intentions they might have. The question calling for urgent consideration was how social, economic and political developments could be channelled, so that revolution would occur, but its fruits be rescued for the people, its rightful benefactors.[11]

The anarchist way to socialism, by definition according to Reclus, avoided the hazards of the parliamentary arena and the tragedy of despotism. Anarchists understood that historical phenomena could not be altered before the necessary transformations had taken place in the hearts and heads. Young people mistakenly believed in the possibility of rapid changes, he said to an interested student in 1895. No, he declared, 'transformations are made slowly, and consequently, it is necessary to work with so much more consciousness, patience and devotion'.[12] He saw a growing divide between the anarchists and other socialists, a divide for which he readily found historical comparisons. It was a process similar to that which had earlier split the French republican party into opportunists and socialists. Now it was the socialists who were being divided into two main groups: 'one group, to sweeten their programme and to render it acceptable to the conservatives; the other, to guard their spirit of free evolution and sincere revolution'. The anarchists had experienced their moments of discouragement and even scepticism. However, they had become conscious of the need to abandon their efforts to work within the framework of a body (the Second International) which had launched itself upon a course which was hazardous, if not treasonous, to the revolutionary cause. Having allowed 'the dead to bury the dead', anarchists would take their place 'at the side of the living'.[13] They were aware of the development of historical laws, he wrote elsewhere, and seeing the gradual changes in society, never despaired, however small their influence might appear to be on passing events.[14]

In the 1870s Reclus had felt that it was necessary to tolerate all approaches to socialism. By the 1890s, however, he felt that the time had arrived to become an outspoken critic of 'non-anarchist' socialism. We are used to tracing the Marxist/anarchist dispute back to the Marx/ Bakunin quarrel, but it is important to note that the great cleavage was fully and irrevocably established only with the rise of the Second International in the 1890s. The year 1896 marked the final parting of the ways. Those anarchists who were reluctant to devote their energies to anarcho-syndicalism now had to decide what direction to take. Some thought they should carry on as before. Upon his release from prison in early 1895, Jean Grave was full of enthusiasm 'to take up the propaganda where we had left it, to remake the newspaper', *La Révolte*. When he requested Reclus' support, he was told that 'times had changed'. Grave replied that he saw nothing changed: 'We are fifteen months older, that is all.'[15] None the less, he was persuaded by Reclus to call the proposed paper *Les Temps Nouveaux* (New Times), and the first issue appeared on 4 May 1895. Reclus' influence upon Grave's perception of the changing times can be seen in the name of the paper, as well as in its tone. 'It is the new phase of the struggle that we are entering . . . Human emancipation cannot be the work of any legislation. It must be the product of the individual will . . . It is sufficient for them [the people] to wish to be free in order to find the means of succeeding.'[16] Reclus was listed among the collaborators of *Les Temps Nouveaux*, although he was an infrequent contributor. According to Grave, he also continued to provide financial assistance so far as he was able.[17] With his financial position having deteriorated after 1894, this must have been small. In any event, his account book contains no entries for the newspaper or for Grave after 1894.

This lack of enthusiasm shown by Reclus with regard to renewing the old anarchist movement was not based upon a fading interest in the anarchist cause. It was rooted in a re-assessment of the old forms of propaganda. By early 1894 he had come to the conclusion that newspaper propaganda was no longer necessary, if it ever was, to the growth of anarchism, and that in some instances, it might even be harmful. The newspaper, he claimed, had the fault of expressing a 'collective thought', and thus a somewhat 'castrated' thought. There was an unavoidable tendency to undermine the powerful springs of individual initiative.[18] 'In a word', he said in December 1895, 'organisation is always unsound, regressive, in proportion to the individual presumptuousness and authoritarian violence which it contains; always beautiful and good in proportion to the spirit of freedom which moves it.'[19] He also warned that every 'party' had its *esprit de corps* and, consequently there existed within it a solidarity in evil, as well as in good. Each member of the party could not help but share responsibility for the errors, lies and ambitions of the other members.[20] Even the New

University was not immune to his vigorous denunciation of all organisation. 'Without doubt', he wrote to a friend on 1 July 1895, 'our
University is an institution like any other — therefore bad — but for
the moment it represents the struggle. We enter it anarchically and
personally in order to take part in the combat, and we shall come out
tomorrow.'[21]

As a teacher Reclus could explain to students why the course of
human history had taken one direction and not another. He could
also demonstrate the mistaken assumptions which had supported this
development and suggest how people might be directed towards an
undreamed of happiness. He was disappointed that students showed
so little enthusiasm for the social question, but believed that this
could be partly explained in light of their training as 'exploiters', a
process in which even the New University participated.[22] Yet the fact
that students and intellectuals generally were playing a less important
role than formerly in the world of ideas and politics he welcomed as a
sign of the changing times. This role was being assumed by the increasingly active working class, from whom, it was maintained, the
students could learn much.[23] But Reclus continued to find it difficult
to be precise about what could be done to bring about revolutionary
change. His own revolutionary strategy amounted to energetic
agitation with a view to eliminating traditional prejudices, so that the
people, having become 'purified', would be capable of thinking and
judging for themselves. This he recommended to others. 'At least',
he said, the anarchist 'can act upon himself — work to free himself
personally from all preconceived or imposed ideas, and gradually
group around himself friends who live and act in the same fashion. It
is step by step, through small, loving and intelligent societies that the
great fraternal society will be established.'[24]

Anarchist revolutionary agitation could be fairly satisfying in the
period up to the early 1890s, but it was extremely limiting in an
age when the working class was becoming more tolerant of the
parliamentary system. Some anarchists, disillusioned at the prospects,
believed that anarchist 'colonies' would establish units in which
they might put their beliefs into practice. Reclus sympathised with
their motives, but was merciless in his condemnation of 'backwoods
utopias'. This we saw in Chapter 2. Anarchists must not vacate the
scene of the battle; they had to stand their ground and continue to
press for ever greater social change. The small loving societies which
he advocated — really just groups of good friends — had to take
root within the existing order, not in some monastery-like retreat.

Reclus could be understanding with regard to the mistaken assumptions underlying the attempts to establish anarchist colonies, but he was appalled at the move towards neo-Malthusianism which was propagated in the early 1900s by such prominent anarchists as Paul Robin and (from 1903) Sébastien Faure.

Robin accepted Malthus' proposition that the population of the world increased by geometric progression while the supply of food increased by arithmetic progression. However, he rejected the second part of the original theory which postulated that the population, because it tended to grow too large to be maintained by the available food supply, would be repeatedly reduced by a variety of disasters as it searched for a stable equilibrium. The solution proposed by Robin to counteract this supposed inevitability was the regulation of the birth rate by selective breeding in the best possible conditions, so that the working people, having been reduced in number would become healthier, better educated and a more valued part of society. It was hoped that the result would be more happiness for all. A number of anarchists were recruited to this new creed, and neo-Malthusianism was proclaimed as *the* revolution, a pacific revolution. It is hardly necessary to point out that the theory diverged in practically every respect from Reclus' anarchism. He felt − correctly − that the thrust of the new movement was directed at the development of an elite and aimed to produce social integration rather than revolution.[25] Moreover, he had always maintained that even the original Malthusian argument was untenable, that there would be 'bread for all' once the private appropriation and wastage associated with capitalism had been eliminated, and industrial society run on the principle of solidarity rather than that of profit for a few.[26] Just before his death, he replied to the neo-Malthusians, a matter which he considered most urgent, and attacked their main premise. He called for revolution as 'the only means of winning bread'.[27]

The intransigence which Reclus demonstrated on the question of revolutionary strategy in the post-1894 period was a logical extension of his assessment of developments in the years just prior to it. The attentats had no doubt stirred the blood in his veins. However, it was not the terrorism itself which gave him cause for hope, so much as it was his view of the terrorism as a further manifestation of more widespread social progress. Even before 1892 he was confident and happy. He was especially thrilled by the example of the 1 May celebrations of 1890. 'The 1st May was a great historical date. For the first time there was a conscious solidarity between all internationalists of the world, and all the bourgeois instinctively trembled.'[28] There is a note of extreme optimism in his preface to Kropotkin's *La Conquête du Pain*; the preface was probably written in January 1892,[29] before the outbreak of the *attentats*. The 1890s, he said in the preface, represented something quite different from that which the doomsday talk of the 'end of the century' would have one believe. It was true that people were experiencing 'the end of an epoch, of an era of history', but this old civilisation was giving way to a new era which held forth great possibilities. Science was coming to form the basis of the faith of all people in search of truth, and this would surely lead them to see that this truth was anarchism. By a thousand different phenomena, by a thousand profound modifications 'the anarchical society has for a long time been in full growth', in thought divorced from dogma, in independent research, in the refusal to submit to imposed authority. 'All that is anarchy, even when it is not conscious of itself, and more and more it comes to know itself.'[30] Into this pattern stepped the political terrorists who expressed their solidarity with humanity as a whole and nobly laid down their lives for the cause. It was the intention behind their acts which Reclus found to be progressive and so inspiring.

The political terrorists of the 1890s stood at the crossroads of instinct and consciousness. They represented the instinctive grasping after justice characteristic of past revolutions, as well as the 'reasoned' revolution of the future. They also provided the clue to the failure of the past and suggested lessons for the future. The revolutionary forces had thus far never been able to triumph completely, said Reclus in 1898, because no revolution had been absolutely reasoned. In 1848 too many peasants had been unprepared.[31] In 1871 only half Paris and the industrial areas had been revolutionary, and the Commune had ended in a deluge of blood.[32] It was not sufficient to repeat old formulae in the hopes of raising revolutionary ardour. Successful revolution depended upon the development of 'conscious' forces.[33] 'The transformations must be accomplished in the heads and hearts before muscles are stretched and change is brought about in historical phenomena.'[34] The battle for socialism consisted not only in an awareness of oppression, but also in an understanding of it. The conviction was that, basically, no one wished to be deceived, and that once the truth were known, there would be a desire to act upon it. The more thoroughly ancient prejudices and fears were examined and demolished, the weaker would be the forces of reaction and the less resistance there would be to revolutionary change. At a certain point in the future there would be no more than a few greedy capitalists facing the mighty hordes who demanded retribution.[35] Science had to be used to explain the past and the present, and most importantly, to point to the possibilities for the future.

For Reclus 'science and knowledge was not an abstract matter, to be pondered upon in the quiet study, but a *reality*, to be applied and utilised for the increase of the happiness of all'.[36] Science by its very nature belonged to the human race. Using it for the benefit of the capitalists was seen as a perversion. The dehumanising effects of this sort of applied science were readily observable in the factory where excessive division of labour was a monstrosity, practised by the capitalists in order to maximise profits. Similarly, at the University level, Reclus saw how students were being forced into narrow specialisations to prepare themselves to take up positions as cogs in the great bourgeois wheel. The oppressors of tomorrow were themselves the victims of a dehumanising process, as the bourgeois educational system ensured its survival by emphasis upon career preparation. Any enthusiasm for justice, any interest in the social question were stifled; even the joy of learning was a pleasure that students were denied.[37] Scientific specialisation within a capitalist society simply led down dead-end streets, and did little to create happiness for humanity. It represented a waste of physical and intellectual effort.

This was not an objection to the principle of specialisation. As in the economy, division of labour within science was seen as both inevitable and desirable for the advancement of the human race. The physical, mathematical and social sciences all made their various contributions to a knowledge of the actualities and potentialities of human existence. Moreover, so long as each individual scientist perceived his own work as a contribution to the common product, the specific nature and scope of that work did not matter. What he left unsaid would be taken up by others who would draw upon the available pool of existing knowledge. The main point was that science and the specialisations within it had to become more concerned with general human happiness and not serve capitalism and capitalist institutions.

It is not difficult to imagine how Reclus' approach to geography would make him sensitive to the efforts of the countless numbers of individuals, named and unnamed, in the production of any scientific project. His geography drew upon history, economics, anthropology and especially sociology, and these were mingled with the intimacy of his own personal experience. As a synthesiser he was continually filling in the larger picture, and with such care, sensitivity and eloquence that he has been called an artist who painted in words and pictures,[38] and who raised geography to literature.[39] His was a literature in which imagination was fused with the most intense observation of the earth and its inhabitants. When he could not observe directly, he sought contact with those whose personal experiences he could share. As a result he had a concrete knowledge of all that he presented to the reader, and it is this concreteness, rather than any one particular intellectual gift, which sets him apart in the world of scholarship.

> For though Reclus could not rival the historic insight of Comte, the imagination of Michelet, the technical mastery and interpretation of Le Play, the psychology of Taine, the abstract power of Spencer, or the like, he had the advantage of knowing in his own way more of the concrete world than any of these, perhaps than all put together.[40]

Reclus' whole life may be viewed as an obsession with gaining knowledge. Guérineau, a workingman comrade, caught this spirit when he remembered him as 'an indefatigable worker of intellect'.[41] The vast store of knowledge which he already possessed was never sufficient cause for relaxation; always he was in pursuit of what he did not know. He would talk to Guérineau about the earth, the sky, the trees, the water and the animals, and in turn query him about the lives of the workers and their different mentalities. 'Always, one learns, he said, that the more one knows the less he believes he knows; in short the characteristic of the anarchist is never to pause and always to desire to know more.'[42] And so Reclus lived in his final years. In a letter of 14 November 1895 Elie reported that his brother spent every evening at the University, 'not only to give courses, but also to take them'.[43] Paul Reclus has recorded his uncle's work habits;

> He worked with remarkable regularity, only with great difficulty allowing himself to be diverted by the daily events; 'every day its page' was his line of conduct, and he could write in pencil in the most unlikely places, when a train stopped, in the waiting-room of a rail-way station, on a corner of the table in a public house. He had in his pocket, disposed after the manner of the cartridge-box of a Caucasian soldier, a whole paraphernalia of different pencils. His

memory was prodigious; to verify a sentence, he rose from his table, took the exact book from his library, opened it at the desired page, and had taken up his pen again in an instant.[44]

The lucidity of Reclus' writing and the insatiable thirst for knowledge which he displayed should not lead us to believe that the work was accomplished without effort. One family friend wrote: 'He owned up to his daughter [Jeannie] that in the morning, when he set out to work, he felt as though before an abyss; yet every night the abyss was crossed, the daily task was done . . .'[45]

The rumours that the New University was the Anarchist University and that anarchism would be the creed preached by the professors were soon squashed.[46] It is absolutely essential to see that for Reclus, anarchism was not a mere belief; it was the truth as revealed by science. If his arguments for anarchism were valid, and he believed they were, they would be verified through the scientific method. If they were flawed, which they might conceivably be, science would reveal how they might be improved. It is worth noting that Kropotkin's science never carried him to this singular pursuit of freedom of thought. Shortly after his release from prison in 1886, he wrote to William Morris that '. . . there is so much work to do for elaborating the principles of our Anarchist philosophy which, like each new system of thought, require so much labour'.[47] Kropotkin was preparing to build a 'new system'; Reclus was in revolt against all systems. Nettlau saw this distinction (although he failed to understand it). Reclus, he wrote, lived in a 'more distant epoch', one of anarchy where it was no longer necessary to become involved with dogmas, while Kropotkin 'closer to our epoch' and had elaborated a detailed system of dogmas and hypotheses.[48] Reclus' refusal to consider anarchism a dogma did not preclude an unshakeable conviction in the essential correctness of the anarchist position. 'Not only was he a convinced anarchist, but he could hardly comprehend that an honest, well-meaning human being could fail to be one.'[49]

The anarchist way to revolution was not through the parliamentary system, nor through anarcho-syndicalism, but through a persistent effort to eliminate traditional prejudice. Thus, it was with a re-awakened enthusiasm and excitement that Reclus immersed himself in scholarship and teaching in the final years of his life. As the principal speaker at the opening ceremony of the New University in October 1895 he defined the 'common purpose' of all those connected with the University;

> Science, as we conceive it, and as we seek to interpret it, possesses that supreme bond of union which is found in a boundless respect for human thought. It [the University] will also have the bond which arises from community of method, the firm resolve to draw no conclusion that is not derived from observation and experiment, and to set aside scrupulously all preconceived ideas of merely traditional or mystic origin. Finally, we count on a third bond, that which our pupils and auditors will knit by their love of truth, and by the lofty spirit of sincere, disinterested study.[50]

Reclus was enjoining the students to participate with him in the search for truth through the use of the scientific method. But it was also a call to revolution, to the establishment of a society based upon the principles of anarchism.

## Notes

1.  For the proceedings of the meeting see *Le Révolté*, 17 Oct. 1880.
2.  See the programme of *Le Travailleur*, May 1877.
3.  James Guillaume, *L'Internationale. Documents et Souvenirs (1864–1878)*, 4 vols. (Paris, 1905–10), vol. II, p. 279. It is to be noted that Reclus was very enthusiastic about Guillaume's plans to write a book of commentary and documentation on the anti-authoritarian and anarchist trends within the First International.
4.  Letters of Reclus to Louise in the summer of 1896, *Papiers ER, NAF* 22912.
5.  Reclus to Louise, Aug. 1896, *Papiers ER, NAF* 22912. Reclus made short trips to England in 1894 and at least twice in 1895. See Reclus to Grave, 19 Sept. 1894, *Fonds ER*, 14 AS 232, *IFHS*; Anne Cobden-Sanderson, 'Elie and Elisée Reclus' in J. Ishill, *Elisée and Elie Reclus: In Memoriam* (Berkeley Heights, 1927), p. 45; Reclus to Louise, July 1895, *Correspondance*, 3 vols. (Paris, 1911–25), vol. III, p. 187. Reclus delivered an address on anarchy for the first time in England at South Place in London on 26 July 1895. See report, *P.Po.* B a/1237. The Paris police continued to keep a close watch on Reclus, taking an interest in his activities outside France, but especially surveying his movements when he visited Paris.
6.  *Freedom*, Aug.–Sept. 1896. At the reunion on Tuesday, 28 July, the speakers included Kropotkin, Reclus, Louise Michel, V. Gori, Keir Hardie, Tom Mann, Domela Nieuwenhuis, Bernard Lazare, Gustave Landauer. It was decided that the anarchists should come together every evening as long as the London Congress was in session and that, moreover, those anarchists excluded (some had been admitted as trade unionists) should meet every day in St Martin's Hall, in the same hall, Tcherkesoff reminded them, where the First International had been founded, 32 years previously. The anarchists held meetings until Friday, 31 July. See *Les Temps Nouveaux*, 22 Aug. 1896.

7. Reclus is not mentioned in the report of the proceedings given in *Freedom*.

8. Reclus, *Idéal anarchique*, p. 171 ff.

9. Ibid., pp. 176–7.

10. Ibid., p. 177.

11. Ibid., p. 43 ff.

12. Reclus to Clara Koettlitz, 12 Apr. 1895, *Corr.* III, p. 182.

13. Reclus, *Idéal anarchique*, pp. 177–8.

14. Reclus to Clara Koettlitz, 12 Apr. 1895, *Corr.* III, p. 182. Cf. Reclus to Buurmans, 17 Feb. 1878, *Corr.* II, p. 198.

15. Jean Grave, *Quarante Ans de Propagande Anachiste* (Paris, 1973), p. 338 ff.

16. *Les Temps Nouveaux*, 4 May 1895.

17. Grave, *Quarante Ans*, p. 339.

18. Reclus to Gross, n.d. (Mar. 1894), *Fonds ER*, 14 AS 232, *IFHS*.

19. Reclus to Renard, 27 Dec. 1895, *Corr.* III, pp. 192–3.

20. Reclus, *Idéal anarchique*, pp. 178–9.

21. Reclus to Roorda van Eysinga, 1 July 1895, *Corr.* III, p. 186.

22. Reclus to Grave, 6 Oct. 1894, *Corr.* III, p. 172.

23. Elisée Reclus, *L'Idéal et la Jeunesse* (Brussels, 1894), *passim.* Cf. his address at the official opening of the New University in 1895: *Université Nouvelle de Bruxelles, Séance solennelle du rentrée du 22 octobre 1895, Discours de M. Elisée Reclus* (Brussels, 1895).

24. Reclus to Koettlitz, 12 Apr. 1895, *Corr.* III, p. 182.

25. Reclus to Henri Fuss, n.d. (1904), *Corr.* III, pp. 295–6. Cf. Reclus to Fuss, n.d., *Corr.* III, p. 299.

26. Cf. Reclus' remarks at the 1880 Congress of the Jura Federation in *Le Révolté*, 17 Oct. 1880; Reclus to Heath, n.d. (1884), *Corr.* II, p. 325. See also Reclus, *Idéal anarchique*, p. 128 ff. and his 'Quelques Mots d'Histoire' in *La Société Nouvelle*, Nov. 1894.

27. Elisée Reclus, 'A grande mistificaçao' in *Aurora* (Brazil), Apr. 1905. When Reclus agreed to present an article, he had reserved the right to expand upon it in another review and to bring out a further version in a pamphlet. See Reclus to Neno Vasco, 3 Mar. 1905, *Corr.* III, pp. 310–11. Cf. a response to Reclus by a neo-Malthusian: G. Giroud, 'La Grande Erreur' in *La Régénération*, Dec. 1905 (organ founded by Paul Robin). Reclus had a continuing interest in the problem of population and food supply. He made some contribution to the pamphlets: *Les Produits de la Terre* (Geneva, 1885), *Les Produits de l'Industrie* (Paris, 1887) (article in *La Révolte*, 26 Feb. to 26 Mar. 1887) and *La Richesse et la Misère* (Paris, 1888) (article in *Le Révolté*, 25 June 1887 to *La Révolte*, 5 Nov. 1887). These were translated several times and usually published anonymously, occasionally under Reclus' name. Max Nettlau, *Bibliographie de l'Anarchie* (Brussels, 1897), pp. 70–1, claims that Reclus collaborated in the writings of the pamphlets. Reclus, who wrote the preface to this book, must have been aware of Nettlau's statements and may even have provided the information himself. However, it is doubtful that he collaborated very heavily. In 1901 he wrote to Grave that *Les Produits de la Terre* was not his work, but had been republished under his name, he thought, by some of his friends in Geneva. (The same was probably true for *Les Produits de l'Industrie*.) In any case, he was not satisfied with the work, and expressed the desire to revise it. Reclus to Grave, 19 Dec. 1901, *Fonds Jean Grave*, 14 AS 184b, *IFHS*. Cf. Reclus to Roorda van Eysinga, 16 Mar. 1891, *Corr.* III, p. 91. Grave, *Quarante Ans*, p. 557, claims that *Les Produits de l'Industrie, Les Produits de la Terre* and *La Richesse et la Misère* were written by Reclus.

28. Reclus to Paul Régnier, 6 May 1890, *Corr.* III, pp. 81–2.

29. Reclus to Louise, 15 and 20 Dec. 1891, *Papiers ER, NAF* 22912.

30. Peter Kropotkin, *La Conquête du Pain* (Paris, 1892), Preface by Reclus, pp. IX–XI.

31. Reclus, *Idéal anarchique*, p. 61.

32. Ibid., p. 62.

33. Ibid., p. 44.

34. Ibid., p. 63.

35. Ibid., pp. 63–4.

36. Quoted in Pierre Ramus, 'In Commemoration of Elisée Reclus' in J. Ishill, *Elisée and Elie Reclus*, p. 124.

37. Reclus, *Jeunesse*. Cf. his address at the official opening of the New University in 1895.

38. See, for example, N. Roubakine, 'Elisée Reclus and the Russian Readers' in Ishill, *Elisée and Elie Reclus*, p. 166.

39. Patrick Geddes, 'A Great Geographer: Elisee Reclus' in Ishill, ibid., p. 155.

40. Ibid., p. 158.

41. L. Guérineau, 'Recollections of Elisée Reclus' in Ishill, *Elisée and Elie Reclus*, p. 119.

42. Ibid.

43. Elie Reclus to Daniel Baud-Bovy, 14 Nov. 1895, *Archives Baud-Bovy* 36, *BPU*, Geneva.

44. Paul Reclus, 'A Few Recollections', pp. 3–4.

45. Lilly Zibelin-Wilmerding, 'Elisée Reclus', in Ishill, *Elisée and Elie Reclus*, p. 1103.

46. See the discussion in Lazare.

47. Kropotkin to William Morris, 11 Apr. 1886, Morris Papers VIII, Brit. Mus. Add. Ms. 45, 345.

48. Nettlau to Gross, 17 July 1905, *Fonds Jacques Gross, IISG*.

49. Lilly Zibelin-Wilmerding, 'Elisée Reclus' in Ishill, *Elisée and Elie Reclus*, p. 102.

50. Reclus' address at the official opening of the New University in 1895, p. 6; English from Thérèse Dejongh, 'The Brothers Reclus at the New University' in Ishill, *Elisée and Elie Reclus*, p. 228.

# 12 THE SEARCH FOR TRUTH

The anarchist movement is generally held to have reached an abrupt end with the trial of leading French anarchists in 1894. The groups had been thrown into confusion, their press silenced, and many activists were either in prison or in exile. The anarchist movement failed, so it would appear. However, the terrorists had not envisaged their attacks as constituting a revolution which would immediately bring down the bourgeois order, but rather as acts of propaganda, to inform, rouse to action, prepare for the 'coming' battle. From this perspective, putting the anarchists out of commission was not a sufficient indicator of ultimate failure. Reclus spent the final years of his life inspecting the condition of the troops. Everywhere he found evidence that progress was on the side of the rebels against injustice. A world was taking shape whose resources were increasing and whose inhabitants were developing a mentality favourable to the placing of these resources at the disposal of all. The fight was on to liberate people's minds from centuries old prejudices, to assist them to become conscious of what was rightfully theirs.

It was clear to Reclus that the arguments for communism must stand or fall on the essential equality or inequality of human beings. A central issue touching on that problem concerned the new racial theories which emerged in the late nineteenth century. In that era of nationalism and imperialism a simultaneous battle had to be waged against traditional prejudices and against those conservative critics of democracy who abused science in the name of sanctifying these very same prejudices. He vigorously opposed suggestions that the process of evolution and adaptation of the species had led to the development of specific racial characteristics and that this 'racial soul', as Gustave LeBon described it, was a determining factor in forming national characters. In this period race theory was used to support the claims that the more 'advanced' nations had achieved their superiority on the basis of natural selection and that the theory of the survival of the fittest demanded imperialist policies for fear of losing advantages. It was also used to caution imperialist nations against assimilating subject peoples who, it was said, had their own peculiar racial make-up which should not be disturbed, but allowed to develop at its own rate. It was not difficult for Reclus to see that these were arguments conveniently designed to protect the established interests, even to assuage the cry of their consciences, so that they might rest easily in their exploitation of the weak. The same arguments were used to defend class and sex privileges within countries. He rebelled against such lies and self-deceptions, and plunged into the debate on race, continuing the line of argument which he had begun almost a half century earlier. In Chapter 2 we saw how, in contrast to people such as Gobineau, he had championed the fusion of the races rather than racial purity. It now became important for him to show why it was that people who were fundamentally 'equal' could manifest themselves so 'unequally'.

An underlying assumption of all Reclus' writings was that the elements which went to constitute a national character were largely determined by the environment in which people lived, in particular that the geographical location helped to determine the social and political institutions which developed throughout the history of these peoples. In his preface to Léon Metchnikoff's *La Civilisation et les Grands Fleuves Historiques* (Civilisation and the Great Historical Rivers) (1889) he drew attention to the chapter on the influence of the environment on races as 'the part of the book which appears to me to have the most importance in the history of human thought'.[1] In the 1890s he maintained that the nature of all people, though frequently disguised or apparently distorted by the social and political conditions in which they lived, was essentially the same. All people could be located somewhere on the spectrum of social evolution, the highest existing level being that of Western Europe. However, the advances of the Europeans had not been due to any racial superiority, but to the fact that, for various geographical and historical reasons, institutions favourable to human progress had happened to be developed among them.[2] The question was whether the advantages which were enjoyed by the Europeans were of a temporary or a permanent nature. Since he could not conceive that the Europeans would maintain their lead forever, it therefore became important to show why the factors which had formerly supported their impressive leaps forward were no longer operable. He attempted to prove this by demonstrating that the entire world was becoming 'Europeanised'.

In October 1894 he pointed out that Western Europe had become 'the centre of equilibrium between the forces of the human race' and that from this area radiated 'not only all the roadways of commerce, but also the ideas and influences of social life, in its collective solidarity'. While the contrasts between East and West were still sharp, and at many points reconciliation appeared impossible, travel and commerce were slowly contributing to a 'mutual understanding between the race of men which points to their unification'. In India, for example, England's homogenisation of the people was reducing the contrasts and providing moral unity.[3] In 1898 he saw the same unifying forces at work with even more positive results. Japan had been transformed into a European power — 'if not in language, history, and traditions, in the complete recasting of its administration, institutions, customs and theories, in its devotion to science, in its entire and unreserved acceptance of a policy based on observation and experience'. This was the 'great event of the century' and would be no 'solitary avatar'. There were unmistakeable signs that similar transformations were about to take place in China and in all those countries where different races, yellow, red or black, were being brought into close contact with people of the Aryan-Greco-Latin civilisation. 'So vanished the oft-repeated assertion that *race* is a final and irreducible fact, and that no possible progress in the perception of scientific or moral truths can ever prevail against it.' The transformation in China was not taking place at the governmental level, but where it really mattered, among the people. The steamboats on her rivers and the factories along their banks were 'engines of revolution'. Science had penetrated into the schools, and its precepts had begun to compete with those of Confucian philosophy. Although the number of Europeans in China was extremely small, these foreigners, whatever their moral worth as individuals, were frequently 'torch-bearers of learning and harbingers of ideas'.[4]

It was becoming increasingly meaningless to speak of the history of a particular country. The process of Europeanisation was dissolving the former relative isolation between countries and creating an inter-related world. Henceforth history would be universal, the record of the relations between the peoples of the entire world.[5] Reclus must have grinned as he remarked that the conventional boundaries between countries were gradually being eroded by the force of circumstances, and that the most ardent patriot was becoming a 'citizen of the world'.

> In spite of his aversion to the foreigner, in spite of the tariff which protects him against outside business, in spite of the cannon facing the two sides of the tabooed line, he eats bread which comes from India, drinks coffee which is harvested by the

Negroes or the Malaysians, dresses himself in material made from American fibre, uses devices which are the product of the combined work of a thousand inventors of every time and race, experiences the sentiments and the thoughts which millions of men experience with him from one end of the world to the other.[6]

As the many local histories became fused into a universal history, people were coming to recognise their common humanity. In spite of the national hatreds which persisted, they understood the 'same scientific laws formulated in a language of precision and consequently with a perfect identity', they researched the same intellectual origins, the same historical figures, and were preoccupied with the same political and social problems.[7]

It is a fact of the first importance, showing as it does how the very shrinkage of the earth, brought about by the progress of science and by increased facilities of communication, has the effect of enlarging men's minds and of broadening every question. Contemporary history is far outstripping the narrow conceptions of the Monroe Doctrine.[8]

This shrinkage of the world was not in itself to be applauded. It might indicate no more than that a greater proportion of the world's population had become the unwitting victims of capitalist exploitation. But, with the combined efforts of the oppressed of the entire world, this would be only a temporary, if regrettable, stage in the course of human development. Henceforth the relations between capital and labour would be played out upon a broader stage. All social questions would be exposed to open, public discussion, and the enemy would become fully aware that they had to deal with the disinherited of the world. In the 1870s Reclus had expressed some anxiety about the exploitation of cheap, foreign labour by the more highly industrialised countries.[9] By 1898 this fear had been allayed by the speed with which the Chinese in New York or Boston had learned to bargain for the same wages as their white counterparts. The pattern of developments in the Far East, and he made particular reference to the role of the Americans, logically led back to the larger human question of 'bread and justice' for all. Once again he was suggesting how an evil situation could be made to yield good, if the will were sufficiently strong. Not only would all people come to know each other as brothers and sisters, but together they would hasten their emancipation through concerted action against their common enemy. The question of race clouded the issue of the relations between capital and labour.[10]

Attention was also drawn to the ways in which race was being used to mask social-economic concerns between bourgeois. At the time of the Dreyfus affair Reclus applied himself to uncovering the real motives behind the recent outbursts of anti-Semitism. In a lecture of 3 March 1898 he sought first of all to clear up misconceptions about who the Jews really were. Tracing their history back to the earliest times, he demonstrated that only a very small proportion of them were entitled to call themselves Semites. Anti-Semitism was not a response to any set of racial characteristics peculiar to Jews, he said, because Jews were a mixture of many peoples, including Aryans. Another approach had to be taken. For various historical reasons, he explained, those who professed the Jewish religion had undergone repeated persecution. This victimisation had drawn them together in a spirit of solidarity, which had acted as a means of self-preservation, but which had also ensured them a separate identity. As middlemen they had had contact with a wide number of people, but it had not been possible to become assimilated as a group into these societies. While the role of middlemen had been assumed out of necessity, it had also provided the Jews with certain specific skills which had prepared them as keen businessmen and commercial dealers. Having lived by their wits among foreign peoples for many generations, they had developed strong desires to excel and could boast of noteworthy accomplishments in the arts and sciences, as well as in business. The desire to excel, sometimes coupled with a need to display conspicuous habits of consumption, had gradually worked towards their elevation as a highly visible, rich and influential minority. Jews had become identified with the 'monopolising of the commonweal'; it was the covetousness of this social position, real or perceived, which was at issue in the late nineteenth-century attacks upon Jews. The question of anti-Semitism could be reduced to the struggle between bourgeois Christians and bourgeois Jews. Both groups had the 'identical desire egotistically to appropriate the goods of the earth to themselves'. The hatred against the Jews was not a reflection of the antipathy of races: 'As for the question of races, it becomes lost in the social question.'[11]

When asked about events surrounding the Dreyfus affair in France, Reclus replied that every social phenomenon had a complex origin and varied according to time and place. At that time in France (early 1898) anti-Semitism was a very superficial movement, due almost

entirely to 'the base envy of candidates outdistanced in the competition, of officials eliminated in the distribution of places'. It was
understandable that wage-earners and the unemployed were not
interested in the movement 'because the holders of capital, masters
and parasites, all resemble each other, whether they be Jews or
Christians'. While recognising the viciousness of the attacks of French
anti-Semites, he felt that the movement would produce no more than
a momentary emotion and that the Jewish question would only
temporarily divert energies away from 'la grande question' of bread
and justice for all people, Jews, Christians, Muslims or pagans.[12]

The question of race, as Reclus was well aware, is intimately connected with that of sex; rarely does one encounter a racist who is
not also sexist, or vice versa. He was perhaps the most progressive
of all prominent nineteenth-century revolutionaries in his views on
women and marriage. From an early age he had been cognizant of the
vital role played by women in the transmission of traditional culture, and
he had believed that they might eventually wield a powerful influence
in human emancipation.[13] However, on only a few occasions did he
refer specifically to the situation of women in society.[14] In June 1868
he showed some interest in *La Société de la Revendication des Droits
de la Femme* (Society for the Demand of the Rights of Women) in
which Champseix and Elie and Noémi were directly involved.[15] In
July 1882 he criticised a friend for making an allusion to Proudhon's
remarks on the position of women 'since his pages on woman are still
for all of us that which weighs most heavily upon the memory of the
socialist writer'.[16] In a letter on the subject of education in September
1894 he declared that 'the question of sex . . . is the question of
importance'. Did not women have just as much right as men to the
fruits of liberation, such as the right to a full education? 'Outside co-
education, there is no education.'[17] This education was intended to
counteract the traditional prejudices against women, to open up
opportunities for them to realise their potentialities as human beings,
rather than meekly to accept their traditional roles.

In the period after 1894 we find Reclus probing into the origins
of the relationship between men and women. He noted that a diversity
of marriage forms had existed in primitive society, but held that there
were two fundamental facts diametrically opposed to each other:
'The brutal sexual force of the man: origin of patriarchy' and 'the
natural attachment of the child to the mother which suckles it: origin
of matriarchy'. Throughout the ages the conflict between these two
opposing forces had produced the most 'unequal' results. Even

where matriarchy prevailed in principle, it was often patriarchy which existed in practice.[18] Reclus used the terms, patriarchy and matriarchy, in the sense of influence by the man or by the woman respectively. When he referred to the natural attachment of the child to the mother as the origin of matriarchy, he was referring to the development of woman's sphere of influence. This domain he did not assume to be limited to the children and indicated that it could be, and sometimes was, extended to other social relations.

In *L'Homme et la Terre* (Man and the Earth), his final statement to the world of scholarship, Reclus put forth his objections to the view that the institution of patriarchy was the mature result of a slow evolutionary process from primitive forms of marriage. He insisted that patriarchy had come into existence at the point where the man had exerted force over the woman and had claimed her as his private property.[19] The most barbarous society was that in which the male ruled simply because he had the greater physical strength, provided the food and meted out blows to his enemies and the weak, while the female was bearer of children, nurse and servant to the absolute master.[20] The introduction of elements of matriarchy, or the opening up of the woman's influence, was based upon a 'natural fact', the birth of the child, rather than brute force. Matriarchy, he said, contrary to widespread belief, was a development towards a refinement of mores and represented a higher stage in social evolution.[21] It is unfortunate that he referred to the attachment of the child to the mother as a 'natural' phenomenon and failed to employ his own principle concerning the influence of the environment a little more thoroughly. He might have seen that the development of both male and female roles was environmentally conditioned. But he himself was a product of his milieu, and however open his attitudes, occasionally showed signs of a slightly chivalrous way of referring to women by the use of a certain phrase or term.

As in the wider sphere of the economy the root of the evil between the sexes could be traced to the rise of private property, and no real progress could be achieved until it had been eliminated. Goods and services had to be collectivised, produced and enjoyed in common. Fortunately, women were not to be included in this collectivisation; they were to be emancipated as human beings. Women had to undergo a double emancipation, since not only were they among the disinherited of the earth, but they themselves had been reduced to private property. Reclus did not envisage post-liberated society as one of atomised individuals, however. It was natural for a man and a woman to come together freely, to establish a family based 'solely upon affection, upon its free affinities'. Every aspect of the family which rested upon the power of prejudice, the intervention of laws or the interests of fortune ought to disappear: 'Here, as in every other thing, liberty and natural élan are the elements of life.'[22] A man and a woman were to form a free union, two equals, setting forth together to complete themselves as human beings and to make their individual and collective contribution to the higher development of humanity.[23] The year before his death Reclus described the union of the sexes as the joy 'of feeling oneself absolutely one with another self'.[24] Such a relationship could not be artificially regulated, and he shocked his more conservative contemporaries in 1870 and again in 1875 by 'marrying' with neither official nor religious recognition. In October 1882 his two daughters decided, as free and rational beings according to their father, upon a similar form of marriage.[25]

Reclus had three wives, Clarisse (1858–69), Fanny (1870–74) and Ermance (1875–1905). Late in life he also enjoyed the companionship of the Belgian school-teacher Florence de Brouckère. The evidence suggests, however, that it was Fanny with whom he came to understand the depth of the intimacy between a man and woman who confronted one another not as master to servant, but as equals. In February 1878 Reclus described Fanny in moving terms as

the woman who, during the siege and the Commune, defended my honour so admirably, the woman who made me love life, the one of whom I was proud, because she always gave me counsels of courage and rectitude and because she was the better part of my being . . . but I have changed a great deal. In animated conversation, when it is a question of the cause, I am still the same: but in day-to-day life I am the most taciturn of men.[26]

Although he had married Ermance Beaumont-Trigant in 1875,[27] the memory of Fanny continued to haunt him, and he grieved for many years.[28] In a letter of January 1880 he confided to a friend that he was 'very unhappy, and life has been so difficult for me that I very often ask myself if it would not be better to go to bed and die'. However, he added bravely, he did not have any right to complain, for he was blessed with family and friends, and above all there was as a consolation the 'joy of fighting and suffering for a good cause'.[29]

Throughout his life and work there was a preoccupation with the question of progress. It was one thing to argue that progress was coincident with the movement of society towards anarchist communism. He also felt obliged to isolate general (natural) laws of development, in order to be able to show how progress was achieved, and to assess the prospects for the future. *L'Homme et la Terre* stated that there were three main factors or laws which determined the development of the human race: 'The "class struggle", the search for equilibrium and the sovereign decision of the individual.'[30] The class struggle had arisen out of an unequal development among individuals and within societies, with the consequence that human collectivities divided into classes or castes, not only different but with opposing and conflicting interests. The second law was a necessary consequence of the division of the social body. As the equilibrium was upset from individual to individual, from class to class, it was constantly being re-established around the axis: 'The violation of justice always demands vengeance.' From that point of departure there were incessant oscillations. While rulers attempted to maintain their position, the ruled fought to win their liberty, but as soon as the latter had won, they attempted to reconstitute the power to their own profit. Either the oppressed submitted, or the 'demands of free men' prevailed. In the chaos of events it was possible to discern 'real' revolutions, changes of a political, economic and social nature which were the result of heightened con-sciousness and individual initiative. Thus the third law revealed through a study of human history was that no evolution would have been possible but for individual effort. It was in the human person that it was essential to search for the 'impulsive shock' of the milieu, which would translate itself into the voluntary activity responsible for the diffusion of ideas and social change. The instability of societies was caused by the constraint imposed upon the free expression of individuals. The 'free' society would only exist when full liberty was provided for everyone.[31]

The key to all progress was individual initiative, and the way to promote progress was to remove all constraints upon the individual. This could not be done without a struggle because all masters, religious or bourgeois, perceived it to be in their interests to retain their privileges through the forceful suppression of individual initiative. The most frequently employed means, and that which was found to be the most successful, was the diverting of national anger about domestic affairs into hostility against foreigners.[32] Revolutionary opposition to the state might be undermined by harmless or even attractive expressions, such as 'patriotism', 'social peace' or 'order'. The quite natural and even very beautiful sentiment, love of one's country, had come to signify a necessarily accompanying hatred of one's neighbours; patriotism was easily transformed into chauvinism. At the turn of the century socialists everywhere were having to defend themselves (and socialism) against the charge of disloyalty to their native land.[33] In addition, such activities as gambling, drink and debauchery created a depravity and demoralisation which, conveniently for the dominant class, tended towards the weakening of the spirit of revolt and thus individual initiative.[34]

Disappointed but not discouraged by these incidences of human frailties, Reclus judged that the forward movement of history might be delayed but never brought to a halt.[35] Nor was he thrown off course by the sheer number of different social and political tendencies which he observed to be present in society at any one time. Within the general evolution, he said, there were a great many groups at different levels of evolution, and thus there were many opposing movements. Progress did not take place in a straight line, but in complicated curves, and thus it was all the more necessary to examine the record with care.[36] Even the ugliness and shame of the Dreyfus affair might be seen as progress because it exposed to the world evils which might otherwise have remained hidden for a time from full view. The hastening of the death of a society without justice was progress, even if it were not replaced by the society which anarchists aimed to create.[37] In the larger movement of history Reclus could perceive that periods of reaction were followed by periods of action, and reversals by progress; 'the general thrust is accomplished by a sort of oscillation, by a series of comings and goings, comparable to the movement of waves in the flood-tide; always an alternation of temporary reversals is produced in the collective march of men'.[38] Sometimes the periods of regression endured a long time and were so extensive that there was a temptation to believe in an 'irremediable decadence', to suffer the illusion that the present so-called iron age had been preceded by a golden age and that it would be followed by an age of mud. But even the darkness of the Middle Ages had given way to the light of science. And it was clear from a study of history that the periods of reaction were increasingly shorter. It was possible to become more conscious of their rhythm, to forecast their expected length, even to attempt to avert them.[39]

In the meantime, the incessant battle continued: successful revolution was directly dependent upon the liberation of the spirit from prejudices, which were essentially atavisms or survivals of an earlier, more primitive age. Some survivals, such as modesty in dress,[40] were not of fundamental importance and would tend to disappear in time. However, there were others which had to be tackled immediately. One of these was the primitive fear of the foreigner which lay at the basis of racism. Another was religion.

In the 1870s, in an effort to establish the precise nature of the struggle between capital and labour, Reclus had resisted being diverted into a discussion of religion.[41] In 1884 he said that religion no longer had any power.[42] However, in the late 1880s he came to see that religion was not going to disappear as easily as he had once believed. Travelling in North America in 1889, he came into contact with several groups of methodists, and perceived that religion, through such movements as spiritualism and neo-Buddhism, was able to survive by accommodating itself to the milieu. The same was true of the Salvation Army in England. By means of joyous refrains, dances, common outings, religion was able to feed upon natural feelings of solidarity, to present itself as blending with liberty, poetry and love. Even Catholicism was attempting to keep in step with the century and was able to persuade some socialists to remain in the church for fear of excommunication.[43]

By 1894 Reclus was searching for scientific explanations for religion's remarkable hold. In an address to the *Ecole des Libres Etudes* (School of Free Studies) in Brussels, he attempted to place religion within the context of universal evolution.[44] Not content to explain religion simply in terms of organised religion, he traced it back to what he regarded as its earliest form, to superstition, or a fear of the unknown. As time went on, superstitions passed into myths and symbols and crystallised into dogmas and theologies. (Compare his critique of parliamentary socialism.) In its strict etymological sense, superstition designated those ideas and sentiments which had survived the distant ages; they existed in the child because 'every man develops as humanity develops'.[45] Contemporary society, he insisted, was increasingly capable of ridding itself of survivals. The origins and development of religion had to be scientifically explained and its premises demolished; otherwise an attack on official religion would be much less effective.[46]

The question of religion came to assume some importance the more he recognised its durability and the more the dispute over clericalism gained momentum in France. On Christmas Day 1899 he wrote to Grave, criticising an article on religion in *Les Temps Nouveaux*. The article had claimed that the battle against clericalism and Christianity was of secondary importance in the economic struggle, a view which Reclus himself had put forth some fifteen years previously, but which he now believed contained an error of judgement. From an historical point of view, he said, the fear of the unknown had preceded the regime of private property. 'If a man finds it so difficult to rebel against Injustice, it is because he always feels dominated by mystery.'[47] To attack religion, the unknown, would be equivalent to undermining the foundation of the system of private property, especially since, as he wrote elsewhere, the Church was actually in league with the defenders of property.[48] The faith of old was quickly disappearing, but the Church remained a power in society, directly through its recruitment of the privileged and indirectly through the survival of religious superstition. The function of religion had come to be the reinforcement of the authority of the bourgeois order.

The attack on religion, as fierce and decisive as it was, should not blind us to the inspiration which religion continued to provide for Reclus' social and political theories. He had been tremendously impressed with the Christian ideals to which he had been introduced as a boy, and he suffered acutely once he saw that religion had no place for the concrete needs of human beings. While the church was abandoned, the ideals remained. And as he matured, his early determination to see the realisation of these ideals was strengthened through the passionate faith in science which he shared with many of his contemporaries. In his boyhood Reclus had imagined the Heavenly Father sending down the daily bread; several decades later he suggested 'The Conquest of Bread' as the title for Kropotkin's well-known book which was published under that name in 1892. In 1894, he summed up his view of the aims of the revolutionary struggle by insisting that anarchists had a triple ideal. The first was bread for the body, since everybody had a right to eat. The second was education, or 'bread for the spirit', since everybody had a right to develop to his full capacities. The third was brotherhood, what he might have called 'bread for the heart'.[49] The daily bread had become nourishment for the whole person, physical, spiritual and emotional, and a healthy person was also an equal person, not in the sight of God — there was no God — but in the eyes of his brothers (and sisters!).

As they marched into the future men and women had to overcome the survivals of primitive societies. However, it was not a straightforward question of overcoming the past. While some primitive elements lingered which would be better left behind, other elements had been abandoned at a loss. In particular humans had become the poorer through attitudes which rigidly separated them from the animals whom they then proceeded to debase and enslave. The noble wild boar had become the filthy pig, the 'intrepid' mouflon the 'timid' sheep. The great preoccupation of flesh-eaters was 'to augment certain four footed masses of meat and fat . . . stores of walking flesh, moving with difficulty from the dung-heap to the slaughterhouse'. Through thoughtlessness and cruelty whole species of animals became extinct. Most dogs had become 'degraded beings that tremble before the stick', some of them taught to be savage or vain or stupid. But ever searching for the ray of light as he probed every dark corner, Reclus believed that there had been some progress. The dog that was brought up in 'generosity, gentleness, and nobility of feeling' might frequently 'realise a human or even superhuman ideal of devotion and moral greatness'. Cats surpassed dogs by far in learning to safeguard their 'personal independence and originality of character', to become 'companions rather than captives'. Moreover, since their days in the wilderness, they had made moral and intellectual advances which were miraculous. 'There is not a human sentiment which on occasion they do not understand or share, not an idea which they may not divine, not a desire but what they forestall it.'[50] (Cat lovers will agree.) These are touching sentiments. They are also arguments in support of an increased sensitivity to animals and to nature in general.

Although an enthusiastic proponent of technological advancement, Reclus could also cringe at the havoc which a 'pack of engineers' could wreak upon a 'charming valley'.[51] One must be wary of placing this student of human geography within the Western humanist tradition. The hero of Reclus' work was not a God-man, for whom the animals and trees existed to serve his greater glory. In many ways man is the villain of the piece, as for example when he needlessly slaughters would-be companions for food. While the inspiration for Reclus' work was hope for the future, he also longed to re-establish certain characteristics of the primitive, especially his respect for nature, his nobility and his savage pride. Here we can also detect that spirit which led him to elevate a Ravachol. Once the bankruptcy of the present had been declared, he said, and wealth had been forsaken for friendship, people would be reminded of the animals which had been left behind and seek anew to make companions of them.[52] There was much to be learned about life by looking backwards and downwards. 'The study of primitive man has contributed in a singular degree to our understanding of the "law and order" man of our own day, the customs of animals will help us to penetrate deeper into the science of life, will enlarge both our knowledge of the world and our love.'[53]

Reclus' vegetarianism was not based solely upon convictions which grew out of his studies of nature. He himself tells us that he was a 'potential vegetarian while still a small boy wearing babyfrocks'.

> I have a distinct remembrance of horror at the sight of blood. One of the family sent me, plate in hand, to the village butcher, with the injunction to bring back some gory fragment or other. In all innocence I set out cheerfully to do as I was bid, and entered the yard where the slaughtermen were. I still remember this gloomy yard where terrifying men went to and fro with great knives, which they wiped on blood-besprinkled smocks. Hanging from a porch an enormous carcass seemed to me to occupy an extraordinary amount of space; from its white flesh a reddish liquid was trickling into the gutters. Trembling and silent I stood in this blood-stained yard incapable of going forward and too much terrified to run away. I do not know what happened to me; it has passed from my memory. I seem to have heard that I fainted, and that the kind-hearted butcher carried me into his own house; I did not weigh more than one of those lambs he slaughtered every morning.
>
> Other pictures cast their shadows over my childish [*sic*!] years and, like the glimpse of the slaughterhouse, mark so many epochs in my life. I can see the sow belonging to some peasants, amateur butchers, and therefore all the more cruel. I remember one of them bleeding the animal slowly, so that blood fell drop by drop; for, in order to make really good black puddings, it appears essential that the victim should have suffered proportionately. She cried without ceasing, now and then uttering groans and sounds of despair almost human; it seemed like listening to a child.
>
> ˙. . . One of the strongest impressions of my childhood is that of having witnessed one of those rural dramas, the forcible killing of a pig by a party of villagers in revolt against a dear old woman who would not consent to the murder of her fat friend. The village crowd burst into the pigstye and dragged the beast to the slaughter place where all the apparatus for the deed stood waiting, whilst the unhappy dame sank down upon a stool weeping quiet| tears. I stood beside her and saw those tears without knowing whether I should sympathise with her grief, or think with the crowd that the killing of the pig was just, legitimate, decreed by common sense as well as by destiny.[54]

These recollections at the age of 71 demonstrate Reclus' early sensitivity and suggest how childhood experiences remained with him and became fused with scholarly investigation. Along with emotional revulsion at the sight of the slaughterhouse and the learned arguments which went together to produce his vegetarianism, we might also include the influence of his early encounter with Christianity. 'Do we understand the meaning of the traditions which place the first man in a garden of beauty, where he walks in freedom with all the animals, and which tell us that the "Son of Man" was born on a bed of straw, between the ass and the ox, the two companions of the field-worker?'[55] And the powerful realism of the descriptions of those acts arising out of the needs of meat-eaters — do we detect traces of ecstacy amid the agony?

## Notes

1. Léon Metchnikoff, *La Civilisation et les Grands Fleuves Historiques* (Paris, 1889), Preface, pp. XIV–XV.

2. Cf. for example, Elisée Reclus, *Hégémonie de l'Europe* (Paris, 1894).

3. Elisée Reclus, 'East and West' in the *Contemporary Review*, Oct. 1894.

4. Elisée Reclus, 'The Vivisection of China' in *The Atlantic Monthly*, Sept. 1898.

5. Reclus, 'd'Histoire', p. 489.

6. Ibid., pp. 489–90.

7. Ibid., p. 490.

8. Reclus, 'Vivisection'.

9. Elisée Reclus, 'L'Internationale et les Chinois' in *Almanach du People pour 1874* (revised in *Le Travailleur*, Mar./Apr. 1878).

10. Cf. Elisée Reclus, *La Chine et la Diplomatie Européene* (Paris, 1900), p. 16.

11. As reported in François Bournand, *Les Juifs et nos contemporains* (Paris, 1898), pp. 217–21. Cf. report in *La France*, 4 Mar. 1898. Cf. Karl Marx, 'On the Jewish Question' in David McLellan, *Karl Marx, Early Texts* (Oxford, 1971), p. 85 ff.

12. Reclus to Henri Dagan, n.d. (1898), published in *Les Droits de l'Homme*, 22 Apr. 1898. See also Elisée Reclus, *Les Arabes* (Cours de M. Elisée Reclus à l'Institut des Hautes Etudes de l'Université Nouvelle de Bruxelles (année 1897–1898) – 6e Conférence) (Brussels, 1898), especially pp. 3 and 14.

13. See references in *Correspondance*, 3 vols. (Paris, 1911–25), vol. I.

14. See Reclus' comments on Josephine Butler. While he supported her work among the prostitutes of England, it was his feeling that she was attacking 'a simple consequence of the social regime. As for us [anarchists] . . . we attack the regime itself, property, law.' Reclus to Heath, 2 Aug. 1882, *Corr.* II, p. 258.

15. Elisée to Elie, June 1868, *Corr.* I, p. 276. Louise Michel also became involved in this society.

16. Reclus to Heath, 8 July 1882, *Corr.* II, pp. 254–5.

17. Reclus to Baud-Bovy, 19 Sept. 1894, *Archives Baud-Bovy* 36, *BPU*, Geneva.

18. Reclus to Kropotkin, 8 Jan. 1901, *Corr.* III, pp. 232–3.

19. Reclus, *L'Homme et la Terre*, vol. I, p. 239.

20. Ibid., pp. 242–3.

21. Ibid., p. 251.

22. Reclus to Clara Koettlitz, 12 Apr. 1895, *Corr.* III, p. 183.

23. See the address delivered by Elisée and Fanny at their marriage on 26 June 1870 in *Papiers ER, NAF* 22909 (document in Fanny's handwriting).

24. Reclus to Clara Mesnil, 25 Oct. 1904, *Corr.* III, p. 293.

25. See, for example, Reclus to Nadar, 19 Dec. 1882, *Corr.* II, pp. 263–4. Elie acted as adviser to Elisée's daughters, while Elisée remained in the background in order to avoid the role of a paternal figure which might exert pressure on them. After the death of Elie, the editors of *La Société Nouvelle* published as a brochure his address to his nieces at their wedding: Elie Reclus, *Le Mariage tel qu'il fut et tel qu'il est. Avec une allocution d'Elisée Reclus* (Mons, 1907). It appeared as *Souvenirs du 14 octobre 1882* (Paris, 1882), beginning with forward 'Unions Libres', followed by 'Exposé des Motifs' and 'Allocution du Père à ses Filles et à ses Gendres', and in the same form in *Les Arts de la Vie*, July 1905.

26. Reclus to Buurmans, 17 Feb. 1878, *Corr.* II, p. 199.

27. See the document dated 10 Oct. 1875 which seems to have been the address delivered by Reclus at the wedding; *Papiers ER, NAF* 22911.

28. See the correspondence in *Corr.* II, *Fonds ER*, 14 AS 232, *IFHS*; *Papiers ER, NAF* 22913. Cf. Paul Reclus, 'Biographie', p. 12.

29. Reclus to Heath, 30 Jan. 1880, *Corr.* II, p. 223.

30. Reclus, *L'Homme et la Terre*, Preface to vol. I, p. IV.

31. Ibid., pp. II–III.

32. Elisée Reclus, 'Metamorphoses du Progrès' in *Almanach de la Question Sociale pour 1899* (Paris, 1899), p. 17.

33. Reclus, *Idéal anarchique*, p. 112 ff. Cf. his preface to *Patriotisme, Colonisation, Bibliothèque Documentaire*, no. 2 (Paris, 1903).

34. Reclus, 'Metamorphoses'.

35. Ibid.

36. Ibid., p. 18.

37. Ibid., pp. 18–19.

38. Reclus, 'd'Histoire', p. 490.

39. Ibid., pp. 490–1.

40. Cf. Reclus to Roorda van Eysinga, 16 Mar. 1891, *Corr.* III, p. 89 ff.

41. See above, Chapter 6.

42. Reclus, *Anarchist*, p. 7 ff.

43. Reclus to his daughter Jeannie, 18 June 1889, *Corr.* II, p. 494. Cf. Elisée Reclus, 'Quelques Mots sur la Révolution Boudhique' in *L'Humanité Nouvelle*, June 1897.

44. Elisée Reclus, *La Formation des Religions, Conférence à l'Ecole des Libres Etudes* (Brussels, 1894), See also his 'Origines de la religion et de la morale' in *Les Temps Nouveaux*, 27 Feb.–19 Mar. 1904.

45. Ibid., p. 11.

46. Ibid.

47. Reclus to Grave, 25 Dec. 1899, *Corr.* III, p. 215.

48. Elisée Reclus and Georges Guyou (pseudonym of Elisée's nephew, Paul), 'L'Anarchie et l'Eglise' in *Les Temps Nouveaux*, 8–14 Sept. 1900. See also Elisée Reclus, 'Nouvelle proposition pour la suppression de l'Ere chrétienne' in *Les Temps Nouveaux*, 6 May 1905.

49. Reclus, 'd'Histoire', p. 492 ff.

50. Elisée Reclus, 'La Grande Famille' in *Le Magazine International*, Jan. 1897 (English from translation, 'The Great Kinship' by Edward Carpenter, London, 1900).

51. Reclus, 'Vegetarianism'.
52. Reclus, 'Grand Famille'.
53. Ibid.
54. Reclus, 'Vegetarianism'.
55. Reclus, 'Grand Famille'.

# 13 MAN AND THEORETICIAN

On several occasions throughout his life Reclus achieved notoriety
because of his social and political views. He developed into a controversial figure of major proportions as links came to be increasingly
drawn between what anarchist theoreticians were saying and what
political terrorists were doing. The unprecedented scale of terrorist
activity in the early 1890s heightened the controversy, so that his
arrival in Brussels in the spring of 1894 to deliver geography lectures
was greeted with mass demonstrations and riots. Needless to say, such
a sensational introduction ensured that the lectures would be publicised
and well attended at the very least. Indeed, they were a resounding
success. A witness recalled that first memorable lecture on 2 March
1894, the enthusiastic crowds, the tensions and the excitement, 'the
serenity of the professor in his triumph'.[1] Throughout the summer
the lectures continued before students young and old, as well as
curious citizens from a wide variety of backgrounds.[2] Such a
reception was no doubt of some satisfaction to Reclus, entering
what was to be the last decade of his life. However, while the years
at Brussels were a period of feverish activity, they also reveal the
limitations of a revolutionary strategy which neither the man nor the
theoretician was able to overcome.

The New University brought the Reclus brothers together again in
the same place when Elie accepted an offer to give a course in
Comparative Mythology. The contrast which the pair made in
physical appearance, temperament and intellectual outlook, fascinated
all who met them. One friend, who remembered them from the 1870s,
commented that they were 'so conspicuously different that nobody
who did not know could have believed them to be brothers'. Elie was
tall, 'with a monumental head which by its noble form would have
formed the delight of a sculptor in marble'. He had black hair, 'dark
tranquil serious and yet friendly-looking' eyes. Elisée was 'under
middle size, had bright brilliant eyes, fair hair'. Elie was unusually
reflective and 'spoke with meditation, slow, clear, using an un-
commonly fine vocabulary, never losing the noble calm of the
philosopher', while his younger brother 'seized things quickly, with
genius, his talk was quick and ardent, he was always stirring, could
not be held to a point and he possessed to all appearance a never-tiring

energy and force of work'.[3]

Elie the pessimist and Elisée the optimist did not contrast so much as they complemented one another. Their nephew Elie Faure described them as 'so pure that the pessimist retained until his charming old age the freshness of feeling and the dreams of childhood – while nothing, not even sad experience, could keep the optimist from believing, whenever he witnessed the first stirring of a revolutionary movement, that it was the seventh blast of the horns of Jericho'.[4] It is frequently noted that Elisée's prodigious scholarship did not obliterate the simplicity of his early years, that he 'remained to the last as direct and straightforward as a child'.[5] However, Faure's remark that Elie also retained the characteristics of childhood adds an interesting perspective. At Brussels Elie was affectionately called 'Old Elie' and referred to as the Patriarch.[6] However, his personality, while it had softened, was essentially as it had always been, and his interest in primitives, myths and religions was an extension of the preoccupations of his early years. In fact, the aged brothers presented a charming picture, evoking, each in his own way, the two boys who had romped together in rural France. Thérèse Dejongh, a former student and friend explained how Elisée would leave his students 'under the spell of his thunderous prophesies', and the next day Elie would draw their attention to the 'humble beginnings of our changeful humanity'. 'For two straws he [Elie] would have said to us: "My brother tells you whither we are going . . . if the fates consent. For my part, I shall tell you where we come from . . . " '[7] The good-natured Elie was a 'quizzical old character', a treasure to those who appreciated him,[8] but Elisée was, and remained, the Anarchist Prophet.

Up until 1894 Elisée Reclus had spent most of his life travelling and writing, and he had not delivered a great number of speeches. A story has been passed down about a faculty meeting at which it was decided that lectures ought not to be read. Reclus who had kept his silence until that point said quietly, 'Gentlemen, I have been in the habit of reading my lectures; I shall have need of indulgence'. This caused his colleagues some anxiety, and they proceeded to rectify the situation by making an exception for the Institute of Advanced Studies where Reclus lectured. But henceforth he never read another lecture[9] – to the delight of his students, for while he was not a 'practised' orator, he certainly was effective:

His improvised discourses were yet more vivid than the others had been. When he hesitated a moment in quest of the fittest, most expressive word, the listener seemed, even in that instance of silence, to see further into his thoughts. It seemed as if the glance of his clear blue eyes shed a portion of his genius and his ardour over his audience. His face was that of an apostle or a prophet, with its halo of fine white hair. And when he was moved to indignation, his look had a wild nobility. His eyes were magnetic and revealed a world of human love.[10]

Those who thronged into the lecture hall, and who recorded their impressions of the ageing geographer, were generally struck by his extraordinary blue eyes, shining all the more brilliantly next to his white hair and beard, and by his ability to change from an animal ferocity at one moment to a tender, all-embracing love. One student wrote: 'He was small and ethereal, and his power showed only in his blue eyes, which glowed beneath his white hair like the gentian beside the Alpine snow, and in which the love of mankind flashed, now in tenderness, now in revolt.'[11]

Dejongh remembered that those who frequented Reclus' lectures 'listened with wonder to the lesson which showed them the earth as "rhythm and beauty expressed in a harmonious whole" ', and that they anxiously awaited the customary 'appeal to justice and mutual kindness' at the end.[12] From another student we learn: 'He always ends a lecture with some sweeping flight of intellect, whereby he discovers and reveals the cosmic bearings of his particular subject.'[13] A friend and colleague, Jacques Mesnil, described him as a man who 'spoke well, but without affectation. He spoke as a sincere man who sways the public and achieves the most oratorical effects only by the warmth of his heart, only by the force of his convictions.'[14] It is not surprising that Reclus' lectures could be so successful. He himself looked upon lecturing as a joyful way of communicating, as a co-operative enterprise between speaker and audience. The listener, he used to say, 'holds up the mirror in which our thoughts take life before our eyes'.[15] Elisée Reclus had at last found the pulpit for which he had vainly searched in his youth. An Englishman who heard him speak in 1896 in London was struck by this 'Grand Old Man without rival or peer; never elsewhere have I seen such magnificent energy and enthusiasm combined with such lofty intellectual gifts'.[16]

The energy was all the more impressive because Reclus' body was frail and his general bearing was mild, dignified and quietly reserved. The eminent biologist Alfred Russell Wallace described his first meeting with him in 1895:

> He was a rather small and very delicate-looking man, highly
> intellectual, but very quiet in speech and manner. I really did not
> know that it was *he* with whose name I had been familiar for
> twenty years as the greatest of geographers, thinking it must have
> been his father or elder brother; and I was surprised when, on
> asking him, he said that it was he himself.[17]

The fiery anarchist Johann Most who met Reclus in the late 1880s in
New York told the following story:

> I was sitting in my poor editorial chair in William Street, where at
> that time the *Freiheit* was published. Suddenly someone tapped
> me on my back, while I was writing. Turning angrily around, I saw
> before me a small-sized personality of advanced age, but with
> striking features whose eyes streamed kindness and fraternity.
> 'I am Reclus', says he, with absolutely no air of pride or affection,
> as though he would be the most commonplace visitor.
> 'Excuse me for disturbing you', he added modestly. I must say,
> I was happy to be thus disturbed. I embraced Elisée Reclus, and
> the hours which I enjoyed in his company belong to the brightest
> and happiest in my life. His whole personality is invigorating. His
> eyes penetrate the universe and give one the feeling that one is, in
> the struggle for the emancipation of the workers, in unity and
> harmony with cosmic forces. Elisée Reclus I count as one of the
> greatest inspirers, since I became an anarchist.[18]

The use of the term 'modestly' implies that Reclus regarded himself as
less than his worth. Reclus would have maintained that he was equal,
neither superior, nor yet inferior to others. His powerful will was
directed towards the maintaining of his 'ordinariness' among the great,
and this was the source of his strength.

None the less, it must have been trying at times to remain ordinary.
Though he reminded himself that 'nothing depraves like success',[19]
Reclus was constantly reminded of his achievements by the great
numbers of scholars, artists and dignitaries who would seek audience
with him, as well as by the formal distinctions for which he was
singled out. The decision of the Paris Geographical Society to award
him a gold medal had been taken just before the period of the
attentats had begun, in February 1892. While he anticipated the

suffering to his vanity which would result from his participation in the 'absurd' ceremony, he was placed in a particularly embarrassing position with regard to this 'large gold medal', for he had failed to return the small medal which the Society had earlier sent to him. In the end he was persuaded by the arguments put to him by the explorer Henri Duveyrier: 'We wished to be fair to the geographer and without putting on airs, to treat ourselves to the delicate pleasure of sympathising with the anarchist. Would it not be a veritable injustice on your part to offend us?'[20] Once he had accepted a gold medal from the French, it was extremely awkward to refuse one from the British. He no doubt comforted himself in the knowledge that he was accepting recognition on behalf of humanity, not merely for himself; he was no more than a collaborator in the common product which was to be put at the service of all.

In his behaviour towards others, Reclus was meticulous. 'For shame', he wrote in 1882 to a young woman who had called herself his disciple. 'Is it thus right for some to be subordinated to others? I do not call myself "your disciple" . . . '[21] A friend of his daughter Jeannie remembered: 'Never shall I forget the perfect courtesy of his manner as he bowed to the slip of a girl I was then [1880]. Towards the old and feeble, this courtesy remained the same. I can see him, advancing gaily towards his aged mother-in-law [Ermance's mother], helping her up, and slipping her arm through his, as he led her, with cheerful words in to dinner.'[22] His workingman friend Guérineau viewed him thus: 'He did not encase himself in the superiority which a great many savants believe they possess . . . He inclined toward simple men, toward workingmen before all others.'[23] As might be expected, Reclus set out to approach his students not as a master to disciples, but as an equal. From his first lecture on 2 March 1894 he invited the students to work together with him and to challenge his conclusions.[24] The programme of his Geography Institute[25] stated that 'as large a part as possible is to be reserved for individual initiative in the organisation of the courses, or rather the informal discussions'.[26] One lifelong friend reported: 'While to those who claimed superiority of any kind he could be terrible in the scathing contempt or mocking bitterness with which he spoke, to the unhappy – the moral failures – he was gentle and much enduring.'[27]

With his time and money Reclus was extremely generous. 'One could come and find him at any hour, and he interrupted himself in the midst of his work to discuss with people whose conversation must frequently have been without any interest to him.'[28] He spent com-

paratively little of the money which he earned on himself, was forever
contributing to worthy causes, and was reduced to near poverty when
a small cartography project which he was persuaded to finance had to
be liquidated.[29] According to some observers he had a 'naive
confidence'[30] which allowed him to become the 'easy prey of
schemers'.[31] On the whole, however, his friends were generally able
to grasp that he was acting in accordance with his principles, though
they tended to view the scrupulous avoidance of the corruption of
success as nothing less than saintliness. 'In another age, Reclus would
have been considered a saint; he had all the characteristics.'[32] 'One of
the most truly religious spirits of this age, he was of the race from
which springs saints and martyrs . . . He practiced all the virtues, simply
and naturally . . . He saw the future as a dawn rising over a world of
men, good, simple, and brotherly — made in his own image.'[33] Elisée
Reclus 'belonged to the greater order of men: he was a man sui
generis — one whom the pagans would have made a demigod or hero'.[34]

Those who have left their impressions of Reclus were friends and
admirers. There is no such record from his critics, and even he had a
few. The evidence suggests that there were some who rebelled at his
saintliness and insinuated that he was setting himself up as a model for
everyone else to follow.[35] Reclus may have been willing to be patient
with those who failed to understand how they were demeaning him
and themselves by holding him up as a superior being. However, his
critics' observations, as few as these appear to have been, caused him a
good deal of pain, partly because, I suspect, as a sensitive man he could
not help but see that there was an element of truth in them. He seems
to have reacted by blaming himself for a failing, and to have attempted
to correct it by becoming even more perfect[36] — which of course
would have exacerbated the situation. It was a bitter-sweet experience
to live the life of a revolutionary according to Reclus' formula.
Perfection became the more elusive the more he struggled to achieve
it. Shortly before his death, he wrote to a comrade: 'Are not even
revolutionaries bourgeois in spirit?'[37]

Reclus has had many admirers, but he asked only for respect, not
admiration, for fellow workers, not disciples. Few people could respond
to this without some sort of adulation (or occasionally its opposite,
contempt). This response is unfortunate, if understandable, for it
tended to focus attention upon the halo and to reduce the frequently
compelling and attractive figure beneath it. Some of us might prefer
to see him through the eyes of a woman who has left her impressions
of his encounter with the artist Verhaeren just after the triumphant

arrival in Brussels in 1894.

> I was living at Knocke when Elisée was called to Brussels; so I did
> not meet him there; but in the spring of that year he was on the
> Belgian coast and, knowing that Verhaeren was staying with me,
> he came to visit him. I do not think that Verhaeren had met him
> before; but when we saw him coming, as we sat in front of the house,
> we recognised him at once. He advanced, with his hands in the
> pockets of his every-day clothes, bare headed, with his hair and his
> loose tie floating in the breeze; and he looked, as he would have
> had everybody look, the type of a 'free man'. His salutation was
> simple and cordial, with a suggestion of youthful ardour; but his
> bearing had great nobility. Verhaeren and he greeted each other
> with the generous warmth of kindred spirits . . . I see him yet, on
> the beach, close to the waterside, making islands, capes and
> archipelagoes in the sand with his stick, to amuse some child, and
> saying: 'This is the ideal place to teach geography'.[38]

At this point in his life, 1894, Elisée Reclus was the anarchist theorist
who was shocking the world by the sympathy which he was showing
for terrorism. The theoretician and the primitive rebel were fellow
workers, each striving to advance the great cause of humanity. But this
was a satisfaction which Reclus was never again to enjoy as fully.
However fiercely he might resist being denied a flesh and blood existence, in the final decade of his life he was transformed into the
legendary anarchist saint.

To be 'canonised' a saint was doubtlessly a painful experience for a
man who believed so intensely in equality and who fought so
vehemently to achieve it. This surely was something of a defeat for
Reclus. The equality at which he aimed was an objective reality, a
world in which all people would be equal in theory and practice, in
their own view and in that of others. 'As for my definition of
Equality', he had written in 1887, 'I am only able to give it from my
point of view which is that of the Revolution. But as is my way, I
restrict myself to indicating the effects: Equality is the ensemble of
social facts which permit each man to look another man in the eyes
and to extend his hand to him without second thought.'[39] Thus one
person could not find salvation in isolation from the rest of humanity.
Moreover, the brotherhood of equals might be farther from realisation
than ever before, if the one perfected brother were made into an idol.
The drive for perfection ultimately led to defeat for the man who

attempted to live as though the universal brotherhood were already established, as well as for the theoretician who insisted that the brotherhood had to be achieved without resort to the 'circuitous' ways of the bourgeois order.

Reclus' insights are extremely perceptive, frequently brilliant. Without the fanatical insistence upon perfection, the fundamentals of his social theory might be nicely fitted to a political theory which at least tolerated party-political activity, even if the aim was eventually to dispense with it. It might be helpful, if we reflected a little upon his views on the use of the franchise. His break with the parliamentary system came swiftly, and in agonisingly painful circumstances, and it was at least a partial reversal of his earlier position. We also know that Reclus was extremely obstinate, and that once he had made up his mind he never wavered in his resolve. His rejection of the parliamentary system was largely emotional, and although he attempted to build an intellectual basis for it, he never really succeeded. It is a mistake to rely too heavily upon the few comments which he made with regard to the Commune as the great example of the evil of governments. In the period 1870 to 1871 he was well aware of how governments operated, as the material presented in Chapter 4 amply demonstrates. He could give no satisfactory assessment of the role of government because his views on government were rooted in a response to the Paris Commune which was, and continued to be, emotional. Consider, for example, his reply in 1882 to the accusation that he did not visit Paris because he did not love the city. 'I love Paris very much', he insisted, 'and it is precisely because I love it so much that I would like to find myself there again in conditions similar to those which I have known' – that is, in those which had existed during the early days of the Commune.[40] In the latter part of 1895 or early 1896 Grave asked Reclus to give an address in Paris in order to help *Les Temps Nouveaux* out of financial difficulty. A reasonable request, one would think, but it was refused. Grave believed that Reclus held a 'sort of hatred against the people of Paris'.[41]

In the 1870s Reclus rarely went into detail or spoke with clarity on the subject of electoral abstention, although it was clear to those around him that he was unconditionally opposed to working through the parliamentary system. Even so, it was originally conceivable that, given time, he might modify his position. There were others, Brousse for example, who had been intransigent anarchists, but had relented when the Jura movement went into decline. Moreover, the depth of Reclus' antagonism to party politics was not comprehended even by

Brousse who in late 1879 was planning a newspaper project for which
he was hoping to gain the collaboration of such a varied lot as Reclus
and Kropotkin, Costa, Malon, Guesde and Xavier de Ricard.[42] Reclus
had little to say in defence of his position other than to remind us that
power corrupts, hardly a startling revelation. In *An Anarchist on
Anarchy* he declared:

> It is now a matter of common knowledge that power, whether its
> nature be monarchic, aristocratic, or democratic, whether it be
> based on the right of the sword, or inheritance, or of election, is
> wielded by men neither better nor worse than their fellows, but
> whose position exposes them to greater temptations to do evil.
> Raised above the crowd, whom they soon learn to despise, they
> end by considering themselves essentially superior beings;
> solicited by ambition in a thousand forms, by vanity, greed and
> caprice, they are all the more easily corrupted that a rabble of
> interested flatterers is ever on the watch to profit by their vices.
> And possessing as they do a preponderant influence in all things,
> holding the powerful lever whereby is moved the immense
> mechanism of the State — functionaries, soldiers, and police —
> every one of their oversights, their faults, or their crimes repeats
> itself to infinity and magnifies as it grows.[43]

It is surprising to learn that as late as 1885 Reclus' position on the
parliamentary system was so unclear that his name was placed on the
electoral list of Lissagaray's *La Bataille*. Reclus, Kropotkin and
several others who were being sponsored without their permission in
the 5 October 1885 general elections vehemently objected and
declared that they did not intend to stand as candidates under any
title.[44]

This notice was not sufficient for Reclus, and he gave his views
on electoral abstention in a letter of 26 September to Grave. The
letter was enlarged into an electoral placard and published in *Le
Révolté*.[45] To vote, it was declared, was to abdicate one's
sovereignty, to be a dupe in believing that representatives were wise
enough to legislate on all things, to invite treachery because power
corrupted the most sincere and honest. The people were called upon
to defend their own interests, to act themselves and to accept
responsibility for their actions. The letter was overwhelmingly
approved by the anarchist groups in late 1885 and early 1886.
According to a police report of 25 February 1886, it 'was peddled

in the meetings and greeted with unanimous approval'.[46]

From an early age Reclus had sensed the delusions associated with the ballot box. By 1851 he had balked at the notion that democracy (read brotherhood) consisted in the 'sham' of universal suffrage.[47] Following the brutal repression of the Commune, he must have felt that he himself had also been deluded into believing that significant social change could be effected in this way. He could hardly argue that the use of the franchise brought progress to a halt; it merely slowed down the revolutionary process — it was a 'circuitous' route. The factors responsible for this circuitousness did not lie in the franchise itself, however. They were rooted in the unliberated attitudes of the people which conditioned them to submit to those whom they placed in positions of authority, and in their vanities and other weaknesses which politicians had to exploit in order to win their favour. The franchise was circuitous because people were weak; they had to be made strong before it might become acceptable. Theoretically, when all were fully conscious, fully anarchist, it would not be possible to dupe or to be duped.

As painstaking as he was with detail and so avid in his thirst after every scrap of knowledge, Reclus was at ease only when dealing with the larger picture. Just as he shunned the routine administration of the anarchist press, so he also squirmed on the question of the day-to-day revolutionary strategy. It was largely because his great knowledge of the forward movement of history had made him sensitive to the eddies that he merely waded ankle-deep in the stream. And yet the logic of his own theories also led him to admit that he might plunge in deeper — if he wished. The anarchist view of morality, according to Reclus, tolerated no 'outside' constraint upon behaviour, so that any particular anarchist might be directed to the ballot box by the 'interior voice'. Moreover, the end justified the means, and the franchise qualified as a neutral means. He recognised the validity of such arguments when he wrote in 1897: 'But, to come to the question of voting, I would comment on this act as I would on all others, that is that it is neutral in itself and ought to be studied in its movements and its relations with circumstances and men. In such and such a circumstance, the conscience of this one or that one, among the anarchists, may justify, even approve it.'[48]

In view of the moral and intellectual progress which Reclus perceived all around him at the turn of the century, he ought to have conceded that the use of the franchise was less hazardous to the revolutionary cause than it had been in former years. However, even though he had viewed Bakunin as a noble relic of the past, he himself, when the time came, was little inclined to vacate the field which he had tended for over four decades. Bakunin died in disillusionment; Reclus said his farewell amid the excitement of one more harvest, the revolutionary events of 1905 in Russia. When the events broke out in January of that year, Reclus was an old man, suffering from acute spells of angina pectoris and still shaken by the loss of Elie who had died the year before. But the unrest following 'Bloody Sunday' roused his spirits, and he set out for Paris, 'revolutionary' Paris, where he had been reluctant to address gatherings ever since the suppression of the Commune. 'Alas!' he wrote to Kropotkin, 'I should speak to them in words of fire, and I only have an asthmatic puff to give them. None-theless, I shall do it with my whole spirit. It is no mistake to repeat: "The Revolution has begun." '[49] At the meeting he began to speak, but too ill to withstand the excitement, had to ask a friend to read out his prepared address.[50]

The comrades were reminded of the terrible end of the Paris Commune, and a comparison was made between it and the bloody events around the Winter Palace on 9 January. St Petersburg had become, like Paris, a revolutionary city. The great question was the magnitude which the revolution in Russia would ultimately assume, since all revolutions, although similar in movement and rhythm, differed in detail and scope. He was convinced that it would certainly rank with the French Revolution among the great epochs of humanity. Moreover, this time the issue was not simply the entrance of the Third Estate into the social body. The workers, as well as the intellectuals and the bourgeoisie, were demanding their share of liberty; the peasants too would take part. Furthermore, the Russians would be forced to consider the question of the cultural and linguistic groups confined within the borders of the Russian Empire. All the different peoples would be first emancipated and then joined in a free association.

> . . . a federal tie will unite them, assuring each human person, of whatever race he is, the absolute fullness of his liberty. The French Revolution theoretically proclaimed the 'right of man'; we demand the Slavic Revolution to make a living reality of it; we prophesy for it the joy of achieving the greatest accomplishment of history, the conciliation of races in a federation of equity.

Finally, the historical development of Russia, its vast domains enveloping

many peoples and its extensive contacts with East and West, held out
the promise that the revolution would develop a universal character:

> Here is the promise of a national revolution, which, by the force
> of circumstances, will evolve in the sense of 'globality', that is to
> say of a real liberty which will no longer be the prerogative of
> some whites, but the right of all men, whether they be white,
> yellow, or even black, whether they be Arab, Turkish or whether
> they even belong to the category of the 'hereditary enemies', such
> as the English or the Germans.

The events of 1905 were a dream come true, the theory of the
International Working Men's Association fused with practice, the
concrete proof that 'the emancipation of the Workers will be made
by the Workers themselves'.

In the second half of June 1905 Reclus' physical condition
rapidly deteriorated. His last days were spent at Thourout in the
countryside west of Brussels, at the home of Florence de Brouckère.
Shortly before he died, he completed the preface to the Russian
edition of *L'Homme et la Terre*, and a few hours before death on 4
July listened to his daughter read the telegram which carried the glad
tidings of the revolt of the sailors on the battleship Potemkin in the
Black Sea. 'Elisée Reclus was luminously smiling . . . He had no more
strength to speak. After a few hours he died peacefully and in full
consciousness.'[51] On the morning of 6 July his body was taken,
accompanied only by his nephew Paul, to the cemetery of Ixelles.
In accordance with his wishes, there was no procession.[52]

## Notes

1. Edmond Picard, quoted in Thérèse Dejongh, 'The Brothers Reclus at the
New University' in J. Ishill, *Elisée and Elie Reclus: In Memoriam* (Berkeley
Heights, 1927), p. 225.
2. Ibid., pp. 225–6.
3. Albert Heim, 'Recollections on Elie and Elisée Reclus' in Ishill,
*Elisée and Elie Reclus*, p. 32.
4. Elie Faure, 'Elie Reclus' in Ishill, ibid., pp. 28–9.
5. C. Wm. Owen, 'Elisée Reclus' in Ishill, ibid., p. 127.
6. Dejongh, 'The Brothers Reclus', p. 232 ff.
7. Ibid., pp. 232–3.
8. Ibid., p. 234 ff.
9. Ibid., p. 229.
10. Ibid., pp. 229–30.

11. Quoted in ibid., p. 230.
12. Ibid., p. 237.
13. Edmond Picard, quoted in ibid., p. 230.
14. Mesnil, 'Elisée Reclus', in Ishill, *Elisée and Elie Reclus*, p. 185.
15. Zibelin-Wilmerding, 'Elisée Reclus', in Ishill, ibid., p. 102.
16. Henry S. Salt, 'The Many-sided Man of Genius' in Ishill, ibid., p. 68.
17. Alfred Russell Wallace, *My Life, A Record of Events and Opinions*, 2 vols. (London, 1905), vol. II, pp. 207–8.
18. Quoted in Ramus, pp. 124–5.
19. *Le Travailleur*, Feb./Mar. 1878. Cf. Reclus, *Elie Reclus*, pp. 21–2. According to Elisée, from an early age Elie had observed the motto: 'And especially, my friend, especially guard yourself well against success!'
20. Reclus to Louise, n.d. (Feb. 1892), *Correspondance*, 3 vols. (Paris, 1911–25), vol. III, p. 103.
21. Reclus to Mlle. De Gérando, 1 Jan. 1882, *Corr.* II, p. 238.
22. Zibelin-Wilmerding, 'Elisée Reclus', p. 101.
23. L. Guérineau, 'Recollections of Elisée Reclus' in Ishill, *Elisée and Elie Reclus*, p. 117.
24. Elisée Reclus, *Leçon d'Ouverture du Cours de Géographie Comparée, Extrait de la Revue Universitaire* (Brussels, 1894), pp. 3–4.
25. See Reclus to Nadar, 18 Apr. 1899, *Corr.* III, pp. 210–11.
26. Quoted in Albert François, *Elisée Reclus et l'Anarchie* (Ghent, 1905), pp. 23–4.
27. Richard Heath, 'Elisée Reclus' in *Humane Review*, Oct. 1905.
28. Mesnil, 'Elisée Reclus', p. 189.
29. See Reclus to Paul Regnier, 2 July 1900, *Corr.* III, p. 225.
30. Mesnil, 'Elisée Reclus', p. 189.
31. Dejongh, 'The Brothers Reclus', p. 239; also Mesnil, 'Elisée Reclus', p. 192.
32. Emile Cammaerts, quoted in Dejongh, ibid., p. 238.
33. L. Descaves, quoted in ibid.
34. Heath.
35. Zibelin-Wilmerding, 'Elisée Reclus', pp. 238–9.
36. Mesnil, 'Elisée Reclus', p. 191 ff.
37. Reclus to Luigi Galleani, 19 May 1905, *Fonds ER*, 14 AS 232, *IFHS*.
38. Madam Theo van Rysselberghe, quoted in Dejongh, 'The Brothers Reclus', p. 238.
39. Reclus to Louise, 21 Nov. 1887, *Fonds ER*, 14 AS 232, *IFHS*.
40. Reclus to Heath, 18 Feb. 1882, *Corr.* II, pp. 242–3.
41. Jean Grave, *Quarante Ans de Propagande Anarchiste* (Paris, 1973), pp. 359–60.
42. David Stafford, *From Anarchism to Reformism, A Study of the Political Activities of Paul Brousse 1870–1890* (London, 1971), p. 144.
43. Reclus, *Anarchist*, p. 7 ff.
44. Reclus, Ferré, J.B. Clément, Audejean, Jance and Kropotkin requested that their names be removed from the *La Bataille* list. See *Le Télégraphe*, 8 Oct. 1885 and report in *P.Po.* B a/1237.
45. *Le Révolté*, 11 Oct. 1885; an English version was inserted in *The Anarchist* also in 1885 and reproduced in *Freedom*, Jan. 1910.
46. *AN* F7 12504.
47. Reclus, 'Développement'.
48. Reclus to B.P. Van der Voo, Apr. 1897, *Corr.* III, p. 201.
49. Reclus to Kropotkin, 6 Feb. 1905, *Corr.* III, p. 300.
50. For a copy of the address, see *La Terre* (Mons), 24 June–1 July 1906

and *Corr.* III, p. 302 ff.

51. Zamfir C. Arbore (Ralli), 'Elisée Reclus — Reminiscences' in Ishill, *Elisée and Elie Reclus*, p. 164.

52. Paul Reclus to Kropotkin, 6 July 1905, *Corr.* III, pp. 326−7.

# AFTERWORD

Since its appearance 100 years ago European anarchism has been
viewed primarily as a doctrine in an 'anti-statist' tradition. Almost from
the beginning there was a tendency to see late nineteenth-century
anarchists as concerned with an assault upon the political superstructure
without much thought for the substructure. They have also been
pigeon-holed as representatives of an individualist rejection of authority
— hence their supposed affinity with liberalism and appeal to the middle
class. Moreover, their participation in an 'anti-statist' tradition of
dubious validity in any case has highlighted what might be termed the
quixotic element in their theory. My study of Elisée Reclus has demonstrated that his hostility to authority, party-political activity and the
state must be seen within the context of his socialism. He was an
extreme socialist, not a 'saintly' protector of anything which smacks of
*laissez-faire* liberalism. In fact, his theory of anarchism was a carefully
elaborated *attack* upon a social order guided by *laissez-faire* principles.
I would suggest that there is a need to rethink many of the old
assumptions about the nature of European anarchism, especially in
light of the fact that he was so very 'representative' of the theory. In
the eyes of his comrades he was the 'perfect' anarchist!

The desire for an earthly brotherhood of equals which Reclus
expressed in his boyhood presupposes an awareness of social inequalities, the belief that they are morally wrong, and the conviction
that the promised rewards in the Afterlife are no substitute for a
solution to the evils of the here and now. The social and political
theory which he began to develop from his youth was a response to a
rapidly expanding European industrialisation, and represented a fierce
determination to remove all misery, forever. The religious overtones
of his theories should come as no surprise, once we remember that it
was Calvinism which provided the vehicle through which he became
aware that there was a social question and which helped shape the
nature of his response. 'How good it would be', he used to say, 'with
no god and no master to live like brothers.'[1] No doubt, he was part
of a long tradition of utopians who dreamt of what might be. What
placed him squarely in the nineteenth century, however, was his
rejection of a religion which promised the masses that utopia came
after death and his espousal of a position which insisted that it must

come in this world.

Like all socialists in the nineteenth century, from the Saint-Simonians and the Fourierists to the Marxists, Reclus was utopian in the sense that he came to believe that human effort would be able to transform the evil present into a 'perfect' order at some point in the future. In the latter part of the century, he departed from the utopian tradition, as did the Marxists, in basing his views upon a 'scientific' analysis of how society worked, how change would come, and how the struggle would be conducted. The social sciences came to replace faith and metaphysics as the medium which conferred the new certainty in the rightfulness of the cause and in the assurance of final victory. Perhaps in our own day of an all-pervasive scepticism with regard to neat diagnoses and prognoses, we will say that socialists of all kinds were deluding themselves. Indeed, Carl Becker's description of the eighteenth century's enlightenment thinkers as being captives of 'religious' views[2] might as well fit anarchist and Marxist socialists, their positivism notwithstanding. In their own context, of course, they were convinced that they had discovered the final truth and equally certain that their dream of a better world could be realised. Their theories combined elements of utopianism and positivism, but this assessment is valid for all socialists in late nineteenth-century Europe, not just the anarchists.

The determination which Reclus expressed so early in life to rid the world of social ills was developed into a sophisticated call for co-operation in the destruction of the capitalist social, economic and political order. At the same time he was advocating the establishment of a society based upon solidarity rather than competition, the interests of all rather than egoism, freedom for all people rather than license for the few to subject the many to physical and moral degradation. 'Fundamentally, anarchy is nothing but perfect tolerance, the absolute acknowledgement of the liberty of others.'[3] In a world which had abolished private property, and the greed and aggressiveness promoted by a capitalist system, humanity would be able to fulfil its higher nature. Of course to do as one pleased, as Reclus constantly urged his comrades, would, in the 'perfect' society, always amount to acting within the context of a consideration of the welfare of all. This was never conceived of as a constraint, since he was firmly convinced that the individual experienced his highest satisfaction as a human being in 'gratifying himself in the general good'.[4] Reclus did not simply say that people were naturally co-operative, but rather that they had shown important signs of co-operativeness and that they had the potential to become far more so. And given the fact that the capitalist order was pathological to human society itself, it was not merely desirable, but also necessary, to develop the co-operative side of human nature. Survival had become a moral imperative – a message we can ill afford to neglect.

European anarchism was a theory of socialism which aimed, like all socialism, to arrive at a state of anarchy, an order which would spring naturally from the movement of free beings, responding to the needs of their nature. In the 1870s, anarchism differentiated itself from other socialist theories through its insistence that the existing bourgeois governmental apparatus should not be used to effect the transition to the future society. The immediate decentralisation of decision-making within revolutionary organisations, which was demanded by many socialists, was carried to its logical conclusion by the anarchists – the abandonment of all organisation. They literally became extremists. If the vote could produce anomalous results, no voting should be permitted. If the ideals of political parties tended to become corrupted, all political parties must be shunned. If organis-ation tended to ride roughshod over individuals, then all organisation must be abandoned. In time even newspapers became suspect for Reclus. While he was surely correct in his rational defence of the utility of the principle of mutual aid in the revolutionary struggle, his steadily growing aversion to all organisation mitigated any desire he might have had to elaborate on how co-operation might be en-couraged. He became so 'authoritarian' in his 'anti-authoritarianism' that he failed to develop the theory of mutual aid which, in spite of its 'under-development', remains the most important legacy of late nineteenth-century European anarchism.

Science provided Reclus with the basis for a belief that utopia could be attained. However, as the saying goes, a little – even a lot of – knowledge can be a dangerous thing. The depth of his commitment to science and the ability of science to provide indisputable evidence of the natural laws to which people ought to submit resulted in an overpowering self-righteousness and inflexibility. The faith of old was transferred to science in an astonishingly brutal fashion. We might add that this was not completed until the period following 1871 when science became the great – or last? – hope for revolutionary success, as indicated in his correspondence with Bakunin. We might also men-tion that the transition was made all the easier through his early experiences in the strictly regimented home of his father the Pastor which brought out and reinforced certain personality traits which were

to remain with him the rest of his life, in particular his penchant for
perfectionism and his obstinacy. It was here too that he was introduced to the world of oppressive authority figures. The interesting
thing is that, in the final analysis, science could not tell people what
to do to establish justice and equality, but merely what not to do. The
existing parliamentary structures, producer and consumer co-
operativism, trade unionism, eventually the bourgeois educational
system, all became 'circuitous' ways to revolution.

In a search for the 'direct ' way to revolution Reclus lost sight of
the sufferings of human beings which had led to the rise of the social
question in the first place. He came to love people for what they
might become, not for what they were. Amid mutterings about the
corruption of power, it was out of a recognition that people were weak,
vain and naive that he abandoned all party-political activity after 1871.
This view also formed an important part of his critique of parliamentary
socialism — the franchise meant an appeal to the unliberated crowd.
With the rejection of party politics and soon every form of organisation,
all avenues for the amelioration of day-to-day ills were closed off.
Reclus defended himself by maintaining that anarchists were out to
destroy the whole system, not to tidy it up. Was there no room, we
might ask, to remove the worst social evils in the long interval between
the now and the day of reckoning? Small wonder that Reclus scrupled
about being a thief when he observed the sufferings which went on all
around him and for which he could offer no word of comfort. It was
the *future* for which he worked; the imperfect present occupied him
less and less.

The anarchism which Reclus preached comes out sounding very
much like the religion which it rejected, precisely because it promised
everything and delivered nothing. For the wretched of society, those
people sacrificed before the god of profit, those whose sufferings were
sanctified in the name of progress, was there much difference, after all,
between Christianity which failed to provide the daily bread and
anarchism which promised it in the indefinite future? A theory which
began as a humanistic response to suffering, in the event, does nothing
about it — and that at a time when real possibilities were opening up.
How sterile is it to put off political activity because it will corrupt the
theory, and how curious, especially by Reclus who said that (under
special circumstances only?) the end justified the means. Perhaps
never has the doctrinaire reached such dizzying heights!

As the anarchists differentiated themselves from the social democratic movement which was to become the main carrier of socialist

ideals into the twentieth century, their theories tended to reduce them to the role of spectators. Increasingly trapped in the circularity of his own analysis, the logic of Reclus' arguments left him no choice but to leave the course of the revolution up to the people. A curious thing. Even though the people had come to be at the mercy of the ideal, the anarchist theorist came to be at the mercy of an 'imperfect' people and obliged to justify their acts of violence in the name of social progress. Such was the consequence of an absolute insistence upon 'natural' rather than 'artificial' laws. Reclus was so concerned about finding the natural, or the direct, way to revolution that he effectively decided to go nowhere. According to his own theory, he really ought not to have said − as he did in his old age − how the revolution ought *not* to be made. He himself would not have seen matters this way, but such a conclusion is difficult to avoid when one looks at the effects, not the causes, of his political decisions. As an anarchist thinker, as well as a highly-regarded scholar, Reclus was no fool and intellectually he had a ready defence for what he did and what he failed to do. And his is no simple theory, even if it has turned out to be, politically speaking, suicidal.

With the abandonment of all organisational activity, anarchists pushed themselves out of the active struggle and on to the fringes where they were to remain. Socialism was denied an important and potentially fruitful impulse which it was only to regain sporadically in the future. This has been tragic because it was the 'anarchist' socialists who saw so clearly what in modern terms are referred to as the bureaucratic and obligarchical tendencies at work in *all* political parties, even in those dedicated to revolution. Far better to have socialists participating in party politics who are aware of the hazards of the parliamentary arena than those who are not. But the lessons need not be lost. Indeed, Reclus can still speak to us in a powerful voice. He was poignant in his critique of parliamentary socialism, and his remarks on a phenomenon which we have come to know as 'Bolshevism' were truly prophetic. His central message, the importance of consciousness in the revolutionary struggle, is as vital now as it was then. But, alas, consciousness too was taken to its logical and ridiculous conclusion, so that, in the end, anarchism became more of a struggle to raise consciousness of oppression than a struggle to overcome it. Perhaps we are being rather harsh. However, it is important to see that a consciousness outside an organisational framework is ineffectual in the battle for social justice.

Elisée Reclus speaks to us from a century whose social and political conditions are rapidly becoming more remote from those of our own day. The issue of party politics is increasingly less relevant for people who confront the problems of advanced capitalism, environmental pollution, scarce resources, transnational corporations, political terrorism, worsening relations between capital and labour within and between countries, not to mention the threat of nuclear war. Certainly, he was correct in his critique of the 'circuitous' ways, but was he displaying courage or cowardice in his unwillingness to travel them? After a difficult journey one might arrive at one's destination none the less. The insistence upon excellence in revolutionary strategy was a fatal weakness, because it was beyond the reach of human beings and condemned them to await a millenium which they were increasingly powerless to bring into existence. Those of us who are part of the non-authoritarian left-wing tradition ought not to cling to the comfort of a programme for action which was worked out in another setting very different from our own, and more importantly, has shown itself a programme of non-action. Being correct is not enough.

## Notes

1. Feliks Gross, *European Ideologies* (New York, 1948), p. 86.
2. Carl J. Becker, *The Heavenly City of the Eighteenth-century Philosophers* (New Haven, 1932).
3. Reclus to Renard, 2 June 1888, *Correspondance*, 3 vol. (Paris, 1911–25), vol. II, p. 445.
4. Reclus to Heath, 14 Aug. 1903, *Corr.* III, p. 263.

# BIBLIOGRAPHY

## PRIMARY SOURCES

### I. Archives

A. *Archives de la Préfécture de Police*

B a/66 and B a/67, *Explosions* 1888–1901
B a/73, *Les activités anarchistes* 1882–1884
B a/74, *Les activités anarchistes* 1885–1886
B a/75, *Les activités anarchistes* 1887–1888
B a/76, *Les activités anarchistes* 1889–1890
B a/77, *Les activités anarchistes* 1891–1892
B a/78, *Les activités anarchistes* 1893
B a/79, *Les activités anarchistes* 1894
B a/80, *Les activités anarchistes* 1895–1896
B a/138, *Explosions* 1881–1898
B a/139, *Explosions* 1889–1892
B a/140, *Explosions* 1892
B a/141, *Explosions* 1893–1894
B a/142, *Explosions* 1894–1895
B a/143, *Explosions* 1895–1897
B a/303, a/308, a/309, *Rapports sur les anarchistes*
B a/394, *Menées des socialistes et des anarchistes révolutionnaires à Lyon*
B a/508  a/509, a/510, *Lettres de menaces* 1892
B a/928, Joseph Albert, dit: Libertad
B a/944, Michel Bakounine
B a/996, Caserio Santo
B a/1132, Ravachol
B a/1183, Louise Michel
B a/1216, Fernand Pelloutier
B a/1497, *Rapports et informations concernant les menées anarchistes* 1897–1898
B a/1498, *Rapports et informations concernant les menées anarchistes* 1899–1906
B a/1499, *Anarchistes en Province* 1892–1894
B a/1500, *Listes et états d'anarchistes*
B a/1501, *Anarchistes étrangers*

B a/1502, *Alphabets et chiffres secrets de correspondance entre les anarchistes; Propagande anarchiste par la parole*

B a/1503, a/1504, *Surveillance des anarchistes*

B a/1505, *Procès des Trente; Groupes anarchistes du 5ème arrondissement*

B a/1506, *Rapports sur des groupes anarchistes*

B a/1507, *Groupes anarchistes du 18ème arrondissement*

B a/1508, *Anarchistes en Angleterre jusqu'en 1893; Groupes anarchistes du 20ème arrondiseement*

B a/1509, *Anarchistes à l'Etranger; Anarchistes en Angleterre 1894–1896*

B a/1510, *Anarchistes en Angleterre, Allemagne, Belgique*

B a/1511, *Association internationale antimilitariste; anarchistes aux Etats-Unis; Anarchistes en Espagne*

B a/1512, *Association internationale antimilitariste*

B a/1513, *Fédération Anarchiste Communiste Révolutionnaire*

B a/1660, *Sébastien Faure*

B. *Archives de l'Etat, Neuchâtel*

Fonds Guillaume, five boxes
Letter Reclus to Louis Jeanrenard, pièce privée

C. *Archives Générales du Royaume, Brussels*

*Rapports de police sur l'Internationale*

D. *Archives Historiques du Ministère de la Guerre, Vincennes*

*Dossier Elisée Reclus, 7e Conseil de Guerre Permanent, dossier no. 46*
*Dossier Elie Recus, 3e Conseil de Guerre Permanent, dossier no. 2084*

E. *Archives Nationales, Paris*

BB24 732 *Dossier Elisée Reclus*
BB24 875 *Troubles de Montceau-les-Mines 1882;* Peter Kropotkin
BB24 876 *Meeting des Invalides 9 mars 1883*
BB24 881 *Articles de journaux anarchistes*
B7 12487 *La Ligue des Droits de l'Homme*
F7 12488–12503 *Agissements socialistes, congrès, etc. 1876–1915*
F7 12504–12518 *Agissements anarchistes 1880–1913*
F7 12522–12525 *Congrès divers 1878–1914*
F7 12526 *Evénements de Montceau-les-Mines 1882–1883*
F7 12528–12534 *Premier mai 1898–1911*
F7 12535 *Retraites ouvières 1901–1910*

F7 12581–12601 *Police des étrangers 1886–1906*
F7 12553 *Notes sur la situation politique 1899–1905*
F7 12554–12559 *Rapports quotidiens de la Préfecture de police 1904– 1913*
F7 12560–12565 *Notes de police 1901–1909*
F7 12579–12580 *Relations avec la Suisse 1871–1899*
281 AP(1) *Fonds Edouard Charton*

F. *Bibliothèque Nationale, Salle des Manuscrits, Paris*

*Autographes XIXème-XXème Siècles NAF* 25101
*Autographes Félix et Paul Nadar XXIII NAF* 24282
*Autographes Félix et Paul Nadar XXIV NAF* 24283
*Cent Lettres à Gabriel Faure 1936–1947 NAF* 16421
*Correspondance de Joseph Reinach NAF* 13577
*Correspondance de Louis Blanc NAF* 11398
*Correspondance Germain Bapst XIV NAF* 24538
*Correspondance Louis Havet NAF* 24504
*Lettres adressées à Ossip-Lourié II NAF* 15682
*Lettres à F.A. Cazals NAF* 13152
*Mélanges – XIXe Siècle NAF* 14824
*Mélanges Littéraires – XIXe Siècle NAF* 15892
*Papiers Elisée Reclus I, Notes et Documents Biograhpiques NAF* 22909
*Papiers Elisée Reclus II, Lettres 1849–1869 NAF* 22910
*Papiers Elisée Reclus III, Lettres 1870–1890 NAF* 22911
*Papiers Elisée Reclus IV, Lettres 1891–1905 NAF* 22912
*Papiers Elisée Reclus V, Lettres à ses trois femmes NAF* 22913
*Papiers Elisée Reclus VI, Correspondance A–Z NAF* 22914
*Papiers Elisée Reclus VII, Université Libre de Bruxelles NAF* 22915
*Papiers Elisée Reclus VIII, Globe Terrestre pour l'Exposition de 1900 NAF* 22916
*Papiers Elisée Reclus XIX, Mémoires Divers NAF* 22917
*Papiers Elisée Reclus XX, Premiers Manuscrits NAF* 22918
*Papiers Elisée Reclus XXI, Premiers Manuscrits NAF* 22919
*Papiers Nadar XVII, NAF* 25002
*Papiers Nadar XXXI, NAF* 25016
*Papiers Jehan Rictus, NAF* 24570
*Paul Martine – Mémoires I–V, NAF* 12712–12716

G. *Bibliothèque Publique et Universitaire, Geneva*

*Album domicorum de Jules Perrier, Ms. suppl.* 886
*Archives Baud-Bovy* 23, 36, 214, 216, 237

*Archives BPU*, K15
*Correspondance adressée au peintre Charles Giron, Ms. fr.* 1825
*Jacques Gross*, L10
*Lettres d'Elisée Reclus a Ch. Perron 1889–1904, Ms. suppl.* 119
*Ms. fr.* 4209
*Ms. fr.* 4491/18
*Ms. suppl.* 886
*Papiers Gross, Dépôt du CIRA 1964*
*Papiers Ph. Plan, Ms. fr.* 4297
*Ville de Genève, Coll. B. Reber*

H. *British Museum, London*

Miscellany 1939, Brit. Mus. Add. Ms. 45,498
Miscellany 1947, Brit. Mus. Add. Ms. 46,473
Morris Papers VIII, Brit. Mus. Add. Ms. 45,345
Morris Papers IX, Brit. Mus. Add. Ms. 45,346
Morris Papers, X, Brit. Mus. Add. Ms. 45,347

I. *Institut Français d'Histoire Sociale, Paris*

*Fonds Elisée Reclus* 14 AS 232, five *dossiers*
*Fonds Jean Grave* 14 AS 184b

J. *Internationaal Instituut voor Sociale Geschiedenis, Amsterdam*

Nettlau Archives, which includes *Archief Elisée Reclus*; *Archives de la Fédération Jurassienne*; Kropotkin — Robin correspondence
*Fonds Descaves*
*Fonds Jacques Gross*

II. **Newspapers and Periodicals**

*L'Association*
*L'Avant-Garde*
*Bulletin de la Fédération Jurassienne*
*Ca Ira*
*La Coopération*
*Le Cri du Peuple*
*Le Droit Social*
*L'Egalité* (Geneva)
*Freedom*
*L'Humanité Nouvelle*
*L'Hydre Anarchiste*
*L'Intransigeant*

*Le Libertaire*
*Le Monde Libertaire*
*La République des Travailleurs*
*La Révolte*
*Le Révolté*
*La Revue des Deux Mondes*
*La Revue Socialiste*
*La Rive Gauche*
*Les Temps Nouveaux*
*Le Travailleur*
*Le Vengeur*
*La Vie Naturelle*

## III. Works by Elisée Reclus

'De l'Action humaine sur la géographie physique. L'Homme et la Nature' in *La Revue des Deux Mondes*, 1 December 1864

'Amis et Compagnons' in *La Terre de Mons*, 24 June 1906

*L'Anarchie* (Paris, 1896)

'L'Anarchie et l'Eglise' (with Georges Guyou) in *Les Temps Nouveaux*, 1900

*An Anarchist on Anarchy* (Boston, 1884); as article in the *Contemporary Review*, May 1884

'Aperçu géographique [sur le Mexique]' in *Le Mexique au début du XXe siècle* (Paris, 1904)

*Les Arabes* (Brussels, 1898)

'D'un atlas à échelle uniforme' (with Georges Guyou) in *Bulletin de la Société Neuchâteloise de Géographie*, T. IX, 1896–1897

'Atlas de la Colombie, publié par ordre du gouvernement colombien' in *Bulletin de la Société de Géographie de Paris*, 3 August 1876

'Attila de Gérando' in *La Revue de Géographie*, January 1898

'L'Avenir de nos enfants' in *La Commune. Almanach Socialiste pour 1877* (Geneva, 1877)

'Les Basques. Un peuple qui s'en va' in *La Revue des Deux Mondes*, 15 March 1867

'Le Bosphore et la mer Noire' in *Le Globe* 1875

'Le Brésil et la colonisation' in *La Revue des Deux Mondes*, 15 June and 15 July 1862

*La Chine et la Diplomatie Européanne* (Paris, 1900)

'Les Chinois et l'Internationale' in *Almanach du Peuple*, 1874; revised version in *Le Travailleur*, March/April 1878

'La Cité du bon accord' in *Almanach de la Question Sociale (Illustre) pour 1897* (Paris, 1897)

'Les cités lacustres de la Suisse' in *La Revue des Deux Mondes*, 15 February 1861

'De la Configuration des continents sur la surface du globe' (translation of article by Carl Ritter) in *La Revue Germanique*, November 1859

'Les Colonies anarchistes' in *Les Temps Nouveaux*, 7–13 July 1900

'Considérations sur quelques faits de géologie et d'ethnographie. Histoire du sol de l'Europe, par M. Houzeau' in *La Revue Philosophique*, 1857

*Correspondance*, 3 vols (Paris, 1911–25)

'Le Coton et la crise américaine' in *La Revue des Deux Mondes*, 1 January 1862

'Deux années de la grande lutte américaine' in *La Revue des Deux Mondes*, 1 October 1864

'Développement de la Liberté dans le monde' in *Le Libertairé*, 28 August–1 December 1925

'East and West' in the *Contemporary Review*, October 1894

'Un écrit américain sur l'esclavage' in *La Revue des Deux Mondes*, 15 March 1864

'L'Election présidentielle de la Plata et la guerre du Paraguay' in *La Revue des Deux Mondes*, 15 August 1868

*Elie Reclus 1827–1904* (Paris, 1905); also as 'Vie d'Elie Reclus' in Reclus, Paul, *Les Frères Elie et Elisée Reclus* (Paris, 1964)

*L'Empire du Milieu, le climat, le sol, les races, la richesse de la Chine* (with Onésime Reclus) (Paris, 1902)

'De l'Esclavage aux Etats-Unis' in *La Revue des Deux Mondes*, 15 December 1860 and 1 January 1861

'Etude sur les dunes' in *Bulletin de la Société de Géographie de Paris*, March 1865

'Etude sur les fleuves' in *Bulletin de la Société de Géographie de Paris*, August 1859

*Evolution et Révolution* (Geneva, 1880; Geneva, 1884; Paris, 1891)

*L'Evolution, la Révolution, et l'Idéal anarchique* (Paris, 1898)

'L'Evolution légale et l'anarchie' in *Le Travailleur*, January/February 1878

'The Evolution of Cities' in the *Contemporary Review*, February 1895

'Excursions à travers le Dauphiné' in *Le Tour du Monde*, 1860

*Extension universitaire de Bruxelles. Année académique 1894–1895. Cours de géographique. Amérique meridionale* (Brussels, 1894)

*L'Extrême-Orient, résumé d'une conférence faite, le 28 avril 1898, a la Société Royale de géographie d'Anvers* (Anvers, 1898)

'La Fin triomphante de la Grèce' in *L'Education Sociale de Lyon*, 15
    February and 1 March 1902
'Les Forces souterraines. Les Volcans et les tremblements de terre' in
    *La Revue des Deux Mondes*, 1 January 1867
*La Formation des Religions* (Brussels, 1894)
'Fragment d'un voyage à la Nouvelle-Orleans, 1855' in *Le Tour du
    Monde 1er semestre*, 1860.
'La Géographie' in *Almanach de l'Encyclopédie Generale* (Paris, 1869)
'Le Gouvernement et la morale' in *Le Révolté*, 1883
'La Grande famille' in *Le Magazine International*, January 1897;
    translated as *The Great Kinship* by Edward Carpenter (London,
    1900)
'A grande mistificaçao' in *Aurora* (S Paulo, Brazil), 1 April 1905
'La Grève d'Amérique' in *Le Travailleur*, September 1877
'La Guerre du Paraguay' in *La Revue des Deux Mondes*, 15 December
    1867
*Guide du Voyageur à Londres et aux Environs* (Paris, 1860)
*Hégémonie de l'Europe* (Brussels, 1894)
'Histoire des états américains' in *La Revue des Deux Mondes*, 1866
*Histoire d'une Montagne* (Paris, 1880)
*Histoire d'un Ruisseau* (Paris, 1869)
'Histoire du peuple américain, par Auguste Carlier' in *Bulletin de la
    Société de Géographie de Paris*, February 1865
*L'Homme et la Terre*, 6 vols (Paris, 1905–8)
*L'Idéal et la Jeunesse* (Brussels, 1894)
'Insurrection de Cuba' in *La Revue Politique*, 1868
'John Brown' in *La Coopération*, 14 July 1867
'Sur le lac de Lugano. Extrait d'une lettre de M. Elisée Reclus au
    président de la Société de Géographie de Paris' in *Bulletin de la
    Société de Géographie de Paris*, December 1873
*Leçon d'Ouverture du Cours de Géographie Comparée dans l'Espace
    et dans le Temps* (Brussels, 1894)
'Le Littoral de la France' in *La Revue des Deux Mondes*, 15 December
    1862–1 September 1864
*Londres Illustré. Guide Spécial pour l'Exposition de 1862* (Paris, 1862)
*Le mariage tel qu'il fut et tel qu'il est. Avec une allocution d'Elisée
    Reclus* (with Elie Reclus) (Mons, 1907); also as 'Unions libres' in
    *Les Arts de la Vie*, July 1905
'Le Méditerranée caspienne et le canal des steppes' in *La Revue des
    Deux Mondes*, 1 August 1861
'Metamorphoses du progrès' in *Almanach de la Question Sociale pour*

*1899* (Paris, 1899)

'Le Mississipi, études et souvenirs' in *La Revue des Deux Mondes*, 15 July and 1 August 1859

*A mon Frère, le paysan* (Geneva, 1893)

'Le Mont Etna et l'éruption de 1865' in *La Revue des Deux Mondes*, 1 July 1865

*Nice, Cannes, Monaco, Menton, San Remo* (Paris, 1870)

'Les Noirs américains depuis la guerre' in *La Revue des Deux Mondes*, 15 March 1863

'Note relative à l'histoire de la mer d'Aral' in *Bulletin de la Société de Géographie de Paris*, August and November 1873

*Notice pour la carte physique de l'Amérique du Nord* (Paris, n.d.)

'Notre Idéal' in *Almanach de la Question Sociale (Illustré) pour 1898* (Paris, 1898)

*La Nouvelle Géographie Universelle*, 19 vols (Paris, 1878–94)

'La Nouvelle-Granade, paysages de la nature tropicale' in *La Revue des Deux Mondes*, 1 December 1859–1 May 1860

'L'Océan, étude de physique maritime' in *La Revue des Deux Mondes*, 15 August 1867

'L'origine animale dell'uomo' in *Almanaco populare socialista* (Turin, 1897)

'Origines de la religion et de la morale' in *Les Temps Nouveaux*, 27 February–19 March 1904

'Les Oscillations de sol terrestre' in *La Revue des Deux Mondes*, 1 January 1865

*Ouvrier, prends la machine! Prends la terre, paysan!* (Geneva, 1880)

'Pages de Sociologie préhistorique' in *L'Humanité Nouvelle*, February 1898

'Le Panslavisme et l'unite russe' in *La Revue*, 1 November 1903

'La Passe du sud et le port Eads dans le delta mississipien' in *La Revue Lyonnaise de Géographie*, 12 January 1878

'Paysages du Taurus Cilicien' in *La Revue Germanique*, 15 May 1861

*La Peine de Mort* (Geneva, 1879)

'La Perse' in *Bulletin de la Société Neuchâteloise de Géographie*, 1899

'La Phénicie et les Pheniciens' in *Bulletin de la Société Neuchâteloise de Géographie*, 1900

*Les Phénomènes Terrestres*; vol. I, *Les Continents* and vol. II, *Les Mers et les Météores* (Paris, 1870 and 1872)

'Les Pluies de la Suisse' in *Bulletin de la Société de Géographie de Paris*, January 1873

'La Poésie et les poètes dans l'Amérique espagnole' in *La Revue des*

*Deux Mondes*, 15 February 1864

'Pourquoi nous sommes anarchistes!' in *La Société Nouvelle*, 31 August 1889

'The Progress of Mankind' in the *Contemporary Review*, 1 December 1896

*Projet de construction d'un globe terrestre à l'échelle du Cent millième*, Edition de la Société Nouvelle, 1895

'A propos des Tuileries' in *Bulletin de la Société des Amis des Monuments parisiens*, 1885, no. 1

'A propos d'une carte statistique' in *Bulletin de la Société Neuchâteloise de Géographie*, T.V. 1889–1890

'Proposition de dresser une carte authentique des volcans' in *Bulletin de la Société Belge d'Astronomie*, 1903

*Quelques écrits*, introduction by Hem Day (Paris–Brussels, 1956)

'Quelques mots d'histoire' in *La Société Nouvelle*, November 1894

'Quelques mots sur la propriété' in *Almanach du Peuple pour 1873* (St Imier, 1873)

'Quelques mots sur la révolution bouddhique' in *l'Humanite Nouvelle*, June 1897

'La Question d'Orient' in *La Marseillaise*, 3 April 1878

'Recent books on the United States' in *The Geographical Journal*, November 1895

*Renouveau d'une Cité* (with Elie Reclus) (Brussels, 1896)

'Report on the Physics and Hydraulics of the Mississippi River' in *Bulletin de la Société de Géographie de Paris*, 5 February 1862

'Les Républiques de l'Amérique du Sud, leurs guerres et leur projet de fédération' in *La Revue des Deux Mondes*, 15 October 1866

'Russia, Mongolia and China' in the *Contemporary Review*, 1895

'Du Sentiment de la nature dans les sociétés modernes' in *La Revue des Deux Mondes*, 15 May 1866

'La Sicile et l'éruption de l'Etna en 1865, récit de voyage' in *Le Tour du Monde*, 1866

'The Teaching of Geography: Globes, Discs and Reliefs' in *The Scottish Geographical Magazine*, August 1901; also as *L'Enseignement de la géographie, globes, disques globulaires et reliefs* (Brussels, 1902)

*La Terre*, 2 vols (Paris 1868–9)

'A tous les démocrates' in *L'Agriculteur* (1866)

*Université Nouvelle de Bruxelles. Séance solennelle de rentrée du 22 octobre 1895*. Discours. (Brussels, 1895)

'On Vegetarianism' in *The Humane Review*, January 1901; as 'A propos

du végetarismé' in *La Réforme Alimentaire*, March 1901
'Verra'!' in *Cronacca Sovversiva*, 3 July 1905
*Les Villes d'Hiver de la Méditerranée et les Alpes Maritimes* (Paris, 1864)
'The Vivisection of China' in *The Atlantic Monthly*, September 1898
'Les Voies de communication' in *Almanach de la Coopération pour 1869*
*Les Volcans de la Terre* (Brussels, 1906–10)
*Voyage à la Sierra-Nevada de Saint-Marthe. Paysages de la nature tropicale* (Paris, 1861)
'Voyage aux regions minières de la Transylvanie occidentale' in *Le Tour du Monde*, 1874

*Introductions and Prefaces by Elisée Reclus to:*

Bakunin, Michael, *Dieu et l'Etat* (Paris, 1882) (preface by Reclus and Carlo Cafiero)
Gaussen, Louis, *Soyons Laïques!* (Paris, 1903)
Gerlache, Adrien de, *Voyage de la 'Belgica'. Quinze mois dans l'Antarctique* (Paris, 1902)
Joanne, Adolphe L., *Dictionnaire des Communes de la France* (Paris, 1864)
Joanne, Adolphe L., *Dictionnaire Géographique de la France* (Paris, 1869) (introduction by Elisée and Elie Reclus)
Joanne, Adolphe L., *Itinéraire Général de la France* (Paris, 1862)
Joanne, P.B., *Dictionnaire Géographique et Administratif de la France* (Paris, 1905)
Kropotkin, Peter, *La Conquête du Pain* (Paris, 1892)
Kropotkin, Peter, *Paroles d'un Révolté* (Paris, 1885)
Levasseur, E., *Le Mexique au Début du XXe Siècle* (Paris, 1905)
Malato, Charles, *Religion et Patriotisme* (Rome, 1906)
Metchnikoff, Léon, *La Civilisation et les Grands Fleuves Historiques* (Paris, 1889)
Myrial, Alexandra, *Pour la Vie* (Paris, n.d.)
Nettlau, Max, *Bibliographie de l'Anarchie* (Paris, 1897)
Nieuwenhuis, F. Domela, *Le Socialisme en Danger* (Paris, 1897)
Noel, Eugène, *Fin de Vie (Notes et Souvenirs)* (Rouen, 1902)
*Patriotisme. Colonisation, Bibliothèque Documentaire*, no. 2 (Paris, 1903)
Walker, George, *La Dette Américaine et les Moyens de l'Acquitter* (Paris, 1865)

## IV. Other Primary Sources

Amore, Henri, 'La Correspondance d'Elisée Reclus' in *La Vie Ouvrière*, 5 October–20 December 1913

*Anarchism: A Bibliography of Articles 1900–1975, Political Theory*, February 1976

Arbore, Zamfir C. (Ralli), 'Elisée Reclus – Reminiscences' in Ishill, Joseph, *Elisée Reclus and Elie Reclus: In Memoriam* (Berkeley Heights, 1927)

Bakunin, Michael, *Gesammelte Werke*, 3 vols (Berlin, 1921–4)

────── *God and the State* (New York, 1970)

────── *Oeuvres*, 6 vols (Paris, 1907–11)

Baldelli, Giovanni, *Social Anarchism* (London, 1971)

Baldwin, Roger N. (ed.), *Kropotkin's Revolutionary Pamphlets* (New York, 1970)

Berkman, Alexander, *What is Communist Anarchism?* (New York, 1972)

*Bibliographie des Ouvrages de Géographie et de Sociologie d'Elisée Reclus* (Ms. et dactylographie) (n.1, n.d.)

Bournand, François, *Les Juifs et nos contemporains* (Paris, 1898)

Brisson, Adolphe, *Les Prophètes* (Paris, 1902)

*Bulletin sténographique du deuxième Congrès de la Paix et de la Liberté. Stenographisches Bulletin des zweiten Friedens- und Freiheits-Kongresses* (Berne, 1868)

Cattelain, P., *Mémoires inédits du chef de la Sûreté sous la Commune* (Paris, n.d. 1900)

Cobden-Sanderson, Anne, 'Elie and Elisée Reclus' in Ishill, Joseph, *Elisée and Elie Reclus: In Memoriam* (Berkeley Heights, 1927)

Coeurderoy, Ernest, *Hurrah! ou la Révolution par les Cosaques* (London, 1854)

Darnaud, E., *Notes sur le Mouvement* (Foix, 1891)

Daudet, Léon, *Salons et journaux* (Paris, 1917)

Day, Hem, *Essai de Bibliographie de Elisée Reclus* (Brussels–Paris, 1956)

Dejongh, Thérèse, 'The Brothers Reclus at the New University' in Ishill, Joseph, *Elisée and Elie Reclus: In Memoriam* (Berkeley Heights, 1927)

Delfosse, Charles, *Elisée Reclus, Géographe* in series *Hommes du Jour* (Brussels, n.d.)

*The Doctrine of Saint-Simon*, translated and with an Introduction by Georg G. Iggers (New York, 1972)

*Documents of the First International*, 5 vols (Moscow)

Dubois, Félix, *Le Péril Anarchiste* (Paris, 1894)

Dumartheray, François, 'Elisée Reclus' in Ishill, Joseph, *Elisee and Elie Reclus: In Memoriam* (Berkeley Heights, 1927)

—— *Aux travailleurs manuels, partisans de l'action politique* (Geneva, 1876)

'Elisée Reclus, 1830–1905' in *Bulletin de la Société Belge d'Astronomie*, 1905

*Elisée Reclus (1830–1905). Savant et Anarchiste* (Paris–Brussels, 1956)

*1871. Enquête sur la Commune de Paris* (Paris, 1897)

Fabrequettes, P., *De la complicité intellectuelle et des délits d'opinion. De la provocation et de l'opologie criminelles. De la propagande anarchiste* (Paris, 1894–5)

François, Albert, *Elisée Reclus et L'Anarchie* (Ghent, 1905)

Freymond, Jacques, *Etudes et Documents sur la Première Internationale en Suisse* (Geneva, 1964)

—— (ed.), *La Première Internationale. Recueil de Documents*, 4 vols (Geneva, 1962–71)

Galleani, Luigi, 'A Recollection of Elisée Reclus' in Ishill, Joseph, *Elisee and Elie Reclus: In Memoriam* (Berkeley Heights, 1927)

Garraud, R., *L'Anarchie et la Répression* (Paris, 1895)

Gaumont, Jean, *Histoire Générale de la Coopération en France*, 2 vols (Paris, 1924)

Geddes, Patrick, 'A Great Geographer: Elisée Reclus' in *The Scottish Magazine*, September and October 1905

Ghio, Paul, *Etudes italiennes et sociales* (Paris, 1929)

—— 'In Memory of Elisée Reclus' in Ishill, Joseph, *Elisée and Elie Reclus: In Memoriam* (Berkeley Heights, 1927)

Giroud, G., 'La Grande Erreur' in *La Regénération*, December 1905

Goldman, Emma, *Anarchism and Other Essays* (London, 1911)

Grave, Jean, 'Elisée Reclus' in Ishill, Joseph, *Elisée and Elie Reclus: In Memoriam* (Berkeley Heights, 1927)

—— *Quarante Ans de Propagande Anarchiste* (Paris, 1973)

Greef, Guillaume de, *Eloges d'Elisée Reclus et de De Kelles-Krauz, Discours* (Ghent, 1906)

—— *Elogie d'Elie Reclus, Discours prononcé le 31 octobre à la séance de rentrée* (Brussels, 1904)

Gross, Jacques, 'Elisée Reclus' in Ishill, Joseph, *Elisée and Elie Reclus: In Memoriam* (Berkeley Heights, 1927)

Gubernatis, Angelo de, *Fibre, Pagine di Ricordi* (Rome, 1900)

Guérineau, L., 'Recollections of Elisée Reclus' in Ishill, Joseph, *Elisée and Elie Reclus: In Memoriam* (Berkeley Heights, 1927)

Guillaume, James, *Idées sur l'Organisation sociale* (La Chaux-de-Fonds, 1876)

——— *L'Internationale. Documents et Souvenirs (1864—1878)*, 4 vols (Paris, 1905—10)

Hamon, A., *Psychologie de L'Anarchiste-Socialiste* (Paris, 1895)

Heath, Richard, 'Elisée Reclus' in *The Humane Review*, Oct. 1905 (also in Ishill, Joseph, *Elisée and Elie Reclus: In Memoriam*, Berkeley Heights, 1927)

Heim, Albert, 'Recollections on Elie and Elisée Reclus' in Ishill, Joseph, *Elisée and Elie Reclus: In Memoriam* (Berkeley Heights, 1927)

Hess, Moses, *Briefwechsel* (The Hague, 1959)

Horowitz, Irving (ed.), *The Anarchists* (New York, 1964)

Huxley, Thomas H., 'The Struggle for Existence and Its Bearing Upon Man' in *The Nineteenth Century*, February 1888

Ishill, Joseph, *Elisée and Elie Reclus: In Memoriam* (Berkeley Heights, 1927)

Jousseaume, Robert, *Etude sur les lois contre les menées anarchistes et sur les modifications que ces lois ont apportees à la legislation pénale* (Paris, 1895)

*Karl Marx, Chronik seines Lebens* (Frankfurt, 1971)

Krimerman, Leonard I. and Perry, Lewis (eds), *Patterns of Anarchy* (New York, 1966)

Kropotkin, Peter, *La Conquête du Pain* (Paris, 1892)

——— 'Elisée Reclus' in *Les Temps Nouveaux*, 15 July 1905

——— *Fields, Factories and Workshops* (London, 1898)

——— *Memoirs of a Revolutionist* (New York, 1971)

——— *Mutual Aid* (London, 1902)

——— *Paroles d'un Révolté* (Paris, 1885)

Lazare, Bernard, 'A School of Liberty' in Ishill, Joseph, *Elisée and Elie Reclus: In Memoriam* (Berkeley Heights, 1927)

Lehning, Arthur, *Archives Bakounine*, 4 vols (Leiden, 1961—71)

Leroux, Pierre, *Quelques Pages de Verité* (Paris, 1859)

Lissagaray, *Histoire de la Commune de 1871* (Paris, 1876)

Lombroso, Cesare, *Les Anarchistes* (Paris, 1897)

Maillard, Firmin, *Affiches, professions de foi, documents officiels, clubs et comités pendant la Commune* (Paris, 1871)

Maitron, Jean (ed.), *Dictionnaire Biographique du Mouvement Ouvrier Français* (Paris)

Marx, Karl, *Economic and Philosophic Manuscripts of 1844* (ed. Dirk J. Struik) (London, 1970)

Marx, Karl and Engels, Frederick, *Marx Engels Werke* (Moscow)
—— *Selected Works* (London, 1970)
Maximoff, G.P. (ed.), *The Political Theory of Bakunin* (New York, 1954)
*Mémoire de la Fédération jurassienne* (Sonvilier, 1873)
Mesnil, Jacques, 'Elisée Reclus' in Ishill, Joseph, *Elisee and Elie Reclus: In Memoriam* (Berkeley Heights, 1927)
Miller, Martin (ed.), *Selected Writings on Anarchism and Revolution P. A. Kropotkin* (Cambridge, Mass., 1970)
*Miscegenation: The Theory of the Blending of the Races, Applied to the American White Man and Negro* (New York, 1864)
*Les Murailles Politiques Françaises* (Paris, 1873)
Nadar, Félix, 'Elisée Reclus' in *Les Temps Nouveaux,* Supplément no. 33, December 1905
Nettlau, Max, *Der Anarchismus von Proudhon zu Kropotkin* (Berlin, 1927)
—— *Anarchisten und Sozialrevolutionäre* (Berlin, 1931)
—— *Bibliographie de l'Anarchie* (Brussels, 1897)
—— *Elisée Reclus, Anarchist und Gelehrter* (Berlin, 1928)
—— 'Elisée Reclus and Michael Bakunin' in Ishill, Joseph, *Elisée and Elie Reclus: In Memoriam* (Berkeley Heights, 1927)
—— *Eliséo Reclus. La Vida de un Sabio. Justo y Rebelde* (Barcelona, 1928)
—— *Histoire de l'Anarchie* (Paris, 1971)
—— *Michael Bakunin, Eine Biographie*, 3 vols (London, 1898–1900)
—— *Der Vorfrühling der Anarchie* (Berlin, 1925)
Owen, C. Wm., 'Elisée Reclus' in Ishill, Joseph, *Elisée and Elie Reclus: In Memoriam* (Berkeley Heights, 1927)
Pierrot, M., 'Elisée Reclus' in Ishill, Joseph, *Elisée and Elie Reclus: In Memoriam* (Berkeley Heights, 1927)
Plechanoff, George, *Anarchism and Socialism* (Chicago, 1909)
Poster, Mark (ed.), *Harmonian Man, Selected Writings of Charles Fourier* (New York, 1971)
*Procès des Anarchistes devant la police correctionnelle et la Cour d'Appel de Lyon* (Lyons, 1883)
*Les Produits de la Terre* (Geneva, 1885)
*Les Produits de l'Industrie* (Paris, 1887)
Proudhon, Pierre-Joseph, *Du Principe Fédératif* (Paris, 1863)
—— *Qu'est-ce que la Propriété?* (Paris, 1873)
Read, Herbert, *The Philosophy of Anarchism* (London, 1940)
Reclus, Elie, *La Commune de Paris au jour le jour 1871 (19 mars—28*

*mai)* (Paris, 1908)

—— *Le mariage tel qu'il fut et tel qu'il est. Avec une allocution d'Elisée Reclus* (Mons, 1907)

Reclus, Paul, 'Biographie d'Elisée Reclus' in Reclus, Paul, *Les Frères Elie et Elisée Reclus* (Paris, 1964)

—— 'A Few Recollections on the Brothers Elie and Elisée Reclus' in Ishill, Joseph, *Elisée and Elie Reclus: In Memoriam* (Berkeley Heights, 1927)

—— *Les Frères Elie et Elisée Reclus* (Paris, 1964)

*La Richesse et la Misère* (Paris, 1888)

Roubakine, N., 'Elisée Reclus and the Russian Readers' in Ishill, Joseph, *Elisée and Elie Reclus: In Memoriam* (Berkeley Heights, 1927)

Salt, Henry, S., 'The Many-sided Man of Genius' in Ishill, Joseph, *Elisée and Elie Reclus: In Memoriam* (Berkeley Heights, 1927)

Schurz, Carl, *Lebenserinnerungen* (Berlin, 1952)

Tchernoff, I., *Le Parti Républicain au coup d'Etat et sous le Second Empire* (Paris, 1906)

Wertheim, W.F., *Evolution and Revolution, The Rising Waves of Emancipation* (London, 1974)

Vandervelde, Emile, *Souvenirs d'un Militant Socialiste* (Paris, 1939)

Vaughan, E., 'The Criminal Record of Elisée Reclus' in Reclus, Elisée, *An Anarchist on Anarchy* (Boston, 1884)

Zibelin-Wilmerding, Lilly, 'Elisée Reclus' in Ishill, Joseph, *Elisée and Elie Reclus: In Memoriam* (Berkeley Heights, 1927)

## SECONDARY SOURCES

Abramsky, Chimen and Collins, Henry, *Karl Marx and the British Labour Movement* (London, 1965)

Ansart, Pierre, *marx et l'anarchie* (Paris, 1969)

Apter, David E., 'The Old Anarchism and the New — Some Comments' in Apter, David E. and Joll, James (eds), *Anarchism Today* (London, 1971)

Arvon, Henri, *L'Anarchie* (Paris, 1951)

Bartsch, Günter, *Anarchismus in Deutschland*, 2 vols (Hanover, 1972–3)

Becker, Carl J., *The Heavenly City of the Eighteenth-Century Philosophers* (New Haven, 1932)

Bergère, Marie-Claire, 'La Chine, du mythe de référence au modele d'action' in *International Review of Social History*, vol. XVII, 1972,

Parts 1—2

Berstein, Samuel, *Auguste Blanqui and the Art of Insurrection* (London, 1971)

Bestor, A.E., *Backwoods Utopias* (Philadelphia—London, 1950)

Bossu, Jean, *Elisée Reclus* (Herblay, S. et O., n.d.)

Bourgin, Georges, *La Commune* (Paris, 1953)

Braunthal, Julius, *History of the International 1864—1914* (London, 1966

Brenan, Gerald, *The Spanish Labyrinth* (Cambridge, 1962)

Campion, Léo, *les anarchistes dans la F.M.* (Marseilles, 1969)

Carr, E.H., *Michael Bakunin* (New York, 1961)

—— *The Romantic Exiles* (Boston, 1961)

—— *Studies in Revolution* (New York, 1964)

Carr, Reg, *Anarchism in France: The case of Octave Mirbeau* (Montreal, 1977)

Carter, April, *Direct Action and Liberal Democracy* (London, 1973)

—— *The Political Theory of Anarchism* (London, 1971)

Cole, G.D.H., *A History of Socialist Thought*, 5 vols (London, 1958 ff)

Caute, David, *The Left in Europe Since 1789* (London, 1966)

Dautry, L. and Scheler, L., *Le Comité central républicain des vingt arrondissements de Paris* (Paris, 1960)

Day, Hem, *Deux Frères de Bonne Volonté, Elisée Reclus et Han Ryner* (Paris—Brussels, 1956)

—— *Elisée Reclus en Belgique* (Paris—Brussels, 1956)

Dolléans, E., *Proudhon* (Paris, 1948)

—— *Histoire du Mouvement Ouvrier*, 3 vols. (Paris, 1957)

Dommanget, Maurice, 'La Premiere Internationale à son declin' in *La Revue d'Histoire Economique et Sociale*, vol. XLIII, 3, 1964

Drachkovitch, Milorad M. (ed.), *The Revolutionary Internationals 1864—1943* (Stanford, 1966)

Durkheim, Emile, *Socialism* (New York, 1962)

Eltzbacher, Paul, *Anarchism* (London, 1960)

Escher, Hans, *Ravachol, Ein Zyklus* (Vienna—Munich, 1969)

Fowler, R.B., 'The Anarchist Tradition of Political Thought' in *Western Political Quarterly*, December 1972

Freymond, Jacques, *Etudes et Documents sur la Première Internationale en Suisse* (Geneva, 1964)

Freymond, Jacques and Molnár, Miklós, 'The Rise and Fall of the First International' in Drachkovitch, Milorad M., *The Revolutionary Internationals 1864—1943* (Stanford, 1966)

Gross, Feliks, *European Ideologies* (New York, 1948)

Gysens, Guy, 'Elisée Reclus, un coeur d'or', stenciled brochure, 1974

Horne, Alistair, *The Fall of Paris* (London, 1965)

Howard, Michael, *The Franco-Prussian War* (London, 1967)

Joll, James, 'Anarchism between Communism and Individualism' in *Anarchici e Anarchia nel Mondo Contemporaneo, Atti del Convegno promosso dalla Fondazione Luigi Einaudi (Torino 5, 6, e 7 dicembre 1969)* (Turin, 1971)

—— *The Anarchists* (London, 1964)

—— *The Second International* (London, 1955)

Kolakowski, Leszek and Hampshire, Stuart (eds), *The Socialist Idea* (London, 1974)

Laidler, Harry W., *History of Socialism* (New York, 1934)

Landauer, Carl, *European Socialism*, 2 vols (Berkeley, 1959)

Langhard, J., *Die Anarchistische Bewegung in der Schweiz* (Berlin, 1903)

Lefranc, Georges *Le Mouvement Socialiste sous la Troisième République, 1875–1940* (Paris, 1963)

Lichtheim, George, *Marxism in Modern France* (New York, 1966)

—— *A Short History of Socialism* (New York, 1970)

Lida, Clara E., *Anarquismo y Revolución en la España del XIX* (Madrid, 1972)

Ligou, Daniel, *Histoire du Socialisme en France* (Paris, 1962)

Longoni, J.C., *Four Patients of Dr Deibler* (London, 1970)

Louis, Paul, *L'Avenir du Socialisme* (Paris, 1905)

—— *Histoire du Socialisme en France* (Paris, 1901)

Maitron, Jean, 'L'Anarchisme français 1945–1965' in *Le Mouvement Social*, January–March 1965

—— *Le Mouvement Anarchiste en France*, 2 vols. (Paris, 1975)

—— 'Das Leben Ravachols' in Escher, Hans, *Ravachol, Ein Zyklus* (Vienna–Munich, 1969)

Malia, Martin, *Alexander Herzen and the birth of Russian Socialism* (Cambridge, Mass., 1965)

Manuel, Frank E., *The Prophets of Paris* (New York, 1962)

Masters, Anthony, *Bakunin, The Father of Anarchism* (London, 1974)

McLellan, David, *Karl Marx, His Life and Thought* (London, 1973)

—— *Karl Marx, Early Texts* (Oxford, 1971)

Miller, Martin A., *Kropotkin* (Chicago, 1976)

Nicolaevsky, Boris, 'Secret Societies and the First International' in Drachkovitch, Milorad M. (ed.), *The Revolutionary Internationals 1864–1943* (Stanford, 1966)

Nicolaevsky, Boris and Maenchen-Helfen, Otto, *Karl Marx, Man and Fighter* (London, 1973)

Nomad, Max, 'The Anarchist Tradition' in Drachkovitch, Milorad M. (ed.), *The Revolutionary Internationals 1864–1943* (Stanford, 1966)

—— *Apostles of Revolution* (New York, 1961)

Nye, Robert, A., *The Origins of Crowd Psychology, Gustave LeBon and the Crisis of Mass Democracy in the Third Republic* (London, 1974)

Paterson, R.W.K., *The Nihilistic Egoist, Max Stirner* (London, 1971)

Prolo, Jacques, *Les Anarchistes* (Paris, 1912)

Richards, Vernon (ed.), *Errico Malatesta, His Life and Ideas* (London, 1965)

Rihs, Charles, *La Commune de Paris: sa structure et ses doctrines* (Geneva, 1955)

Rocker, Rudolf, *Johann Most, Das Leben eines Rebellen* (Berlin, 1924)

Rougerie, Jacques, 'L'A.I.T. et le mouvement ouvrier à Paris pendant les événements de 1870–1871' in *International Review of Social History*, 1972, Parts 1–2

—— *Procès des Communards* (Paris, 1964)

Rubel, Maximilien, *Karl Marx, Essai de Biographie Intellectuelle* (Paris, 1957)

Ruggiero, Guido de, *The History of European Liberalism* (Boston, 1966)

Ryner, Han, *Crespuscolo di Eliseo Reclus* (Florence, 1954)

—— *Elisée Reclus (1830–1905)* (Paris, 1928)

Schraepler, Ernst, *Quellen zur Geschichte der sozialen Frage in Deutschland 1800–1870* (Göttingen, 1955)

Schulkind, Eugene (ed.), *The Paris Commune of 1871* (London, 1972)

Segall, Marcelo, 'En Amérique' in the *International Review of Social History*, 1972, Parts 1–2

Sergent, Alain and Harmel, Claude, *Histoire de l'Anarchie*, vol. I (Paris, 1949)

Stafford, David, *From Anarchism to Reformism, A Study of the Political Activities of Paul Brousse 1870–1890* (London, 1971)

Stekloff, Y., *History of the First International* (London, 1928)

Taylor, Michael, *Anarchy and Cooperation* (London, 1976)

Varennes, Henri de, *De Ravachol à Caserio* (Paris, n.d.)

Venturi, Franco, *Roots of Revolution* (New York, 1966)

Vizetelly, Ernest Alfred, *The Anarchists* (New York, 1972)

Vuilleumier, Marc, 'Les Archives de James Guillaume' in *Le Mouvement*

*Social*, July—September 1964

———— 'Elisée Reclus et Genève' in *Musées du Genève*, April 1971

———— 'La Première Internationale en Suisse' in *La Revue Syndical Suisse*, 9, 1964

———— 'Les Sources de l'Histoire sociale, Max Nettlau et ses Collections' in *Cahiers Vilfredo Pareto*, no. 3, 1964

Wolff, Robert Paul, *In Defence of Anarchism* (New York, 1970)

Woodcock, George, *Anarchism* (London, 1963)

———— *Proudhon* (London, 1956)

Woodcock, George and Avakumović, Ivan, *The Anarchist Prince, Peter Kropotkin* (London, 1971)

Zenker, E.V., *Anarchism* (London, 1898)

Zévaes, A.L., *Socialisme en France depuis 1871* (Paris, 1908)

Note: The following appeared too late for consultation.
Gary S. Dunbar, *Elisée Reclus, Historian of Nature* (Hamden, Conn., Archon 1978).

# INDEX